THE BEST IN
MEDICAL ADVERTISING AND GRAPHICS
Selections from THE R$_X$ CLUB SHOWS

THE BEST IN
MEDICAL ADVERTISING AND GRAPHICS
Selections from THE R$_X$ CLUB SHOWS

Text by Richard Bayan

Design Press International
Division of Literary House, Inc.
Centerport, New York

Rockport Publishers
Rockport, Massachusetts

1507 Dana Avenue
Cincinnati, Ohio 45207
Telephone: (513) 531-2222
Fax: (513) 531-4744

*Distributed to the book trade and art trade throughout the rest of the
world by:*
Hearst Books International
105 Madison Avenue (20th Floor)
New York, New York 10016
Telephone: (212) 481-0355
Fax: (212) 481-3826

Other distribution by:
Rockport Publishers, Inc.
P.O. Box 396
5 Smith Street
Rockport, Massachusetts 01966
Telephone: (508) 546-9590
Fax: (508) 546-7141
Telex: 5106019284 ROCKORT PUB
Easy Link: 62945477

The Best in Medical Advertising and Graphics was developed and prepared
by Design Press International, a division of Literary House, Inc.

Address sales inquiries to:
Rockport Publishers, Inc.
P.O. Box 396
5 Smith Street
Rockport, Massachusetts 01966
Telephone: (508) 546-9590
Fax: (508) 546-7141
Telex: 5106019284 ROCKORT PUB
Easy Link: 62945477

Address editorial inquiries to:
Design Press International
   Division of Literary House, Inc.
P.O. Box R
Centerport, New York 11721

Library of Congress Cataloging-in-Publication Data

The Best in medical advertising and graphics.

   Includes index.
   1. Advertising—Drugs—Pictorial works. 2. Advertising—Medicine—Pictorial works. 3. Advertising copy.
4. Commercial art. I. Bayan, Richard.
HF6161.D7B47   1989   659.1'961   89-5911

ISBN 0-935603-20-4

Type set and pages composed by PM Imagesetters, Ltd., Ridge, New York

PRINTED IN HONG KONG

STAFF

Publisher
Virginia Christensen
President, Literary House, Inc.

Executive Editor
William Kowalsky

Art Director/Designer
Gary Viskupic

Editor
Diana Puglisi

Artist
Patricia Brodesky

Production Consultant
Bruce Richheimer

CONTENTS

INTRODUCTION

This book is a celebration of contemporary medical advertising and graphics. These pages abound with the best work of today's top creative talents—the most distinguished ads, promotions, direct-mail packages, editorial work, illustrations, and photography recently produced in the service of medicine. And, as you will shortly discover, there is much to celebrate.

At a time when so many leading social and cultural indicators are pointing distinctly downward, it becomes all the more heartening to find something that has actually undergone a renaissance over the past decade or two. Medical advertising has emerged as a splendid oasis of creativity—one of the most dynamic and innovative areas of the advertising industry today. Gone are the stodgy technical copy and the routine clinical illustrations; in their place are vibrant headlines and dazzling visuals, ingenious ads, and powerhouse direct-mail packages that deliver response rates of 40% or more.

How did all this happen? To find the answer, one must look at the marketplace. Today's advertisers are competing feverishly for a share of a healthcare market now estimated to have annual revenues of a half-*trillion* dollars.

In this vast arena, established pharmaceuticals must continually contend with new entries on the market, including a rising tide of generics. And the new entries must be launched with memorable campaigns that quickly position them favorably against the competition. Producers of medical equipment and diagnostic procedures vie with one another in supplying physicians with state-of-the-art technology. Even hospitals are getting into the act, actively promoting outpatient programs and other community services in a bid for revenues. (One recent study revealed that over 90% of the hospitals in the U.S. now advertise.)

Obviously, then, the new vitality of medical advertising can be at least partially explained by the scope of the competition—and the urgency of gaining a respectable market share. There is far too much at stake to justify lackluster advertising.

But one can see another factor at work in these inspired ads, promotions, mailers, and graphics. It is simply this: physicians are being appealed to as *consumers*—as human beings with the same needs, passions, and emotional responses as their patients.

The humor in these ads—and especially in the direct-mail packages (direct mail has traditionally been a strictly no-nonsense medium)—will come as an exhilarating surprise to anyone who might prejudge medical advertising as a solemn and joyless enterprise. And why not? The practice of medicine does not provide much opportunity for laughter; any advertising that can cause the good doctor to break into a grin—or a guffaw—will be welcomed, appreciated, and most likely *read* by its target audience.

The human, emotional side of medical advertising can be seen in the many examples using case studies of patients who have been treated with the advertised medication. As we follow the struggles of these individuals to overcome their illnesses, the products become more than pills or chemical preparations; they can now be defined in terms of relief from suffering. These ads appeal to the caring, nurturing side of the physician, conveying product benefits in uniquely fleshed-out form.

This focus on the patient raises an interesting point: that, especially in pharmaceutical advertising, the person who reads the ad (i.e., the physician) is not the one who will be buying the product. The true beneficiary is the patient, who in most cases will never see the advertising. Thus the physician takes on the role of intermediary—one who must be persuaded to *recommend* the product to others, usually in the form of a prescription.

This third-party factor is almost unique in advertising. If the patient is the one who ultimately reaps the benefits, how does the advertiser appeal to the physician-intermediary as a consumer?

By successfully understanding the psychology of the physician audience. The practice of medicine is partly an altruistic effort to serve the needs of patients, and partly a personal quest for professional achievement. But, happily for advertisers, the two are inextricably linked: by helping his or her patients, the physician achieves a sense of professional accomplishment. The role of the medical advertising team, then, is to convince physicians that the product will help them help their patients. In other words, the same product can be perceived as benefiting both the patient and the physician.

Given the targeted nature of direct mail, along with the highly specialized readership of many professional journals (cardiologists, OB/GYNs, nurses, psychiatrists, and other healthcare professionals are all served by separate publications), it becomes an easy matter for advertisers to zero in on a potentially responsive audience. But the creative talents behind the copy and graphics face a more difficult challenge: how to break away from the copious competitive advertising and establish a positive, memorable impression in the minds of the readers.

Compounding that difficulty, of course, is the fact that such a large proportion of medical advertising is aimed at the physician-as-intermediary—in other words, someone who will not even be purchasing the product. This is why the "top of mind" factor is paramount in medical advertising. The creative team, instead of asking directly for an order, implants an automatic triggering device in the physician's mind. Then, when it comes time to prescribe medication, the trigger goes off: the physician associates the patient's medical condition with the memorably advertised product, writes out a prescription for that product, and hands it over to the patient—who then makes the purchase at the local pharmacy. The circuit is complete; the ad has sold the product.

Of course, not everything in this book is targeted at the physician-as-intermediary. The ads placed in pharmacy journals, for example, appeal directly to the pharmacist. Campaigns for various hospital services and community health programs are aimed at the public, as are the majority of posters and a sizable percentage of the editorial features. The book also includes a sampling of corporate reports directed at shareholders, as well as single-sponsored publications that may reach physicians *or* the public. Complicating matters are the frequent promotional pieces that contain both an advertising message for the physician and educational information for the patient. And occasionally—as in the case of medical equipment, for instance—we will be looking at advertising addressed to the physician as the end consumer.

In each case, the creative team has taken stock of the audience and shaped the message—both visual and verbal—to conform with the background and needs of that audience. But the actual strategies, concepts, and graphic techniques employed to create these messages are wonderfully varied and distinctive.

As you explore the contents of this book, you'll gain a deeper appreciation of the creative dynamism in today's medical advertising and graphics. You'll be able to analyze the creative strategies behind each work. You'll see how copy and graphics blend to produce a unified whole. And you'll even come away with the insights you need to develop memorable advertising of your own.

The ads, promotions, and graphics in this volume were originally chosen to appear in the prestigious Rx Club Show, an annual competition held to honor the best examples of medical advertising and graphics created during the preceding year. The entries are grouped according to categories set up for the purposes of this book, which in most cases correspond to the original categories featured in the Rx Club Show.

Here is a brief chapter-by-chapter overview of the contents of this book:

CHAPTER 1: ADVERTISEMENTS

Here you will discover how leading agency talents position new products against the competition, and promote established products in the face of rivalry from newcomers and generics. Note the use of visual and verbal puns, humor, distinctive design elements, and other attention-getters to make the advertised product stand out from the crowd.

CHAPTER 2: AD CAMPAIGNS AND INSERTS

To create a sense of continuity over space or time, agencies make use of repeated design and/or copy elements: for example, running headlines, special ink colors, and recognizable graphic symbols. As you'll see, these devices help each unit gain recognition as part of the whole.

CHAPTER 3: EDITORIAL GRAPHICS

Selling isn't limited to ads. In today's magazine covers and editorial features, copy and graphics join forces to attract readership—much the way advertising attracts potential customers. At the same time, editorial graphics must sum up the contents of an article with a single memorable image.

CHAPTER 4: PROMOTIONS

What's the difference between an ad and a promotion? In the latter, the selling message accompanies some item of value being distributed to the prospective customer. As you'll see, free kits, posters, pamphlets, anatomical models, and similar giveaways are commonly used as medical promotions. They serve a useful purpose in the physician's office, and they stay visible long enough to promote the product.

CHAPTER 5: DIRECT MAIL

Only in the past decade or so has medical advertising begun to capitalize on the distinct advantages of this medium. And the results—both in terms of creative innovation and bottom-line response—have been spectacular. Because of the small target audiences for most mailings, medical advertisers have been able to dazzle their prospects with expensive, innovative, three-dimensional packages—many with interactive features that impart a sense of fun to the proceedings.

CHAPTER 6: POSTERS AND POSTER CAMPAIGNS

Nothing can rival the large-as-life impact of a poster, and you'll find some exceptional ones in this chapter. As used in medical advertising and promotion, posters can convey educational information to patients in the doctor's waiting room. Or they can speak directly to the physician, announcing upcoming events of interest.

CHAPTER 7: ART AND ILLUSTRATION

A good graphic illustrator can distill difficult concepts into a single powerful image—one that rouses the emotions or stimulates the senses. The outstanding examples in this chapter span the spectrum of styles and methods: from classical realism to *sur*realism. You'll encounter many examples of sleek state-of-the-art medical graphics, as well as amusingly rendered satirical pen-and-wash sketches.

CHAPTER 8: PHOTOGRAPHY AND SPECIAL EFFECTS

This concluding chapter focuses on some of the more innovative graphic techniques used to command the reader's attention: mixed media, dimensional models, photographic tricks—even special art created to resemble photographs. You'll be intrigued by these arresting attempts to outdo nature.

ESSAY

CREATIVITY IN MEDICAL ADVERTISING—SEVEN OBSERVATIONS

December 1982. The year-end review meeting at Doyle Dane Bernbach. From DDB offices all over the world, delegates have arrived on 49th Street to "show-and-tell" outstanding campaigns of the recent past. As the newest member of the family, KPR too has been invited to participate. And so my partner, Jerry Philips, has selected what he considers to be our most sparkling ads, worthy to be shown to this elite of consumer agencies. I watch Jerry's presentation from the last row of the auditorium. And overhear one creative director saying to his friend, "Can you imagine, having to do this kind of work *for the rest of your life?!*"

So much for creativity! Outsiders find it difficult at times to appreciate that this specialized form of advertising, with its multisyllabic terminology, governmental restrictions, and self-censorship, does also require a high degree of imagination. Eloquent proof that this is indeed the case may be found in the present volume, in which the efforts of the best writers and designers in our industry are being presented for the first time.

When I became a medical copywriter (at the old Klemtner agency in Newark, N.J.), what appealed to me was just that: this ever-challenging fusion of science, language, graphics, and salesmanship. And yet, there was no doubt in my mind that, having gathered experience on such accounts as B. F. Ascher and Central Pharmacal of Indiana, I would then move on to the world of "real" advertising. Well, that time never came, and I certainly have no regrets. I still enjoy writing and interacting with art directors and fellow writers. What have I learned in all those years? Is there a common denominator to all those ads and detail pieces and self-mailers? Let me share with you some observations (they happen to add up to the magic Seven) in the hope that they may be of help to other creative people.

1. Look for a picture. It's easy to show a consumer product in action—the scouring pad turning a grimy pan into a shiny mirror. The action of prescription drugs can be measured (the inevitable graphs and tables!) but

seldom seen. We often have to deal in abstractions, such as the passage of time, and must try to find their visual equivalents. Of course, I prefer to see real people in our ads, rather than three-dimensional formulas floating in outer space. Unfortunately, they too can turn into visual cliches.

I once tried to find a visual equivalent for the concept of *prophylaxis* in angina pectoris. How to illustrate something that could have happened but didn't! So I thought of analogies: prophylaxis in dental practice, in infant nutrition, in internal medicine, etc. A terrible idea! The illustration showed a baby (my daughter Jane) getting her vitamin drops, but the product was Peritrate®, a coronary vasodilator. Moral: never use one medical situation to illustrate another! The doctor has no time for visual puns.

2. Positioning means excluding. We find the chink in our competitor's armor. We apply our resources to the segment from which we expect the highest return. Of necessity, that means neglecting the other segments. You can't have it both ways. A well-known campaign once proclaimed: "A Man's Coffee!" OK, that's positioning. But then someone got cold feet and the complete slogan actually ran:"A Man's Coffee—And Women Love It, Too!" When you try to be all things to all people, you wind up with exactly nothing.

3. Stay with a good idea. The idea for Parafon Forte® that helped KPR to land the McNeil account remained constant over a period of 15 years! The interpretation underwent periodic changes—from clinical to humorous and back again—but the theme, once found to be on target, did not change. That takes a lot of courage, on the part of both agency and client! A corollary: graphic symbols become effective through repetition and consistent use. A cartoon in *The New Yorker* showed Betsy Ross submitting her flag to a review committee of Founding Fathers. "I don't know," one of them said, "to me, it's just a bunch of stars and stripes. It doesn't say, The United States of America!" In pharmaceutical terms: a rose is

a rose is a rose is an antidepressant! A rose became the symbol for the lifting of depression through consistent association with Ludiomil®.

4. Don't expect ads to put out brush fires. Listen to your sales force. They have their fingers on the pulse of our customer group. But don't get carried away when the D.M. in Seattle tells you his local problems. Journal ads must find a common denominator. They shouldn't belabor problems that aren't perceived as such by the majority of the audience.

5. Dare to be simple. Puns, word plays, allusions, hidden quotations, are an occupational disease of copywriters. Occasionally, very occasionally, they work. When you've coined an extraordinarily clever phrase, ask yourself: does it make things clearer? Am I running the risk of being misunderstood? In fact, it's a mistake to assume that our audience necessarily thinks like us. Frank Mann, long-time ad manager of A. H. Robins, once told me, "When I use a picture of a horse, I like to run a caption underneath: 'this horse is a horse'!" Excellent advice!

6. An idea that's truly different can't be tested. I realize, in today's climate, that's heresy. MBAs are convinced that *everything* can be improved by testing. I do believe in market research, to get our facts straight. In pre- and posttesting of the communications objective. But it's in the very nature of originality to cause a certain degree of discomfort. Against his better judgment, Bill Bernbach agreed to test the now-famous line "Avis is only Number 2. We try harder!" The test turned out badly. And the client said, "Never mind, Bill. We'll run it anyway!" Which brings me to my last observation.

7. Find creative clients! The secret of longevity is to be careful in selecting one's ancestors. The secret of creative advertising is to pick the right clients. A writer, an art director, a creative department, and an advertising agency are only as good as the person(s) who can accept or reject their ideas.

BY JOHN KALLIR
Kallir, Philips, Ross, Inc.

No significant changes in vital signs in cardiovascular patients*

One of many benefits that comprise the distinctive Ativan profile.

In seven common-protocol, double-blind studies of anxious cardiovascular patients (212 patients on placebo, 211 on Ativan), those on Ativan were found to have statistically significant relief of moderate-to-severe anxiety associated with cardiovascular disorders, with no significant changes in vital signs or serious adverse reactions noted.†

*Benzodiazepines have not been shown to be of benefit in treating the cardiovascular component.

†Data on file, Wyeth Laboratories.

Only
Ativan®
(lorazepam) C-IV

offers <u>all</u> these benefits...

Control
with
once-a-day
dosage...

KIDSPIRIT!

A 15-month calendar presented with the compliments of McNeil Consumer Products Company, makers of Children's and Junior Strength TYLENOL® acetaminophen

(Above left) KPR sought the imaginative talents of renowned artist Jean-Michel Folon for a series of symbolic illustrations depicting the benefits of Ativan®, a drug used to treat anxiety associated with depressive symptoms. (All six stunning illustrations and credits appear on page 66.) (Above right) This intensely colorful cover is one of three created by KPR for a series of direct-mail pieces touting the benefits of Micronase® in the treatment of type II diabetes. The strong graphic on each cover symbolically represents a particular benefit of the medication. (All three covers and credits appear on pages 170–71.) (Left) To promote Children's and Junior Strength TYLENOL®, KPR featured large, colorful photographs of children in this graphically dynamic calendar, which was designed not only to boost doctors' recommendations but also to appeal to children and mothers in their pediatrician's waiting room. (Credits appear on page 156.)

ESSAY

MARKETING, MAGIC MARKERS, AND MAGIC

Graphic communication at Ciba-Geigy has long been considered to be the best in the industry. This glowing reputation, born in Switzerland and brought to the United States by Swiss designers, now has to be maintained by vigorous new efforts. One must not be lulled into complacency but must meet the challenge and the need for constant change.

The designer of today, who is sometimes called upon to be a magician, has been involved in some of the most rapid changes in graphic communications history. The Renaissance person of the past—a person able to do anything and do it well—is just about extinct today. Our current age of specialization seems to narrow one's creative space and obliterate the past. We are living in an explosion of electronic and computer technology, which demands that the designer learn new ABC's: for instance, Alias (Computer Animation System), DVE (Digital Video Effects), and CGI (Computer Graphic Images).

In the early years of the print profession, designers used pencils and pastels, which were later side-tracked for quick and clean Magic Markers. Similarly, the Macintosh and Lightspeed PC's are side-tracking the Magic Marker, but with far more impact on the designer. Some designers are afraid of computers because these machines represent a different language and a completely different way of using hand and eye movement. Some people, calling themselves designers, are very proficient with the computer; however, they lack the skills in design and conceptualization that provide the foundation for the professional craft, regardless of what medium is used. At this time, the computer is a great tool for "roughing out" concepts, ideas, or even a mechanical, but one cannot consider it a do-it-all medium.

Two of the most sophisticated media to evolve in the advertising industry in recent years are TV production and computer animation. Each has a language of its own, and it is necessary to understand the basic concepts of each in order to obtain the best production quality and cost effective communications. Because of the significant technological advances made in the last five years, the industry knows the least about these media. They represent, however, the most important means of communication available to the pharmaceutical/healthcare community. With regard to TV production, video results are immediate and the image appears to be live. Computer animation can be completed in far less time than traditional film animation. It enables the art director actually to meet deadlines!

With all these new developments, the graphic designer must constantly update his education. But, despite the explosion of technology, a good designer cannot permit himself or herself to rely strictly on synthetic imagery. A good designer must expose himself to life, so that he can be stimulated by all that is around him. Developing a curiosity for life allows him to grow and to create imaginative concepts and designs.

A discussion of corporate advertising would not be complete without mention of the marketing people. A well-known lecturer once talked about marketing types using the left side of their brain while the creatives use the right side! This oversimplification does bring up a dramatic point: the creatives and the marketing types are often diametrically opposed when it comes to design. Marketing people would greatly benefit from courses in the principles of advertising, creative writing, journalism, graphic design, and art history. Similarly, the creative types would greatly benefit from taking courses in marketing. Perhaps this interdisciplinary sharing of knowledge would not only enhance communication, but also lay the groundwork for understanding and role clarity between these traditionally dissonant factions.

In my opinion, there can be real teamwork when a swinging door exists between the marketing people and the designer and the copywriter. Today, graphic communication is as sophisticated as the people approving the work; therefore, there must be two-way communication.

I am sympathetic toward the need to utilize research in order to have statistical data on which to base decisions; however, one must not forget that statistics may be biased in a variety of ways. The expertise of the designer and the writer must be taken into consideration.

Following my recovery from the shock of hearing a young product manager say that mediocre was good enough, I began to take a harder look at other corporate advertising. What I saw was dismaying: everything looked the same! Many companies seem to be exhausting their budgets on expensive printing and production when the concepts and the designs are mediocre. It doesn't have to be expensive to be good. In fact, having less money can be a stimulating creative challenge.

If you think you have something good, fight for it. If you don't, you will wind up with what can be called the "Pinocchio Effect." What begins as a simple concept winds up completely distorted after it has been redesigned numerous times.

In spite of everything, however, graphic communication remains a splendid profession. Just keep your door swinging!

BY BOB TALARCZYK
Design Director/Producer,
Ciba-Geigy Pharmaceuticals/C & G Advertising Inc.

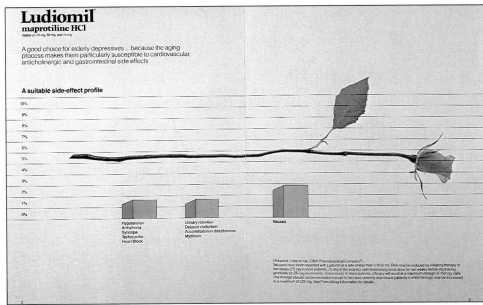

(Above left) To promote the antidepressant Tofranil-PM®, C & G Advertising Inc. created a giveaway memo pad with the image of a faceless man printed down the side, and housed it in an even more ingenious box. The outside of the box reads, "Breaking Down the Walls of Depression," and indeed, the "walls" of the box break down to reveal an inner room with a featureless human figure in the background. (Credits appear on page 177.)

(Above right) The watery blues and whirlpool effect symbolize the depressive side of manic depression in this ad for Lithobid®. Positioning the art on its side added an intriguing off-balance effect. (Credits appear on page 65.) (Below) Shown here are the cover and the first inside spread from a promotional booklet for the antidepressant Ludiomil®. The riveting close-up of an elderly face drives home the seriousness and danger of depression in older

patients. The first inside spread presents data on the favorable side effects of the medication and introduces a rose, which acts as a symbol for the lifting of depression by Ludiomil®. (Credits appear on page 137.) (All the graphics shown here were created by C & G Advertising Inc. under the art direction of Bob Talarczyk.)

THE FIELD OF MEDICAL ILLUSTRATION

Some art buyers may think that a medical illustrator is simply an artist with an interest in medicine. While that is not completely false, it is only a half truth. We medical illustrators can never, of course, be the consummate medical specialists. We can never know all there is to know about general medicine or surgery or anatomy or pathology or whatever. But we do know the basics and we strengthen our foundation as we move through our career. Of more importance is our knowledge that every line is a statement of fact. *A trained medical illustrator would not put a line down on paper without knowing what it means.* We are trained to ask questions, to find answers. We read through masses of literature whenever we embark on a new assignment. We build up a mountain of facts, often more than what is seemingly needed for the job. This gives us more options and allows us to better assess our approach to the visual presentation. It lets us walk around the mountain of information that we've created and figure out our approach. This reading and building and growing is what keeps the field fresh and exciting for me and my colleagues. It pays off for the client.

ACCURACY AND COMMUNICATION

The first and most obvious way it pays off is through accuracy. There is nothing worse than a mistake appearing in print; mistakes never die, they don't ever seem to fade away! But while knowledge is necessary to eliminate inaccuracies, it is also important for another reason. It enhances our ability to know what is important to the story and what can be eliminated. By featuring the important, we move information. And conveying information to the reader or viewer is what our job is all about. The static presentation of facts is not our job, and only when you know a subject well can you tailor it to the audience. We are in the communication business, we are communicators.

The buyer can have an important story to tell, but if we can't get it off the page and into the audience's mind, the buyer has wasted his time and money. Depiction of facts will work

to an extent, but only to a very committed audience. And certainly the plain, total, and bare presentation of scientific material can be uninviting and overwhelming. It can actually get in the way of learning. If plain dissemination was all that was needed, judgment and creativity would be dead. And our job as illustrators would be easy.

If depiction was everything, the camera would suffice. But the camera does not bring judgment to bear. For the most part, it is undiscerning. Of course, that quality is its value and its strength—and one that allows it to play a very important part in the dissemination of information. But our strength, as communicators, is the ability to emphasize, to highlight, to underplay, to bring the important material to the forefront. We don't just draw pictures, we move information. We move that information from the page or the screen to the mind of the viewer. And we use approaches that help to keep it there.

Our ability to turn the spotlight on the message and to make everything else fade away is what we do best. To do that without losing orientation and without losing our audience— all the while retaining accuracy—is the challenge, adventure, and satisfaction of this career.

THE APPROACH

First must come the knowledge, the training, the background, and the information necessary to develop the concept. This concept, however, is dependent upon more than that. Something the client must supply, to wit: information about the interests, education level, and breadth of the audience. We also need to know whether we are to inform or attract. Are we selling a product or educating a student? Or both? Is our viewer studying or just glancing through a journal? Or both? Each bit of information, and every one of the client's needs, must be considered in our presentation of the medical subject matter. And that matter will look different for each audience and will change as that audience learns and its needs change. It is this dynamic

approach that provides meaningful visuals. There is no shortcut.

MEMORABLE ILLUSTRATIONS

How do we create an illustration that clicks into the memory grid of the viewer so that he retains the image and the message encompassed? One part of the answer is to know the audience. That's a phrase that we've all heard so often and yet it is so difficult to accomplish. Our audience and the knowledge that it has is variable, constantly changing, changing as we teach. But, in general, if we know the level of the audience (and that is a constant pursuit of publishers and buyers), then we can create illustrations for that audience. This means that the amount of information put in, and the amount of material left out, is tailored to the audience. For it is what is left out as well as what is included that determines whether the art hits the target or misses. It may even be that what is left out makes it more memorable. We must never lose orientation for the audience. We must keep enough of the familiar so that our image has a spot to slide into and bring the new material along with it. But think about the awesome task of knowing your audience. The students are all different, whether medical, dental, or paramedical. The postgraduate student, the high-prescribing physician, the specialist, the general practitioner receiving 50 to 100 magazines per week— all of these audiences are different. All of our illustrations must be targeted, and different as well, if they are to reach these audiences.

SPECIALIZATION

There are many specialists within our field, although some of us may be able to do a wide variety of assignments. But, in general, we follow our interests, or perhaps our ability and talent draw us into specific areas of expression. Textbook illustration must look different from illustration for pharmaceutical advertisements. Its role is different. The job of the book illustration is to convey information. And while it must look inviting and well done, information dissemination is its primary objective. An advertisement is there first to attract attention and second to impart informa-

BY ROBERT J. DEMAREST
Director, Medical Illustration, College of
Physicians and Surgeons, Columbia University

tion. And while these proportions may vary and the components may change, each illustrator will find his or her niche and usually specialize in it. The client will benefit if he recognizes this.

TEXTBOOK ILLUSTRATION

Once we move away from straight depiction of anatomy we are usually called upon to demonstrate an action or a process. Take surgical illustration, for example. The illustrator is called upon to depict a procedure of, perhaps, some six hours in length—a dynamic event that, as in all surgery, involves as much tactile sense as it does visual. The procedure is temporal and three-dimensional. We are called upon to reduce it to a small number of illustrations that compress time, turn three dimensions into two, and make it comprehensible to a reader who is geographically and perhaps culturally removed from the author. It must be so understandable that the reader can repeat the procedure without firsthand assistance from the author. I know of no comparable challenge in the field of illustration. For the illustrator it is the ultimate in satisfaction, the most rewarding illustration assignment, and the most difficult. The reader can't move his head and look under things the way the surgeon does. He can't press his finger into the muscle to feel the bony attachment. He must see and feel and understand on the basis of a flat two-dimensional work. No representational illustrator, no matter how technically proficient, can do that without complete understanding of the material. No author can bring that visual continuity, that skill in dynamic communication, to an artist. No content expert holds the illustrator's hand and guides it.

CONTROLLED-CIRCULATION MEDICAL MAGAZINES

When we look at controlled-circulation medical magazines we find an interesting new set of circumstances. This is a very substantial and rewarding area for the medical illustrator. There are a great many of these magazines, and while they each strive for a unique profile, many of them use and need medical illustration.

The cover gets the most attention from the illustrator. It is a front line of sorts, and the battle is for attention. It is here on the cover that the fight for attention begins, and if it is supported with quality editorial material on the inside, the magazine can flourish. Inside, the illustrations are more content-oriented. There is less imperative to get the reader's attention inside, more need to impart information.

Good cover illustrators do not necessarily make good inside illustrators and vice-versa. The attention-getting cover illustration embodies an approach to presenting the material that is somewhere between the scientific illustration of the textbook and advertising illustration. It must call out to the reader and say "pick me up and look at me" but it shouldn't have the same intensity as an ad. The cover should have some scientific content and hint at more on the inside. The inside art, like the textbook illustration, should bring information to the reader and make the subject matter easily digestible and memorable.

ADVERTISING ILLUSTRATION

With advertising illustration we are faced with yet another facet of medical illustration. Here, technique and creative ways of showing material become very important. The advertisements that fill the magazines and the detail pieces that promote drugs need a different look. They need illustrators that have a flair for the unusual and the spectacular. For an illustrator to be successful here he needs a faultless technique and a contemporary style. This is a valuable arena for the illustrator and one that may often be less content-oriented than textbook illustration—not less important, perhaps, but with a somewhat different emphasis.

MEDICAL-LEGAL ILLUSTRATION

This is a relatively new area and one that seems to be picking up momentum. The emphasis in medical-legal illustration is on presentation of factual material to a lay audience, a jury. Illustration in this arena must cut through the verbiage and the medical nomen-

clature to help in the understanding of complex medical issues. The illustrations are used by an attorney and expert witnesses, although the illustrator often plans the content and the way the message is to be presented. A mistake by an illustrator can lose him a client forever, lose a case, and do irreparable harm to our field.

CHOOSING AN ILLUSTRATOR

It behooves the client to know the interests, the strengths, and the limitations of the artists that he is considering for a project. Most will be honest—no illustrator is interested in embarrassing either the client or himself. But a word of caution: don't let flashy technique blind you to a lack of solid education and training in the fundamentals. Accuracy must underlie the technique.

How do you recognize the competent illustrator if you're a client without a great deal of experience dealing with visuals? Will the illustrator's work give you a clue? Usually. If a medical illustrator is a communicator, then *understanding must come easily.* If the illustration doesn't communicate to you, the client, then it will never come across to the intended audience.

Much has been said about the Information Age in which we live. New material is constantly flooding the medical field. I believe that the medical illustrator is riding the crest of an information wave in medicine. It's an exciting ride!

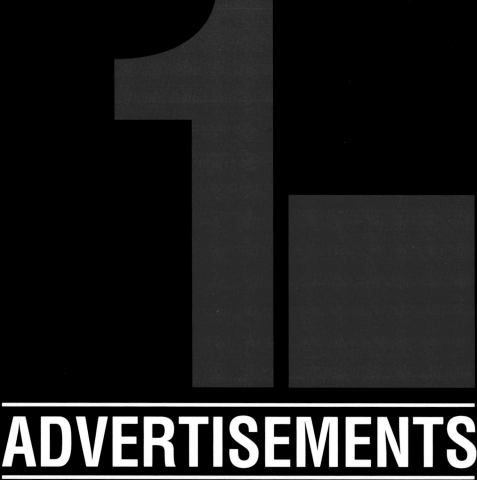

1.

ADVERTISEMENTS

BUSINESS MAGAZINES
TRADE MAGAZINES
CONSUMER MAGAZINES

In medical advertising, as elsewhere in the advertising industry, the client usually has a specific purpose for placing an ad in the media. The company may want to launch a new product, or create "top of mind" memorability for an established one. It may wish to dispel negative publicity about a specific drug, or change prevailing perceptions about its use. And, of course, there's the matter of confronting the competition—whether it's a young, unproven product going face-to-face with a time-tested standard, or the old standard staving off the erosion of market share by generics.

Once the client sets the purpose of the ad, the agency must deliver a potent message along those lines to the targeted readers. And this is no easy proposition. An ad must sell the virtues of a product or service—or even an entire company—within the confines of a limited amount of media space. What's more, the ad must compete against a noisy flock of rival ads shouting for the reader's attention. So, even though the medium is carefully chosen to deliver the target audience, there's no guarantee that the ad will capture the attention of that audience.

This is where creative strategy comes into play. In the hands of a talented creative team, copy and art join forces to project a vibrant and memorable message—one that not only engages the audience but creates a pronounced desire for the advertised product. After all, an ad must do more than inform. It has to *sell*.

The ads assembled in this chapter reflect a stunning variety of approaches to salesmanship in print.

As with most modern space advertising, visuals dominate the scene. The visual can take the form of a metaphor (the intestinal tract becomes a winding river in a PHILLIPS'® Milk of Magnesia ad) or simply a potent attention-getter (those drops of bright red blood oozing from sutures in the ad for Stadol®). It can amuse (see the back-scratching Statue of

Liberty in the Atarax® ad), or evoke sympathy (the helpless babies who need MYLICON® DROPS), or neatly sum up the benefits of the product (a single prescription for Lopressor HCT® replaces two separate prescriptions for other drugs). In short, pictures have acquired the power to do much of the talking, sometimes to the virtual exclusion of copy (see the Transderm-Nitro® "clock" ad).

But copywriters aren't about to give up the ghost, either. A strong, compelling headline still works like magic. Often, the illustration joins forces with the headline to deliver a memorable visual/verbal pun (the "articulate" hands signing for Feldene®, or the warning that drug abuse is "collar blind"—i.e., that it affects white and blue collar workers alike.)

A good headline, backed by an appropriate visual, can break through the audience's apathy barrier and command readership. Note the ominous urgency of Bayer®'s "This is not a headache," coupled with the angiogram showing a blocked coronary artery. Or the simple, deadening impact of seeing a thigh bone riddled by osteoporosis, accompanied by the simple headline message, "Too late."

Because competition is an omnipresent factor, agencies will often go out of their way to differentiate their clients' ad from the dozens of "lookalikes" in medical journals and trade publications. One ad for Berlex Imaging used a sharp reproduction of a 500-year-old Flemish portrait to convey the quality of the company's diagnostic images; a less imaginative agency might simply have photographed the equipment.

For the same reason, interactive ads are emerging as a force to contend with. They invite the reader to play, to explore, to get involved. They appeal to the child in all of us, and they get noticed at the expense of the more mundane competition. For a good example, see the ad for TONOCARD® with its "tear-open" flap disclosing underlying heart trouble.

One age-old strategy for establishing an identity—and one that obviously still works— is to create a recognizable symbol or character that stands for the product. The makers of e.p.t.® (the home pregnancy test) have been using a golden rabbit; the promoters of the Stomach tlc™ program dreamed up a lovable Claymation stomach character for multimedia use.

The ads reviewed on the following pages represent the best work in an immensely fertile field. They should prove beyond doubt that medical ads don't have to be dull or clinical—or even solemn. They can be scintillating, colorful, alarming, engrossing, whimsical, or poignant. And, as you'll soon discover, the very best of them have the power to *astonish*.

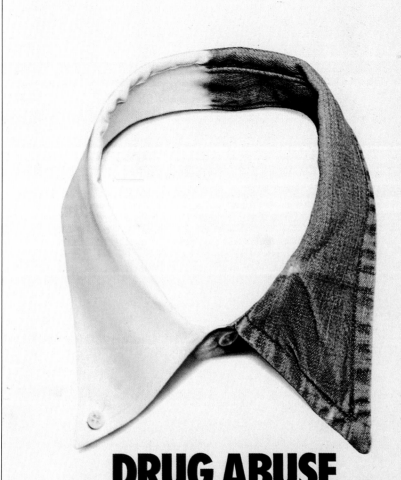

DRUG ABUSE IS COLLAR-BLIND

Drug abusers can be high on the corporate ladder or somewhere near the bottom. One thing's for certain. They're crafty about their addiction. They've learned to hide their habit from friends and co-workers. Drug abusers think they can even outsmart you. But you know better. Confront them before it's too late. If you don't, who will?

Partnership for a Drug-Free America

Title: **"Drug Abuse Is Collar-Blind"**
Ad Agency: **Sudler & Hennessey**
Client: **Partnership for a Drug-Free America**
Art Director: **Dick Russinko**
Photographer: **John Olivo**
Copywriter: **Diane Cooney**

GOLD. A clever pun ("color-blind" becomes "collar-blind") serves as the springboard for a serious message about drug abuse in this ad created for Partnership for a Drug-Free America. Aimed at occupational health physicians, the ad uses a simple yet ingenious graphic device—a collar that's blue on one side, white on the other—to warn the audience that drug abuse knows no occupational boundaries. The copy touches on the telltale signs of drug abuse and stresses the need for confronting drug abusers in the workplace. According to Diane Cooney, creative director (copy) at Sudler & Hennessey, "telling physicians to do what they should already be doing is a touchy matter"—and one that was handled here with great skill.

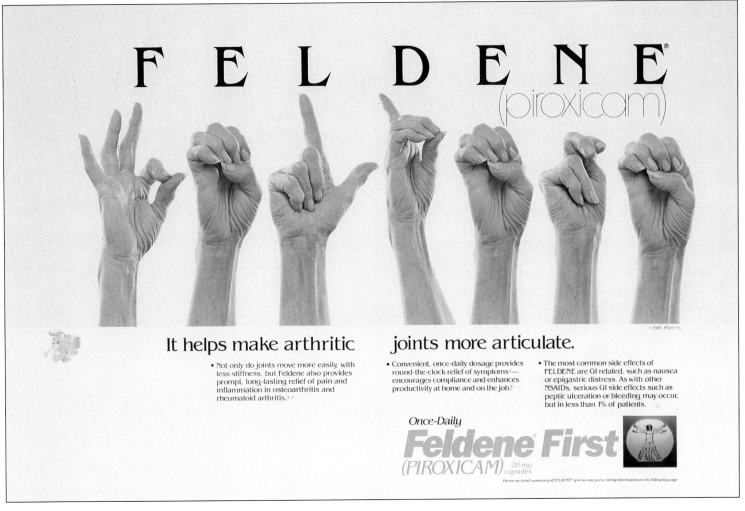

Product: **Feldene**®
Ad Agency: **Dorritie & Lyons, Inc.**
Client: **Pfizer Laboratories**
Art Director: **Mike Lyons**
Photographer: **Al Francekevich**
Copywriter: **Bill Brown**

GOLD. Created by Dorritie & Lyons, Inc., this award-winning ad cleverly capitalizes on the double meaning of the word *articulate* (i.e., "jointed" and "well-spoken"). Using sign language, these "well-spoken" hands spell out the word Feldene®, which happens to be the name of the preparation being promoted here for relief of arthritic symptoms. An interesting sidelight: the model whose hands were photographed for the ad was an arthritic sign language teacher who actually underwent treatment with Feldene®.

Product: **PHILLIPS'**® **Milk of Magnesia**
Ad Agency: **Dugan Farley Communications Associates, Inc.**
Client: **Glenbrook Laboratories**
Art Director: **Eric Rathje**
Illustrator: **Lou Bory**
Copywriter: **Frank Cordasco**

SILVER. This lighthearted look at the intestinal tract as a meandering internal waterway is based firmly on physiological fact: that PHILLIPS'® Milk of Magnesia aids elimination by drawing part of the body's natural water supply into the intestines. According to Copy Group Supervisor Frank Cordasco, this award-winning ad was designed to boost physician recommendations for PHILLIPS'® Milk of Magnesia in a market with several new entries, most notably, bulk laxatives. The graphic was spun off in a direct-mail campaign that offered a sailboat as one of the prizes.

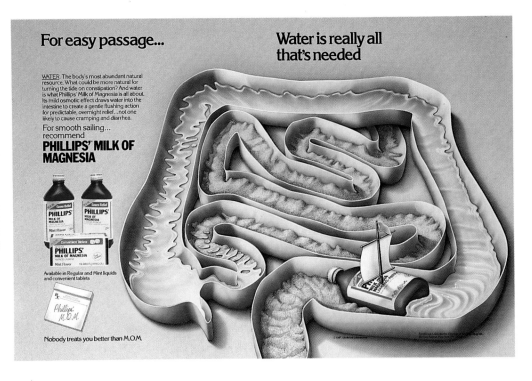

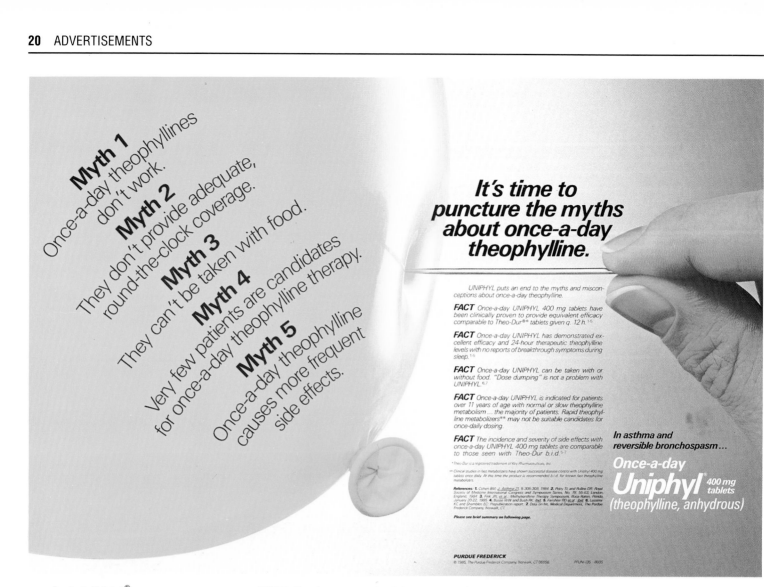

It's time to
puncture the myths
about once-a-day
theophylline.

UNIPHYL puts an end to the myths and misconceptions about once-a-day theophylline.

FACT Once-a-day UNIPHYL 400 mg tablets have been clinically proven to provide equivalent efficacy comparable to Theo-Dur** tablets given q. 12 h.[1-6]

FACT Once-a-day UNIPHYL has demonstrated excellent efficacy and 24-hour therapeutic theophylline levels with no reports of breakthrough symptoms during sleep.[1-6]

FACT Once-a-day UNIPHYL can be taken with or without food. "Dose dumping" is not a problem with UNIPHYL.[6,7]

FACT Once-a-day UNIPHYL is indicated for patients over 11 years of age with normal or slow theophylline metabolism ... the majority of patients. Rapid theophylline metabolizers** may not be suitable candidates for once-daily dosing.

FACT The incidence and severity of side effects with once-a-day UNIPHYL 400 mg tablets are comparable to those seen with Theo-Dur b.i.d.[6,7]

*Theo-Dur is a registered trademark of Key Pharmaceuticals, Inc.

** Clinical studies in fast metabolizers have shown successful disease control with Uniphyl 400 mg tablets once daily. At this time the product is recommended b.i.d. for known fast theophylline metabolizers.

References: **1.** Cohen BM: J. Asthma 21, 5:305-308, 1984. **2.** Petry TJ, and Rollins DR: Royal Society of Medicine International Congress and Symposium Series, No. 78, 55-63, London, England, 1984. **3.** Fink JN, et al.: Methylxanthine Therapy Symposium, Boca Raton, Florida, January 20-22, 1985. **4.** Busse WW and Bush RK: ibid. **5.** Fleisher RD et al.: ibid. **6.** Lazarus KC and Shambain EC: Prepublication report. **7.** Data on file, Medical Department, The Purdue Frederick Company, Norwalk, CT.

Please see brief summary on following page.

In asthma and
reversible bronchospasm...

**Once-a-day
Uniphyl® 400 mg tablets**
(theophylline, anhydrous)

PURDUE FREDERICK
© 1985, The Purdue Frederick Company, Norwalk, CT 06856.   PFUNI-135 - 8035

Product: **Uniphyl®**
Ad Agency: **Gross Townsend Frank Hoffman, Inc.**
Client: **Purdue Frederick**
Art Director: **David Frank**
Photographer: **Andy Spreitzer**
Copywriter: **Ronnie Hoffman**

SILVER. How does an agency break through prevailing misbeliefs and skepticism among physicians? Gross Townsend Frank Hoffman, Inc., came up with a symbolic depiction of "myth-bursting" in this successful ad for Uniphyl®, a drug used in treating asthma. The balloon about to be popped represents the common misconceptions about theophyllines, the generic class of drug to which Uniphyl® belongs. Note that the negative "myths" refer only to the generic drug: "Myth 1—Once-a-day theophyllines don't work." On the other hand, the facts used to dispel the myths refer to Uniphyl® by name: "FACT—Once-a-day Uniphyl® 400 tablets have been clinically proven..." As a result, the ad cleverly lifts the client's product above the controversy and positions it as a safe, effective treatment in a crowded category.

Product: **Transderm-Nitro®**
Ad Agency: **C & G Advertising Inc. (In-house)**
Client: **Ciba-Geigy Pharmaceutical Co.**
Art Director: **Ron Vareltzis**
Photographer: **Denny Harris**
Copywriter: **Nancy Benton**

SILVER. The notion of angina sufferers as semi-invalids is quickly dispelled by this award-winning ad from C & G Advertising Inc., the in-house agency at Ciba-Geigy Pharmaceutical Co. The ad combines the surefire effectiveness of a customer endorsement with the upbeat, high-energy image of an angina patient happily tubing down an amusement park waterway. If you look closely, you'll see that he's wearing a Transderm-Nitro® nitroglycerin patch on his chest. What better way to show that the product enables angina sufferers to enjoy life? Since the picture says it all, the copy is limited to a few brief statements of benefits.

"You've made life easier for angina sufferers."
— H.B. from Ridgewood, NY

Reduces frequency of anginal attacks

Reduces need for sublingual nitroglycerin

Convenient, once-daily application

Improves exercise performance

Transderm-Nitro®
nitroglycerin

Winning the hearts of patients everywhere

C I B A

Please consult Brief Summary of Prescribing Information on the following page.

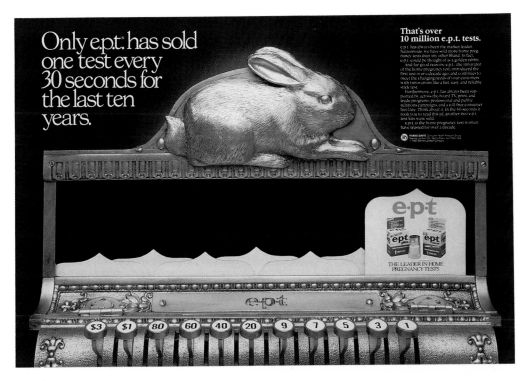

Only e.p.t. has sold one test every 30 seconds for the last ten years.

That's over 10 million e.p.t. tests.

THE LEADER IN HOME PREGNANCY TESTS

Product: **e.p.t.**®
Ad Agency: **Thomas G. Ferguson Associates Inc.**
Client: **Parke-Davis**
Art Director: **George Courides**
Model Maker: **Suzanne Couture**
Photographer: **Fred Kenner Studio**
Copywriter: **Robert Krell**

SILVER. The profit potential of e.p.t.®, the well-established home pregnancy test, is depicted as a golden rabbit atop a cash register in this colorful ad targeted at pharmacists. The rabbit, of course, is a familiar symbol for pregnancy testing and had been used in prior e.p.t.® promotions. The copy emphasizes the wide public acceptance of e.p.t.®, as well as the promotional plans that would soon be sending new waves of customers into pharmacies to purchase the product.

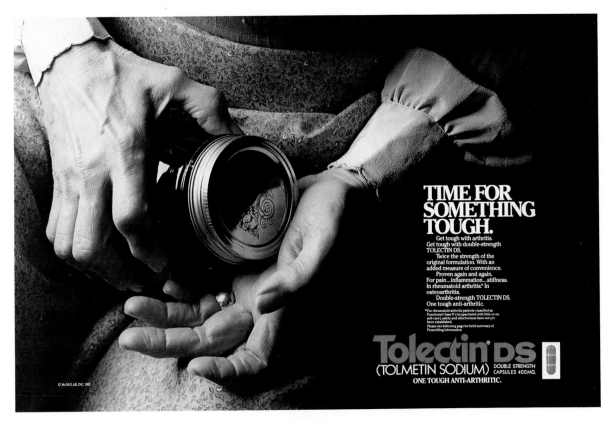

TIME FOR SOMETHING TOUGH.

Get tough with arthritis. Get tough with double-strength TOLECTIN DS.
Twice the strength of the original formulation. With an added measure of convenience.
Proven again and again. For pain...inflammation...stiffness. In rheumatoid arthritis* In osteoarthritis.
Double-strength TOLECTIN DS. One tough anti-arthritic.

*For rheumatoid arthritis patients classified as Functional Class IV (incapacitated with little or no self-care), safety and effectiveness have not yet been established.
Please see following page for brief summary of Prescribing Information.

Tolectin® DS
(TOLMETIN SODIUM) DOUBLE STRENGTH CAPSULES 400MG.
ONE TOUGH ANTI-ARTHRITIC.

Product: **Tolectin**® **DS**
Ad Agency: **Sudler & Hennessey**
Client: **McNeilab, Inc.**
Art Director: **Ernie Smith**
Photographer: **Dick Frank**
Copywriter: **Bob McCaffrey**

SILVER. A powerful close-up of human hands dramatizes the message "Time for Something Tough" in this two-page ad for Tolectin® DS, a double-strength anti-arthritic formula. Beautifully lit and rendered larger than life, the massive hands struggle to open a jar—at once suggesting the ravages of arthritis and the power of the remedy in a single memorable image.

Product: **Transderm-Nitro**®
Ad Agency: **C & G Advertising Inc. (In-house)**
Client: **Ciba-Geigy Pharmaceutical Co.**
Art Director: **Ron Vareltzis**
Photographer: **Ed Gallucci**
Copywriter: **Nancy Benton**

SILVER. We've all heard about medications that work "round the clock." In this ad for Transderm-Nitro®, a nitroglycerin skin patch for angina patients, the creative team at C & G Advertising has gone a step further: they've transformed the product *into* a clock. This simple but ingenious device, coupled with the exceptionally brief copy ("Puts in a full day's work"), tells physicians at a glance that Transderm-Nitro® offers 24-hour benefits.

Product: **LIORESAL**®
Ad Agency: **C & G Advertising Inc. (In-house)**
Client: **Geigy Pharmaceuticals**
Art Director: **Ron Vareltzis**
Photographer: **Image Bank**
Copywriter: **Ellen Schultz**

SILVER. A dramatic panned shot captures the speed and dynamism of a wheelchair athlete in this inspirational ad for LIORESAL®, the antispastic muscle relaxant. The blurred background conveys a sweeping sense of action, while the headline ("Determination, hard work, and LIORESAL®") gives off a positive yet realistic message: that the patient's attitude and perseverance, coupled with drug therapy, can make a big difference. The copy by Ellen Schultz stresses the safe, nonaddictive nature of the drug, with the added message that LIORESAL® "helps them meet the challenge."

Product: **LANOXIN**®
Ad Agency: **Lavey/Wolff/Swift Inc.**
Client: **Burroughs Wellcome Co.**
Art Director: **Ken Lavey**
Illustrator: **Ken Lavey**
Photographer: **John Gotman**
Copywriter: **Al Gerstein**

SILVER. You won't find any meticulously crafted models or punning headline copy in this campaign for LANOXIN®, a digoxin preparation for treating congestive heart failure (CHF) in the early stages. A simple pen-and-ink sketch of a heart by Chairman/Creative Director Ken Lavey is the key visual; the bright red arrow shows a healthy surge of blood from the left ventricle into the aorta. Inside, the no-nonsense copy expands on the benefits introduced on the first page, and the heart graphic is enlarged for greater impact. According to Lavey, the agency's goals were to "create a unique graphic that looks different in a field of slick anatomically rendered hearts" and to "get the doctor to take a new look at a very old product." (Digoxin has been around for two centuries.) The ad was aimed at GPs and internists as well as cardiologists.

New clinical studies[1,2] continue to confirm the essential value of digoxin in CHF and show:

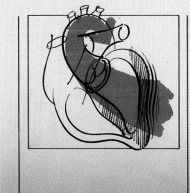

In patients with normal sinus rhythm...

- **Improved ejection fraction.**

- **Improved cardiac output.**

- **Improved exercise tolerance.**

New evidence continues to confirm the essential value of LANOXIN® in CHF.[1,2]

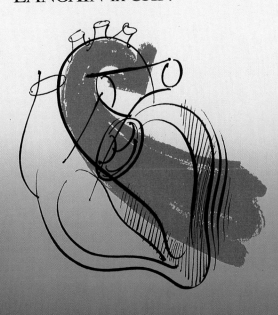

Improved ejection fraction
In a recent double-blind, placebo-controlled study[1] in patients with normal sinus rhythm, digoxin produced a significant increase in ejection fraction compared to captopril ($P<.05$) and placebo ($P<.01$). By contrast, there was no significant difference between captopril and placebo.

Improvement in ejection fraction represents improvement in myocardial contractile performance and better emptying of the left ventricle.

Percent Improvement in Ejection Fraction*

Digoxin[1] 17% Captopril 7% Placebo 3%

*Adapted from the Captopril-Digoxin Multicenter Research Group study.[1]
† $P<.05$ compared to captopril; $P<.01$ compared to placebo.

Improved cardiac output
The positive inotropic effect of digoxin (as measured in part by improved cardiac output) was associated with improved left ventricular (LV) function.[3] This significant improvement in cardiac output was seen in patients at rest as well as during exercise. Long-term therapy with digoxin contributed to the maintenance of LV function as indicated by both a decrease in cardiac output when digoxin was stopped and a restoration to treatment levels with readministration of the drug.

Improved exercise tolerance
In a new placebo-controlled study[2] of CHF patients with normal sinus rhythm and on diuretics, exercise tolerance (treadmill) was improved 14% ($P<.05$) by digoxin. In this study, digoxin produced favorable effects on cardiac function beyond those of the diuretic alone. Another study[4] showed that digoxin significantly improved exercise tolerance and O_2 consumption over placebo. In the latest digoxin/captopril study, there was no significant statistical difference between the two drugs with regard to effects on exercise tolerance and functional class.[1]

Percent Improvement in Exercise Tolerance*

Digoxin 14% Diuretic Baseline

*Adapted from DiBianco et al.[2]

References: 1. The Captopril-Digoxin Multicenter Research Group: Comparative effects of therapy with captopril and digoxin in patients with mild to moderate heart failure. *JAMA* 1988;259:539-544. **2.** DiBianco R, Shabetai R, Kostuk W, et al: Oral milrinone and digoxin in heart failure: Results of a placebo-controlled, prospective trial of each agent and the combination, abstract. *Circulation* 1987;76(suppl 4):256. **3.** Arnold SB, Byrd RC, Meister W, et al: Long-term digitalis therapy improves left ventricular function in heart failure. *N Engl J Med* 1980;303:1443-1448. **4.** Alicandri C, Fariello R, Boni E, et al: Comparison of captopril and digoxin in mild to moderate heart failure. *Postgrad Med J* 1986;62(suppl 1):170-175.

IN THE EARLY TREATMENT OF CHF
LANOXIN®
(digoxin) Tablets
Unique inotropic support for the failing heart.
See brief summary of prescribing information on following page.

Product: **PREMARIN®**
Ad Agency: **Sudler & Hennessey**
Client: **Ayerst Laboratories**
Art Director: **Carveth Kramer**
Illustrator: **Cynthia Turner**
Copywriters: **Nina Padukone, Dan Sturtevant**

"Too Late," warns the ominous headline of this attention-getting ad for PREMARIN®, an estrogen replacement product used in early treatment of osteoporosis. According to V.P./Copy Supervisor Nina Padukone, the ad was intended to "alert MDs to the irreversible and debilitating bone loss that occurs if osteoporosis is not treated early." While a striking illustration depicts a thigh bone turned into a brittle sponge, the copy adds a hopeful note by suggesting that PREMARIN® can halt osteoporosis before bone loss occurs. The copy's emphasis on early treatment of the disease, coupled with newsy subheads like "10 million women could benefit," manages to convey a selflessly crusading message while it primes physicians to prescribe the drug.

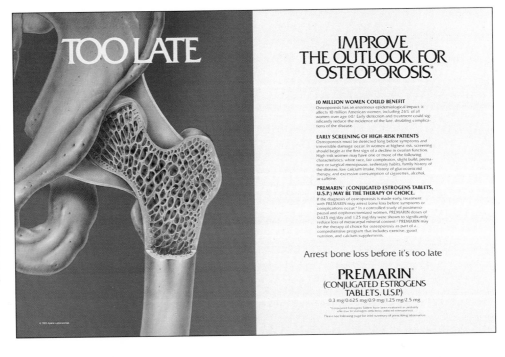

Product: **Olympus URF-P**
Ad Agency: **Sutton Communications**
Client: **Olympus Corp.,**
Medical Instrument Div.
Art Director: **Stan Dornfest**
Illustrator: **Caspar Henselmann**
Photographer: **Clayton Price**
Copywriter: **Nort Bramesco**

A sense of high-tech adventure pervades this colorful ad for the Olympus URF-P, a flexible ultrathin fiber-scope that enables urologists to peer farther into the kidney than ever before. Since this was a new product launch, the client wanted to dramatize the advantages of the URF-P and make urologists receptive to forth-coming visits by company sales representatives. In the striking visual developed by Sutton Communications, a brightly illuminated kidney cross section shows the instrument probing beyond the ureter and well into the kidney itself. The bulleted copy clearly enumerates the benefits of the new scope.

Product: **CEA-ROCHE**® **EIA System**
Ad Agency: **William Douglas McAdams Inc.**
Client: **Roche Diagnostics**
Art Director: **Carl Opalek**
Illustrator: **David Noyes**
Photographer: **Murray Shear**
Copywriter: **Ruth Grossman**

For an ad promoting a specific blood technology used in diagnosing cancer, the creative team at William Douglas McAdams Inc. developed a dramatic visual that suggests some extraterrestrial war—or possibly the formation of stars following the Big Bang. What this turbulent scene *actually* depicts is the action of the product inside the test tube. With its free, hand-sketched quality, the art stands apart from today's silky-smooth airbrushed renderings of cells and organs. Senior Art Director Carl Opalek writes that the client "liked the intentional vigor and roughness...of the original comprehensive color art. We retained it in the finish." The copy stresses the accuracy of the CEA-Roche® EIA System—as well as its reasonable cost.

Product: **Alupent**®
Ad Agency: **Barnum Communications, Inc.**
Client: **Boehringer Ingelheim**
Art Director: **Monica Garb**
Illustrator: **Alex Grey**
Copywriter: **Melissa De Fiebre**

A cross section of a bronchial tube, its lining highlighted in healthy pink, snakes its way back to an imaginatively rendered (but anatomically accurate) human lung in this eye-catching ad for Alupent®, an inhalation aerosol for relief of asthma symptoms. The bold perspective and intricacy of Alex Grey's illustration capture attention immediately. The headline, "60 seconds to relief," emphasizes the fast-acting nature of the product, while the brief copy backs up this selling point with the added benefit of sustained relief.

The Sun Never Sets On Feldene®
(piroxicam)

All around the world, day after day, Feldene® (piroxicam) **effectively and dependably relieves the pain and inflammation of osteoarthritis and rheumatoid arthritis.**

- FELDENE has been used in more than 90 countries and in an estimated 12 million patients.

- Convenient single daily dose of FELDENE enhances patient compliance.

- Patients sleep through the night because of reduction of nighttime arthritis pain and awake with less morning stiffness.¹

- Patients are more productive on the job and in their daily activities.²

- The most common side effects of FELDENE are GI related. Other side effects (as indicated in the prescribing information) include dizziness, somnolence, vertigo, tinnitus, headache, malaise, edema, pruritus and rash.

Start one-a-day

 **Feldene®** (PIROXICAM) 20 mg capsules **For full anti-arthritic action**

© 1985. Pfizer Inc.

Please see a brief summary of FELDENE® (piroxicam) prescribing information on the following page.

Product: **Feldene®**
Ad Agency: **Dorritie & Lyons, Inc.**
Client: **Pfizer Laboratories**
Art Director: **Mike Lyons**
Photographer: **Emil Schultheiss**
Copywriter: **Bill Brown**

A visually stunning time-lapse photomontage of the midnight sun by Emil Schultheiss supports the headline message in this colorful two-pager for Feldene®,

the antiarthritic formula. The familiar headline/slogan (originally applied to the British Empire) works well here. In fact, it suggests multiple meanings later reinforced by the copy: that the product is used around the globe, that it works steadily and dependably, that a single dose gets you through the day, and that its beneficial effects last throughout the night. One might also note the implication that, unlike the British Empire, Feldene® will always be with us.

Title: **"Hope...Through research"**
Ad Agency: **Dugan Farley Communications Associates, Inc.**
Client: **Lederle Laboratories**
Art Director: **Eric Rathje**
Illustrator: **Sal Catalano**
Copywriter: **Fran Dyller**

"Hope...Through research" is the uplifting theme of this corporate image ad for Lederle Laboratories. The "hope" is for a cure for cancer, visually expressed by a lone flower peeking out from a parched brown field. In the second frame, "research" has transformed the barren waste into a fresh green meadow spangled with thriving flowers. According to Eric Rathje, executive creative director (art) for Dugan Farley Communications Associates, Inc., the ad was aimed at oncologists as a reminder of "the dedicated effort Lederle Laboratories has continued to put forth in discovering and perfecting effective anti-cancer agents."

Hope...

Through research

Lederle Laboratories
Developers of some of the most widely used anticancer drugs of today.

Currently investigating a variety of new antineoplastic agents for tomorrow.

© 1992 Lederle Laboratories

Lederle Laboratories
A Division of American Cyanamid Company, Wayne, New Jersey 07470

A SOURCE OF CONFIDENCE IN PERILOUS SEAS.

Early warning and treatment of colorectal cancer–the #2 cancer in incidence and mortality–can save lives. In fact, the American Cancer Society estimates up to 85% of patients could be saved. Clearly, the reliability of your screening test is paramount.

Hemoccult® provides a foundation of confidence unapproached by any other fecal occult blood test. A foundation built on hundreds of documented studies and millions of tests performed in over 18 years of clinical use.

FOR YOUR PATIENTS AT RISK, INSIST ON HEMOCCULT.

SKD

Product: **HEMOCCULT**®
Ad Agency: **Rainoldi Kerzner & Radcliffe**
Client: **SmithKline Diagnostics, Inc.**
Art Director: **Charles Schmalz**
Illustrator: **Nick Gaetano**
Copywriter: **Diane Koerner**

HEMOCCULT® had attained an almost generic identity during its 18 years as the leading test for fecal occult blood. In fact, its very success posed a problem: how to re-establish the product as a name brand. The visual that would attempt to do this had to be arresting if it were to stand out among the clutter of promotional material aimed at primary care physicians. And, it had to be flexible enough to be used throughout a series of ads and promotions (including T-shirts). The lighthouse with its gleaming beacon not only creates a memorable image but also parallels the purpose of HEMOCCULT®: to serve as a reliable early warning device. In this one-page ad, the lighthouse dominates a powerful color visual, which is topped by a headline that applies to both the beacon and the product.

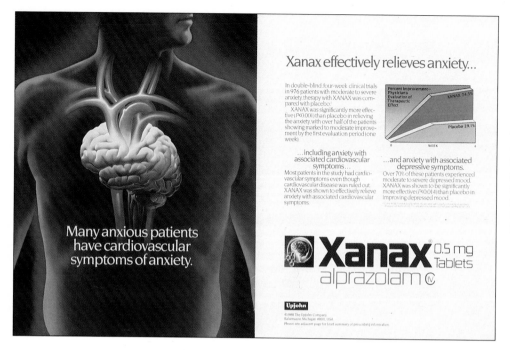

Product: **Xanax**®
Ad Agency: **Frank J. Corbett, Inc.**
Client: **The Upjohn Company**
Art Director: **Bill Harrison**
Illustrator: **The Art Staff**
Copywriter: **Dick Jacobs**

Many patients who run to their physicians complaining of cardiac symptoms are simply suffering from easily treatable anxiety. To interpret this problem visually, Art Director Bill Harrison cleverly placed the brain where the heart should be. What the ad says, in effect, is that apparent heart symptoms can often be produced by an overanxious mind—and that Xanax® can measurably relieve the problem. The colorful visual is supported by copy that substantiates the findings with statistics from a double-blind test.

Product: **Stadol**®
Ad Agency: **Sieber & McIntyre**
Client: **Bristol Stadol**
Art Director: **John Bernegger**
Photographer: **Tom Arma**
Copywriter: **Steve West**

Here's a real attention-getter: what surgeon would not respond to the sight of bright red blood oozing through sutures on an otherwise perfect female body? For maximum impact, the headline was positioned right next to the photograph's most salient detail. The negative side of the message (i.e., that postoperative vomiting can break sutures) is immediately clear; for the solution, the audience must read the copy, which explains how Stadol® provides postoperative pain relief while generally eliminating nausea.

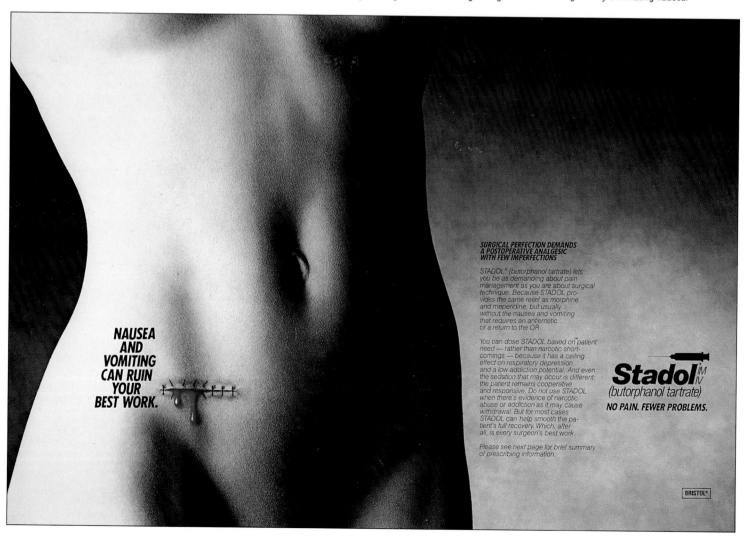

Product: **Operating Room CO₂ Patient Monitor**

Ad Agency: **Giardini/Russell Inc.**

Client: **Hewlett-Packard, Medical Products Group**

Art Director: **Eric Nord**

Photographer: **John Holt**

Copywriter: **Carol Patch**

A solitary tightrope artist steps across open space, the moment frozen in an atmospheric photograph by John Holt. According to Account Supervisor William E. Green, the high-wire man represents "the precarious and lonely situation of the anesthesiologist when it comes to the responsibility of patient safety…." The message in this corporate ad for Hewlett-Packard is that the company understands the concerns of anesthesiologists and has developed accurate monitoring equipment (the "net" referred to in the headline) and extensive training materials to support them in their work. As groundwork for this dramatic ad, Giardini/Russell Inc. actually interviewed numerous anesthesiologists for insights into their concerns and responsibilities.

Product: **LASIX®**

Ad Agency: **William Douglas McAdams Inc.**

Client: **Hoechst-Roussel Pharmaceuticals Inc.**

Art Director: **Patrick Creaven**

Illustrator: **Radu Vero**

Copywriters: **Bill Wolf, Gwenne Freiman**

Because LASIX®, the leading diuretic used in treating congestive heart failure, was a mature product and off patent, its market share faced potential erosion. According to Patrick Creaven, V.P./group head art director at William Douglas McAdams Inc., the client opted for strong graphic approaches in its antigeneric campaign. The creative team responded with a stunning illustration of a heart writing its own prescription. Their remarkably graphic ad made the strong argument that physicians must insist on the LASIX® brand of furosemide in order to achieve the precise dosing necessary when prescribing the classic furosemide-digitalis regimen. LASIX® has, in the face of generics and brand-name competitors, continued to hold a significant market share.

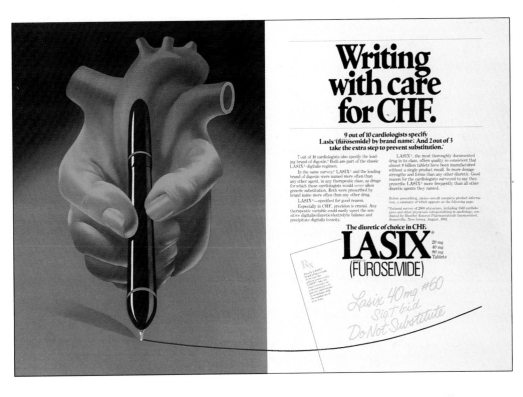

Title: **"Clarity"**
Ad Agency: **Sudler & Hennessey**
Client: **Berlex Imaging**
Art Director: **Dick Russinko**
Illustrator: **Rogier van der Weyden, courtesy of the National Gallery of Art**
Copywriter: **NancyKay Shapiro**

Why would Sudler & Hennessey use a 500-year-old face to advertise state-of-the-art equipment? According to copywriter NancyKay Shapiro, the agency wanted to position Berlex Imaging as "a company dedicated to the subtle nuances and artistry of radiologic imaging." Limited to a single page without accompanying technical data, the agency conceived a simple yet distinctive corporate image ad that effectively stands out from the more conventional (and more expensive) competition in radiology journals. The ultrasharp portrait image and dignified copy work together to create a positive message that suits the nature and purpose of the client's products—without mentioning them by name. (A footnote for students of art history: The painting used in this ad is Rogier van der Weyden's *Portrait of a Lady*.)

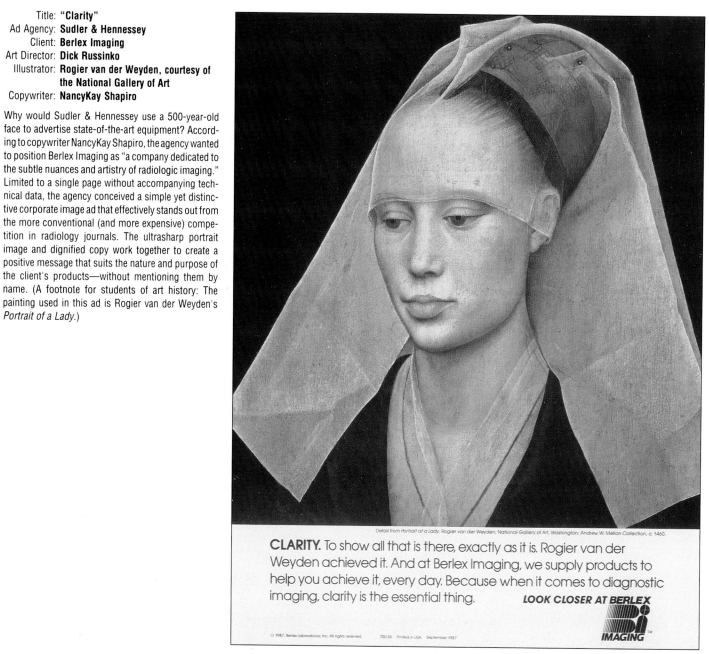

Detail from *Portrait of a Lady*, Rogier van der Weyden; National Gallery of Art, Washington; Andrew W. Mellon Collection, c. 1460.

CLARITY. To show all that is there, exactly as it is. Rogier van der Weyden achieved it. And at Berlex Imaging, we supply products to help you achieve it, every day. Because when it comes to diagnostic imaging, clarity is the essential thing. **LOOK CLOSER AT BERLEX**

© 1987, Berlex Laboratories, Inc. All rights reserved.   700-35   Printed in USA   September 1987

BI IMAGING™

Product: **Tolinase**®
Ad Agency: **Kallir, Philips, Ross, Inc.**
Client: **The Upjohn Company**
Art Director: **Gerald Philips**
Illustrator: **Michael Deas**
Copywriter: **Jack Domeshek**

A spectacular wilderness scene serves as the backdrop in this handsome spread for Tolinase®, a tablet medication for type II (noninsulin-dependent) diabetics. According to Gerald Philips, vice chairman/creative director of Kallir, Philips, Ross, Inc., the purpose of the ad was to impress physicians with the convenience of the 24-hour medication; just one tablet each day would enable diabetes patients to relax about their condition and focus on the activities they enjoy. The copy stresses not only the convenience but the safety of Tolinase®. The illustration is one of a series of U.S. outdoor scenes commissioned from young American artists.

Tolinase works   one day at a time

Each once-a-day dose of *Tolinase* is effective for about 24 hours once steady state has been achieved— an important consideration in the management of type II diabetic patients. Most of the urinary excretion occurs within the first 24 hours after administration.

When diet and exercise fail to control glucose levels adequately in type II (non-insulin-dependent) diabetes, TOLINASE Tablets (tolazamide) are a sound addition to the regimen—not only because they provide effective, once-a-day therapy, but also because the action of each dose lasts about

24 hours. Proper patient selection, dosage, and instructions are important in order to avoid hypoglycemic episodes.

Tolinase **causes a mild diuresis**— an added advantage in patients whose condition may be aggravated by fluid retention (patients with hypertension or congestive heart failure, for example).

Although the interpretations are controversial, the UGDP study reported in 1970 that the use of tolbutamide, an oral hypoglycemic drug, was associated with increased cardiovascular mortality.

In type II diabetes

Tolinase 100, 250 & 500 mg tablets
(tolazamide)
One tablet...one day's therapy

Please turn page for brief summary of prescribing information.

Upjohn The Upjohn Company
Kalamazoo, MI 49001 U.S.A.

Product: **BuSpar**®
Ad Agency: **Robert A. Becker Inc.**
Client: **Mead Johnson**
Art Director: **Frank O'Blak**
Photographer: **F.P.G.**
Copywriter: **Liz Lemay**

Here's an ad with no overt message—just the name of the product and the tranquil beauty of a swan at sunset.

Created by Robert A. Becker Inc. for an audience of physicians, the ad assumes familiarity with BuSpar® and serves solely as a reminder—to achieve "top of mind" memorability, an all-important factor in medical advertising. According to Art Director Frank O'Blak, the photo utilizes "the graphic associated with the product name"—i.e., the swan—thus adding visual reinforcement to the boldly displayed name.

Closing the gap
in cancer detection and treatment.

Because of their ability to seek out and attach to cancer cells within the body, monoclonal antibodies offer tremendous potential for revolutionizing cancer detection and treatment.

At NeoRx, we're overcoming the obstacles that have prevented this potential from being fully realized. In a remarkably short period of time, we have made significant progress in using monoclonal antibodies to deliver diagnostic and therapeutic agents directly to tumor sites with much greater specificity.

As a result, we are drawing ever closer to the introduction of cancer detection and treatment products that will offer levels of effectiveness unmatched by current methods.

NeoRx
THE VITAL CONNECTION™

NeoRx CORPORATION
410 West Harrison
Seattle, Washington 98119
(206) 281-7001

Title: **"Closing the gap"**
Ad Agency: **Gerbig, Snell/Weisheimer & Associates, Inc.**
Client: **NeoRx Corp.**
Art Director: **Jim Lutz**
Illustrator: **Kevin Burke**
Copywriter: **Joe Ashley**

Designed to create interest in a new company, this two-page ad for NeoRx Corporation uses a compelling visual to attract readership. The zipper motif shows how the firm is harnessing monoclonal antibodies to "deliver diagnostic and therapeutic agents directly to tumor sites with much greater specificity." By doing so, NeoRx Corporation is "closing the gap" in cancer detection and treatment. Targeted at oncologists and nuclear medicine specialists, the ad avoids any mention of specific products. As Account Supervisor Gregory J. Longenecker writes, it was intended to "help identify the company and its area of expertise," preparing the audience for "the entry of the company and its products into the marketplace."

Product: **Adapin®**
Ad Agency: **Sieber & McIntyre**
Client: **Pennwalt Pharmaceutical Division**
Art Director: **Lin Kossak**
Illustrator: **Jeanette Adams**
Copywriter: **Steve West**

How do you make one drug stand out from a virtually identical (and better known) competitor? That was the problem tackled by Kossak Design Group in this two-page ad for Adapin®, a drug used in doxepin therapy. An attractive visual twist on the old "peas in a pod" theme—one pea glows like a light bulb—tells us that Adapin® has something more to offer. That "something"—according to the headline on the second page—is a much lower price. The copy explains that Adapin® and its competitor, Sinequan®, are bio-equivalent, but that when it comes to cost, the two are "worlds apart." Add the assurance of *"quality* backed by the Pennwalt name," and a solid case has been made.

Adapin® (doxepin HCl)
or
Sinequan®?
(doxepin HCl)

Adapin® (doxepin HCl)
costs a lot less!

When it comes to doxepin therapy, Adapin and Sinequan are like two peas in a pod because they are bioequivalent. They provide equal efficacy and safety profiles in relieving depression and associated anxiety.

But when it comes to cost, Adapin and Sinequan are worlds apart. With Adapin you can save your patients an average of 23%* on every prescription.

In addition to these savings, you and your patients can be assured of the quality backed by the Pennwalt name.

For doxepin therapy, specify the cost-effective choice... Adapin from Pennwalt.

Specify **Adapin®** (doxepin HCl)

Product: **CEFOTAN**®
Ad Agency: **Sudler & Hennessey**
Client: **Stuart Pharmaceuticals**
Art Director: **Joe Paumi**
Photographers: **Ed Rysinski, Irv Bahrt**
Copywriter: **Lisa Melilli**

The old versus the new is the theme of this attractive four-pager for CEFOTAN®, a cephalosporin used in treating abdominal and pelvic infections. To make the point that CEFOTAN® is superior to Cefoxitin, its predecessor, the ad uses a clever visual metaphor: antique surgical tools (once "the best there was") are contrasted with their sleek modern replacements ("Now there's something better"; i.e., CEFOTAN®). On the third page, the copy starts to unfold the story, using clearly stated benefits and bold, simple graphics to convert physicians to CEFOTAN®.

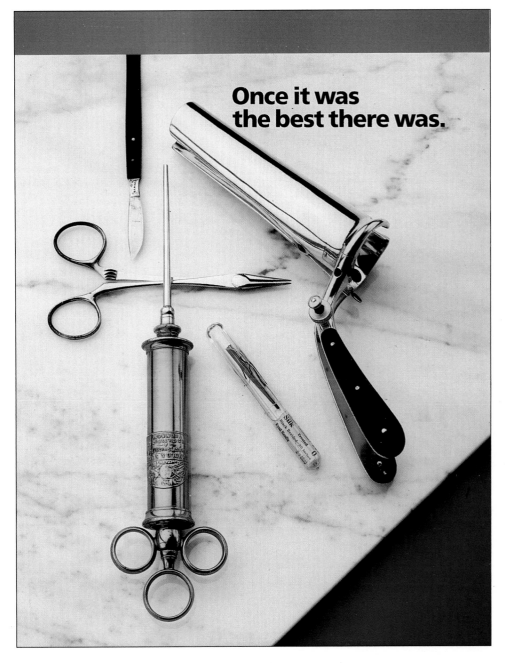

Product: **PHILLIPS'**® **Milk of Magnesia**
Ad Agency: **Dugan Farley Communications Associates, Inc.**
Client: **Glenbrook Laboratories**
Art Director: **Eric Rathje**
Photographer: **Bernie Gold**
Copywriter: **Fran Dyller**

The headline sounds vaguely familiar...but this two-page spread for PHILLIPS'® Milk of Magnesia puts it to novel use: to contrast the safe, simple virtues of M.O.M. with the wild profusion of laxatives on the market—many of them harsh and unpredictable. The "war and peace" theme is echoed by the graphics, which display a chaotic battleground of pills and powders alongside the familiar M.O.M. bottle and a spoon. The copy picks up this theme: "PHILLIPS'® Milk of Magnesia promotes peace of mind as well as peace in the gut." The ad was intended to increase usage among primary care physicians.

Title: **"Concern is what it's all about."**
Ad Agency: **Sudler & Hennessey**
Client: **Parke-Davis**
Art Director: **Dick Russinko**
Photographer: **Tom Caravaglia**
Copywriter: **Jack Speiller**
Account Services: **Don Masterson**

The human touch works wonders in this successful corporate ad for Parke-Davis. The muted figures of two children, the older one gently guiding the younger, serve as a poignant backdrop for the ad's intent: to communicate the company's 120-year legacy of concern for human healthcare needs. In addition to conveying the positive corporate message, the copy increases awareness of the firm's rapidly growing over-the-counter product line.

Product: **Alupent®**
Ad Agency: **Barnum Communications, Inc.**
Client: **Boehringer Ingelheim**
Art Directors: **Monica Garb, David Barnum, Celia Hirsch**
Photographer: **Gary Kufner**
Copywriter: **Melissa De Fiebre**

The headline says, "Fast Action"—and so does the colorful action photo of a beaming young ballplayer sliding into home plate. (We'll assume he's safe.) In this ad for Alupent®, an inhalation aerosol for relief of asthma symptoms, Barnum Communications, Inc., has played off the double implication of the headline: that Alupent® is not only fast-acting, but permits asthma sufferers to enjoy healthy, action-filled lives. There's even an extra dimension to the visual: the safe slide into home dramatizes the safety of the medication as stated in the copy. ➤

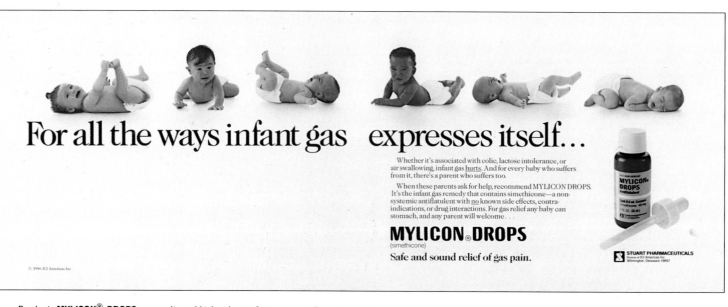

Product: **MYLICON® DROPS**
Ad Agency: **Sudler & Hennessey**
Client: **Stuart Pharmaceuticals**
Art Director: **Judith Sweeney**
Photographer: **Elizabeth Hathon**
Copywriter: **Steve Abbruscato**

It would take a heart of stone to turn the page on a half-dozen helpless infants, all of them in a state of obvious distress. In this ad for MYLICON® DROPS, an over-the-counter medication for relief of gas pain, Sudler & Hennessey arranged an assortment of young models—all of them under six months of age (infant colic disappears after that age). According to V.P./Account Supervisor Douglas M. Burcin, the photography was not an easy proposition, since all the babies had to be photographed while crying, and in a variety of positions. The copy underscores the safe, dependable nature of the product for a target audience of pediatricians.

Product: **PARLODEL**®
Ad Agency: **M.E.D. Communications, Inc.**
Client: **Sandoz Pharmaceuticals, Inc.**
Creative Director: **Edward B. Cohen**
Art Director: **Warren McLeod**
Photographer: **Barbara Campbell**
Copywriter: **Sally Paull**

The universally appealing image of mother and child helps promote the fertility drug PARLODEL® in this multi-page ad sequence aimed at OB/GYNs. Appearing on consecutive pages, the photographs show mothers of different races in tenderly affectionate poses with their young progeny—accompanied by the triumphant headline, "SUCCESS AT LAST!" By coupling the warm human images with bottom-line results, the agency has created an interesting two-pronged strategy for reaching the target audience. As Edward B. Cohen, executive director/creative services, puts it, the ad was intended to communicate with OB/GYNs "by appealing to their medical/scientific side through an emotional window."

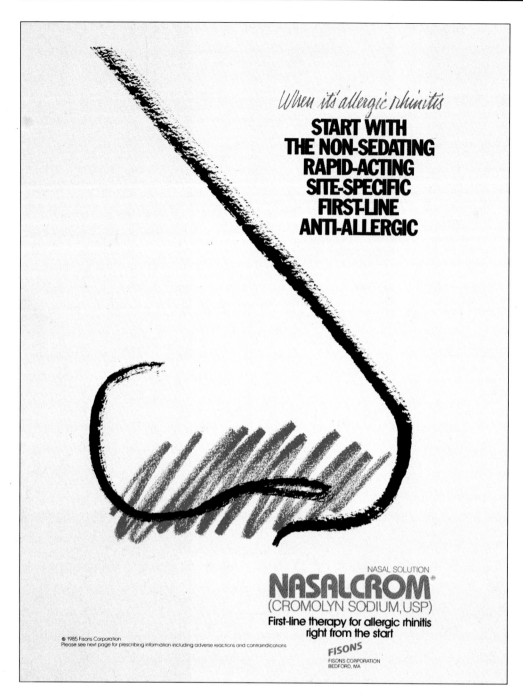

Product: **NASALCROM®**
Ad Agency: **Sandler Communications Inc.**
Client: **Fisons Corporation**
Art Director: **Jerry Malone**
Illustrators: **Bob Walker, Jerry Malone**
Copywriter: **Michael Metelenis**

Aimed at physicians treating allergy patients, this ad from Sandler Communications Inc. is remarkable for its visual economy. With a simple black outline for the nose, and a dash of red to indicate inflammation, the art immediately establishes the purpose of NASALCROM®. The copy further positions the medication with a short burst of hyphenated terms ("non-sedating rapid-acting site-specific first-line anti-allergic").

Product: **proctoCream®•HC**
Ad Agency: **M.E.D. Communications, Inc.**
Client: **Reed & Carnrick**
Creative Director: **Edward Cohen**
Art Director: **Jim Crispo**
Photographer: **Neil Molinaro**
Copywriter: **Richard Dotz**

How does one make a new product stand out from the crowd? To promote proctoCream®•HC, a proctological pain relief formula, M.E.D. Communications, Inc., set up a row of boys easing their sore posteriors on pillows. The only boy without a pillow—and the only one isolated in color in an otherwise black-and-white photograph—is obviously the only one who has tried proctoCream®•HC, the "Ahhhh-nesthetic!™" If there's any doubt, the copy is placed directly below this boy's pain-free posterior. All of the above devices, plus the tagline ("The one *with* an anesthetic"), help position the newcomer favorably against the competition.

Product: **Benadryl**®
Ad Agency: **Sudler & Hennessey**
Client: **Parke-Davis**
Art Director: **Steve Brothers**
Photographer: **Irv Bahrt**
Copywriter: **Jack Speiller**

The makers of Benadryl® wanted to achieve "top of the mind" recognition for their well-known decongestant. The creative team at Sudler & Hennessey responded by placing their copy right where the product goes to work—that is, on a startling close-up photograph of a nose. The headline identifies the site of the action ("Relieves congested symptoms here!"), while the copy cleverly conforms to the shape of the nose. Light-hearted but effective, the ad establishes an immediate link between the product and the proboscis.

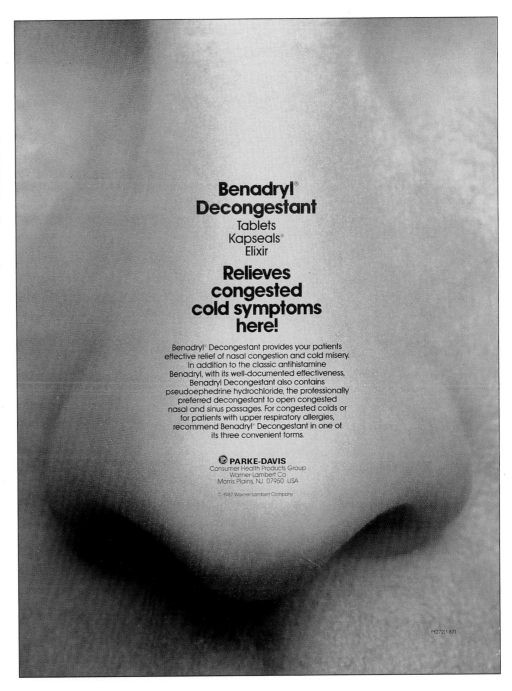

Product: **Anusol**®
Ad Agency: **Sudler & Hennessey**
Client: **Parke-Davis**
Art Director: **Steve Brothers**
Photographer: **Carmine Macedonia**
Copywriter: **Robin Silverman**

At a time when many ingredients in hemorrhoidal preparations were being questioned, the makers of Anusol® wanted their product to be thought of as a simple, basic remedy. The blue jean graphic used in this half-page spread serves several functions: it reinforces the "down to earth" message of the headline, allows for tasteful treatment of delicate subject matter, and adapts readily to cost-saving two-color printing. Sudler & Hennessey V.P./Copy Supervisor Robin Davenport notes that the client had originally requested a one-page ad, but that the final half-page spread across two pages was chosen because of the graphic used.

SOME ALLERGY PATIENTS THINK IT'S "SAFE" TO GO INDOORS...

But it isn't. For the majority of allergy patients there is no "end" to the allergy season. The menacing house dust mite (or alternaria or cat dander) causes as much nasal discomfort as the seasonal flareups brought on by tree, grass, and weed pollens.

In fact, recent studies report that most allergic rhinitis patients suffer substantial nasal symptoms more than 40 weeks each year.[1,2]

Yet there is a way to safely and effectively offer these patients relief, year round. Proven, non-sedating, site-specific NASALCROM* Nasal Solution. It delivers rapid, symptomatic relief of nasal congestion, rhinorrhea, nose blowing, and sneezing...all with virtually no serious or complicating side effects.

NASALCROM®
NASAL SOLUTION
(cromolyn sodium / FISONS)
For allergic rhinitis...year round.

Scanning Electron Micrograph of the House Dust Mite (x300)

Product: **NASALCROM®**
Ad Agency: **Sandler Communications Inc.**
Client: **Fisons Corporation**
Art Director: **Jerry Malone**
Photographer: **Phil Harrington**
Copywriter: **Michael Metelenis**

Restricted by a limited budget, Sandler Communications Inc. came up with a rather riveting visual to carry this ad for NASALCROM®, an antiallergenic nasal medication. According to President Kenneth Sandler, the goal was to find a new way to promote the product and to associate it with "nonseasonal" allergies. The strategy: to create a monster out of the humble house dust mite (magnified 300 times in the actual ad), reminding physicians that allergic rhinitis can occur year-round, triggered by indoor culprits as well as weeds and pollen. The ad achieved its goal of boosting "off-season" sales.

Product: **Atarax®**
Ad Agency: **Robert A. Becker Inc.**
Client: **Roerig Div., Pfizer Pharmaceuticals**
Art Director: **Dave Charney**
Copywriters: **Norman Franklin, Dave Charney**

"Freedom from itch" is the theme of this whimsical ad for Atarax®. And what better symbol of this precious freedom than Lady Liberty herself, reaching to scratch her colossal back with her free hand. According to Creative Director David H. Charney, the ad attempted to boost physician awareness of the drug in a market where generics were gaining ground. It worked. It also represents one of the rare successful uses of broad humor in medical advertising.

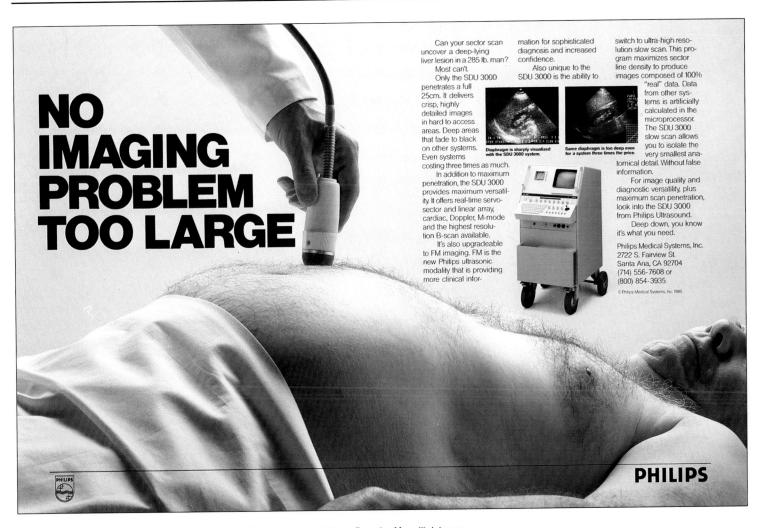

NO IMAGING PROBLEM TOO LARGE

Can your sector scan uncover a deep-lying liver lesion in a 285 lb. man? Most can't.

Only the SDU 3000 penetrates a full 25cm. It delivers crisp, highly detailed images in hard to access areas. Deep areas that fade to black on other systems. Even systems costing three times as much.

In addition to maximum penetration, the SDU 3000 provides maximum versatility. It offers real-time servo-sector and linear array, cardiac, Doppler, M-mode and the highest resolution B-scan available.

It's also upgradeable to FM imaging. FM is the new Philips ultrasonic modality that is providing more clinical infor-

mation for sophisticated diagnosis and increased confidence.

Also unique to the SDU 3000 is the ability to

Diaphragm is sharply visualized with the SDU 3000 system.

Same diaphragm is too deep even for a system three times the price.

switch to ultra-high resolution slow scan. This program maximizes sector line density to produce images composed of 100% "real" data. Data from other systems is artificially calculated in the microprocessor. The SDU 3000 slow scan allows you to isolate the very smallest anatomical detail. Without false information.

For image quality and diagnostic versatility, plus maximum scan penetration, look into the SDU 3000 from Philips Ultrasound.

Deep down, you know it's what you need.

Philips Medical Systems, Inc.
2722 S. Fairview St.
Santa Ana, CA 92704
(714) 556-7608 or
(800) 854-3935
© Philips Medical Systems, Inc. 1985

PHILIPS

Product: **Philips SDU 3000**
Ad Agency: **Forsythe Marcelli Johnson Advertising, Inc.**
Client: **Philips Medical Systems, Inc.**
Art Director: **Vic Marcelli**
Photographer: **Bill Braly**
Copywriter: **Jim Forsythe**

A potbellied patient serves to demonstrate the effectiveness of the Philips SDU 3000 scanning system in this memorable ad from Forsythe Marcelli Johnson Advertising, Inc. If the SDU 3000 can produce sharp images from this stout fellow, it's obviously worth looking into. The arresting visual and tongue-in-cheek headline ("No Imaging Problem Too Large") are supported by President Jim Forsythe's convincing benefits-intensive copy. In fact, the copy and inset photos show that the SDU 3000 outperforms systems costing three times as much—no small accomplishment.

Product: **Stomach tlc™**
Ad Agency: **Northstar Productions**
Client: **Smith Kline & French Laboratories**
Art Director: **Mike Lazur**
Claymation: **Will Vinton Productions**
Photographer: **Peter Stone**
Copywriter: **Mike Norton**

If Gumby had a stomach, it might well resemble this lovable Claymation organ. This rotund little fellow is the official spokesman for Stomach tlc™, Smith Kline & French's large-scale, multifaceted program for stomach care. Aimed at both physicians and the public, the program encompasses products for the detection and treatment of peptic ulcers, as well as educational materials for stomach patients and the public at large. (The "talking stomach" character is slated to appear in TV commercials and promotional literature.) In the background of this integrated professional/consumer campaign is the promotion of Tagamet®, Smith Kline & French's antiulcer medication.

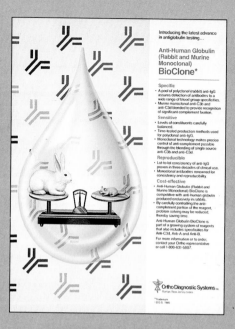

Product: **BioClone™**
Ad Agency: **Falcone & Associates**
Client: **Ortho Diagnostic Systems Inc.**
Art Director: **William Falcone**
Illustrator: **Daniel Kirk**
Copywriter: **Margaret Treacy**

According to William Falcone, Jr., president of Falcone & Associates, this colorful ad for BioClone™ had three goals: to describe visually a new manufacturing technology, to "catch the reader," and to convey the "up style" of the Ortho corporate image. The brief copy above the product name quickly defines the purpose of BioClone™; the technical copy utilizes short crossheads to sum up the benefits.

Title: **"Picture Perfect..."**
Ad Agency: **Lavey/Wolff/Swift Inc.**
Client: **Janssen**
Art Director: **John Kane**
Photographers: **Norman Gorbaty, Edward Rysinski**
Copywriter: **Linda Culvert**

It's not a work from the Op Art school, but this introductory ad for Janssen Gold leaps from the page like a painting by Vasarely. What we're actually looking at is a model that depicts a new diagnostic technology developed by Janssen Life Sciences Products: a process in which molecules of gold (those brilliant points of light in the model) adhere to selected chemicals for easy detection in lab procedures. Created by Lavey/Wolff/Swift Inc., the introductory ad effectively conveys the message that Janssen Gold enhances laboratory technology—without giving away too much information at this point. It's a simple, provocative statement that arouses curiosity about the new product.

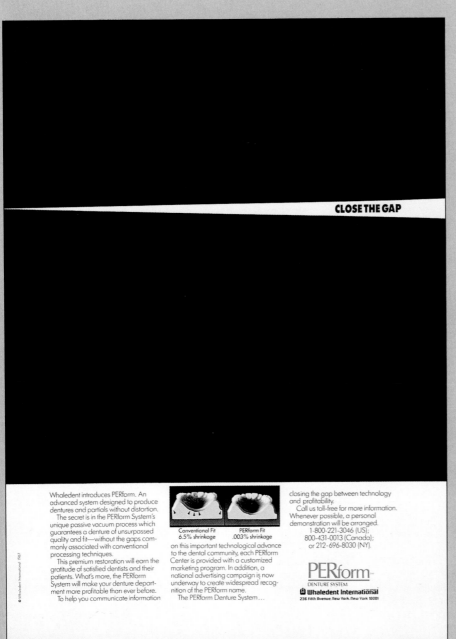

CLOSE THE GAP

Whaledent introduces PERform. An advanced system designed to produce dentures and partials without distortion.

The secret is in the PERform System's unique passive vacuum process which guarantees a denture of unsurpassed quality and fit—without the gaps commonly associated with conventional processing techniques.

This premium restoration will earn the gratitude of satisfied dentists and their patients. What's more, the PERform System will make your denture department more profitable than ever before.

To help you communicate information

Conventional Fit	PERform Fit
6.5% shrinkage	.003% shrinkage

on this important technological advance to the dental community, each PERform Center is provided with a customized marketing program. In addition, a national advertising campaign is now underway to create widespread recognition of the PERform name.

The PERform Denture System...

closing the gap between technology and profitability.

Call us toll-free for more information. Whenever possible, a personal demonstration will be arranged.
1-800-221-3046 (US);
800-431-0013 (Canada);
or 212-696-8030 (NY).

PERform
DENTURE SYSTEM
Whaledent International
236 Fifth Avenue, New York, New York 10001

Product: **PERform™ Denture System**
Ad Agency: **Ad Lab, Inc.**
Client: **Whaledent International**
Art Directors: **Cindy Ho, Elliot Weinstein**
Copywriter: **Barbara Griffing**

A simple but powerful visual, coupled with an equally simple but strategically placed headline, adds clout to this ad for PERform™ Denture System. The creative team at Ad Lab, Inc., has capitalized on the product's leading benefit—its "unsurpassed...fit"—to meld headline copy and art into an organic whole. If the main visual is abstract, the inset photos and captions add concrete evidence of PERform™'s superior fit. The body copy fills out the story and adds a call to action for additional information.

Now, no patient should be restricted to life at 70 beats a minute.

Now, Activitrax® single chamber rate responsive pacemaker is the most-prescribed pacemaker in the world.

Every 15 minutes, an Activitrax is implanted somewhere in the world. Just a year after its release, over one out of four single chamber pacemakers implanted in the United States is an Activitrax, and the numbers are growing. Physicians have been quick to realize that patients no longer have to endure the limitations of a constant rate pacemaker. When disease or trauma take away your patient's natural heart rate response to daily activity, you can restore it with rate responsive pacing.

Rate responsive pacing proved superior to VVI pacing.

Eight independent published studies show that single chamber rate responsive pacing provides significant improvement over VVI pacing in enhancing cardiac output and work capacity. They also show that this improvement is due primarily to rate response. The unique patented signal processing circuitry makes it possible.

Activitrax can safely improve life, not just maintain it, for a broad range of patients.

Activitrax can benefit pacemaker patients who also have coronary disease, angina pectoris, congestive heart failure, and even those with the ability to increase heart rate with exercise. Since Activitrax uses standard leads, it can be used to upgrade an existing VVI system at replacement time. Activitrax can help older, less active patients be self-sufficient and can help younger patients lead more normal lives.

Because the rate responsive mode is optional, the rate patient who doesn't benefit can be reprogrammed to VVI pacing.

Activitrax
Single chamber rate responsive pacemaker
Makes VVI pacing obsolete.

Product: **Activitrax®**
Ad Agency: **Girgenti, Hughes, Butler & McDowell**
Client: **Medtronic**
Art Director: **Mark McDowell**
Photographer: **Mark David Cohen**
Copywriter: **Lynn Franks**

To the uninitiated layman, "life at 70 beats a minute" doesn't exactly sound like hard punishment. But, as the ad explains, most pacemakers can't keep up with the increased cardiovascular demands experienced during exercise or other strenuous activity. By contrast, the Activitrax® is positioned as a rate-responsive pacemaker—one that actually changes the heart rate during activity. Obviously, any pacemaker that can accomplish this feat will significantly improve the patient's quality of life. In this ad created by Girgenti, Hughes, Butler & McDowell, the "shackle" visual motif is supported by long copy that emphasizes the Activitrax® pacemaker's wide acceptance, performance benefits, and suitability for all types of patients.

Product: **PANADOL**®
Ad Agency: **Dugan Farley Communications Associates, Inc.**
Client: **Glenbrook Laboratories**
Art Director: **Eric Rathje**
Illustrator: **Jim Hunt**
Photographer: **Bernie Gold**
Copywriter: **Fran Dyller**

Classy competition is the theme of this ad for Maximum Strength PANADOL®, the over-the-counter pain-relief formula. The problem faced by the agency, Dugan Farley, was to create a sense of equivalence in the minds of physicians who would otherwise recommend the better known TYLENOL®. PANADOL® was the new kid on the block at this point; the agency is not claiming superiority for the client's product but simply putting it in the same class as its formidable competitor. The Mercedes/BMW analogy is apt and attention-getting, and the visual economy is pleasing to the eye.

Product: **Halcion**®
Ad Agency: **Frank J. Corbett, Inc.**
Client: **The Upjohn Company**
Art Director: **Bill Harrison**
Illustrator: **The Art Staff**
Copywriter: **Dick Jacobs**

An airliner shuttles across a starry sky, the single light indicating a lone insomniac among the passengers. In this handsome ad for Halcion®, prepared by Frank J. Corbett, Inc., the night flight serves as a fitting illustration of transient insomnia, the disorder for which the drug is prescribed. But—as the headline states—jet lag is only one of the possible factors behind this type of insomnia. The copy names some of the other causes, then goes on to promote the twin benefits of Halcion®: its effectiveness in producing a full night's sleep, and the greater alertness of patients after awakening.

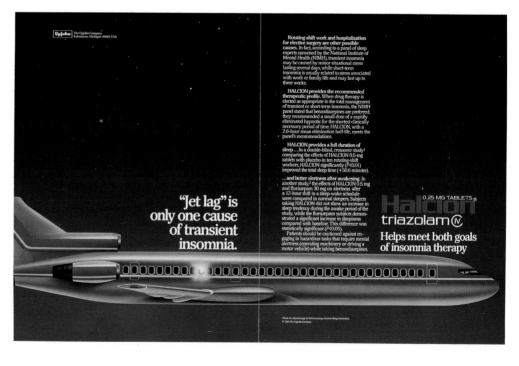

He remembers when his son announced
he wanted to be a fireman. Then, a cowboy...
and a baseball player.

Finally, a doctor like his dad.

This year, their shared dream came true
as he joined his father's practice.

A family tradition begins.

A professional tradition continues as one
more ophthalmologist relies on Blephamide for
treatment of non-specific conjunctivitis.

BLEPHAMIDE®

(sulfacetamide sodium 10%, prednisolone acetate 0.2%)
Liquifilm® sterile ophthalmic suspension

ALLERGAN®

Allergan Pharmaceuticals, Inc., Irvine, CA 92713
© 1986 Allergan Pharmaceuticals, Inc.

Product: **BLEPHAMIDE**®
Ad Agency: **Pacificom (In-house)**
Client: **Allergan Pharmaceuticals, Inc.**
Art Director: **Donald R. Meyers**
Photographer: **Jon Kubly**
Copywriter: **Susan Wesselink**
Photo Retoucher: **Peter Meyerhardt**

A brief story about a father-son ophthalmology practice adds a human touch to this ad for BLEPHAMIDE®, a suspension used in treating conjunctivitis. Copywriter Susan Wesselink conveys a sense of confidence and tradition in the product by establishing BLEPHAMIDE® as a legacy passed from one generation to the next: "A family tradition begins. A professional tradition continues...." At the same time, the photograph—actually shot in an MD's garage—shows two cars side by side, one of them a stately sedan (presumably belonging to the father), the other a flashy Corvette. The license plates quietly link the two cars, representing two generations bound together by reliance on a time-proven product.

New Lopressor HCT®
metoprolol tartrate and hydrochlorothiazide

For hypertensives who need two drugs,
not two prescriptions...

Also: Tablets: 50/25; 100/25
Once or twice daily as titrated.

Combines the standard among
cardioselective* beta blockers with the
standard among thiazide diuretics.

Lopressor HCT®
metoprolol tartrate and hydrochlorothiazide

Geigy

Changing the Course
of Cardiovascular Care

Product: **Lopressor HCT**®
Ad Agency: **C & G Advertising Inc. (In-house)**
Client: **Ciba-Geigy Corp.**
Art Director: **Bob Talarczyk**
Photographer: **Bill White**
Copywriter: **Ellen Schultz**

Visual and verbal economy heighten the impact of this introductory ad for Lopressor HCT®, a combination diuretic and beta blocker from Ciba-Geigy Corporation. Created by the company's in-house agency, the spread uses a simple but clever visual motif to position the product: one prescription for Lopressor HCT® replaces two separate generic prescriptions. The handwriting, while arguably more legible than that of the average MD, is just intricate enough to require some effort—and increased involvement—on the part of the audience. At the same time, the physicians reading the ad can visualize themselves scrawling the name of the drug on their own prescription pads.

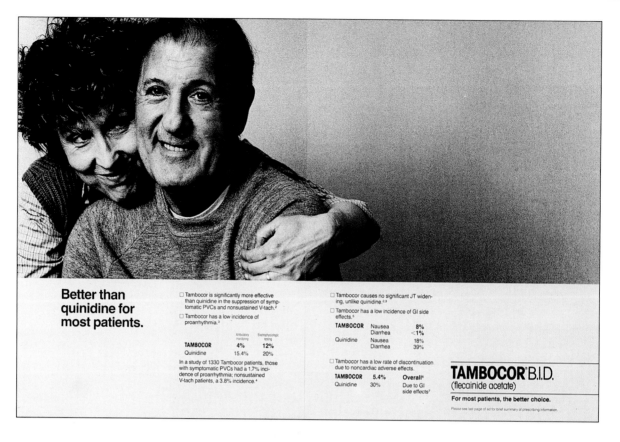

Better than quinidine for most patients.

☐ Tambocor is significantly more effective than quinidine in the suppression of symptomatic PVCs and nonsustained V-tach.[2]

☐ Tambocor has a low incidence of proarrhythmia.[3]

	Ambulatory monitoring	Electrophysiologic testing
TAMBOCOR	4%	12%
Quinidine	15.4%	20%

In a study of 1330 Tambocor patients, those with symptomatic PVCs had a 1.7% incidence of proarrhythmia; nonsustained V-tach patients, a 3.8% incidence.[4]

☐ Tambocor causes no significant JT widening, unlike quinidine.[2,3]

☐ Tambocor has a low incidence of GI side effects.[5]

TAMBOCOR	Nausea	8%
	Diarrhea	<1%
Quinidine	Nausea	18%
	Diarrhea	39%

☐ Tambocor has a low rate of discontinuation due to noncardiac adverse effects.

TAMBOCOR	5.4%	Overall[6]
Quinidine	30%	Due to GI side effects[7]

TAMBOCOR B.I.D.
(flecainide acetate)

For most patients, the better choice.

Please see last page of ad for brief summary of prescribing information.

Better than tocainide or mexiletine for most patients.

☐ Tambocor is more effective than tocainide or mexiletine in the suppression of symptomatic PVCs and nonsustained V-tach.[11,12]

☐ Tambocor has a low incidence of proarrhythmia.[3]

	Ambulatory monitoring	Electrophysiologic testing
TAMBOCOR	4%	12%
Tocainide	10%	6%
Mexiletine	7.6%	20%

In a study of 1330 Tambocor patients, those with symptomatic PVCs had a 1.7% incidence of proarrhythmia; nonsustained V-tach patients, a 3.8% incidence.[4]

☐ Tambocor has a low incidence of GI side effects. For example, Tambocor has an 8.9% incidence of nausea[5]; tocainide a 25% incidence[13] and mexiletine 36%.[14]

☐ Major organ toxicity is not characteristic of Tambocor therapy.

☐ Tambocor has a low rate of discontinuation due to noncardiac adverse effects.

TAMBOCOR	5.4%	Overall[6]
Tocainide	10-20%	Overall[13]
Mexiletine	40%	Overall[15,16]

TAMBOCOR B.I.D.
(flecainide acetate)

For most patients, the better choice.

Please see last page of ad for brief summary of prescribing information.

Product: **TAMBOCOR® B.I.D.**
Ad Agency: **Girgenti, Hughes, Butler & McDowell**
Client: **3M Riker**
Art Director: **Mark McDowell**
Photographer: **Robert Lambert**
Copywriter: **Lynn Franks**

This seven-page ad for TAMBOCOR® B.I.D. combines engaging human-interest photographs with an endorsement (for the generic form of the drug) from the august *New England Journal of Medicine*. In fact, the ad opens with this authoritative quotation, cleverly positioned alongside the photograph of a physician directly addressing the audience. Inside, the evocatively grainy monochrome photographs by Robert Lambert show us an affectionate middle-aged couple, a father and his young son, a woman gesturing—all warm images that make us want to look closer. The copy touts the virtues of the drug against its competitors, based on head-to-head tests, and repeats the tagline, "For most patients, the better choice."

Product: **NORLESTRIN®**
Ad Agency: **Sudler & Hennessey**
Client: **Parke-Davis**
Art Director: **Elissa Querze**
Photographer: **Carl Fischer**
Copywriter: **Karen Irland**

This striking photograph of an attractive young woman—her large eyes gazing directly and somewhat imploringly at the audience—immediately grabs attention and invites readership. The copy, printed in red, which creates contrast and a sense of urgency, suggests that women who experience certain problems with low-dose oral contraceptives can be switched to higher-dose NORLESTRIN® as an alternative to going off the pill. The ad tactfully avoids any overt attack on low-dose oral contraceptives, since the client, Parke-Davis, also produces Loestrin® 1.5/30, a low-dose oral contraceptive.

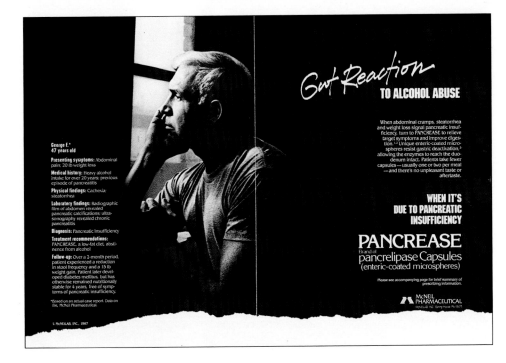

Product: **PANCREASE®**
Ad Agency: **Botto, Roessner, Horne & Messinger, Inc.**
Client: **McNeil Pharmaceutical**
Art Director: **Russell Brightwell**
Photographer: **Mark Malabrigo**
Copywriters: **Susan Mayer Roher, Jennifer Ratcliff**

An alcohol-abuse patient stares aimlessly out the window in this memorable ad for PANCREASE®, a drug used to treat pancreatic insufficiency. Developed by Botto, Roessner, Horne & Messinger, the ad reminds V.A. hospital-based physicians that alcoholism can cause problems in the pancreas (the "gut reaction" referred to in the headline), and that PANCREASE® is the "treatment of choice." The copy picks up the human interest story suggested by the dark, moody photograph, giving us the case history of an alcoholic veteran with pancreatitis.

Product: **Bayer® Aspirin**
Ad Agency: **Dugan Farley Communications Associates, Inc.**
Client: **Glenbrook Laboratories**
Art Director: **Eric Rathje**
Photographer: **Howard Sochurek**
Copywriters: **Mike Marino, Fran Dyller**

"This is not a headache!," warns the headline of this no-nonsense ad for a famous over-the-counter headache remedy, Bayer® aspirin. The drama of "a heart attack waiting to happen," vividly illustrated using digital subtraction angiography, captures attention immediately. Prompted by the recent findings that aspirin can be effective in treating heart patients, this ad was, according to Copy Group Supervisor Michael Marino, "designed to position Bayer®, already well-known in the aspirin category, as serious medicine for the treatment of a serious problem—heart attack." Aimed at internists, cardiologists and FP/GPs, the ad emphasizes brand-name specificity, noting that for just a penny a day more than the cost of generic aspirin, "Bayer® provides assurance of quality and consistency" along with numerous other advantages.

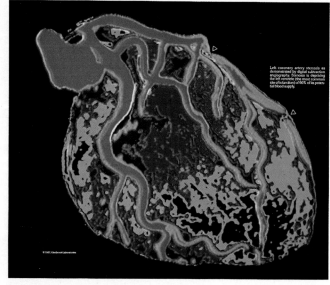

Design Firm: **Janin/Foster Design Communication**
Client: **Providence Hospital—Seton House**
Art Directors: **Susan Foster, Sue Dyer**
Photographer: **Dave Kasamatsu**
Copywriter: **Sue Dyer**

What could be more chilling than the image of a toe tag on a corpse—a human life reduced to an inert object on a shelf. That image, coupled with the powerful irony of the headline, drives home a convincing message in this ad for Seton House, an alcohol treatment program at Providence Hospital in Washington, D.C. According to Designer Susan Foster, the ad was intended to "shock the public into awareness of the danger of drinking and driving…." Because this was a newspaper ad (it ran in the *Washington Post*), the approach had to be "strong and simple and direct"; the photograph and headline are the dominant elements. The ad, which according to Foster was "considered gutsy in its use of a corpse—something one is not supposed to do," received an excellent response.

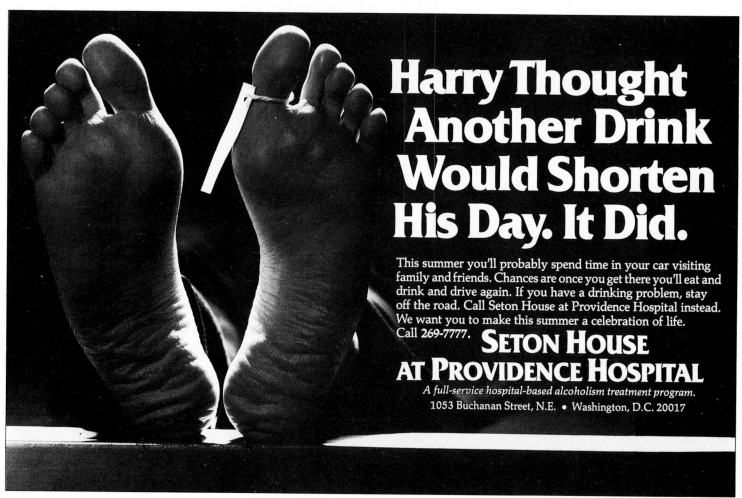

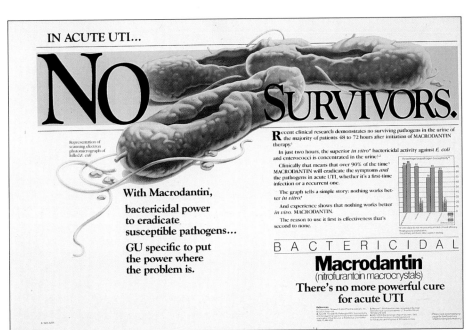

Product: **Macrodantin**®
Ad Agency: **Lally, McFarland & Pantello**
Client: **Norwich Eaton Pharmaceuticals, Inc.**
Art Director: **Jim McFarland**
Illustrator: **Ray Srugis**
Copywriter: **John Lally**

Macrodantin®, a urinary tract anti-infective, had been around for 30 years when Lally, McFarland & Pantello developed this hard-hitting ad. Their purpose: to change the widespread perception of Macrodantin® among physicians from that of a "weak antiseptic" to a "potent antibacterial." Their tactic: to grab attention with the hugely magnified carcasses of killed *E. coli* bacteria, coupled with the simple, unequivocal headline: "No Survivors." The copy then substantiates the message with a comparative graph and strong, no-nonsense selling copy.

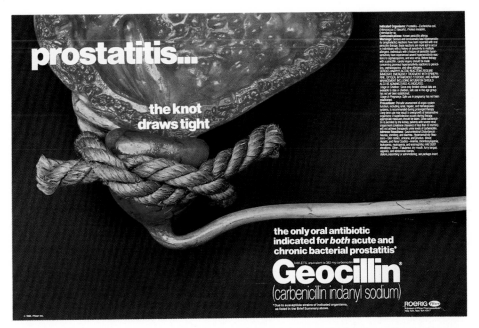

Product: **Geocillin**®
Ad Agency: **Robert A. Becker Inc.**
Client: **Roerig Div., Pfizer Pharmaceuticals**
Art Director: **Dave Charney**
Photographer: **Carl Fischer**
Copywriter: **Norman Franklin**

Geocillin® was an old standard in treating prostate infections. The problem, according to Creative Director David H. Charney, was to keep interest and "top of the mind" memorability. The solution: to dramatize the affliction of prostatitis with a knot drawn tightly around the base of the prostate. This vividly graphic treatment quickly succeeds in creating "top of the mind" memorability while the brief copy deftly sums up both the problem and the remedy.

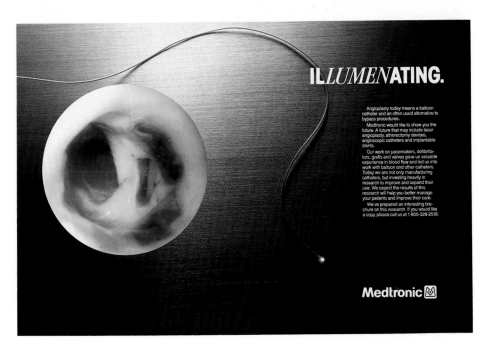

Product: **Catheters**
Ad Agency: **Girgenti, Hughes, Butler & McDowell**
Client: **Medtronic**
Art Director: **Mark McDowell**
Photographer: **Mark David Cohen**
Copywriter: **Frank Hughes**

"Il*lumen*ating" is the operative pun in this corporate ad for Medtronic. The play on words refers to the *illuminated* catheter shown in the photograph, as well as to the *lumen* (the inner passageway) of the artery shown in cross-section. In other words, this catheter is illuminating the lumen, giving physicians the opportunity to explore human blood vessels from within. The copy by Creative Director Frank Hughes emphasizes the important research being conducted at Medtronic, and invites the reader to contact the company for more information.

Product: **Dolobid**®
Ad Agency: **Robert A. Becker Inc.**
Client: **Merck Sharp & Dohme**
Art Directors: **Don Kruzinski, Ben Gooch**
Illustrator: **Weber**
Copywriter: **Steve Tom**

A *New Yorker* style cartoon sets the genial tone of this ad for Dolobid®, a pain-relief formula. While the patient earnestly describes symptoms, the physician simultaneously translates the information into a comparative graph that shows the effectiveness of Dolobid® against the competition. The cartoon balloons above the characters' heads add a whimsical touch, yet the ad never lapses into mere frivolity.

Product: **MECLOMEN**®
Ad Agency: **Sudler & Hennessey**
Client: **Parke-Davis Div.,
Warner Lambert Co.**
Art Directors: **Rudi Sanchez, Steve Brothers**
Copywriter: **Steve Hamburg**

Sometimes less really *is* more, as demonstrated in this well-conceived "minimalist" ad for MECLOMEN®, an

antiarthritic formula. The visual is simply a graph curve that rises sharply from the outset, lending new meaning to the old adage used in the headline. At a glance, the ad tells physicians that MECLOMEN® provides fast relief of arthritis symptoms. At the same time, it creates a simple, high-impact message that sets it apart from the competition.

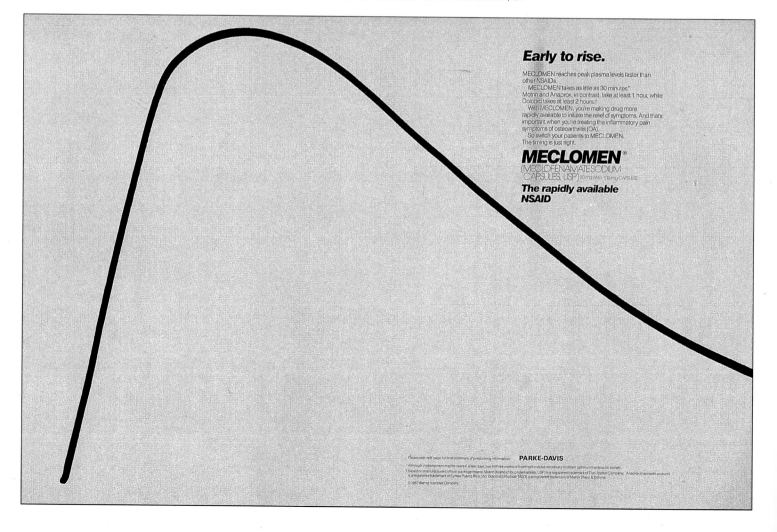

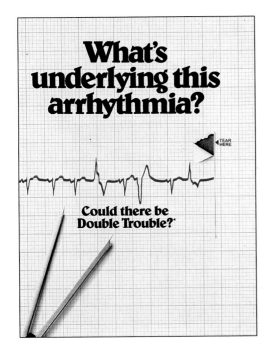

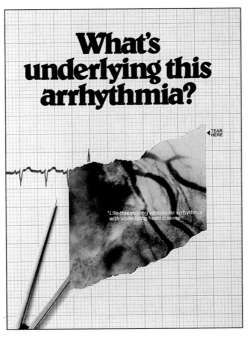

Product: **TONOCARD**®
Ad Agency: **Gross Townsend Frank Hoffman, Inc.**
Client: **Merck Sharp & Dohme**
Art Director: **Jeffrey Pienkos**
Photographer: **Jeff Morgan Photography**
Copywriter: **Zoë R. Graves**

The "double trouble" theme of this clever interactive ad for TONOCARD® refers to arrhythmia coupled with underlying coronary artery disease. But instead of mentioning the problem in such mundane fashion, the creative team at Gross Townsend Frank Hoffman, Inc. has come up with a unique visual reinforcer: the reader responds to the "double trouble" teaser by *tearing open* the pre-cut page and uncovering a photograph of narrowed coronary arteries beneath the wobbly EKG. This perfect involvement device primes the reader for the benefits-and-positioning copy message on the reverse side of the page. There, the "tear-open" visual is picked up again (this time it's only a *trompe l'oeil* effect—the page is actually intact). Here's a prime example of an ad that's fun to experience, yet still fundamentally serious and medically relevant.

Product: **Norpace**® **CR**
Ad Agency: **Sutton Communications**
Client: **Searle & Co.**
Art Director: **Nick Manganiello**
Illustrator: **Don Brautigam**
Copywriter: **Richard Norman**

Norpace® had been losing ground to newer anti-arrhythmic medications, due in part to negative publicity, when Sutton Communications created this arresting two-pager. The attention-getting visual of an EKG strip in the form of a face serves two functions: it humanizes the treatment of cardiac arrhythmia, and it leads the reader to the copy on the right-hand page. Here, using the EKG strips in a bar graph, the creative team spells out the full story: that in a recent series of tests, the active ingredient in Norpace® caused less aggravation of symptoms than any other antiarrhythmic agent.

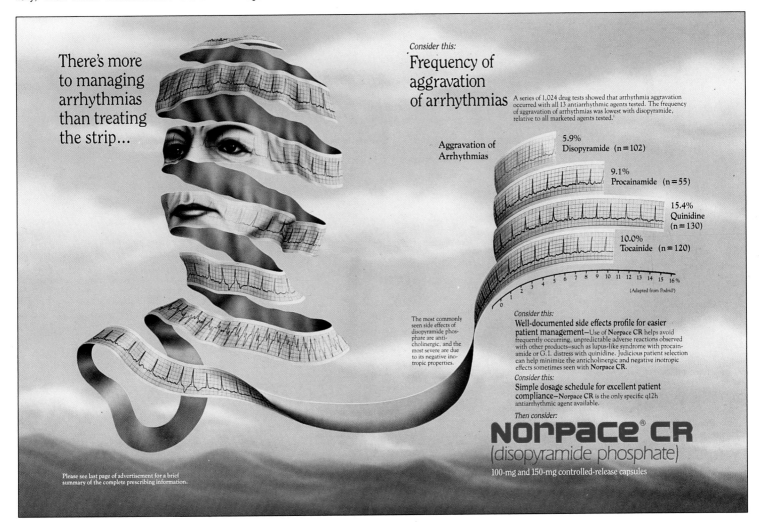

Product: **RESTORIL**®
Ad Agency: **Robert A. Becker Inc.**
Client: **Sandoz Pharmaceuticals Corp.**
Art Directors: **Sal Morello, Julian Molesso**
Photographer: **Clyde May**
Copywriter: **Sam Bromberg**

How do you sell your audience on a sedative without putting them to sleep? V.P./Senior Art Director Sal Morello and Julian Molesso took the leading benefit of RESTORIL®—that it provides the optimum duration of sleep—and humanized it with a warm, friendly image. The merry old Continental chef, whose face and hand dominate the ad, tells us in the international language of cooking that the product is *just right*— "short acting…but not too short." The copy below the face expands on this idea—but not for too long. Just long enough to get the point across to an audience of GPs.

Product: **Permaflex**® **Thin** 43
Ad Agency: **Gross Townsend Frank Hoffman, Inc.**
Client: **CooperVision**
Art Director: **Mark Tripetti**

At a time when contact lenses were receiving adverse publicity because of their tendency to cause corneal ulcers, this startling ad for Permaflex® Thin 43 lenses delivered a welcome message. Here was a lens that, according to the copy, combined "5 unique advantages to keep the cornea healthy." In the opening spread of this eye-catching ad from Gross Townsend Frank Hoffman, Inc., the raised eyebrow of the model communicates surprise, jibing nicely with the tagline, "Surprising options in flexible wear." Aimed at eye care specialists, the ad attempts to surprise its audience with a timely and effective solution to a threatening problem. It works. The third page highlights the fashion side of the story—lenses in an assortment of appealing colors.

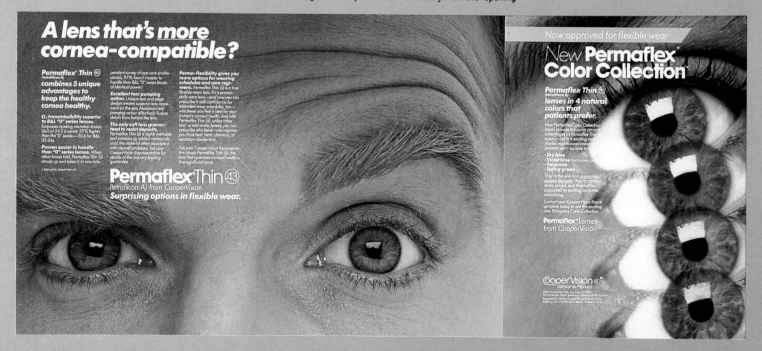

Product: **PANCREASE**®
Ad Agency: **Botto, Roessner, Horne & Messinger, Inc.**
Client: **McNeil Pharmaceutical**
Art Director: **Russell Brightwell**
Photographer: **Steven Mark Needham**
Copywriters: **Peggy O'Driscoll, Susan Mayer Roher, Jennifer Ratcliff**

"Balance" is the headline—and the theme—of this intriguing ad for PANCREASE®, a pancreatic enzyme supplement. According to V.P./Copy Supervisor Susan Mayer Roher, "The client hoped to convince physicians who treat cystic fibrosis that an appropriately balanced enzyme supplement (PANCREASE®) is as important as a balanced diet in treating pancreatic insufficiency." The diet is depicted on the left as a perfectly balanced column of essential food groups. Then we're shown that PANCREASE® is every bit as balanced as the diet, with the pancreatic enzymes lipase, amylase, and protease all present and accounted for.

Product: **DYAZIDE**®
Ad Agency: **Salthouse Torre Norton Inc.**
Client: **Smith Kline & French Co.**
Art Director: **Mike Lazur**
Photographer: **Donato Leo**
Copywriter: **Mike Norton**

"Physicians were no longer interested in stopping to look at DYAZIDE® ads in journals," writes Senior V.P./Account Supervisor Barbara Falco. So Salthouse Torre Norton Inc. developed this colorful attention-getter to rekindle interest in the long-established antihypertensive drug. The agency built its concept around one of the leading benefits of DYAZIDE®: that it works without creating a need for extra potassium in the diet (usually consumed in the form of bananas by hypertensives who take diuretics). The result is a whimsical and highly memorable visual of a peeled-down banana skin with a big DYAZIDE® pill in place of the banana. According to Falco, "the ad tested well and demonstrated strong readership scores."

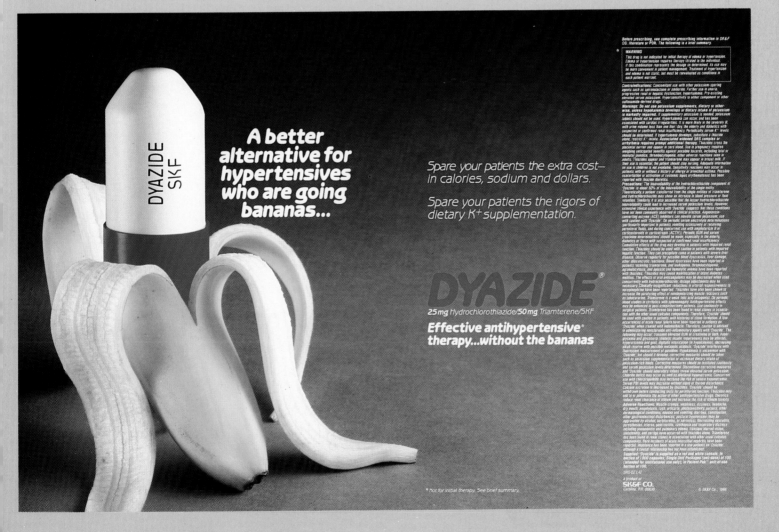

Product: **Karl Storz Ultrasonic Lithotriptor**
Ad Agency: **Forsythe Marcelli Johnson Advertising, Inc.**
Client: **Karl Storz Endoscopy—America, Inc.**
Art Director: **Vic Marcelli**
Photographer: **Stan Sholik**
Copywriter: **Jim Forsythe**

It sure *looks* like a gun, with its long barrel, handgrip, trigger, and sighting scope. But this small bore semi-automatic was designed to relieve pain rather than cause it—specifically by zapping stones in the ureters. That's the point of this eye-catching ad from Forsythe Marcelli Johnson Advertising. The photograph cleverly capitalizes on the superficial resemblance between the Karl Storz Ultrasonic Lithotriptor and a rifle. The copy picks up on this playful idea: "Feel the grip settle firmly in your hand. Admire the smooth trigger action." But then the real benefits are quickly, clearly, and persuasively stated.

Destroy ureteral stones with a small bore semi-automatic.

Karl Storz

Product: **VIVONEX®**
Ad Agency: **Lally, McFarland & Pantello**
Client: **Norwich Eaton Pharmaceuticals, Inc.**
Art Director: **Bill Kerby**
Illustrator: **Enid Hatton**

Equivalence is the key to establishing any medical product against better known (and higher priced) competition. An ad attempting this must supply compelling evidence that the new alternative produces the same (or better) results than the old standard—and at a lower price. That's what the creative team at Lally, McFarland & Pantello has done here: the twin illustrations suggest a head-to-head test of VIVONEX® T.E.N., an intravenous solution, against the more established TPN. (Note the high-tech look of the VIVONEX® T.E.N. packaging, contrasted with the old-fashioned I.V. bottle on the left.) The actual results of such a test are displayed in the graph below, along with the convincing tagline, "The benefits of TPN, at a fraction of the cost."

TPN isn't the only way to get TPN results.

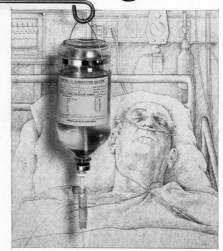

Like TPN, VIVONEX® T.E.N. is truly elemental for rapid return to positive nitrogen balance.

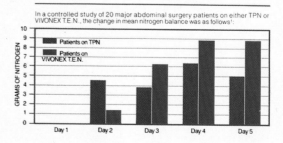

VIVONEX®
T.E.N.
(TOTAL ENTERAL NUTRITION)

The benefits of TPN, enterally... at a fraction of the cost.

Norwich Eaton
Norwich Eaton Pharmaceuticals, Inc.
Norwich, New York 13815-0231
A Procter & Gamble Company

Saving lives when the heart is under attack...

Intravenous Lopressor is now accepted as basic protocol for acute MI in more than 350 hospitals.

Reduces 3-month mortality[1]

Reduces incidence of ventricular fibrillation[2]

Reduces duration of chest pain and need for analgesics[1]

Lopressor in **MI**
metoprolol tartrate

...and protecting healing hearts in the months ahead

The combination of early intravenous administration of Lopressor followed by long-term oral therapy resulted in a 36% reduction of three-month mortality in patients with definite or suspected acute MI in the Göteborg Trial.[1]

Alternatively, oral treatment can begin within 3 to 10 days of the acute event.

Treatment should be continued for 1-3 years.

Lopressor in **MI**
metoprolol tartrate

Changing the Course of Cardiovascular Care

Product: **Lopressor® MI**
Ad Agency: **C & G Advertising Inc. (In-house)**
Client: **Geigy Pharmaceuticals Co.**
Art Director: **Bob Talarczyk**
Photographer: **Michael Furman**
Copywriter: **Pat Blagden**

The in-house agency at Ciba-Geigy Corporation has delivered a powerful one-two punch in this multi-page ad for Lopressor® MI, a drug injected during a heart attack and administered orally thereafter. Note how the high-tech look of the first spread gives way to a gentle human-interest scene in the second spread. This two-tier approach reflects the actual use of the drug, which is first used under emergency conditions in the hospital, then taken by the patient as long-term therapy. The first spread says "emergency!" while the second conveys a positive image of healing, springtime, and familial intimacy. The copy concisely states the benefits, offers evidence of wide acceptance, provides statistics, and furnishes guidelines for therapy.

Product: **LO/OVRAL**®
Ad Agency: **William Douglas McAdams Inc.**
Client: **Wyeth/Ayerst Laboratories**
Art Director: **Jeffrey Lipman**
Photographer: **John Manno**

A graceful bonsai tree, shown in stunning close-up, illustrates the "minimalism" theme of this handsome two-page ad for LO/OVRAL®, a low-dose contraceptive. The headline, the spare beauty of the tree, and the very brief copy all work together to reinforce the minimalist concept, which relates to the pill's properties. Writes Art Director Jeffrey Lipman, "The primary goal in this piece was a borrowed interest visual of something minimal, representing minimal spotting and breakthrough bleeding with LO/OVRAL®."

Product: **LIORESAL**®
Ad Agency: **C & G Advertising Inc. (In-house)**
Client: **Geigy Pharmaceuticals**
Art Director: **Ron Vareltzis**
Photographer: **Ed Gallucci**
Copywriter: **Pat Blagden**

Although the young man in the photograph is wheelchair-bound, he's obviously living life to the fullest. That's the message of this upbeat ad for LIORESAL®, an antispastic muscle relaxant for people with MS or spinal cord injury. Photographer Ed Gallucci has caught the man's enthusiasm at the moment of victory, reminding physicians—and all of us—that a wheelchair isn't necessarily a barrier to the enjoyment of active pursuits, and that LIORESAL® can enhance the quality of life for wheelchair patients.

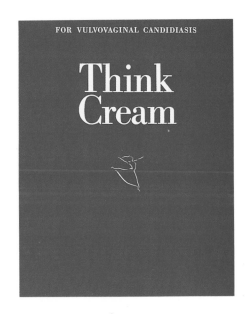

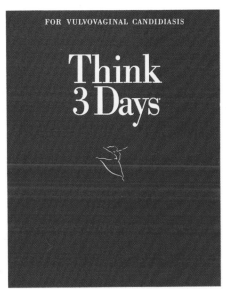

Product: **Femstat**®
Ad Agency: **Vicom/FCB**
Client: **Syntex Laboratories, Inc.**
Art Director: **Penny DeWind**
Copywriter: **Robert Finkel**

When the product is a cream for treating yeast infections in women, an agency must tread cautiously. One must keep the ad tasteful, yet create advertising with impact—something that will establish the product in the top of the physician's mind. This ad for Femstat® succeeds on both counts. Running on three consecutive right-hand pages, the ad positions the product with a simple but powerful three-step memory device: "Think Cream…Think 3 Days…Think Femstat®." In other words, Femstat® is a cream that works in just three days—a fact reinforced by the tagline on the final page. But here's the final clincher: it's the *only* three-day cream. The three pages of the ad reinforce the "three-day" message, and they're linked by a number of common elements: the uniformly bold background colors, the word "think," the overline (stating the purpose of the cream), and the visual motif of a woman who obviously enjoys her body.

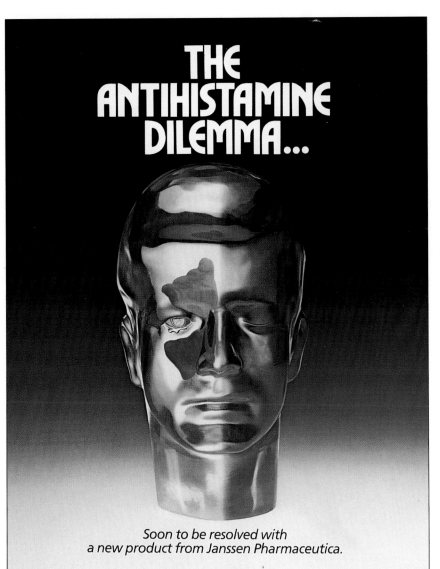

Soon to be resolved with
a new product from Janssen Pharmaceutica.

Title: **"The Antihistamine Dilemma…"**
Ad Agency: **William Douglas McAdams Inc.**
Client: **Janssen Pharmaceutica**
Art Directors: **Patrick Creaven, Diane Lynch**
Photographer: **Shig Ikeda**
Model Maker: **Nick Aristovulos**
Copywriter: **Gwenne Freiman**

A split view of a human head—congested and miserable on one side, heavily sedated on the other—dramatizes the traditional "dilemma" facing allergy patients: whether to suffer the symptoms or trade them for a drug-induced stupor.

In this pre-launch ad for Hismanal®, the creative team at William Douglas McAdams Inc. created this exceptional graphic, which was no easy technical task. According to Patrick Creaven, V.P./group head art director, two clear Lucite heads were cast from a live model—one had closed eyes, the other had eyes sculpted open and sinuses imbedded. Both heads were colorless except for the red sinuses.

The head images were joined photographically and all color in the background and in the heads (except for that of the sinuses) were created on *one sheet of film*. Photographer Shig Ikeda used three 8" x 10" view cameras, precision masking, coloring, and multiple exposure techniques to create this unified image. He even added tears on the left part of the image using corn syrup.

2

AD CAMPAIGNS AND INSERTS

BUSINESS MAGAZINES
TRADE MAGAZINES
CONSUMER MAGAZINES
NEWSPAPERS
PUBLIC SERVICE

Like the examples in Chapter 1, the ads on the following pages were created to fill media space. But there's also an important difference. The Chapter 1 ads were self-contained; they told their stories in a single burst of creativity. By contrast, the ads in Chapter 2 were all designed to extend their messages through space or time.

If this concept sounds like Einstein's theory of advertising, be assured it's not. By *space* we mean, of course, the *media* space filled by the ad. A multi-page advertising insert must generate the selling message over an expanded amount of space—and, simultaneously, the entire sequence must display a visual coherence that ties it together in the mind of the reader.

The reference to *time* simply acknowledges the challenge faced by an ad campaign: to deliver a message in the chosen media, then reinforce it in subsequent publications. In other words, to build a strong, compelling, and internally consistent story over a period of time—usually in more than one publication and often in a variety of media (for example, posters, promotional kits, direct mail, or broadcast commercials).

But whether space-oriented or time-oriented, these extended ads all rely on *continuity* to achieve their desired impact. The reader must be able to recognize any single page from any of these ads as part of the whole—or the cause is lost. Slogans, typography, color, and other design elements all play a role in creating the vital linkage that spells instant recognition—and probable success.

A multi-page ad insert must accomplish all of the above—and, at the same time, stand apart visually and editorially from the medium in which it appears. To establish its unique identity as a "publication within a publication," the contemporary art director will often enhance the insert with specially textured paper, metallic inks, or other visual attention-getters. These devices announce to the reader that he or she is temporarily leaving the publication behind and crossing the border into different, perhaps more visually dynamic terrain. As the reader progresses through the insert, the consistency of design provides reassurance that the message continues. And, of course, the insert must end as dramatically as it began—with a sharp transition back to the mainstream of the publication.

A good example is the insert for Searle, which uses a black background, superior anatomical graphics, and a running headline to establish an identity of its own. The three-page insert for Brevibloc®, a beta blocker, benefits from five ink colors—including a specially mixed metallic green. Not to be outdone, the three-page insert for the antibiotic Claforan® makes use of *six-color* printing. But what makes this example especially noteworthy is the stunning use of glossy black type on a matte black background.

Ad campaigns use a variety of strategies to establish a sense of continuity in the mind of the reader. Rather than take the safe but dull route of simply repeating the same visuals and copy to drive home the message, the best campaigns keep introducing new elements within a recognizable framework.

Often, the visual may vary from ad to ad while retaining a pronounced family resemblance. To advertise its GLUCOSCAN™ blood glucose meters, LifeScan Inc. used a different patient testimony in each ad, with similar design and photographic style. A campaign for the anti-arthritic drug Feldene® made use of stroboscopic photographs of various body joints in motion. Deep red backgrounds, punning headline copy, and dramatic studies of the human back established immediate identity in a series of ads for FLEXERIL®. And, in a campaign for PROPINE®, the recognition factor was the softly grainy texture of the photography.

In some cases, the campaign reached beyond the boundaries of the publication. For a series of space ads promoting Ativan®, an antidepressant, noted artist Jean-Michel Folon dreamed up a wild and colorful group of symbolic visuals, each one corresponding to a single benefit of the drug. These images were then transformed into prints and distributed free to psychiatrists in a successful direct-mail campaign.

This "one benefit, one image" concept figures prominently in a number of campaigns. The makers of NAPROSYN® commissioned illustrator Will Nelson to create a collection of wildlife portraits, each accompanied by a single word that characterized both the animal and the drug (e.g., "powerful" like an elephant). Each animal/trait coupling then became a separate ad in the campaign. Along the same lines, the oral contraceptive TRI-NORINYL® was featured in a memorably beautiful "one benefit, one image" series using lyrical nature photographs.

When the visual element changes more radically from one ad to the next, the copy often assumes the burden for maintaining linkage. Note the repetition of the tagline in the campaign for Partnership for a Drug-Free America.

And sometimes continuity is established by nothing more than a subtle tone in the copy or art—something that tells you the same creative minds are at work throughout the campaign. To see what we mean, take a look at the gently ironic (but nonetheless highly compelling) ads for Torrance Memorial Hospital. Or the wryly comical photographs of women at work in the appealing series for Triphasil®, an oral contraceptive. And for a highly original campaign that approaches its subject from a more oblique angle, be sure to see the "clinical clues" ads for PROCARDIA®, with their understated aura of mystery and suspense.

Now that you're prepared for your trip through "space" and "time," turn the page and discover some of the best medical ad campaigns and inserts of the past few years.

Product: **PROCARDIA**®
Ad Agency: **Dorritie & Lyons, Inc.**
Client: **Pfizer Laboratories**
Art Director: **Thomas Velardi**
Photographer: **Bob Walsh**
Copywriter: **Carol Shepko**

GOLD. Each of the four-page ads in this intriguing series starts with a seemingly innocuous "clue" on the first page: an overturned book, a departing train, and so on. Something's clearly afoot here. The common headline for all the ads tips us off: "Clinical Clues to Mixed Angina." But what do these clues have to do with angina? To solve the mystery, we turn the page, see a dramatic close-up shot of the "victim" clutching his or her chest, and plunge into the copy, which links the initial clue to angina (the angina sufferer has dropped the book, missed the train, etc.). This clever award winner from Dorritie & Lyons, Inc., helps educate physicians about the various causes of angina attacks (effort, stress, cold, and no outward cause), dramatizes the stark terror of such attacks, and promotes the benefits of PROCARDIA® in relieving vasoconstriction. The solid red background conveys urgency, while the mysterious "whodunit" atmosphere commands reader involvement.

The Second in a Series

Clinical Clues to Mixed Angina

The First in a Series

Clinical Clues to Mixed Angina

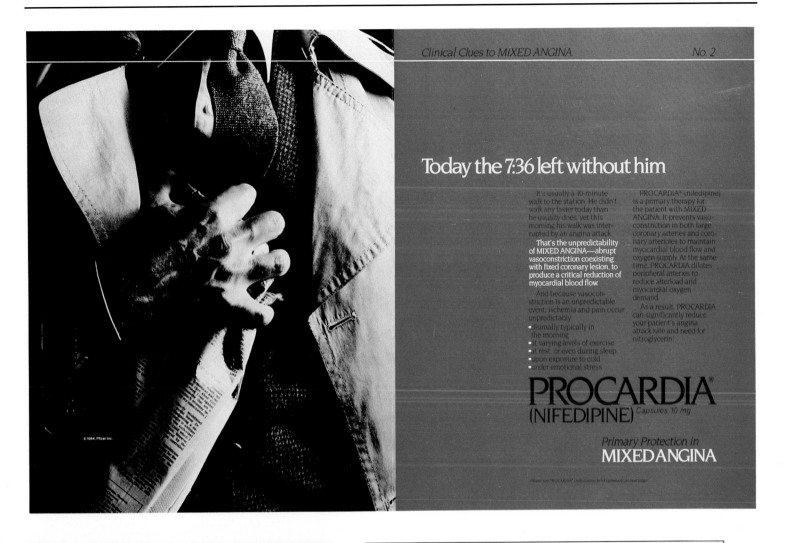

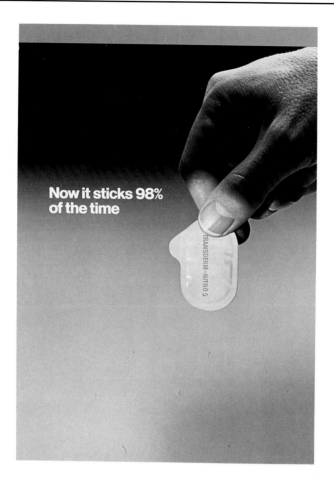

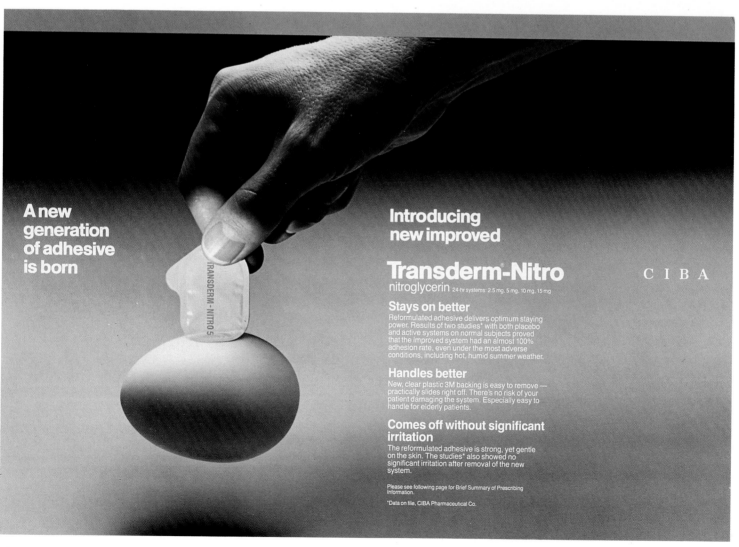

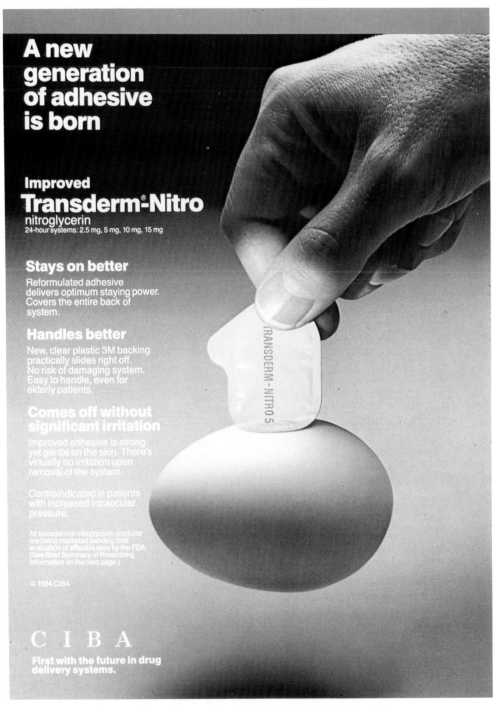

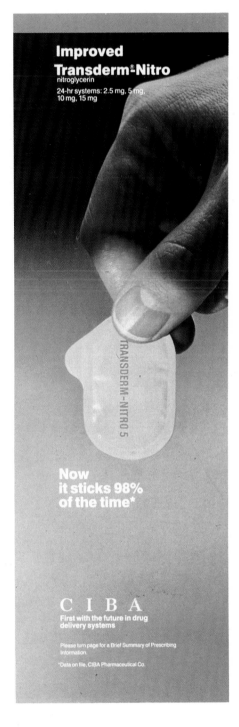

Product: **Transderm-Nitro**®
Ad Agency: **C & G Advertising Inc. (In-house)**
Client: **Ciba-Geigy Pharmaceutical Co.**
Art Director: **Ron Vareltzis**
Photographer: **Ed Gallucci**
Copywriter: **Nancy Benton**

GOLD. Marketing campaigns for "new, improved" products can sometimes leave skeptics wondering, "What was wrong until now?" But the makers of Transderm-Nitro®, the widely accepted skin patch for angina sufferers, announced an upgrade in their product with a campaign that's positive—and disarming—all the way. The simple graphic of the patch supporting a dangling egg is all we need to conclude that the adhesive qualities have indeed been improved. The copy reference to "a new generation of adhesive," coupled with the news about easier removal, says that a good product has been made even better.

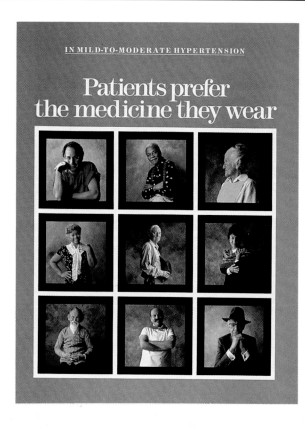

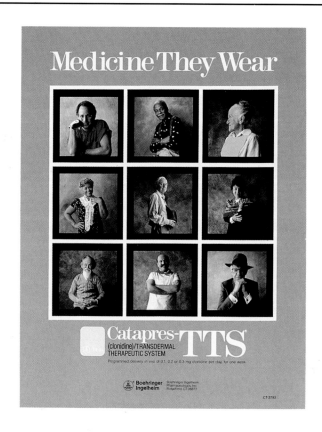

Product: **Catapres-TTS**®
Ad Agency: **Barnum Communications, Inc.**
Client: **Boehringer Ingelheim**
Art Director: **Monica Garb**
Photographer: **Ken Nahoum**
Copywriters: **Melissa De Fiebre, James Pelletier**

GOLD. The theme of patient preference runs through this warmly human ad campaign for Catapres-TTS®, the transdermal patch for treatment of mild to moderate hypertension. Ken Nahoum's color portraits of typical users, most of them smiling directly into the camera, quickly capture the reader's attention in this series of one-page, four-page, and eight-page ads. The multi-page ads then go on to focus on one of three patient types for whom treatment with the product is recommended: the elderly, the active, and those with concurrent disorders. To illustrate each patient type, one of the nine characters from the cover takes center stage. The featured patient, once again beaming into the camera, is shown happily at work—while wearing the Catapres-TTS® patch.

Product: **FLEXERIL**®
Ad Agency: **Vicom/FCB**
Client: **Merck Sharp & Dohme**
Art Director: **Lester Barnett**
Photographer: **David Tise**
Copywriter: **David Lumsden**

SILVER. The human back takes center stage in this award-winning campaign for FLEXERIL®, a drug used in treating back pain. The elegant photographs by David Tise show a variety of backs in motion, all suffused by a warm reddish glow. In each ad, the headline plays off the word "back" to create a deliberate stopper: "Bring her back back to Bach"…"Get his back back on track" and so on down the line. You can glance at these ads casually—even carelessly—and still know immediately what they're for. According to Lester Barnett, creative director of Vicom/FCB, this series was part of a long-term back pain campaign. Each ad had to share some characteristics yet "be so different as to capture new attention."

Feldene® reduces arthritis pain
(PIROXICAM)

The most common side effects of FELDENE are GI related, such as nausea or epigastric distress. As with other NSAIDs, serious GI side effects such as peptic ulceration or bleeding may occur, but in less than 1% of patients.

Artist's interpretation of osteoarthritis of the lumbar spine.

■ FELDENE®(piroxicam) effectively relieves symptoms of osteoarthritis.[1]

■ Patients can perform daily activities better, more comfortably and more productively.[2]

When low back pain is due to osteoarthritis,

Feldene® Works
(PIROXICAM) 20 mg capsules

Please see brief summary of FELDENE® (piroxicam) prescribing information on next page.

© 1987, Pfizer Inc.

Product: **Feldene**®
Ad Agency: **Dorritie & Lyons, Inc.**
Client: **Pfizer Laboratories**
Art Director: **Mike Lyons**
Illustrator: **Cass Henselmann (spine model)**
Photographers: **Peter Vaeth (strobe photos),
Bruno (spine),
Dr. Vise (thermography)**
Copywriter: **Bill Brown**

SILVER. These three elegant studies of the human body in motion were created by photographer Peter Vaeth, who used three strobes to attain the special effects in each panel. The soft, slightly grainy images of an arm, leg and back are not included here for their beauty alone; they're used to demonstrate the effectiveness of Feldene® in restoring easy movement to arthritic patients. The small insets, which add a note of vivid color to the muted flesh tones, are actual before-and-after clinical images of patients who had been treated with Feldene®.

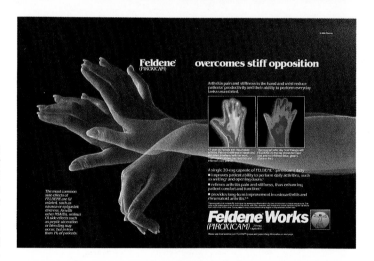

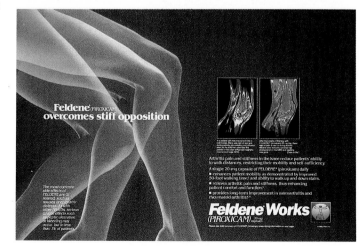

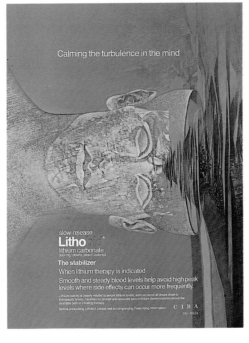

Product: **Lithobid**®
Ad Agency: **C & G Advertising Inc. (In-house)**
Client: **Ciba Pharmaceutical Co.**
Art Director: **Bob Talarczyk**
Illustrator: **Luis Cueva**
Copywriter: **Pat Blagden**

These hypnotic images of a disturbed mind comprise a memorable campaign for Lithobid®, a lithium-based drug used in combating manic depression. In each ad, a powerful illustration by Luis Cueva gives us a literal translation of the headline: copy and art are fused into a single coherent message. The fiery image in one ad effectively conveys the explosive energy of manic depression; the other ad, with its muted blues and whirlpool effect, appears to symbolize the down side of the disorder. By tilting this illustration on its side, Art Director Bob Talarczyk achieved an unsettling off-balance effect.

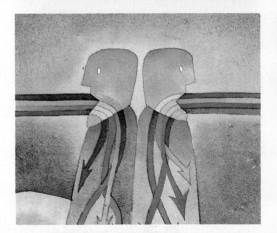

In addition to rapid relief of anxiety...
Only Ativan® (lorazepam) ©
offers <u>all</u> these benefits...

See important information on last page.

Product: **Ativan®**
Ad Agency: **Kallir, Philips, Ross, Inc.**
Client: **Wyeth Laboratories**
Art Director: **John Geryak**
Illustrator: **Jean-Michel Folon**
Copywriter: **Phyllis Wachsman**

Internationally renowned graphic artist Jean-Michel Folon was commissioned to create this stunning series of symbolic illustrations for Ativan®, a medication used to treat anxiety associated with depressive symptoms. Folon's rich imagination transforms each of the drug's major benefits into visual terms, with a full panel devoted to each benefit. Targeted at psychiatrists (who are sure to respond to these playful mental landscapes), this multi-page insert from Kallir, Philips, Ross, Inc., dazzles and entertains while it informs its audience about the multiple advantages of this useful drug.

NOW YOU CAN
SEPARATE THE BEST FROM THE REST

...WITH THE CUTTER
NEOCEL SYSTEM FOR YOUNG RED CELLS.

Now, young red cells can be routinely used to improve the management of chronically transfused patients by decreasing the transfusion requirement and the rate of iron loading... or whenever the best red cell product is indicated. Because now there's a commercially available blood bag system for efficient, reliable separation of red cells by age.

A BETTER RED CELL PRODUCT
The Neocel System delivers a product rich in neocytes (young red cells) with a 31% extension in mean half-life over normal packed red cells.

Color enhanced red cells 4400×. Top, least dense (youngest) fraction. Bottom, most dense (oldest) fraction.

SIMPLE, FAST PROCEDURE
Neocel provides a simple method of separation using a standard centrifuge, significantly reducing cost and technical difficulty compared to present methods.

Provide a better red cell product, with the Neocel System for Young Red Cells...another Component Enhancement Product, only from Cutter.

For more information, contact your Cutter Biological Representative or call our Professional Services Department at (800) 227-1762.

Cutter Biological MILES
A Division of Miles Laboratories, Inc. © 1986, Miles Laboratories, Inc.

NOW YOU CAN
STORE LEUKOPOOR RED CELLS

...WITH THE CUTTER
LEUKOTRAP RED CELL STORAGE SYSTEM.

Now you can cost-effectively produce and store high-quality leukopoor red cells for *42 days*. The Leukotrap closed system efficiently removes leukocytes from fresh red cells, then maintains red cell viability for 42 days in the Nutricel* AS-3 additive solution.

MOST EFFICIENT
CLOSED SYSTEM METHOD
The Leukotrap Storage System removes 91% of leukocytes and 80% of platelets, while recovering 90% of the red cells.*

Leukotrap's closed blood bag system contains an in-line leukocyte removal filter

SIMPLE, RELIABLE
PROCEDURE
The Leukotrap System provides consistent results with only minimal technician time and a standard centrifuge.

Provide a better red cell product with the Leukotrap Storage System...another Component Enhancement Product, only from Cutter.

For more information, contact your Cutter Biological Representative or call our Professional Services Department at (800) 227-1762.

Cutter Biological MILES
A Division of Miles Laboratories, Inc. © 1986, Miles Laboratories, Inc.   *Data on file at Cutter.

NOW THE WAY IS CLEAR FOR
YOU TO PROVIDE LEUKOPOOR PLATELETS

...WITH THE CUTTER
LEUKOTRAP PLATELET POOLING SYSTEM.

Now, leukopoor platelets can be routinely used for treatment of patients on platelet therapy to reduce or eliminate leukocyte-associated transfusion reactions. Leukotrap is the first commercially available system for *routine* production of leukopoor platelets.

MOST EFFICIENT METHOD
The Leukotrap System removes 90% of leukocytes and residual red cells with only 10% platelet loss.

Leukotrap™ Pooling Bag shown after completed procedure with leukocytes and residual red cells trapped in the pouch.

SIMPLE, FAST PROCEDURE
The Leukotrap System requires minimal technician time and a standard centrifuge.

Provide a better platelet product...with the Leukotrap Platelet Pooling System.

For more information, contact your Cutter Biological Representative or call our Professional Services Dept. at (800) 527-7200; in CA (800) 527-7222.

Cutter Biological
A Division of Miles Laboratories, Inc. © 1985, Miles Laboratories, Inc.

Product: **Neocel™ and Leukotrap™ Systems**
Ad Agency: **Rainoldi Kerzner & Radcliffe**
Client: **Cutter Biological**
Art Director: **Charles Schmalz**
Illustrator: **Wilson McLean**
Copywriter: **Diane Koerner**

Three surrealistic dream-visions by illustrator Wilson McLean distinguish this imaginative campaign for a trio of new products from Cutter Biological. Targeted at both physicians and blood bank technologists, the ads had to appeal to *both* audiences simultaneously. Jay Kerzner, V.P. (client services) writes that the new products (all used in blood technology) "gave the agency the opportunity to generate excitement and awareness with a conceptual campaign that tied the family of products together and broke through the mundane 'product photo' advertising generally found in blood banking publications." The ads not only create awareness of the products but help establish an innovative "cutting edge" image for the company as a whole. It's worth noting that the visionary illustrations are complemented by down-to-earth inset photos and selling copy.

Product: **SKD Diagnostic Systems**
Ad Agency: **Rainoldi Kerzner & Radcliffe**
Client: **SmithKline Diagnostics, Inc.**
Art Director: **Charles Schmalz**
Illustrators: **Ricardo Tringali,**
Ed Manning/Watson, Manning, Inc.
Copywriter: **Daniella Thompson**

The visual centerpiece of this corporate image campaign for SKD Diagnostic Systems is a computer-generated image of the human body—a body transformed into pure diagnostic information. (If the image looks vaguely familiar, it's because the agency adapted it from the famed locomotion series by 19th century photographer Edward Muybridge.) According to Account Supervisor Eugene Berman, the determined stride of the walking man suggested the headline. It also echoes the primary purpose of the campaign as stated by Berman: to communicate the client's "determination to be the single source for physician office testing products." The theme of determination runs like a thread throughout the different copy messages in the two ads shown here. Targeted at both physicians and distributors, this was the first corporate image campaign in the history of SmithKline Diagnostics. Berman writes that "the primary campaign visual had to be capable of being successfully applied to journal ads, sales and promotional materials, exhibit graphics, and other marketing communication elements in single as well as four-color reproduction."

Product: **PPG Biomedical Systems**
Ad Agency: **M.E.D. Communications, Inc.**
Client: **PPG Biomedical Systems, Inc.**
Art Director: **Skip Hurley**
Copywriter: **Malcolm Hall**

Ancient pictographs add meaning and a touch of individuality to this advertising insert for PPG Biomedical Systems. Featured on the first page is the Chinese symbol for "coming together," drawn from the *I Ching* (Book of Changes). Depicted on the following pages are the alchemists' symbol for "amalgamation," an Anglo-Saxon rune that stands for "communications and information," and the Ojibwa Indian sign for "I am about to climb." All of these symbols jibe nicely with the nature and goals of the company, as explained in the accompanying text blocks. A very contemporary pictographic symbol is also included—the PPG logo, which the company hopes will "become synonymous with biomedical accomplishment."

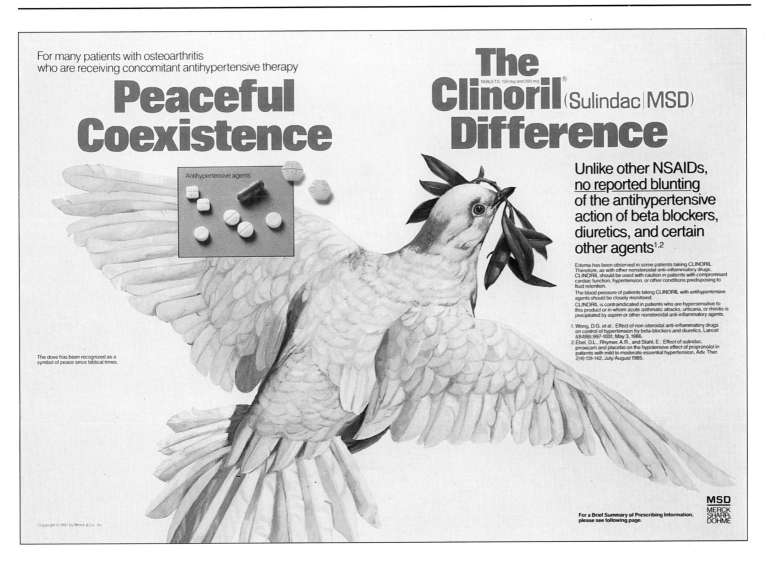

Product: **Clinoril®**
Ad Agency: **Robert A. Becker Inc.**
Client: **Merck Sharp & Dohme**
Art Directors: **Don Kruzinski, John Witt**
Illustrators: **Paul Blakey (olive branch),
Shannon Stirnweis (dove)**

The olive branch and the dove, both time-honored symbols of peace, visually echo the "Peaceful Coexistence" theme of this ad series for Clinoril®, a medication used in the treatment of arthritis. What the "Peaceful Coexistence" refers to is the compatibility of the drug with other types of medication—specifically, prostaglandin (taken by kidney patients) and blood pressure drugs. In one ad, the olive branch is accompanied by an inset of kidneys and prostaglandin pills; the other ad features a plump white dove along with an inset showing high blood pressure medication.

THE HEART AS AN ENDOCRINE ORGAN... WITH THERAPEUTIC POTENTIAL

Searle research contributed to identification of the most recently discovered components of the endocrine system—the atrial natriuretic factors (also called atrial peptides). Granules secreted by cells in the walls of both atria contain cardiac proteins which act to regulate the blood pressure, water and electrolyte homeostasis within the body in response to changes in the atrial pressure.

The atrial peptides have strong vasodilatory properties with an apparent direct relaxant effect on smooth muscle previously constricted by virtually any agent including angiotensin or norepinephrine. The vasodilatory effects contribute to a marked hypotensive action.

In addition, atrial peptides directly antagonize all major antinatriuretic and antidiuretic hormones, producing a brisk diuresis. Pharmacologically different from most existing diuretics, atrial natriuretic factor does not produce nephrotoxicity. It increases rather than diminishes renal function and glomerular filtration rate.

Atrial peptides produced through Searle biotechnology may have major value in the treatment of renal shutdown caused by trauma, abdominal surgery, suprarenal aortic clamping, immunosuppressant therapy and hepatic cirrhosis—without the side effects of current therapy (dopamine). It is possible that molecular modifications of this peptide could be useful in treating edematous and hypertensive disorders.

Because this endocrine system is such a recent discovery, many fundamental questions remain. For example, what function do atrial peptides perform in the brain? The (as yet) untested possibilities provide an exciting area full of therapeutic promise for the future.

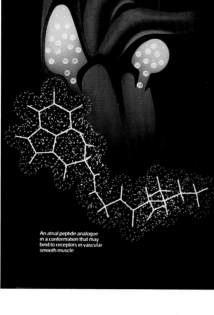

An atrial peptide analogue in a conformation that may bind to receptors in vascular smooth muscle

WHEN MINUTES ARE CRITICAL HOPE OF INSTANT FIBRINOLYSIS

Thrombolytic therapy is one of the most promising new approaches to acute coronary care. Reperfusion of ischemic, but not yet necrotic myocardium, may actually limit the size of the infarct if given soon after the onset.

In a number of randomized trials, streptokinase has failed to produce a significant and uniform reduction in mortality. Interest is moving toward the development of more effective and fibrin-specific thrombolytic agents. The most promising of these to date is tissue-type plasminogen activator (t-PA).

Intravenous t-PA derived from the Bowes melanoma cell line was twice as effective as IV streptokinase in opening occluded coronary arteries in MI patients.[1,2] Now biotechnology has produced a t-PA preparation derived from normal human cells rather than the Bowes melanoma.

Recent animal studies suggest that t-PA also could be useful in treating cerebrovascular problems such as embolism, frequent TIA's with threatened infarction, and stroke in evolution.[3] Yet the full possibilities of this new agent remain to be explored.

1 Thrombolysis in myocardial infarction (TIMI) trial *NEJM* 1985, *312* 932-936
2 Williams DO et al. Intravenous recombinant tissue-type plasminogen activator in patients with acute myocardial infarction: a report from the NSBLI thrombolysis in myocardial infarction trial *Circulation* 1986, *73* 338-346
3 Zivin JA et al. Tissue plasminogen activator reduces neurological damage after cerebral embolism *Science* 1985, *230* 1289-1292

A model for the possible association of a t-PA mimic to its complementary protein. Binding regions are highlighted.

BECAUSE LOSS OF MEMORY IS LOSS OF SELF

Loss of memory, the classic symptom of Alzheimer's disease, destroys a vital component of personal identity. Closely involved with memory loss is impairment of the learning process. Capacity to form new associations, integrate new information, and retain newly acquired material disappears. Recent memory is gone, but a remarkable ability to recollect early life experience remains.

Most efforts to treat cerebral deficits in the aging have been largely symptomatic. For example, attempts to compensate for diminution of cholinergic function in the hippocampus may temporarily improve memory and learning but will not cure or prevent progression of some of these disorders.

Searle scientists are seeking a more fundamental intervention in the disease process. Certain amino acids are known to function as excitatory neurotransmitters in the brain. Excessive activity of these excitatory amino acids may produce nerve cell destruction resembling that which occurs in Alzheimer's, Huntington's chorea, and other degenerative diseases. We are looking for antagonists that might block these amino acid receptor systems and prevent neuronal dysfunction and disruption. Such antagonists might also protect the CNS from ischemic damage in stroke.

Another avenue of approach to cerebral disorders such as Alzheimer's involves the neurotrophic factors. These are larger peptides, such as nerve growth factor, that protect the brain from various types of insults. Deficiencies of these substances may lead to degeneration. Searle scientists are trying to develop protective substances modeled on the nerve growth factor.

In addition, we are evaluating the possibility of using our biotechnology capacities to examine the role of specific proteins found exclusively in Alzheimer's patients. We are also exploring the possible role of slow viruses and autoimmune phenomena in CNS degeneration.

Three-dimensional representation of nerve growth factor showing both molecular detail and the protein backbone as a ribbon.

REMODELING THE ENDORPHINS FOR IMPROVED ANALGESIA

Morphine, a structurally rigid analgesic and addictor operating on brain receptors is depicted in blue. Searle's peptide pain reliever in orange. It targets the same receptors but computation demonstrates that it populates different regions represented by circular vector maps.

In the 1970's, the analgesic potency of certain opiate-like drugs was shown to correlate with the ability to bind to particular brain proteins —opioid receptors. The ligands, or substances naturally bound to these receptors, are the body's endogenous opiates known as the enkephalins or endorphins.

There appears to be a discrete endorphin-mediated network designed specifically to modulate pain; agents such as morphine, meperidine, and oxycodone presumably relieve pain by mimicking the action of endorphin at synapses in this network.

Searle research in enkephalins has developed a compound that promises to represent a substantial advance in analgesic pharmacology. This enkephalin analogue appears to cause less respiratory depression and constipation than the opiates. We expect this line of investigation to produce true non-addictive substitutes for the opiates.

Results of studies of the endorphin system may have other benefits. The compounds Searle scientists develop may also have significant symptomatic benefit in memory and learning disorders.

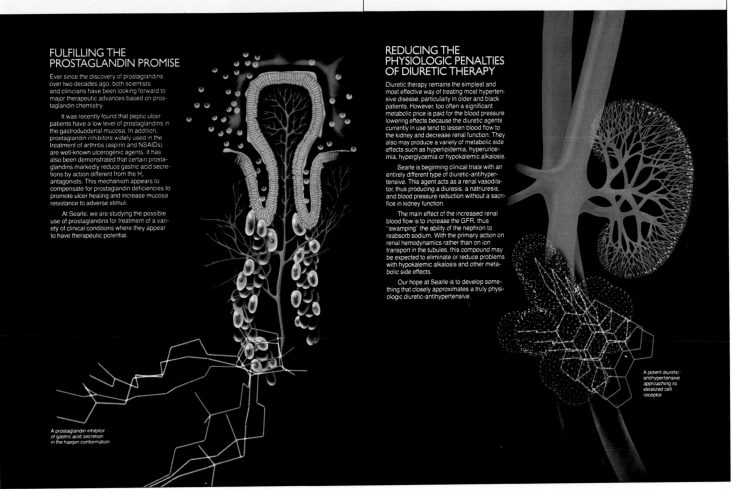

THE   NEW   VISION   OF   RESEARCH   FROM   *SEARLE*

FULFILLING THE PROSTAGLANDIN PROMISE

Ever since the discovery of prostaglandins over two decades ago, both scientists and clinicians have been looking forward to major therapeutic advances based on prostaglandin chemistry.

It was recently found that peptic ulcer patients have a low level of prostaglandins in the gastroduodenal mucosa. In addition, prostaglandin inhibitors widely used in the treatment of arthritis (aspirin and NSAIDs) are well-known ulcerogenic agents. It has also been demonstrated that certain prostaglandins markedly reduce gastric acid secretions by action different from the H₂ antagonists. This mechanism appears to compensate for prostaglandin deficiencies to promote ulcer healing and increase mucosa resistance to adverse stimuli.

At Searle, we are studying the possible use of prostaglandins for treatment of a variety of clinical conditions where they appear to have therapeutic potential.

A prostaglandin inhibitor of gastric acid secretion in the hairpin conformation

REDUCING THE PHYSIOLOGIC PENALTIES OF DIURETIC THERAPY

Diuretic therapy remains the simplest and most effective way of treating most hypertensive disease, particularly in older and black patients. However, too often a significant metabolic price is paid for the blood pressure lowering effects because the diuretic agents currently in use tend to lessen blood flow to the kidney and decrease renal function. They also may produce a variety of metabolic side effects such as hyperlipidemia, hyperuricemia, hyperglycemia or hypokalemic alkalosis.

Searle is beginning clinical trials with an entirely different type of diuretic-antihypertensive. This agent acts as a renal vasodilator, thus producing a diuresis, a natriuresis, and blood pressure reduction without a sacrifice in kidney function.

The main effect of the increased renal blood flow is to increase the GFR, thus "swamping" the ability of the nephron to reabsorb sodium. With the primary action on renal hemodynamics rather than on ion transport in the tubules, this compound may be expected to eliminate or reduce problems with hypokalemic alkalosis and other metabolic side effects.

Our hope at Searle is to develop something that closely approximates a truly physiologic diuretic-antihypertensive.

A potent diuretic-antihypertensive approaching its idealized cell receptor

---

Title: **"New Ideas for the Future from SEARLE"**
Ad Agency: **William Douglas McAdams Inc.**
Client: **Searle**
Art Director: **Walter Scott**
Illustrator: **Radu Vero**
Photographer: **William Franklin McMahon**
Copywriters: **Toby Jacobson, Midge Spaeder**

Without mentioning any products by name, this graphically exciting insert from Searle positions the *company* on the cutting edge of the research revolution. Aimed at physicians, the piece makes effective use of the schematic (yet provocatively vibrant) anatomical/biochemical illustrations by Radu Vero. These exceptional illustrations take the reader on a beautiful and futuristic voyage through mysterious inner landscapes. The jet-black background enhances Vero's clean colors and

makes them appear even more luminous. Compelling headlines (e.g., "The Heart as an Endocrine Organ—with Therapeutic Potential," "Because Loss of Memory Is Loss of Self," "Examining the 'Brain' in the Gut") promote readership of the short articles on Searle's current efforts to provide important new medicines for specific problems. Linking these spreads is a common heading that sums up the theme of the insert in bold black letters: "The New Vision of Research from Searle."

Product: **Aloka 650™**
Design Firm: **The Opus Group**
Client: **Corometrics Medical Co.**
Art Director: **Joe Grasso**
Computer
Graphics: **ACCM Communications Industries Inc.**
Copywriter: **Joe Grasso**

In this handsome insert for the Aloka 650™ ultrasound device, the agency is introducing "breakthrough technology" to a wide audience of diagnostic specialists in all fields—with the purpose of generating inquiries. The first page shows a sharp image on the instrument's screen; inside, each feature is isolated with prominent subheads, a vivid illustration or diagram, and clear explanatory copy. We're also told how multiple technological advances and cooperative research made the Aloka 650™ possible. A high-tech look prevails throughout. According to Joe Grasso, president of The Opus Group, "the graphics were first designed in line form, then generated and regenerated on sophisticated computer equipment until the right look and information were finalized in four-color, three-dimensional graphic form."

Don't let the
miotic side effects
of pilocarpine interrupt
her working day.

She can't afford to set aside needle and thread
to wait for the blurred vision and miosis of
pilocarpine therapy to clear. Her livelihood
depends on good eyesight…her eyesight
depends on regular medication.
Propine has none of the miotic side effects
of pilocarpine so there's no time lost waiting for
these symptoms to subside. And when medication doesn't interfere with a patient's lifestyle,
compliance is likely to improve.

The drug of choice
for concomitant therapy
with beta-blockers.

PROPINE®
(dipivefrin HCl) 0.1%
sterile ophthalmic solution

Please see adjacent page for brief summary of prescribing
information.

ALLERGAN®
Allergan Pharmaceuticals, Inc.
Irvine, CA 92713
© 1985 Allergan Pharmaceuticals, Inc.

Don't let the
miotic side effects
of pilocarpine
keep him from
getting the job done.

The intricacies of his work require a steady
hand and clear, sharp vision. He depends
on his eyesight…his eyesight depends on
regular medication.
Propine has none of the miotic side effects
of pilocarpine so he can work a full day without
losing time waiting for miotic symptoms to
subside. And when medications don't interfere
with patient lifestyles, compliance is likely
to improve.

The drug of choice
for concomitant therapy
with beta-blockers.

PROPINE®
(dipivefrin HCl) 0.1%
sterile ophthalmic solution

Please see adjacent page for brief summary of prescribing
information.

ALLERGAN®
Allergan Pharmaceuticals, Inc.
Irvine, CA 92713
© 1986 Allergan Pharmaceuticals, Inc.

Product: **PROPINE**®
Ad Agency: **Pacificom (In-house)**
Client: **Allergan Pharmaceuticals, Inc.**
Art Director: **Donald R. Meyers**
Photographer: **James Wood**
Copywriter: **Susan Wesselink**

Two evocatively grainy photographs by James Wood establish the human-interest theme of this series of ads for PROPINE®, an ophthalmic solution. Both ads stress the "miotic side effects of pilocarpine" (the drug causes the pupils to overcontract) and recommend PROPINE® as "the drug of choice for concomitant therapy with beta-blockers." The copy by Susan Wesselink begins by expressing the needs of the patient in simple human terms ("The intricacies of his work require a steady hand and clear, sharp vision. He depends on his eyesight…"). Then the advantages of PROPINE® are introduced. Aimed at physicians, the ads are noteworthy for their emphasis on the quality of life of patients.

Product: **Triphasil**®
Ad Agency: **William Douglas McAdams Inc.**
Client: **Wyeth/Ayerst Laboratories**
Art Director: **Jeffrey Lipman**
Photographer: **Mark Kozlowski**
Copywriter: **Elaine Heimberger**

In this engaging pair of ads for Triphasil® oral contraceptive, we're looking at two very different worlds: a bustling diner and a corporate boardroom. The two women who occupy center stage are obviously from different walks of life—yet both find themselves in pressure-packed situations. So why are they smiling? Apparently both of them are using Triphasil®, so they can be confident about getting through the day without breakthrough bleeding. According to Art Director Jeffrey Lipman, the goal was to "depict women in real-life work situations" and emphasize to OB/GYNs that breakthrough bleeding is a "people problem" that can affect a woman's daily life. The touch of humor in Mark Kozlowski's photographs (note the facial expressions on the various "characters" in both photos) adds appeal without sacrificing the seriousness of the message.

GENTLE

Well-tolerated arthritis therapy*

NAPROSYN® B.I.D.
(naproxen) 250 mg/375 mg/500 mg tablets

*The most frequently reported side effects relate to the G.I. tract.
Please see brief summary of prescribing information on next page.

POWERFUL

Effective arthritis therapy

NAPROSYN® B.I.D.
(naproxen) 250 mg/375 mg/500 mg tablets

The most frequently reported side effects relate to the G.I. tract.
Please see brief summary of full prescribing information on next page.

ENDURING

**Proven track record—
over 4.8 billion patient-days* and
13 years of worldwide experience**

NAPROSYN® B.I.D.
(naproxen) 250 mg/375 mg/500 mg tablets

*Cumulative worldwide total based on estimated daily dosage in certain
major markets through October 1985. Data available upon request.
Please see brief summary of prescribing information on next page.

VERSATILE

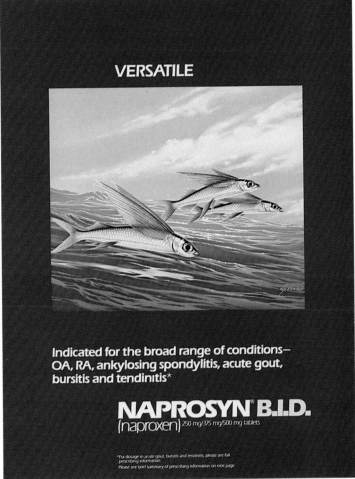

**Indicated for the broad range of conditions—
OA, RA, ankylosing spondylitis, acute gout,
bursitis and tendinitis***

NAPROSYN® B.I.D.
(naproxen) 250 mg/375 mg/500 mg tablets

*For dosage in acute gout, bursitis and tendinitis, please see full
prescribing information.
Please see brief summary of prescribing information on next page.

Product: **NAPROSYN® B.I.D.**
Ad Agency: **Vicom/FCB**
Client: **Syntex Laboratories, Inc.**
Art Director: **Joseph Rozon**
Illustrator: **Will Nelson**
Copywriter: **Cari Weisberg**

We humans have always associated certain animals with certain traits: elephants are powerful, tortoises long-lived, and so on down the line. In this simple yet effective campaign for the antiarthritis drug NAPRO-SYN® B.I.D., the agency singled out the drug's key benefits and linked them to images of wild creatures that exhibit the same traits. Note that a single word suffices for each benefit; an explanatory caption provides some elaboration. An interesting psychological insight: Creative Director Lester Barnett tells us that the colorful illustrations by Will Nelson were specifically designed to "portray the animals in a form which always emphasized strength, yet made them warm and alive."

SELECT FROM OVER 50 EMIT® ASSAYS

Select from the most extensive immunoassay menu available. Anywhere. Over 50 quantitative and qualitative Emit® assays. Reliable and economical assays for therapeutic drug monitoring, toxicology, endocrine, and specific proteins. All from the company that made drug monitoring a practical reality. Syva. Don't settle for less.

SELECT, DON'T SETTLE. **SYVA**

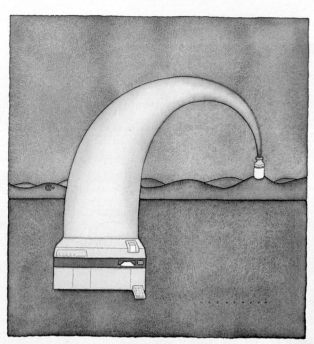

AUTOMATE DIGOXIN ON THE SYVA® ADVANCE™

Select the nonisotopic digoxin assay that's so easy to perform, so rapid and reliable that any laboratory can deliver digoxin results in minutes. No separation or centrifugation means the Syva Advance Fluorescence Immunoassay System does all the work. Automate digoxin, T_4, T_3 Uptake, cortisol, specific proteins, and therapeutic drug assays. For convenient and efficient immunochemistry testing, why settle for less than Syva?

SELECT, DON'T SETTLE. **SYVA**

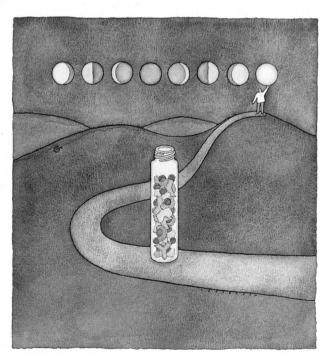

SELECT SYVA® QST™ TECHNOLOGY FOR 30-DAY CURVE STABILITY

With a 30-day standard curve, the Syva Qst System makes drug testing practical and economical — even for single samples. Premeasured and premixed in single vials, Qst powdered drug assays make it easy for any technologist to get a quantitative result in as little as 50 seconds. Instant access to drug monitoring any day on any shift. What's more, the system also performs qualitative Emit'st™ toxicology assays. The Syva Qst System. Another reason why you should never settle for less than Syva.

SELECT, DON'T SETTLE. **SYVA**

ROUTE STAT TRAFFIC TO THE SYVA® QST™ SYSTEM

Select the system that clears the way for both toxicology and therapeutic drug testing in your laboratory. The Qst System is ready for your stat, low-volume, and on-demand needs. Reduced calibration, ready-to-use single vial reagents, and quick turnaround means results can be delivered within minutes—without blocking other lab traffic. For convenient and economical testing of a wide range of drugs, don't settle for less than Syva.

SELECT, DON'T SETTLE. **SYVA**

SYSTEM SELECTIONS FROM SYVA

Select the laboratory system that meets your testing needs. Exactly. Automate high-volume testing on the Syva® Advance™ or the Syva® AutoLab™ System. Provide qualitative and quantitative single test results conveniently on the Syva® Qst™ Perform toxicology assays in one minute with the Emit® st™ Drug Detection System. And, if you own a Cobas® Bio or Parallel® Analytical System, you can still use Emit® Assays. Whichever system you select, don't settle for less than Syva.

SELECT, DON'T SETTLE.   **SYVA**

Product: **Syva® Systems and Products**
Ad Agency: **Gross Townsend Frank Hoffman, Inc.**
Client: **Syva Co.**
Art Director: **Orin Kimball**
Illustrator: **L.S. Johnson**
Copywriter: **Marietta Abrams**

How do you dramatize a wide range of product benefits when many of them are intangible? That was the problem tackled by Gross Townsend Frank Hoffman, Inc., in creating this visually striking campaign for Syva Company. Syva® QST™ technology covers a wide range of systems and products for toxicology and therapeutic drug testing in laboratories. The benefits, while impressive, aren't exactly the stuff of visual drama: "Select from over 50 Emit® assays," "Automate digoxin on the Syva® Advance™," "Route stat traffic to the Syva® QST™ System"...you get the picture. Enter illustrator L.S. Johnson, who proceeded to transform each benefit into a surrealistic, wonderfully pictorial dreamscape that gets the point across. At the same time, the illustrations tie in neatly with the "Select, Don't Settle" theme of the campaign.

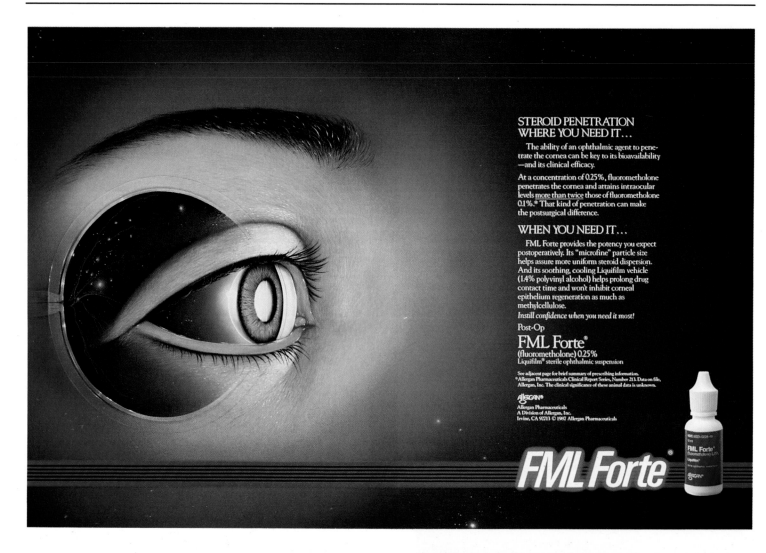

STEROID PENETRATION
WHERE YOU NEED IT...

The ability of an ophthalmic agent to pene-
trate the cornea can be key to its bioavailability
—and its clinical efficacy.

At a concentration of 0.25%, fluorometholone
penetrates the cornea and attains intraocular
levels more than twice those of fluorometholone
0.1%.* That kind of penetration can make
the postsurgical difference.

WHEN YOU NEED IT...

FML Forte provides the potency you expect
postoperatively. Its "microfine" particle size
helps assure more uniform steroid dispersion.
And its soothing, cooling Liquifilm vehicle
(1.4% polyvinyl alcohol) helps prolong drug
contact time and won't inhibit corneal
epithelium regeneration as much as
methylcellulose.
Instill confidence when you need it most!
Post-Op
FML Forte®
(fluorometholone) 0.25%
Liquifilm® sterile ophthalmic suspension

See adjacent page for brief summary of prescribing information.
*Allergan Pharmaceuticals Clinical Report Series, Number 213. Data on file,
Allergan, Inc. The clinical significance of these animal data is unknown.

Allergan Pharmaceuticals
A Division of Allergan, Inc.
Irvine, CA 92713 © 1987 Allergan Pharmaceuticals

FML Forte®

Product: **FML Forte®**
Ad Agency: **Pacificom (In-house)**
Client: **Allergan Pharmaceuticals, Inc.**
Art Director: **Donald R. Meyers**
Illustrator: **Carl Rohrig**
Copywriter: **Eric Chiel**
Production: **Jaqui Keilhold**

"The Cosmic Eye" is Allergan's in-house nickname for
this stunning visual by award-winning West German
illustrator Carl Rohrig. Based on roughs supplied by
Art Director Donald R. Meyers, the illustration penetrates beyond the luminous green iris and takes us into
another dimension: the world of the inner eye, where
the retina sparkles like the starry heavens (or at least
the dome of a good planetarium). Bold and memorable, this unusual graphic links the entire campaign
and shows ophthalmologists how FML Forte® penetrates the cornea to achieve desired results. Rather
than give us a literal rendering of cornea penetration,
the illustration translates this concept into a grand
vision. The copy by Eric Chiel provides a neat summa-
tion of benefits.

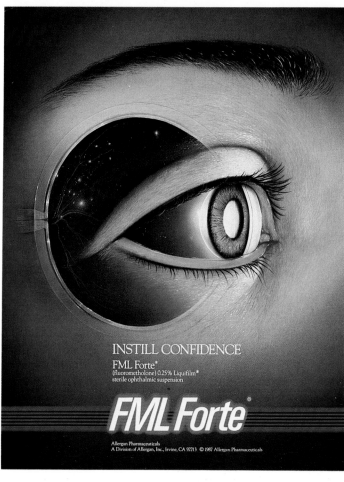

INSTILL CONFIDENCE
FML Forte®
(fluorometholone) 0.25% Liquifilm®
sterile ophthalmic suspension

FML Forte®

Allergan Pharmaceuticals
A Division of Allergan, Inc., Irvine, CA 92713 © 1987 Allergan Pharmaceuticals

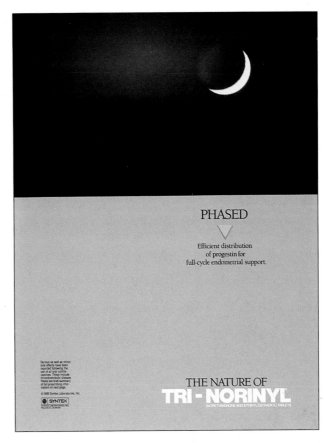

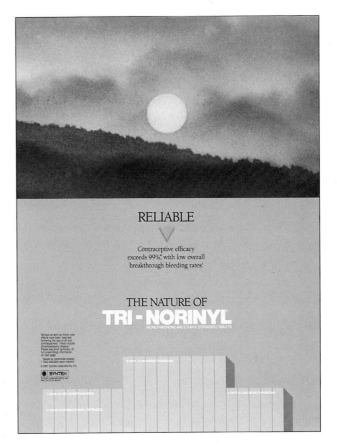

Product: **TRI-NORINYL**®
Ad Agency: **Vicom/FCB**
Client: **Syntex Laboratories, Inc.**
Art Director: **Vanya Akraboff**
Copywriter: **Robert Finkel**

This campaign for TRI-NORINYL®, an oral contraceptive, can serve as a textbook example of congruity between copy and image. In each ad, the key word is a product benefit reinforced by an appropriate visual analogy. We're told that TRI-NORINYL® is "phased" (like the moon), "unique" (like a pink tree in an emerald-green forest), "predictable" (like a crocus blooming each spring), and "reliable" (like the sun rising each day). Each single-word benefit is amplified by a brief caption for greater message clarity. For similar visual treatment of product benefits, see the agency's campaign for NAPROSYN® B.I.D. in this chapter.

Product: **Brevibloc®**
Ad Agency: **William Douglas McAdams Inc.**
Client: **Dupont Critical Care**
Art Director: **Patrick Creaven**
Model Maker: **Nick Aristovulos**
Photographer: **Shig Ikeda**
Copywriter: **Gwenne Freiman**

To create awareness of Brevibloc®, a new intravenous beta blocker from Dupont Critical Care, William Douglas McAdams Inc. prepared this five-color insert featuring a "plug-in" visual motif on the cover. V.P. Group Head Art Director Patrick Creaven writes that the fifth color (a specially mixed metallic green ink) and the gold used "distinguished our campaign from the other, more obvious cardiovascular color schemes." The plug-in graphic suggests not only the general function of beta blockers ("plugging in" to the heart's beta receptors) but the distinctive short-term action of the client's product. The inside copy positions Brevibloc® as "the only ultrashort-acting I.V. beta blocker," and we're shown a graph of heart rate before, during and after administration of the drug.

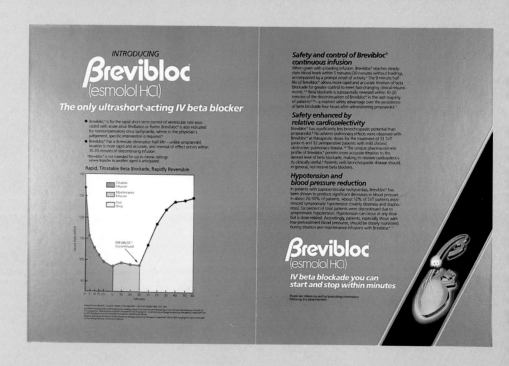

Product: **Claforan®**
Ad Agency: **William Douglas McAdams Inc.**
Client: **Hoechst-Roussel Pharmaceuticals, Inc.**
Art Directors: **Patrick Creaven, Diane Lynch**
Illustrator: **Ed Acuna**
Copywriters: **Gabrielle Strasun, Gwenne Freiman**

What headline could be more compelling than "Life, Death, & the Bottom Line"? Printed in powerful, glossy black type—all caps, naturally—on a *matte* black background, the headline is bisected down the first row of letters by a white I.V. line leading to a tiny patient highlighted in color. The I.V. is delivering the lifesaving benefits of Claforan®, an injectable antibiotic used in hospitals. Inside this dramatic six-color insert, the I.V. motif is repeated—this time it keeps an elderly woman alive. Here the copy picks up the "bottom line" theme and informs the reader about the uses of the drug—as well as its commendable safety profile. V.P. Group Head Art Director Patrick Creaven writes that "the campaign has been highly successful, is into its second year, and continues to win graphic and advertising awards."

The right antibiotic at the right time. The bottom line in infectious disease.

For six years, Claforan® has been the right antibiotic for countless patients—with q8h dosing for moderate-to-severe infections, and q12h dosing for uncomplicated infections. From meningitis in neonates to pneumonia in the elderly, it has established an outstanding record of success. And, Claforan® provides the flexibility of q6-8h dosing for severe infections, and q4h dosing for life-threatening infections.

The efficacy and safety of Claforan® are uncompromised. In neonates it has the potential for less of an impact on fecal flora than ceftriaxone or cefoperazone.[1] That's why Claforan® is preferred by leading pediatric authorities.[2-4] In patients of all ages, it has not been shown to cause coagulation abnormalities, disulfiram-like reactions, nephrotoxicity, ototoxicity, or seizures.

Right for cost containment with q8h/q12h dosing.
The bottom line in today's hospital environment.

Claforan® saves money as well, with economical q12h dosing in uncomplicated infections and q8h dosing in moderate-to-severe infections. In fact, data on over 2,000 cases show that Claforan® q8h for moderate-to-severe infections and q12h for uncomplicated infections consistently maintained a high level of efficacy.[5]

Clearly, what's best about cephalosporins is what you get with Claforan®

q8h/q12h   **Claforan®**
STERILE & INJECTION
(cefotaxime sodium)
Please see following page for references and brief summary of prescribing information.
The bottom line.

Is your kid too big for his britches?

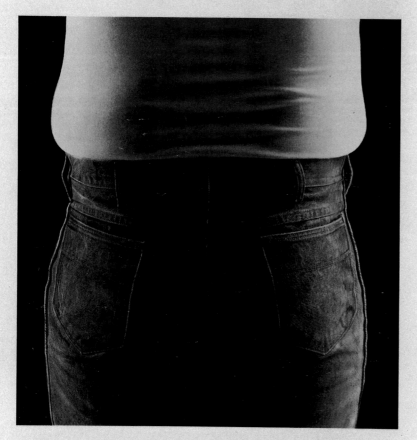

The biggest problem with overweight children is they often grow into overweight adults.

Which usually leads to weighty medical problems. Even to a shorter life

If your youngster is starting to hang out in the wrong places, do something about it now.

The Body Shop is a good place to start.

The Body Shop is a weight control program for youths ages 8-18. The 10-week session helps develop skills that will lead to a slim, healthy, happy future.

More than a diet and workout plan, The Body Shop is a comprehensive program including nutrition, exercise and personal counseling. It is an upbeat approach improving a youngster's physical image and building self-esteem too.

Enrollment is limited and early registration is recommended. Call (213) 517-4738 for complete information on The Body Shop. It's the best way we know to cut kids down to size. For life.

HEALTH ACCESS SYSTEMS
Torrance Memorial Hospital Medical Center

3330 Lomita Boulevard, Torrance, CA 90509-2935

This is no way to live.

Your lifestyle could be taking years off your life.

In fact, you may not be aware of all the risks you're taking. Or the best ways to reduce them.

But you can find out at Torrance Memorial Hospital Medical Center. Our Learn to Live™ programs are specially designed to keep you well.

One class helps you pinpoint factors that influence your well-being. This careful analysis of personal behaviors can lead to better control of harmful habits. Which should make you look younger, feel better and live longer.

Another course teaches you how to recognize and handle stress. You'll learn to take responsibility for your emotional reactions and find ways to reduce pressure even during the most tense times.

Naturally, we offer programs to help you stop smoking or lose weight.

These have proven successful for thousands.

You might even want to learn how to save someone else's life by taking our CPR course.

For a current schedule of classes, call 325-9110, Ext. 2739. Or write: Learn To Live, 3330 Lomita Blvd., Torrance, CA 90509-2935.

Why not come to the hospital before you have to? It's a smart way to really live it up.

 Torrance Memorial Hospital Medical Center
Affiliated with Health Access Systems

Instructions not included.

Having a baby and guiding its growth is a joyful experience. But it also requires lots of preparation.

Fortunately, you can learn all you need to know from your doctor and Torrance Memorial Hospital Medical Center.

Torrance Memorial offers a complete schedule of classes on childbirth and child care. Our courses also deal with the physical and emotional health of new mothers. And the adjustments required from other family members.

Certified instructors will teach you about natural or cesarean childbirth. Lifesaving for infants and other safety strategies. Newborn care and toddler to preschool development.

Our Learn to Live™ programs also include managing the stresses of motherhood and a career. Fitness during and after pregnancy.

Healthy ways for brothers and sisters to adapt to the new arrival.

So call 325-9110, Ext. 7560 for a current schedule of classes. Or write: Learn To Live, 3330 Lomita Blvd., Torrance, CA 90509-2935.

Being prepared means taking better care of yourself and your child. Whether you're a new mother or expecting, we'll show you what to expect.

 Torrance Memorial Hospital Medical Center
Affiliated with Health Access Systems

Ad Agency: **Forsythe Marcelli Johnson Advertising, Inc.**
Client: **Torrance Memorial Hospital Medical Center**
Art Director: **Vic Marcelli**
Photographer: **Bill Braly**
Copywriter: **Bill McGee**

In the best advertising, the whole tends to be greater than the sum of the parts. Case in point: take these three headlines out of context and you can see they're nothing special…just a trio of familiar phrases bordering on cliche. But couple them with their respective photographs and the result is pure dynamite. In this series of ads for public education programs at Torrance Memorial Hospital Medical Center, each headline adds an emphatic twist to the image in the photograph. The reader makes the mental connection, and *bingo!* The poster-like visuals are each accompanied by skillfully written copy that communicates a serious message without sounding the least bit threatening.

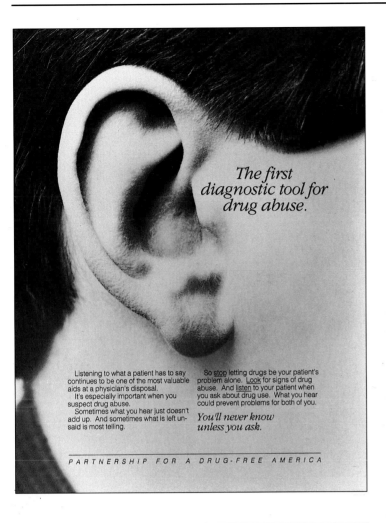

The first diagnostic tool for drug abuse.

Listening to what a patient has to say continues to be one of the most valuable aids at a physician's disposal.

It's especially important when you suspect drug abuse.

Sometimes what you hear just doesn't add up. And sometimes what is left unsaid is most telling.

So stop letting drugs be your patient's problem alone. Look for signs of drug abuse. And listen to your patient when you ask about drug use. What you hear could prevent problems for both of you.

You'll never know unless you ask.

PARTNERSHIP FOR A DRUG-FREE AMERICA

A life of substance? Or substance abuse?

You would like to know that each baby you deliver will have a life of substance. But unfortunately, because of the extent of drug abuse in our society, more and more babies are born drug addicts—sentenced to a life of substance abuse.

You, as a physician, are in a position to do something about it. During her initial workup, simply ask your patient about drug use. It's no more an invasion of privacy than asking about exposure to German measles. It's just as important to her baby's health. And it may prevent serious problems for you, mother, and baby.

Help free this generation—and the next—from drugs.

You'll never know unless you ask.

PARTNERSHIP FOR A DRUG-FREE AMERICA

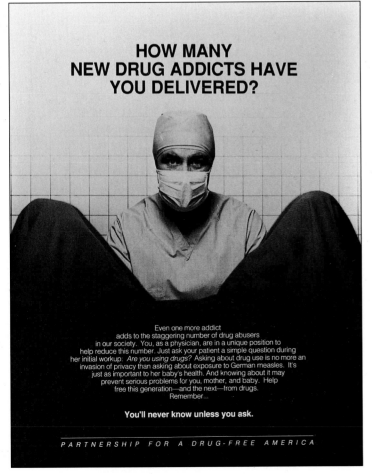

HOW MANY NEW DRUG ADDICTS HAVE YOU DELIVERED?

Even one more addict adds to the staggering number of drug abusers in our society. You, as a physician, are in a unique position to help reduce this number. Just ask your patient a simple question during her initial workup: *Are you using drugs?* Asking about drug use is no more an invasion of privacy than asking about exposure to German measles. It's just as important to her baby's health. And knowing about it may prevent serious problems for you, mother, and baby. Help free this generation—and the next—from drugs. Remember...

You'll never know unless you ask.

PARTNERSHIP FOR A DRUG-FREE AMERICA

Ad Agency: **Lavey/Wolff/Swift Inc.**
Client: **Partnership for a Drug-Free America**
Art Directors: **Neil Lavey, Peter Zamiska**
Copywriter: **Al Gerstein**

At first glance, these three ads on drug abuse bear little resemblance to one another. But each uses an arresting black-and-white visual to break through the reader's apathy and command attention. Art Director Neil Lavey volunteered his ear for the first ad, which urges physicians to "stop...look...listen" for signs of drug abuse among their patients. The mug shots in the second ad serve to remind doctors that many babies are born drug addicts. The third ad, the work of Associate Creative Director Peter Zamiska, tackles the same theme from a different angle—quite literally—in a neatly symmetrical view of an OB/GYN framed by the covered thighs of his patient. Created for Partnership for a Drug-Free America as a volunteer service, all three ads are united by the common tagline, "You'll never know unless you ask."

Product: **National Medical Homecare**
Ad Agency: **Forsythe Marcelli Johnson Advertising, Inc.**
Client: **National Medical Homecare**
Art Director: **Ed Mari**
Photographer: **Jim Porter**
Copywriter: **Jim Forsythe**

The tagline "Caring on a National Scale" sets the human-interest tone of this appealing campaign for National Medical Homecare, an organization that provides medical services in the home. Each ad features a large color photo that illustrates a typical client or service, accompanied by a black-and-white inset photo of National people at work. Each of the brief headlines plays off the word "national" in a manner that's both tongue-in-cheek and image-enhancing. The effective copy by the agency's president, James H. Forsythe, manages to seem engagingly casual while it sells the public on the company without wasting a word.

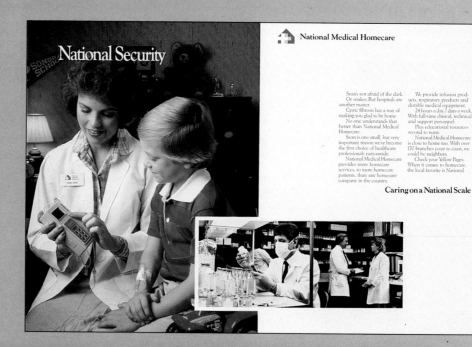

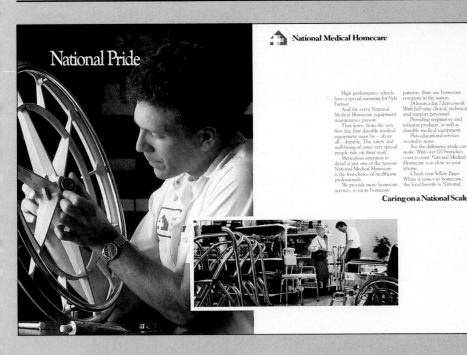

National Pride

National Medical Homecare

High performance wheels have a special meaning for Neb-Farmer.

And for every National Medical Homecare equipment maintenance person.

They learn, from the very first day, that durable medical equipment must be – above all – durable. The safety and well-being of some very special people ride on their work.

Meticulous attention to detail is just one of the reasons National Medical Homecare is the first choice of healthcare professionals.

We provide more homecare services, to more homecare patients, than any homecare company in the nation.

24 hours a day, 7 days a week. With full-time clinical, technical and support personnel.

Providing respiratory and infusion products, as well as durable medical equipment.

Plus educational services second to none.

See the difference pride can make. With over 120 branches coast to coast, National Medical Homecare is as close as your phone.

Check your Yellow Pages. When it comes to homecare, the local favorite is National.

Caring on a National Scale

"I WORK BETTER WHEN MY BLOOD GLUCOSE IS UNDER CONTROL."

"Now, with the GLUCOSCAN Meter, I understand why I feel as I do. Once I was at a large shopping center and I began to feel really shakey. I stopped right there and did a blood glucose test—my blood sugar was very low.

"I carry my GLUCOSCAN Meter with me all the time. Lately, I've been very busy. I find the memory feature of the GLUCOSCAN Meter helps a great deal, especially if I'm on the road and don't have my logbook with me to record my data.

"I was so impressed with the GLUCOSCAN Meter I bought one for my dad, who has diabetes too. He's 86 years old and felt marginally well, his urine tests were OK, but his blood glucose level was very high. Blood glucose monitoring helped him cut his insulin intake nearly in half."

GLUCOSCAN is the blood glucose meter that keeps people with diabetes on the go and in tune with themselves and the rest of the world. It's so easy to use, blood glucose monitoring becomes second nature.

Factory calibrated to help ensure accuracy, you can trust your GLUCOSCAN Meter to take care of your blood glucose test results so you can concentrate on the rest of your life.

GLUCOSCAN Blood Glucose Meters are backed by LifeScan's reputation for prompt and caring service. And, LifeScan offers a **money-back guarantee** with each and every GLUCOSCAN Meter. The GLUCOSCAN Meter is available from over 3,000 authorized distributors nationwide. For the distributor near you, or for more information, call

TOLL FREE:
United States   1 800 227-8862
Canada   1 800 663-5521

Kenneth Davis, age 45, has used the GLUCOSCAN Meter for 6 months. Roy Davis, age 85, for 4 months.

GLUCOSCAN: A friend for life.

LIFESCAN

a Johnson & Johnson company

"MONITORING MY BLOOD GLUCOSE MAKES ME FEEL MORE SECURE."

"My GLUCOSCAN Meter makes me feel more secure. Before I go out, I'll do a blood glucose test. Then I know if I should take orange juice along with me.

"I never leave my GLUCOSCAN Meter home. It gives me a sense of security that I know what I'm doing. I have the 'brittle' type of diabetes. Sometimes I can't tell if my blood sugar is up or down because some of the symptoms are the same. My blood sugar can drop in a moment without notice for no apparent reason.

"You learn to work around the diabetes. Checking my blood sugar helps me everyday to care for my family."

GLUCOSCAN is the blood glucose meter that keeps people with diabetes on the go and in tune with themselves and the rest of the world. It's so easy to use, blood glucose monitoring becomes second nature.

Factory calibrated to help ensure accuracy, you can trust your GLUCOSCAN Meter to take care of your blood glucose test results so you can concentrate on the rest of your life.

GLUCOSCAN Blood Glucose Meters are backed by LifeScan's reputation for prompt and caring service. And, LifeScan offers a **money-back guarantee** with each and every GLUCOSCAN Meter. The GLUCOSCAN Meter is available from over 3,000 authorized distributors nationwide. For the distributor near you, or for more information, call

TOLL FREE:
United States   1 800 227-8862
Canada   1 800 663-5521

Jennie Saltiel, age 62, has had 'brittle' diabetes for 5 years; has used the GLUCOSCAN Meter for 1 year.

GLUCOSCAN: A friend for life.

LIFESCAN

a Johnson & Johnson company

Product: **GLUCOSCAN™ 3000**
Ad Agency: **Marquetry, Inc.**
Client: **LifeScan Inc.**
Art Director: **Yutaka Wada**
Photographer: **David Martinez**
Copywriter: **Mary Jean Pramik**

These happy-looking people aren't models—they're satisfied real-life users of GLUCOSCAN™ blood glucose meters from LifeScan Inc., a Johnson & Johnson subsidiary. According to James O. Bowles, president of Marquetry, Inc., the agency tracked down these customers through warranty cards, then built the ads around their actual testimonials. Aimed directly at diabetic patients, these real-people ads emphasize the reliability of the product, its ease of use, and the money-back guarantee—all essential elements in consumer advertising of technical products. In addition, this campaign accomplished the goal of repositioning the product and extending its life cycle.

3

EDITORIAL GRAPHICS

BUSINESS MAGAZINES
TRADE MAGAZINES
CONSUMER MAGAZINES
NEWSPAPERS
SINGLE-SPONSORED PUBLICATIONS
EDUCATIONAL LITERATURE

Now we temporarily leave the world of advertising to examine the best recent work in the medical editorial field. We'll be looking at some dynamic magazine covers, opening spreads for magazine articles, and newspaper illustrations—along with an attractive selection of educational booklets (for patients as well as physicians) and sponsored publications.

Note that we mentioned leaving the world of *advertising*, not the world of *selling*. It's true that you won't find much in the way of overt product promotion in these pages. No slogans, bulleted benefits, or calls to action. But look closely at the examples in this chapter, and you'll detect more than a hint of selling. That's because the best editorial work sells *itself*.

After all, a magazine article (or a newspaper article, or a sponsored publication) serves its purpose only if it is read. And to break through the reader's natural apathy barrier, the creative staff must deploy many of the same tactics used by advertising professionals.

A powerful, engaging headline is one such weapon in the arsenal. With a combination of terse wording and eye-catching typography, it commands attention and cajoles the audience into reading the story. Viewed in this light, the headline for a magazine article is every bit as much a selling tool as the headline for an ad.

And the visual element is at least as important as the headline. Whether conceived as an illustration, photograph, or model, the visual must not only relate to the contents of the text but *summarize* them—and do so with a single compelling image. The artist must be able to help readers visualize the subject matter and intrigue them enough to continue into the text.

In medical publications, especially, the illustrations should make abstract ideas concrete, and complex concepts readily comprehensible. Often this is accomplished with *symbolic*

visuals—as in the sketch of a "living will" pulling the plug on itself.

Sometimes the symbolism can take on a markedly satirical bent: a good example is the memorably ridiculous image of a plucked eagle (representing the Federal government after its fleecing by a local HMO). It's a long story, but the illustrator neatly summed it up with a visual that's both funny and to the point.

Or take the wry parody of Grant Wood's *American Gothic*—featuring a pair of die-hard rural GPs as the indomitable farmers. Here, as in other such parodies, the artist seizes upon a familiar image with readily comprehended meaning, then gives it a wickedly ironic twist that reflects the editorial content.

It's interesting that the satirical element is noticeably more prominent in editorial art than in advertising. One possible explanation is that an ad—no matter how imaginative—cannot veer too sharply away from product exposition. And when it comes to products (or the company itself), the advertising message must always be *upbeat* and *uncomplicated*. The editorial artist, on the other hand, is free to indulge his mischievous side—especially when treating an object of widespread scorn or criticism. (Note the various gibes at malpractice insurance—a "popular" topic in this field.)

But, as you'll discover, satire is just one of the many approaches to creativity in the editorial sector. The variety of artistic styles represented here is wide: photorealism (see the "Proceed with Caution" road sign), surrealism (Tanya Tewell's "Spare Body Parts"), classicism (the beautifully rendered "Persistent Fever"), cartoons (especially in the patient education booklets), multimedia compositions—even whimsical models (don't miss "Learning to Live with Third Party"). And, of course, all those impeccably rendered airbrushed illustrations of anatomical structures.

Yes, the writers and artists behind editorial work must still shape their words and images to sell the audience on a story. But the nature of their mission allows them to play with a broader, more subtly colored spectrum of styles and attitudes.

Two memos that clinched a countersuit victory

Strategies for hiring top-notch office assistants

The peer reviewer who got nailed by peer review

Has your life insurance died of old age?

OCTOBER 19, 1987

medical economics

WHY THE FEDS LET AN HMO PLUCK THEM CLEAN

Title: **"Why the Feds Let an HMO Pluck Them Clean"**

Design Firm: **In-house**

Publisher: **Medical Economics Co. Inc.—** *Medical Economics*

Art Director: **Roger F. Dowd**

Illustrator: **Joan Steiner**

Photographer: **Ken Schroers**

SILVER. America's national emblem looks more like a plucked chicken in this witty cover art for an article entitled, "Why the Feds Let an HMO Pluck Them Clean." The visual pun reduces the mighty eagle to a fairly ridiculous specimen of a fowl. Roger F. Dowd, art director for *Medical Economics*, fills us in on the story: "On behalf of Medicare patients, the Federal government paid millions to a fraudulent HMO. Joan Steiner's illustration for this cover story pokes fun at the gullibility of the Feds."

A Man Alone

Caring for a Patient with Guillain-Barré Syndrome

...and Afraid

To combat the Guillain-Barré patient's sense of isolation and helplessness, you must offer hope as well as care. But suppose he can't *hear* a word you say.

Susan Drain, RN, BSN: On April 9, Zach Reisman, a 54-year-old man with adult onset deafness, fell in his home—and could hardly pick himself up. Frightened, he asked a neighbor to drive him to the emergency department.

When admitted to a general medical/surgical unit that afternoon, Zach was unable to walk. Because he'd fractured his hip and leg about 5 years earlier, he was used to having some trouble walking. But his legs now felt "useless," he said.

Zach mentioned that he'd had the flu recently. His chest X-ray showed lower right lobe infiltrates; physical examination revealed marked, rapidly progressive muscular weakness. He had a weak grip and poor leg movement, and he couldn't help with his position changes. He said, "I seem to be getting weaker and weaker."

Because Zach's signs and symptoms suggested Guillain-Barré syndrome (GBS), his doctors transferred him to the intensive care unit (ICU). This rare form of polyneuropathy leads to generalized bi-

lateral motor weakness, with cranial nerve involvement, motor incoordination, and hyporeflexia. Improvement usually occurs spontaneously—and as mysteriously as the disease's onset. The insert on page 46, *GBS: Portrait of a Neurologic Thief,* will give you more information about the underlying pathophysiology behind this syndrome.

As I assessed Zach on the ICU, I noted muscular weakness in the face, neck, and torso and flaccid extremities. His respirations were rapid and shallow, with diminished breath sounds in the lung bases. I auscultated wheezes and crackles, which didn't clear even though nasotracheal suctioning yielded large amounts of thick yellow sputum. His cough was very weak.

Cardiac monitoring showed a sinus tachycardia with frequent premature atrial contractions, indicating possible hypoxemia. This was confirmed by a PaO₂ of 65 mm Hg on room air.

Zach's abdomen was flat and soft, with audible bowel sounds. He complained of

Nursing Grand Rounds

The panelists for this Nursing Grand Rounds article work at St. Joseph Community Hospital, Southwest Washington Hospitals, Vancouver, Washington. They are: Teresa P. Grow, RN, BS, nursing education coordinator; Susan Drain, RN, BSN, staff nurse, intensive care unit; Erich Bruckner, CRTT, respiratory therapist; Steven J. Ryder, RN, staff nurse, intermediate care unit; Linda J. Weagant, OTR/L, BS, occupational therapist; and Christine L. Thorndal, RPT, physical therapist. Teresa Grow moderated this panel report.

44 Nursing87, December

Title: **"A Man Alone...and Afraid"**
Design Firm: **In-house**
Publisher: **Springhouse Corp.—***Nursing87*
Art Director: **Ed Rosanio**
Illustrator: **Steve Cusano**

SILVER. Guillain-Barre syndrome is an agonizing nervous system disorder that can strike without warning, rob its victim of basic speech and motor skills, then disappear just as mysteriously as it arrived—if the patient survives. The fear and isolation of the GBS patient are memorably depicted in this award-winning spread from *Nursing87*. The victim seems suspended in a deep blue void, his arms and legs outstretched and useless. Illustrator Steve Cusano has cast his subject in a faint, eerie light, illuminating the face from below and deftly highlighting the folds of the striped robe with a delicate pastel technique. The prevailing blue of the illustration is picked up in the headline on the opposite page.

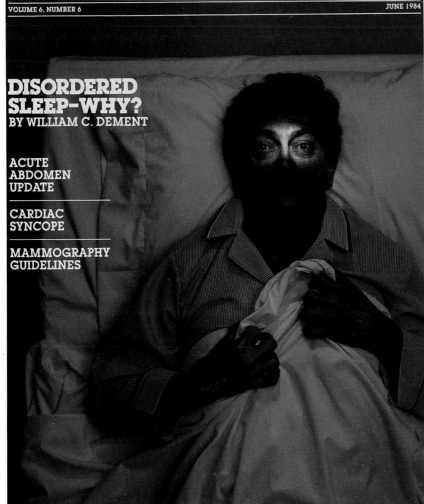

DIAGNOSIS

VOLUME 6, NUMBER 6
JUNE 1984

DISORDERED SLEEP—WHY?
BY WILLIAM C. DEMENT

ACUTE ABDOMEN UPDATE

CARDIAC SYNCOPE

MAMMOGRAPHY GUIDELINES

Title: **"Disordered Sleep—Why?"**
Design Firm: **In-house**
Publisher: **Medical Economics Co. Inc.—** ***Diagnosis***
Art Director: **Susan Kuppler Haber**
Photographer: **Walter Wick**

SILVER. A man lies motionless in bed, his eyes staring blankly into space. Clearly this person is an insomniac, and the photograph transmits a memorable image for the cover article on sleep disorders. Photographer Walter Wick has created a nocturnal mood by casting his subject in a deep blue light—except for the spotlighted eyes, which immediately call attention to the man's condition. The deep eye rings and tense hands add to the overall impact.

Title: **"Herpes"**
Design Firm: **In-house**
Publisher: **Krames Communications**
Art Director: **Carveth Kramer**
Illustrators: **Ellen Going Jacobs (medical),**
Sharon Ellis (cartoons)

SILVER. Two artists collaborated on this profusely illustrated patient information booklet about herpes. Tackling a sensitive subject that lacks intrinsic visual appeal, the artists have filled the booklet with lively and engaging color illustrations—including cartoon herpes viruses with sharp noses and pea-soup complexions. Sharon Ellis contributed the many cartoons; Ellen Going Jacobs did the sophisticated medical illustrations.

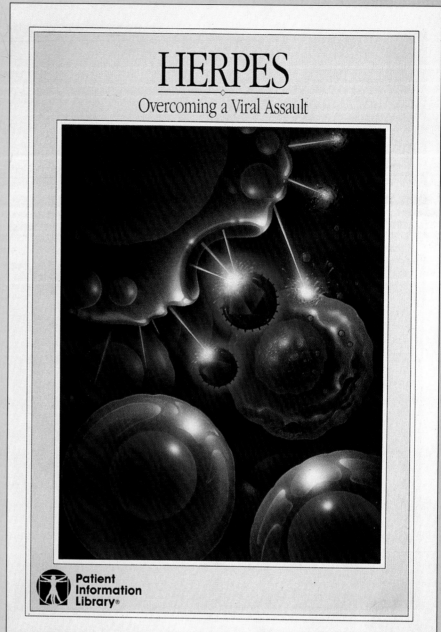

HERPES
Overcoming a Viral Assault

Patient Information Library®

HERPES—IT CAN BE CONTROLLED

Herpes: you've heard about it, you've read about it, and now you think you have it. About 150 million Americans have had at least one bout with the virus. Many people feel guilty or worry that herpes won't allow them to lead a normal life. The truth is, although herpes has no cure, many people who get herpes for the first time are never bothered by another outbreak. And you can learn to control herpes, preventing further outbreaks and curbing its spread.

Herpes in the past. Herpes is not new. The Roman Emperor Tiberius outlawed kissing in public in an effort to stop the spread of oral herpes.

Herpes today. As sexual attitudes change, more people than ever before are being exposed to the herpes virus. This probably accounts for the rising incidence of herpes of the genitals (sex organs), which is fast becoming one of the most prevalent socially transmitted diseases.

Herpes tomorrow. Someday soon, herpes may be treated by new, more effective drugs; or it may be prevented by a vaccine that can give lifetime protection.

In the meantime you can help reduce the chances of herpes outbreaks by learning about the herpes life cycle and how the body's immune defenses rally to meet the viral invasion. Knowing how herpes takes over the cells in the skin and how you can bolster your natural defenses will ensure early control over the virus and help keep recurrences to a minimum. Reducing stress is important. By recognizing when you are most contagious, you can help protect others, too.

This booklet is not intended as a substitute for professional medical care. Only your doctor can diagnose and treat a medical problem. ©1983, 1984, 1986 by Krames Communications, 312 90th Street, Daly City, CA 94015-1898. (415) 994-8800. All rights reserved. 8307/8707

THE HERPES LIFE CYCLE

The herpes virus is an extremely small infectious particle whose only mission in life is to duplicate itself. To do this, the virus tricks a healthy cell into producing thousands of viral copies, each with the potential to infect neighboring cells. If allowed to go unchecked, herpes viruses would eventually spread throughout the entire body. Fortunately, the immune system counterattacks with its army of white cells and forces herpes to retreat.

Common sites of herpes infections are lips (oral herpes) and external sex organs (genital herpes). Neglect of herpes sores can lead to secondary infections that can retard healing. Although rare, the virus may transfer to fingers or nearby areas.

The herpes invasion begins when the virus passes through a break in the skin or the moist membranes of the lips, vagina, or anus. The virus then penetrates a skin cell and heads for its command center (the cell nucleus). There, it reprograms the cell's genes, causing them to direct the manufacture and assembly of new viral particles.

The immune system counterattacks by dispatching a battalion of large white cells called macrophages that destroy the infected cells. The herpes sore that appears on the surface of the skin is a sign of the battle taking place underneath. But the herpes battle isn't over when the sores heal.

Some viruses manage to retreat to nerve cells near the spine or base of the brain. There, they will wait until a lapse in the body's defenses allows them to escape.

Herpes attacks can recur when the body's army of white cells is exhausted from fighting other viral infections, such as a cold, or when the body is under stress from inadequate nutrition, insufficient sleep, or emotional upset.

Herpes Recurrences. Antibodies produced by special white cells of the immune system help minimize the severity and frequency of recurrences by neutralizing the herpes viruses as they emerge from the nerve cells. In 60 percent of all cases, herpes doesn't recur. Of those people who do have recurrences, 90 percent have them infrequently—only one episode every 3 to 12 months. Only 10 percent have recurrences more often than once every three months.

Herpes viruses may escape from the nerve cells. Recurrences often follow stress of some kind.

Macrophages once again are called into action to seek out and destroy the infected cells.

Oral Herpes Type I (90% of all herpes)

Genital Herpes Type II (10% of all herpes)

Other sites may be infected with the virus. These sites include the eyes, fingers, and brain, especially if the immune system has been weakened.

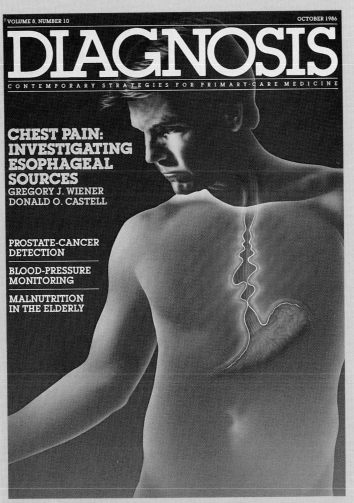

Title: **"Chest Pain: Investigating Esophageal Sources"**
Design Firm: **In-house**
Publisher: **Medical Economics Co. Inc.— *Diagnosis***
Art Director: **Carol Waters**
Illustrator: **Enid Hatton**

By now, whenever we see a picture of a man with a spreading red glow in the center of his chest, we're conditioned to think "heart attack." Similarly, patients who *experience* that pain—and even the physicians who treat them—could erroneously jump to the same conclusion. That's what makes this cover art for *Diagnosis* so instructive: the source of the man's pain is actually his esophagus. In Enid Hatton's elegant illustration, everything is rendered in cool blue tones except for the alarming area of pain and the spastic walls of the esophagus.

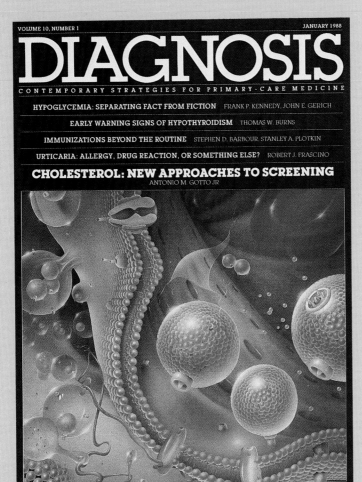

Title: **"Cholesterol: New Approaches to Screening"**
Design Firm: **In-house**
Publisher: **Medical Economics Co. Inc.— *Diagnosis***
Art Director: **Carol Waters**
Illustrator: **Keith Kasnot**

It looks like a fantastic sci-fi vision of air travel on a distant planet. But, in fact, this spectacular cover art actually demonstrates the workings of HDL and LDL in a human artery. According to Art Director Carol Waters, this imaginative depiction of cholesterol at the molecular level was chosen over a more commonplace image of a clogged artery. Framed by a dark border, the vibrant artwork immediately catches the reader's eye and draws it to the title of the article.

Title: **"Chest Imaging"**
Design Firm: **In-house**
Publisher: **Miller Freeman Publications—**
Diagnostic Imaging
Illustrator: **Kevin O'Shea**

For an article on chest imaging (X-rays, ultrasound, magnetic resonance, etc.) illustrator Kevin O'Shea created this stylish cover art in muted blue, white, and beige tones. The patient holds up an image of her own back, with the title of the article directly underneath. The artwork communicates that the standard chest X-ray remains the cornerstone of workups for patients with chest disease.

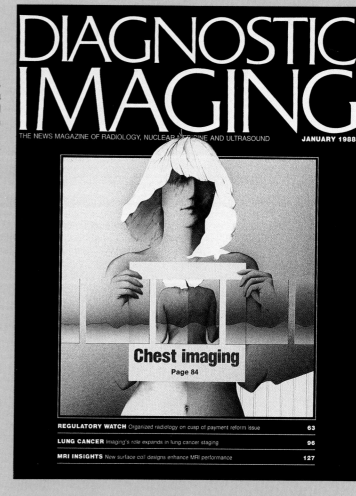

Title: **"Imaging and Therapy of Cancer**
Patients"
Design Firm: **In-house**
Publisher: **Miller Freeman Publications—**
Diagnostic Imaging
Illustrator: **Dick Cole**

Giving the appearance of watercolor, this rendering of an actual CT image (the photograph appears in the accompanying article) depicts a cancerous liver for the cover of Diagnostic Imaging. The article underscores the importance of imaging techniques in treating cancer, and the illustration supports this theme: the grid imposed over part of the image suggests high-tech precision. Illustrator Dick Cole effectively used irregular dark blots to portray the spreading cancer.

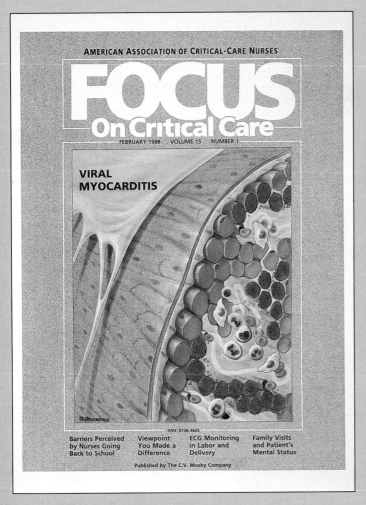

Title: "Viral Myocarditis"
Publishers: C.V. Mosby and the Amer. Assn. of
Critical Care Nurses—*FOCUS on
Critical Care*
Art Director: Diane L. Nelson
Publication
Manager: Ellen French
Illustrator: Diane L. Nelson

This handsome schematic rendering of heart muscle cells being attacked by viruses made the cover of a magazine aimed at nurses. Diane L. Nelson, president of Biomedia Corp., writes that "the challenge was to convince the publisher that their readers (critical care nurses) were capable of understanding a sophisticated medical image...in contrast to the traditional photographic image of a nurse at a bedside." In addition to its compelling graphic qualities, the illustration helps the reader visualize a disease that is difficult to diagnose.

Title: "Cuts, Bites and Abrasions"
Design Firm: In-house
Publisher: American Academy of Family
Physicians
Art Director: H. Marshall Wagoner III
Illustrator: Gustave Falk

For a monograph entitled "Cuts, Bites and Abrasions," illustrator Gustave Falk has depicted a cubic cross section of the skin against a dark background. The epidermis is being ravaged by all manner of injuries (including flying shards of glass), but the underlying layers of the skin seem to be unscathed. The artist himself writes that his purpose was "to tell the clients' story as simply and as beautifully as I could." Not a bad definition of the illustrator's role.

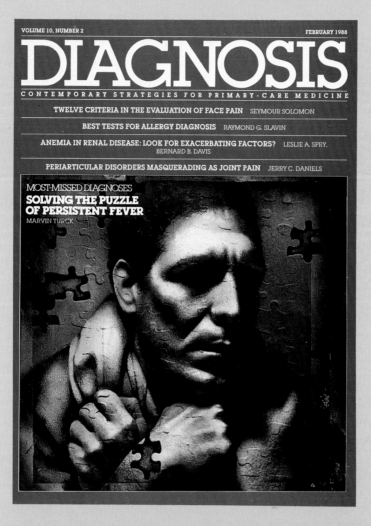

Title: **"Solving the Puzzle of Persistent Fever"**
Design Firm: **In-house**
Publisher: **Medical Economics Co. Inc.— *Diagnosis***
Art Director: **Carol Waters**
Illustrator: **Amy Guip**

This exceptional cover art by Amy Guip displays a classic technique known to students of art history as *chiaroscuro*—a heightened contrast of light and shadow for dramatic effect. The understated suffering of the fever-ridden man is communicated by his hands and his worried brow. The entire illustration is made up of jigsaw puzzle pieces (some of them missing), tying in neatly with the title of the cover article.

Title: **"Dementia—When Is It Alzheimer's?"**
Design Firm: **In-house**
Publisher: **Medical Economics Co. Inc.— *Diagnosis***
Art Director: **Susan Kuppler Haber**
Illustrator: **Sharon Ellis**

To illustrate a cover article on senile dementia (and its relation to Alzheimer's Disease), illustrator Sharon Ellis created this poignant elderly face with a missing mind. Intended to depict loss of memory, the empty space cuts cleanly through the forehead and out to the other side; the sky and clouds behind are plainly visible through the opening.

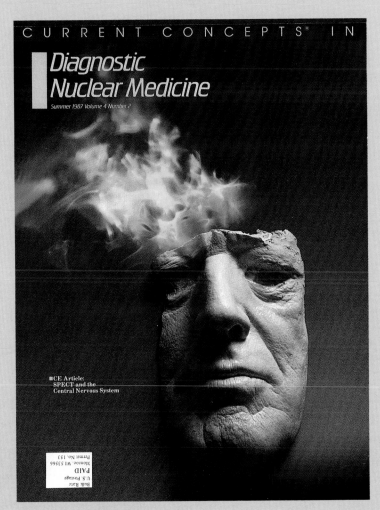

Title: **"Sorting out the Causes of Head and Face Pain"**
Design Firm: **In-house**
Publisher: **Medical Economics Co. Inc.— Diagnosis**
Art Director: **Carol Waters**
Illustrator: **Robert Wisnewski**

The depiction of pain poses an intriguing problem for the medical illustrator. Unlike the tangible bones, cells, and organs typically portrayed in medical art, pain is invisible. Only the *reaction* to pain can be visualized. And that is how artist Robert Wisnewski has handled the subject of head and face pain for the cover of *Diagnosis*. The sufferer presses his hands to his temples; his shadowy face is held in a deep frown; his eyes are closed. (Art Director Carol Waters notes that the subject is shown in darkness because victims of head and face pain are especially sensitive to light.) The actual areas of pain are softly highlighted against the subtle earth tones of the face and background.

Title: **Current Concepts® in Diagnostic Nuclear Medicine (Vol. 4, No. 2)**
Design Firm: **Kossak Design Group**
Publisher: **Macmillan Healthcare Information**
Sponsor: **Medi-Physics**
Art Director: **Lin Kossak**
Photographer: **Fred Burrell**
Editors: **Dorsey Woodson, Karen Izui**

This striking cover is one of a series developed by Kossak Design Group for *Current Concepts® in Diagnostic Nuclear Medicine*. For this issue, the cover article examined advances in Single Photon Emission Computed Tomography (SPECT) and its bearing on the central nervous system. The white life-mask with its jagged edges and sadly mortal features, together with the ethereal cloud of light in all the colors of the spectrum (a visual reference to SPECT), tell us something about the interplay of technology and the human condition.

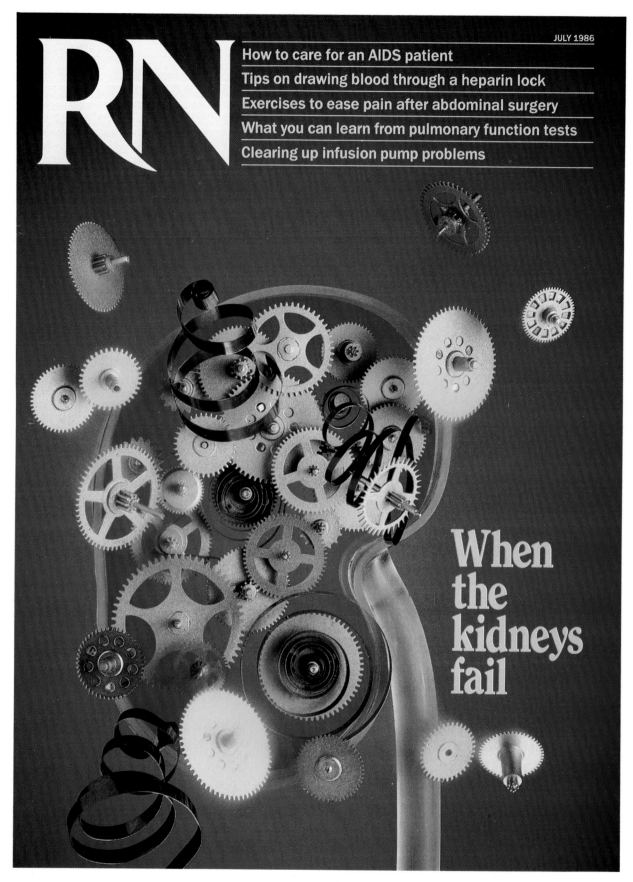

JULY 1986

RN

How to care for an AIDS patient

Tips on drawing blood through a heparin lock

Exercises to ease pain after abdominal surgery

What you can learn from pulmonary function tests

Clearing up infusion pump problems

When
the
kidneys
fail

Title: **"When the Kidneys Fail"**
Design Firm: **In-house**
Publisher: **Medical Economics Co. Inc.—*RN***
Art Director: **Andrea DiBenedetto**
Model Maker: **Bill Schmelk**
Photographer: **Walter Wick**

For the cover article on kidney failure, *RN* magazine ran this visually dramatic depiction of gears and springs flying out of the malfunctioning organ. According to the publication's art director, Andrea DiBenedetto, the mechanical model (designed by Bill Schmelk) serves to illustrate the danger of acute renal failure, "when the kidney's working mechanics go wild." The cover gives us a literal rendering of that idea—a simple yet daring conceptual step that succeeds handsomely.

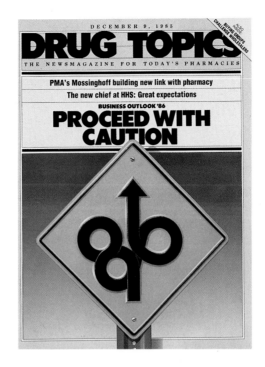

Title: **"Proceed with Caution"**
Design Firm: **In-house**
Publisher: **Medical Economics Co. Inc.—**
Drug Topics
Art Director: **Thomas Darnsteadt**
Illustrator: **Jim Bandsuh**

Imagine confronting a sign like this when you're doing 65 mph on the local expressway. According to the cover article for *Drug Topics*, the business wisdom for the coming year was "proceed with caution." Illustrator Jim Bandsuh chose to depict that uncertainty in the form of the loopy road sign that ultimately points up. The sign is rendered with photographic realism, from the raised highlights to the slightly rounded screws that hold the sign in place.

Title: **"The Hot and Not So Hot in**
OTCs/HBAs"
Design Firm: **In-house**
Publisher: **Medical Economics Co. Inc.—**
Drug Topics
Art Director: **Thomas Darnsteadt**
Photographer: **Walter Wick**

This intriguing "fire and ice" cover shot for *Drug Topics* is the result of a simple but clever idea: take the title of the cover article ("The Hot and Not So Hot in OTCs/HBAs") and create a literal visual interpretation. We see the "hot" pill and HBA item (in this case, lipstick) glowing with the blaze of success; their "not so hot" rivals are encased in a block of ice. The execution proved to be more complicated than the concept; the photographer found that real ice wouldn't work and finally resorted to using a block of acrylic.

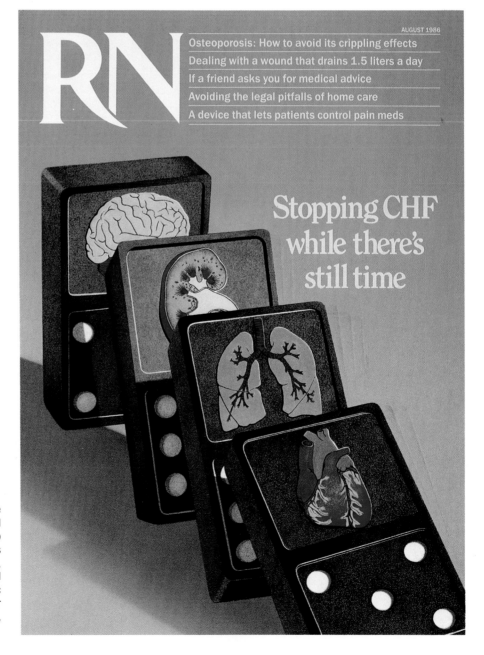

Title: **"Stopping CHF While There's**
Still Time"
Design Firm: **In-house**
Publisher: **Medical Economics Co. Inc.—RN**
Art Director: **Andrea DiBenedetto**
Illustrator: **Sal Catalano**

Falling dominoes fill the frame here, signalling at once that an irreversible sequence of events has begun and may be headed out of control. The reader who turns to the lead story quickly learns that when the heart's pumping action is impaired in congestive heart failure, other organs begin to fail, creating a potentially fatal "domino effect." In Sal Catalano's neatly symbolic illustration, each domino depicts one of the major organ systems that "topples" as a result of CHF: heart, lungs, kidneys, and brain.

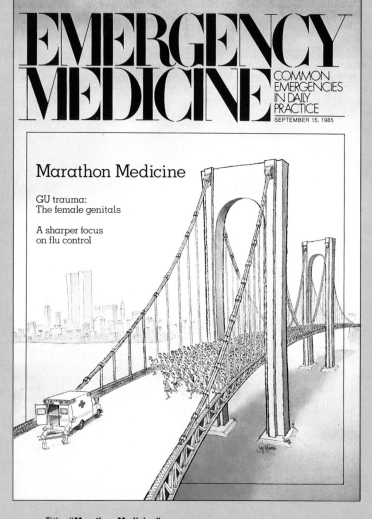

Title: **"Marathon Medicine"**
Design Firm: **In-house**
Publisher: **Cahners Publishing Co.—**
Emergency Medicine
Art Director: **Lois Erlacher**
Illustrator: **Jeff Moores**

An army of marathon runners wheezes its way across New York's Verrazano-Narrows Bridge, where an ambulance team waits for the worst to happen. This semi-whimsical cover for _Emergency Medicine_ calls our attention to an article on the special medical problems of marathon runners. Illustrator Jeff Moores achieves a fine balance between the amusing spectacle of panting marathoners and the seriousness of the subject.

Title: **"The Lowdown on Low Back Pain"**
Design Firm: **In-house**
Publisher: **Cahners Publishing Co.—**
Emergency Medicine
Art Director: **Lois Erlacher**
Illustrator: **Joseph Ciardiello**

A colossus like the legendary Atlas (depicted here holding up the heavens) must have developed a colossal pain in the lower back, as the grimace on his face would suggest. Illustrator Joseph Ciardiello brought off this _Emergency Medicine_ cover with an engaging light touch, successfully attracting the reader to the cover article on lower back pain.

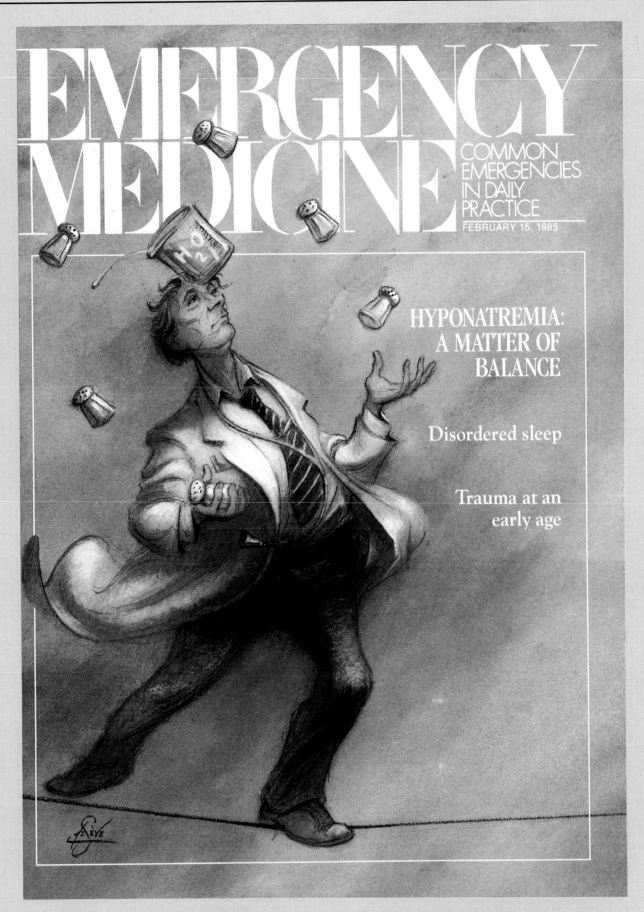

Title: **"Hyponatremia: A Matter of Balance"**
Design Firm: **In-house**
Publisher: **Cahners Publishing Co.—**
Emergency Medicine
Art Director: **Lois Erlacher**
Illustrator: **Peter de Seve**

A physician walks the proverbial tightrope, juggling half a dozen salt shakers while balancing a beaker of water on his forehead. This memorable cover illustration by Peter de Seve accompanies an article on hyponatremia, a deficiency of sodium in the blood. (The teaser copy reads, "Hyponatremia: A Matter of Balance.") This art shows that doctors have to balance salt and water levels in patients with hyponatremia.

Title: **"Do Nurses Have Their Own Living Wills?"**
Design Firm: **B. Martin Pederson Inc.**
Publisher: **American Journal of Nursing Co.— AJN**
Art Director: **Forbes Linkhorn**
Illustrator: **Jean François Allaux**

A living will is the legal means by which a person can, in a sense, pull his own plug in the event of terminal illness. For the cover of *American Journal of Nursing,* illustrator Jean François Allaux has transformed the living will into a hand pulling the plug on the patient. Rendered in a simple color scheme, with delicate cross-hatching on the hand, the illustration calls attention to an article on living wills for nurses.

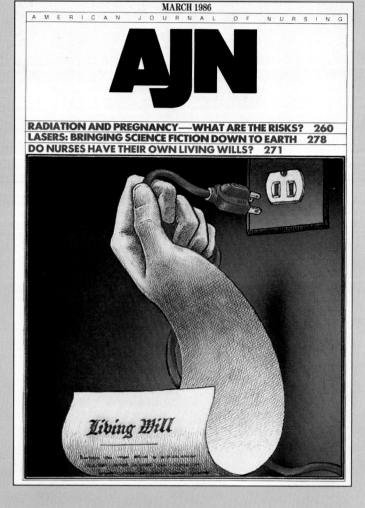

Title: **"Learning to Live with Third Party"**
Design Firm: **In-house**
Publisher: **Medical Economics Co. Inc.— Drug Topics**
Art Directors: **Thomas Darnsteadt, John Newcomb**
Model Maker: **Gordon Swenarton**
Photographer: **Stephen Munz**

Seated across the breakfast table from our friendly pharmacist is his new partner-for-life, third-party payment (in the form of a prescription plan credit card). No vision of loveliness, she makes a less than desirable breakfast companion—as we can see from the "What have I gotten myself into?" look in the pharmacist's eye. But, as the title of the cover article implies, the old boy will eventually learn to live with his new mate. The hilarious model is by Gordon Swenarton.

Title: **"Physician Dispensing Tightening Its Grip"**
Design Firm: **In-house**
Publisher: **Medical Economics Co. Inc.— *Drug Topics***
Art Director: **Thomas Darnsteadt**
Illustrator: **Brian Ajhar**

To convey a disturbing headline message ("Physician Dispensing Tightening Its Grip") to an audience of pharmacists, illustrator Brian Ajhar has created a wicked parody of the *caduceus*—the ancient symbol of the medical profession. Instead of winding around a staff as in the traditional emblem, the serpent grows out of a stethoscope and coils around a prescription bottle, ready to crush it in its grip. This ominous twist on a familiar image adds a sense of drama and urgency to the cover story.

Title: **"What Wall Street Sees Brewing"**
Design Firm: **In-house**
Publisher: **Medical Economics Co. Inc.— *Drug Topics***
Art Directors: **Thomas Darnsteadt, John Newcomb**
Illustrator: **Brian Ajhar**

Everybody's on familiar terms with the bull and bear of Wall Street: the bovine fellow on the left is responsible for the heady upturns in the stock market; his ursine counterpart made headlines on October 19, 1987. This cover art for *Drug Topics*, a magazine aimed at pharmacists, ties in with an article entitled, "What Wall Street Sees Brewing." Together, the two mascots of Manhattan's Financial District stir the brew with a mortar and pestle—traditional symbols of the pharmacist's profession. (The bull seems to be doing most of the work; the bear looks on with hopeful anticipation.)

Title: **"Alzheimer's Puzzle"**
Design Firm: **In-house**
Publisher: **Times-Mirror/Newsday—*Newsday***
Art Director: **Bob Eisner**
Illustrator: **Bob Newman**

The unsolved puzzle of Alzheimer's Disease takes shape in the form of a prosperous-looking man whose head literally "fogs over" at the top. The subtle black-and-white illustration by Bob Newman had to communicate its message within the restricting confines of newsprint (it appeared in *Newsday*). Assistant Art Director Rita Hall writes that the goal was to "concretize an abstract idea and make a grim subject attractive."

Part III

DISCOVERY

New York Newsday

Tuesday   May 10, 1988

The Alzheimer's Puzzle

The most important piece, the cause of the brain disease, still eludes researchers

By Robert Cooke

DESPITE ALL THE progress, recent optimism and pioneering experiments, doctors still do not know what causes Alzheimer's disease. They have found some tantalizing clues, but no "smoking gun."

"We are not there yet, but we are close to understanding how the disease affects the brain," said Dr. Robert B. Terry, a neurologist and leading expert on Alzheimer's disease from the University of California, San Diego. "I believe there are three steps to dealing with the problem of Alzheimer's disease," he said. "The first is to completely and accurately trace the path of the disease from its origin in the body.

"Secondly, a diagnostic screening test must be developed to detect Alzheimer's earlier.

"The final step is to develop a method to interrupt the normal progress of the disease."

When he began work on the disease in the 1960s, Terry said, "we were just beginning to find some of the pieces of the puzzle. Now we are quickly discovering how more and more pieces fit together."

Even as the pieces are being fit together, however, desperate families searching for useful treatments are trying unapproved drugs. The most prominent, called THA (its main ingredient is tetrahydroaminoacridine) has been given to hundreds of patients nationwide, even though its value against Alzheimer's disease is not known and its use has not been approved by the U.S. Food and Drug Administration. A large controlled study of the drug—which can cause serious side effects—is currently under way, with results expected later this year.

In the meantime it has now been well documented that

Please see ALZHEIMER'S on Page 3

Title: **"AIDS Virus: Studies Reveal Extraordinary Complexity"**
Design Firm: **In-house**
Publisher: **The New York Times Co.— *The New York Times***
Art Director: **Nancy Y. Sterngold**
Illustrator: **Judith Glick**
Editor: **Rick Flaste**

All art in the "Science Times" section of *The New York Times* shares the same goal, according to the section's art director, Nancy Y. Sterngold: to communicate information important to the reader's understanding of new developments in science. The illustration here graphically presents the increasingly detailed knowledge of the structure of the deadly AIDS virus—a feat that would be virtually impossible through the use of words alone.

TUESDAY, MARCH 3, 1987
Copyright © 1987 The New York Times

Science Times

With Education, Arts

The New York Times

C1

Data Suggest AIDS Risk Rises Yearly After Infection

By LAWRENCE K. ALTMAN

ANALYSIS of blood and data collected in San Francisco since 1978 suggests that the risk of developing AIDS increases yearly after infection with the virus, dampening hopes that rates of illness might plateau or even drop five years or so after infection.

In fact, the findings have led officials to conclude tentatively that the percentage of infected people who develop AIDS rises steadily over the seven years after infection.

The study, prepared by the San Francisco Health Department and the Federal Centers for Disease Control in Atlanta, indicates that only 4 percent of people who become infected with the AIDS virus will develop the disease within three years but that after five years the figure rises to 14 percent and after seven years to 36 percent.

"The longer one is infected, the higher are the chances of developing AIDS," said Dr. George Rutherford of the San Francisco Health Department.

Dr. Harold S. Jaffe, an AIDS epidemiologist at the Centers for Disease Control who is working on the study with the San Francisco Health Department, said the researchers had been unable to identify any factor other than time that triggers the onset of the disease.

"There doesn't seem to be anything obvious that people can do to stop this disease progression," Dr. Jaffe said in an interview.

The findings, which are scheduled to be presented this year at conferences on AIDS, are believed to provide the longest perspective on the progression of AIDS. Dr. Jaffe said the few studies conducted on other groups had covered shorter periods of time, but their results "look more or less the same — it's in the same ballpark," he said.

The study is rooted in another study, of

Continued on Page C11

AIDS Virus: Studies Reveal Extraordinary Complexity

Research discloses new puzzles but points to avenues of attack.

By HAROLD M. SCHMECK Jr.

AS scientists study the virus that causes AIDS they find greater — often surprising — complexity with each new research advance.

The virus has far more genes than expected and therefore a greater subversive repertoire than had been imagined. It is capable of attacking more different human cells than had been thought, and it has more complex means of destroying its victim's immune defenses than had been appreciated in the past.

The virus can kill cells, but it is also capable of hiding out, inactive, within the human body to emerge later in a flare of deadly infection.

"It is a lot more complicated than anyone thought," said Dr. Jeffrey Laurence of Cornell University Medical Center, an immunologist who has made important contributions to the understanding of AIDS.

The virus's complexity helps explain why acquired immune deficiency syndrome is so dangerous. The seeming ingenuity with which the virus attacks and resists counterattack contributes to the explosive growth of the AIDS epidemic.

But scientists have gleaned a vast amount of knowledge from the virus, and in an incredibly brief time. Although no one thinks the AIDS virus will be conquered soon, each new discovery about it not only gives scientists another possible tactic against it but also expands a scientists' understanding of virus infections in general.

"It has revolutionized our concepts of virus-cell interactions," said Dr. Flossie Wong-Staal of the National Cancer Institute, speaking of the AIDS virus and others like it. Although focused on a grave and immediate health problem, research on the virus is generating important knowledge that should go beyond that virus itself, she noted.

"We may learn a lot about the basic processes of life," said Dr. Wong-Staal, who is a major figure in AIDS research. She is a colleague of Dr. Robert C. Gallo, a discoverer of the AIDS virus, now called HIV for human immunodeficiency virus.

The pace of discovery itself has been remarkable. The disease AIDS was discovered in 1981. By the next year, virus experts were already predicting that the cause would be a retrovirus. Although many retroviruses were known to infect animals, only two human retroviruses were known; the AIDS virus became the third. It has proved to be far more complex than any of the others. Evidence for its existence was first reported in 1983 by Dr. Luc Montagnier and colleagues at the Pasteur Institute in Paris. Its identity and its link to AIDS were proved by the next year by Dr. Gallo's group at the Cancer Institute.

Most virus diseases that have been brought under control have been defeated by vaccines rather than drugs. Yet the emerging portrait of the AIDS virus and its mode of attack show that it will be a difficult vaccine target.

Retroviruses take their name from their unusual means of reproduction within the

Continued on Page C11

The Virus

Envelope   Reverse transcriptase   RNA

Vulnerable to AIDS Infection

T4 Cell
Key cell in immune system

Macrophage
Agent of immune system

Possibly Susceptible to AIDS Virus

Endothlial Cell
Lining of organs, including heart

Neuroglial Cell
Component of brain tissue

Colon cell
Lines colon

By infecting the T4 lymphocytes, the AIDS virus cripples the entire immune defense system. Macrophages usually devour invading viruses, but can sometimes harbor the AIDS virus and contribute to spread of infection. New research also points to other possible cellular victims. Most probable is infection of the neuroglial cells, which are cells of the brain and central nervous system. Other possibly vulnerable cells function in linings of organs. The virus might kill these cells or multiply in them, spreading the virus.

Illustrations by Judith Glick

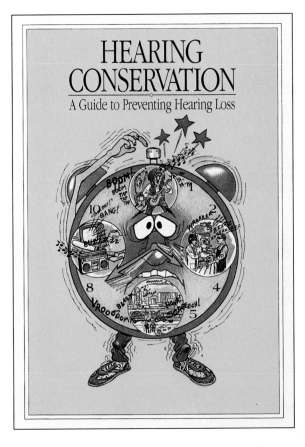

HEARING CONSERVATION
A Guide to Preventing Hearing Loss

Title: **"Hearing Conservation"**
Design Firm: **In-house**
Publisher: **Krames Communications**
Art Director: **Carveth Kramer**
Illustrator: **Sharon Ellis**

Aimed at the general public, this genially illustrated 16-page booklet is packed with helpful tips on preventing hearing loss. Featured prominently throughout the piece is a lovable, ruddy-cheeked cartoon character representing one of the ear's many hair cells—responsible for transmitting sound waves from the inner ear to the brain. The illustrations work in tandem with the brief copy blocks to create inviting, easily managed units of information.

NORMAL HEARING

The outer ear collects sound energy and funnels it into the middle ear where it is transformed into mechanical vibrations. These vibrations, or oscillations, enter the fluid-filled inner ear as undulating waves. It's in the inner ear that thousands of hair cells change the mechanical energy of the waves into electrical impulses that the brain interprets as sound.

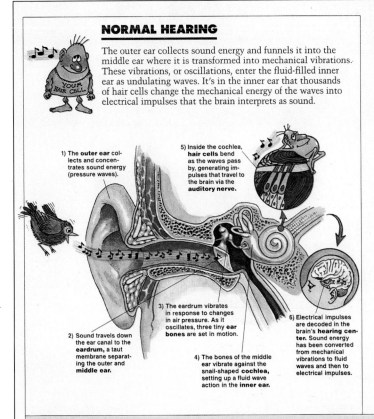

1) The **outer ear** collects and concentrates sound energy (pressure waves).

5) Inside the cochlea, **hair cells** bend as the waves pass by, generating impulses that travel to the brain via the **auditory nerve.**

3) The eardrum vibrates in response to changes in air pressure. As it oscillates, three tiny **ear bones** are set in motion.

2) Sound travels down the ear canal to the **eardrum,** a taut membrane separating the outer and **middle ear.**

4) The bones of the middle ear vibrate against the snail-shaped **cochlea,** setting up a fluid wave action in the **inner ear.**

6) Electrical impulses are decoded in the brain's **hearing center.** Sound energy has been converted from mechanical vibrations to fluid waves and then to electrical impulses.

MEASURING HEARING

Sound has both **frequency** and **intensity.** Frequency, or pitch, is measured as sound vibrations per second, or hertz (Hz). The frequency of a boat whistle or a locomotive horn is approximately 250 Hz, while the frequency of a bird singing or a table saw is 4,000 Hz. Intensity, or loudness, is measured in decibels. A conversational voice is around 65 dBA; a shout is 90 dBA or greater.

The Audiogram

INTENSITY (decibels)

| 0 dB |
| 10 dB |
| 20 dB |
| 30 dB | Vowel sounds | Consonant sounds |
| 40 dB |
| 50 dB | Normal conversation |
| 60 dB |
| 70 dB |
| 80 dB |

250 Hz   500 Hz   1000 Hz   2000 Hz   4000 Hz   8000 Hz

FREQUENCY (hertz)

The Hearing Test

The hearing test measures how loud a sound has to be before you can just hear it. As you sit in a test room wearing earphones, you will be asked to signal to the examiner when each tone can first be heard.

From the results, a hearing profile called the **audiogram** can be plotted. By comparing current to previous audiograms, you can see if hearing loss has occurred, and at which frequencies.

More on decibels (loudness)

Decibels are a measure of sound (how much pressure sound exerts on a surface). As the decibel level rises, the sound increases more rapidly than you perceive it. A sound of 90 dBA is **10 times** stronger than a sound of 80 dBA. A sound of 100 dBA is **100 times** stronger than a sound of 80 dBA.

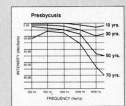

90 dBA

80 dBA

10 9 8 7 6 5 4 3 2 1

The 10 decibel difference

YOUR HAIR CELLS THROUGH LIFE

We start life with a fixed number of hair cells. As we age, they begin to die off naturally, resulting in hearing loss called **presbycusis** (from **presby:** old + **akousis:** hearing). Usually presbycusis isn't noticed until later in life, although premature presbycusis can run in families. Hair cells also can be damaged by head injury, infections, and some medications.

We're born with about 40,000 hair cells.

By adulthood many hair cells have died.

People in their 50s may show some hearing loss.

Others don't show it until their 80s.

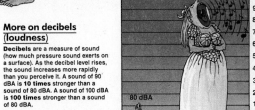

Presbycusis

INTENSITY (decibels)

10 yrs.
30 yrs.
50 yrs.
70 yrs.

250 Hz   500 Hz   1000 Hz   2000 Hz   4000 Hz

FREQUENCY (hertz)

Presbycusis begins in adolescence, but it doesn't become noticeable until years later, when you can't hear high-frequency sounds like a watch ticking or certain consonant sounds.

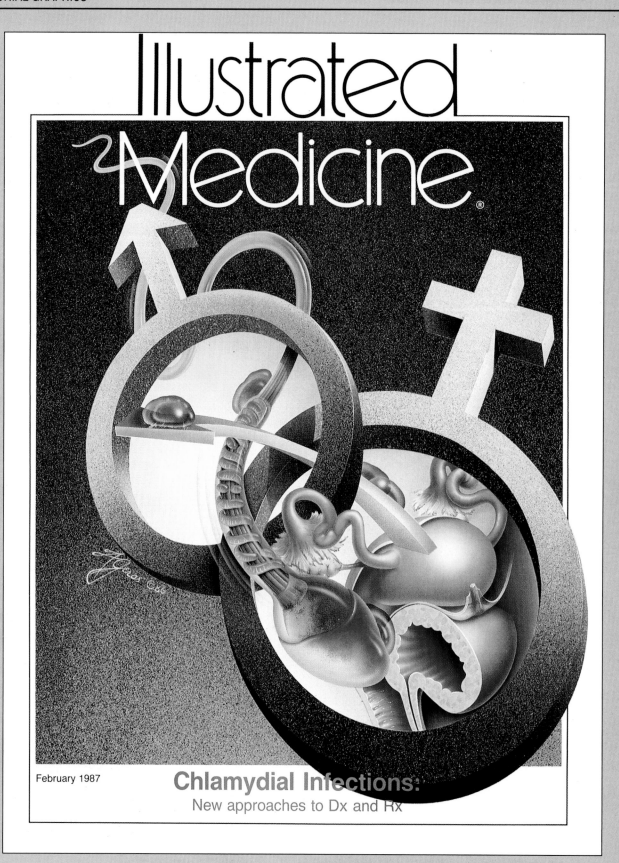

Illustrated Medicine®

February 1987

Chlamydial Infections:
New approaches to Dx and Rx

Title: **Illustrated Medicine—
"Chlamydial Infections..."**
Design Firm: **Focus Communications**
Publisher: **Wynwood Publishing, Inc.**
Sponsor: **Stuart Pharmaceuticals**
Art Director: **Audra Geras**
Illustrators: **Audra Geras (cover),
Edmond S. Alexander**
Executive Editor: **Nancy Agresta Weissflog**

This full-color monograph in the *Illustrated Medicine* series deals with chlamydial infections of the female urogenital tract. The artists have depicted not only the anatomical structures and disorders, but the development cycle of the chlamydia bacterium as well. Subtle highlighting effects and rich colors add visual interest; virtually every feature in the illustrations is labeled to maximize their educational value. Executive Editor Nancy Agresta Weissflog writes that the piece was intended to "help busy physicians keep their knowledge current on practical diagnostic and therapeutic aspects of a common clinical problem." The publication includes a 4-page ad insert (plus prescribing information) on CEFOTAN®, a drug used in treating gynecological infections.

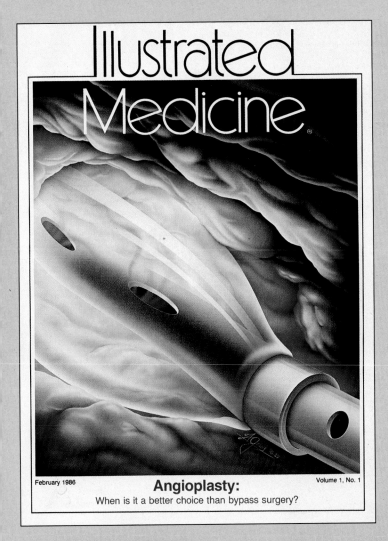

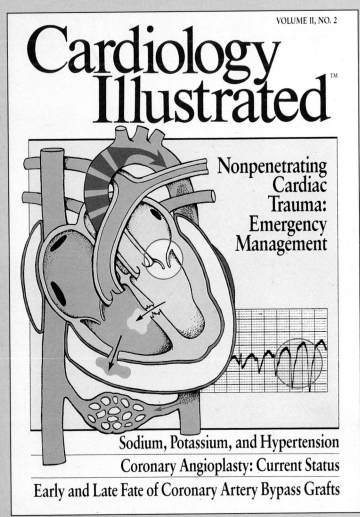

Title: ***Illustrated Medicine—***
"Angioplasty..."
Design Firm: **Focus Communications**
Publisher: **Wynwood Publishing, Inc.**
Sponsor: **Stuart Pharmaceuticals**
Art Director: **Audra Geras**
Illustrator: **Audra Geras**
Executive Editor: **Nancy Agresta Weissflog**

Clear, colorful, skillfully rendered artwork by Audra Geras illuminates this 12-page monograph on angioplasty. Part of the *Illustrated Medicine* series sponsored by Stuart Pharmaceuticals, the piece focuses on the delicate balloon catheter technique for opening a wider channel through diseased coronary arteries. Notable for their uncomplicated depiction of a difficult surgical technique, the illustrations also provide the reader with close-up cross sections of plaque-filled arteries. Insets and multiple callouts add to the educational value of the artwork. The publication includes an advertising spread for TENORMIN®, a beta-blocker used in treating angina.

Title: ***Cardiology Illustrated* (Vol. 2, No. 2)**
Design Firm: **In-house**
Publisher: **Hospital Publications, Inc.**
Sponsor: **Miles Laboratories**
Art Director: **Pat McKiernan**

The cover of *Cardiology Illustrated* shows a heart with ruptured walls resulting from a nonpenetrating injury. Sponsored by Miles Laboratories, the publication is filled with clear, pastel-colored schematic illustrations like the one on the cover. *Cardiology Illustrated* is published quarterly to enhance physicians' knowledge in the cardiovascular field.

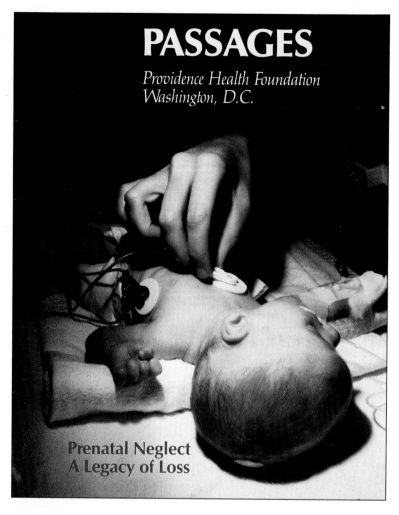

Title: ***Passages***—
"Prenatal Neglect..."
Design Firm: **Janin/Foster Design Communication**
Client: **Providence Hospital**
Art Director: **Susan Foster**
Photographer: **M. C. Valada (cover)**
Editor: **Susan Dyer**
Contributing Editor: **Joan Williams Leslie**

This issue of *Passages*, an occasional publication for Providence Hospital in Washington, D.C., focuses on the topic of prenatal neglect—and its consequences. Intended to awaken the community to "a legacy of loss" (Washington suffers from the second highest infant mortality rate in the country), the publication also projects an image of Providence Hospital as an institution taking action on a major social and medical problem. The "magazine" look of this issue—along with the abundance of human interest photographs (especially of children)—helps enhance reader appeal. Designer Susan Foster writes, "We worked with the editor to break up the manuscript into separate stories that could be presented in spreads."

Title: ***Passages***—
"Diagnostic Imaging..."
Design Firm: **Janin/Foster Design Communication**
Client: **Providence Hospital**
Art Director: **Susan Foster**
Photographer: **George Sumner (cover)**
Editors: **Susan Dyer, John Spragens, Jr.**
Contributing Editor: **Joan Williams Leslie**

Anatomical sketches from Leonardo da Vinci's notebook share page space with state-of-the-art diagnostic images in this issue of *Passages*, the community relations publication of Providence Hospital in Washington, D.C. For instance, Leonardo's drawing of a fetus inside the womb is positioned directly across from an ultrasound scan of a fetus. Devoted exclusively to diagnostic imaging, this issue presents articles on each technology—magnetic resonance imaging, computerized tomography (CT), positron emission tomography (PET), digital subtraction angiography, and several more. The provocative combination of modern and Renaissance graphics works beautifully, and the piece as a whole succeeds in positioning Providence Hospital as a leader in diagnostic imaging.

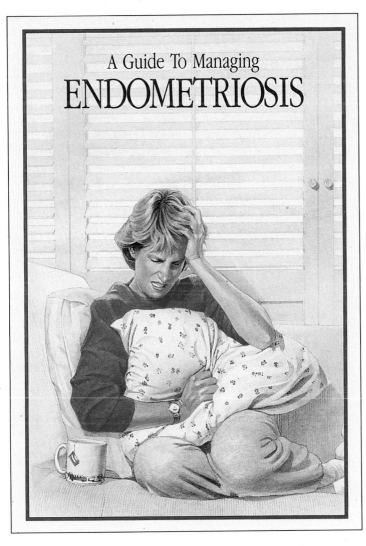

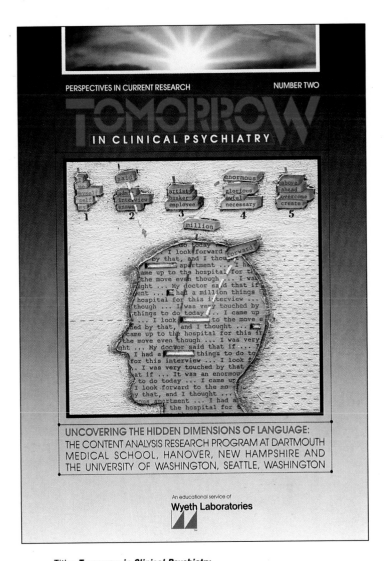

Title: **"A Guide to Managing Endometriosis"**
Design Firm: **In-house**
Publisher: **Krames Communications**
Designer: **Stephanie Zuras**
Illustrators: **Ellen Going Jacobs (medical), Cheolsa-Kim (realistic)**

This patient education publication about endometriosis is distinguished by its brightly colored illustrations of contemporary women—most often shown comfortably interacting with their doctors, friends, and families. The multiracial cast of characters helps the text reach a wide audience, and the generally upbeat faces (the arresting cover image is an exception) convey a supportive, nonthreatening tone throughout. The clear medical illustrations provide more than the usual realism—subtle use of white highlighting adds a glistening effect to internal membranes.

Title: *Tomorrow in Clinical Psychiatry* **(No. 2)**
Design Firm: **Materia Medica/Creative Annex Inc.**
Sponsor: **Wyeth Laboratories**
Art Director: **Don Kahn**
Illustrator: **David Lesh (cover)**

Targeted at psychiatrists, this sponsored publication focuses on a current investigation by a team of scientists into "the hidden dimensions of language"—especially the connection between language and specific illnesses, both mental and physical. The cover collage by David Lesh represents a sampling of the word categories mentioned in the text. Inside the booklet, all charts and tables are printed on beige backgrounds for ease of reference, and direct quotations from the participating scholars are set in blue type. Sponsored by Wyeth Laboratories, this issue of *Tomorrow in Clinical Psychiatry* promotes the firm's antianxiety/antidepressant medication Ativan® while it supplies psychiatrists with professionally significant findings from ongoing research *before* official publication in journals.

FOR SURGEONS

WILL THIS SURGEON'S MALPRACTICE ORDEAL EVER END?

Over the past 14 years, a snapped scalpel and a legal technicality have already cost him more than $500,000 out of his own pocket.

By Mark Crane SENIOR EDITOR

There was nothing unusual about the lumbar laminectomy until, inexplicably, the tip of the scalpel snapped. The neurosurgeon performing the procedure, Robert C. Cantu of Concord, Mass., asked for another, and moments later its tip snapped as well. Both tips became lodged in his patient's back.

Fortunately, the woman suffered no neurological deficit, and Cantu believed there was little chance the tips would migrate. But the May 10, 1973, incident gave the starting push to a row of legal dominoes that are still toppling.

Two years after the surgery, the patient filed suit against Cantu's hospital, the blade manufacturer, her primary physician, and the

hospital's supply company. Then, about a year later, her lawyers added Cantu to the suit.

Even at this stage, Cantu wasn't particularly alarmed. He'd never been sued before. Besides $100,000 in malpractice coverage from a primary insurer, he carried $1 million in excess coverage from another company. In the end, though, he was to find himself out of pocket more than a half million dollars to satisfy a court judgment and pay legal fees. Cantu's experience serves as a painful example of what can happen when a physician fails to make certain his malpractice carrier will back him up.

The "routine" operation

Cantu's ordeal began when the former Harvard Medical School instructor was asked by internist Richard A. Bartlett to provide a consultation for Donna Zeller, a 26-year-old woman complaining of pain in her back and legs. A week of bed rest ordered by Bartlett hadn't helped, and Cantu performed a myelogram at Clinton Hospital, about 20 miles west of Concord, where he held courtesy privileges. He believed it revealed a defect consistent with a herniated intervertebral disk. When pain persisted following another week of bed rest, Cantu recommended surgery to remove the disk.

"The procedure was initially uneventful," he recalls. "As I began to make a cruciate incision in the disk annulus—and it was a soft disk, not hard or calcified—about 4 mm of the tip of a No. 15 knife blade broke off inside the disk space. Because the incision wasn't completed, I then used a No. 11 blade. When I withdrew the knife handle, the tip of that blade was also missing."

The surgical team was unable to spot any metallic objects on X-rays taken in the operating room with a portable machine. Cantu proceeded to excise the disk using straight up-and-down biting pituitary rongeurs. After a lengthy search to locate the scalpel tips, he filled the disk space with methyl methacrylate, which effectively surrounded them with plastic. "I wanted to be positive they'd never migrate backward through the annulus into the spinal canal," Cantu says. Subsequent X-rays revealed the tips at the bottom of the disk space, but

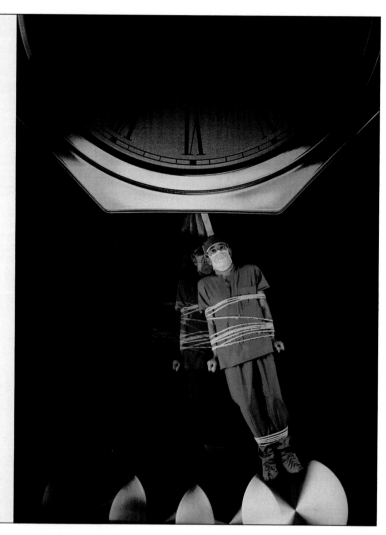

Title: **"Will This Surgeon's Malpractice Ordeal Ever End?"**
Design Firm: **In-house**
Publisher: **Medical Economics Co. Inc.— Medical Economics for Surgeons**
Art Director: **William Kuhn**
Photographers: **Stephen Munz, Lou Marotta**

The story of a surgeon's 14-year malpractice ordeal inspired this apt photographic metaphor. Tied to a swinging pendulum, the defenseless surgeon (who in real life has had to pay over $500,000 out of his own pocket—with no end in sight) dangles helplessly from a clock, a victim of time and fate. The multiple exposure captures four images of the doctor to convey the pendulum movement.

Title: **"Spare Body Parts"**
Design Firm: **In-house**
Publisher: **Vim & Vigor, Inc.—Vim & Vigor**
Art Director: **Robin Bedingfield**
Illustrator: **Tanya Tewell**

The subject of the article—"Spare Body Parts"—sounds like something out of science fiction, and illustrator Tanya Tewell has, indeed, given us a surrealistic sci-fi vision in this piece for Vim & Vigor. A humanoid face, opened like a hinged lid, reveals a black void behind it. The seeing eye (if it looks familiar, check the back of any dollar bill) adds a touch of mysticism, as do the crescent moon and the conjuring hand. In the able hands of this illustrator, a technical subject has taken on a dimension of myth—and obvious reader appeal.

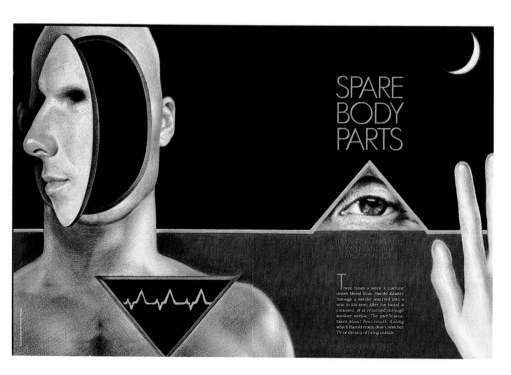

SPARE BODY PARTS

COULD MALPRACTICE PREMIUMS FORCE YOU OUT OF SURGERY?

Though he'd never been sued, this doctor's rates increased tenfold in just three years—to more than he could earn either in or out of the O.R.

By James E. Keasling, M.D.
GENERAL SURGEON, MONTICELLO, ILL.

Until three years ago, I couldn't really complain about the cost of malpractice insurance. For years, I'd been covered by The Medical Protective Company of Fort Wayne, Ind., under an occurrence policy that carried $200,000/600,000 limits. My premium had slowly risen to $4,316 for 1984-85.

In July of 1985, it went to $7,077. Even that wasn't too disturbing, considering the malpractice climate. My premiums had remained relatively modest because I'd never been sued and because Medical Protective had classified me as a general surgeon with a reduced surgical volume. For the previous eight years, I'd averaged only about 40 major operations annually.

My surgical workload lightened in 1977, when, at the age of 51, I moved from Champaign, Ill., to be the only surgeon in this small farming community of 4,800 with a well-equipped 20-bed hospital. In such a small town, I spent about 80 percent of my time in general practice and the rest as a general surgeon. I felt comfortable with this mix: My training had included a rotating internship and a year of medical residency at a county hospital, followed by five years of surgical training and another five providing all types of care as a medical missionary in Iran.

Once in practice in Monticello, I limited myself to general practice and elective general surgery—gallbladders, hernias, colon resections, modified radical mastectomies, and the like. I referred all major trauma, complicated surgical problems, and high-risk patients to the medical facilities I'd left behind.

Being board-certified, I was welcomed aboard by the three GPs in town. Within a few years, a board-certified internist and another GP joined us. We all shared in covering the emergency room.

Though surgery in my new practice required only a fifth of my workweek, it provided about 35 percent of my $150,000 to $160,000 annual gross

APRIL 1988 25

Title: **"Could Malpractice Premiums Force You out of Surgery?"**
Design Firm: **In-house**
Publisher: **Medical Economics Co. Inc.— Medical Economics for Surgeons**
Art Director: **William Kuhn**
Photographer: **Stephen Munz**

Shades of Captain Hook! But instead of being forced overboard by the old one-handed pirate, this hapless surgeon is about to be pushed out of his profession by a well-manicured hand in a pin-striped sleeve. (An oversized scalpel serves as the "plank.") Comical on the surface, this attention-getting photograph sums up the very serious subject of the article: the increasingly prohibitive cost of malpractice insurance.

HOW RURAL GPs STILL FREEZE OUT GOOD SURGEONS

An angry colleague offers a vivid and frightening description of what makes it hard for patients to find competent surgical care in small towns.

When I was still starry-eyed about rural practice, I encouraged a senior resident to open his office someplace where he'd be truly needed and wouldn't face competition from hordes of other general surgeons.

I thought I was doing him a favor. As it turned out, I wasn't.

The small town he picked was nice enough, but the board of directors at its hospital included two general practitioners who were "surgically active." My friend asked them what he could expect in the way of referrals. They patronizingly said they would observe him and, if he measured up, would send him their "tough" cases. It was clear, though, that these GPs had no intention of giving up much of their own surgical activity.

From a chance remark by the clerk at his motel, the resident learned that another general surgeon had recently left town—only six months after opening his office. So he located the other doctor and asked why.

The surgeon who'd left told this story: "One case that was 'too tough' for the GPs was a thyroidectomy. When the superior thyroid artery slipped away, the GP doing the operation was in big trouble. I had to bail him out. I then sent the family a nominal bill for an assistant's fee. But the GP hadn't told the family he'd needed help, and he was outraged at my 'greed.' He advised the family not to pay me."

The disillusioned doctor went on to say that the only cases he was permitted to handle were similar bailouts, along with Saturday-night emergency calls for largely non-paying victims of stabbings, shootings, and automobile wrecks. All of the routine hernia repairs, cholecystectomies, and appendectomies—a surgeon's bread and butter—were performed by the GPs.

My friend didn't have to hear any more of his predecessor's horror stories. He left town, too. "I'd rather take my chances competing with three dozen other surgeons," he said, "than with a couple of small-town GPs like that."

Over the years I've come to realize that such situations aren't uncommon. There still are plenty of rural communities throughout the U.S. where GPs who haven't had a month's worth of surgical training past internship go to ridiculous lengths to freeze out surgeons who have the temerity to

THE AUTHOR, a board-certified general surgeon who's practiced in small towns for 20 years, has been ostracized anonymously to assure him restitution from his generalist colleagues.

34 JULY 1984

Title: **"How Rural GPs Still Freeze out Good Surgeons"**
Design Firm: **In-house**
Publisher: **Medical Economics Co. Inc.— Medical Economics for Surgeons**
Art Director: **William Kuhn**
Photographer: **Walter Wick**

Grant Wood's immortal *American Gothic* has been parodied time and again for half a century; in this recent takeoff for an article in *Medical Economics for Surgeons*, the two indomitable faces are those of rural GPs. As the article informs us, competent surgeons have had a tough time establishing themselves in small towns and rural areas, where GPs still hold sway.

MANAGING THE PATIENT WITH TESTICULAR CANCER

Nursing Grand Rounds

Multidisciplinary teamwork. That's what it takes to help a patient afflicted with the number one cause of death from cancer in men between ages 20 and 40.

This article is based on a *Nursing Grand Rounds* presented at Mercy Hospital in Miami, Fla. The panelists are: Mary Ann Carbonell, RN, CCRN; Lucy Tuseff, RN; Lori Sciarra, RPT; and Ellen Isaac, RN. The panel report was coordinated by Debra Wajcik, RN, MSN, who now works at St. Thomas Hospital in Nashville, Tenn.

Mary Ann Carbonell, RN, CCRN: Steve Morris, age 32, was admitted to our neurology unit from the emergency department (ED) complaining of numbness from nipple to toe. Steve said he'd had back pain for 3 months. He had seen an orthopedic surgeon, who took X-rays and noted a hard right testicle. The surgeon suggested that Steve see a urologist, but Steve put off further treatment for more than 2 months.

Within a day or two of his admission to our hospital, he started losing sensation and motor function in his legs. On admission to the ED, he had paresthesias in his legs and was retaining urine. A neurologic examination revealed neck tenderness on flexion and several abnormal findings in the legs—decreased muscle tone, no voluntary movement, no proprioception, and no response to pinpricks, vibration, or light touch. Response to pinpricks began at the level of the eighth thoracic vertebra (T8); response to vibration, at T6. An initial diagnosis of spinal cord compression was made.

A myelogram showed a complete extradural block at the superior axial level of T8. The vertebral column was X-rayed and found to be otherwise normal. Steve was taken to the operating room; a laminectomy was performed at T7 and T8 to excise an epidural neoplasm engulfing the dura mater. The nerve root to T8, also affected by the lesion, was excised. After surgery, Steve was transferred to the neurologic intensive care unit (NICU).

Tumor identified

Debra Wajcik, RN, MSN: The pathology report described the lesion as metastatic germ cell seminoma, a malignant tumor that originates in the testicle. An oncologist was consulted. He examined Steve and found two enlarged, bilateral, supra-

The patient discussed in this Nursing Grand Rounds developed a malignant tumor in his right testicle. The tumor metastasized to the superior axial level of T8 and to the supraclavicular lymph nodes.

42 Nursing86, August

Title: **"Managing the Patient with Testicular Cancer"**
Design Firm: **In-house**
Publisher: **Springhouse Corp.—Nursing86**
Art Director: **Dyann Craven**
Illustrator: **Brendan Riley**

The headline and opening copy tell the story in no uncertain terms: this article is about caring for patients with testicular cancer, the leading cause of cancer death in men between the ages of 20 and 40. Aimed at an audience of nurses, the article is accompanied by Brendan Riley's graphically understated illustration of a man with an advanced case of the disease. The areas affected by the spreading cancer are isolated in glowing orange. The article and illustration are based on a case study of a man with metastasized testicular cancer.

Title: **"The Dehydration Question"**
Design Firm: **In-house**
Publisher: **Springhouse Corp.—Nursing83**
Art Director: **Ed Rosanio**
Illustrator: **Russell Farrell (illustration), Tom Herbert (logo)**

Part of a special ongoing series entitled "Controversial Issues" that appeared in *Nursing83*, this challenging article helps nurses examine the "dehydration question." The opinion of the author, who spent three years as a hospice nurse, is that dying patients should not necessarily be given intravenous fluids on a routine basis. To illustrate this sensitive issue, Russell Farrell visualized the dehydrated patient as a drying lake, set somewhat ironically in a lush green landscape with rolling hills. The water has almost totally evaporated, leaving only a few isolated pools on the sandy lake bed. The illustration is nicely complemented by the handsome typography and by Tom Herbert's germane graphic symbol.

NEW for 1983
From time to time, we'll publish CONTROVERSIAL ISSUES in nursing. As always, we welcome your reaction.

THE DEHYDRATION QUESTION

If you think we must routinely give intravenous fluids to the dying patient, think again. Read the evidence and make up your own mind on this controversial issue.

BY JOYCE V. ZERWEKH, RNC, MA
Home-Care Nurse, Clinical Coordinator
Hospice of Seattle • Seattle, Washington

I BELIEVE IT'S TIME to question an assumption you've heard as gospel since your days in nursing school. I'm talking about the routine administration of intravenous (I.V.) fluids to the patient who's within days of death. *Is it*, as we've always assumed, more merciful to give the dying patient fluids than to let him experience dehydration?

After 3 years as a hospice nurse, I now believe we should *not* routinely give fluids to all patients. What we *should* do is (1) examine the beneficial effects of dehydration (yes, there are beneficial effects, which we'll list later) and the detrimental effects of hydration; and (2) decide whether or not to administer fluids intravenously in light of the individual patient's condition and reaction to treatment.

The issue can arise when a patient on the unit is approaching death, when a terminally ill patient who can no longer drink fluids is transferred to the hospital, or when a patient is dying at home.

Your nursing role, as you cope with this issue, may become a sensitive, even controversial one. As the patient's advocate, you could be the one to speak for a patient who's beyond speech, or for the family that wants what's best for the patient—but feels unsure of what *is* the best.

Your role, as I see it, is not to take a hard line either for or against giving I.V. fluids. Instead, you must work closely with the entire health team to educate the patient (if he's alert) or the family about the choices.

To help the patient or family understand and make a choice, take a look at what's happening physiologically to the patient close to death.

Physiology of the dying patient

When a patient in the advanced stage of a terminal disease comes within days of death, we expect to see a fluid deficit with reduced circulation in all body systems. Frequently, electrolyte excess and acidosis are concurrent with fluid deficit. Other developments can be nausea and vomiting, neuromuscular irritability with twitching and restlessness, and a progressively lower level of consciousness.

Because fluids play such a critical physiologic role, you can almost predict the oncoming death by observing the patient's reduced fluid intake and output. In the final days, the patient becomes more and more dehydrated. His body fluids diminish as he drinks less and less as a result of any one (or several) of the following problems: dysphagia, vomiting, anorexia, diminishing energy, accompanied by a reduced level of consciousness and a general emotional withdrawal.

At the same time, other physiologic systems can be failing. The fluid deficit may be compounded by bleeding or gastrointestinal losses, or by other fluid and electrolyte changes such as hypernatremia, oliguria, acidosis, hyperkalemia, and hypercal-

Nursing83, January 47

BY PHYLLIS R. CARPENTER, M.D.

PIERCING THE VEIL OF SILENCE

S ilence.
Total, complete, absolute lack
of sound. No voices of family,
friends, lovers, no music,
birdsong, the phone ringing,
with friends no TV....silence
is the reality of life for about
200,000 profoundly deaf persons in the United States. For
some of these persons, cochlear implants may reopen
their ears to hearing.

Title: "Piercing the Veil of Silence"
Design Firm: In-house
Publisher: Vim & Vigor, Inc.—*Vim & Vigor*
Art Director: Robin Bedingfield
Photographer: Chris Bassett

To depict the world of the deaf in visual terms, the staff at *Vim & Vigor* created an oppressive blankness stretching across two pages. But the textured plaster surface that isolates the ear from the rest of the world suggests something more: it is as if the deaf are walled off from life. The silence is, as they say, deafening.

Title: "Prevention in Primary Care"
Design Firm: In-house
Publisher: Hospital Publications, Inc.—*Hospital Medicine*
Art Director: Pat McKiernan
Illustrator: Ray Srugis

An instructive contrast of healthy vs. unhealthy life-styles—centered on a graphic depiction of the most vulnerable organs—helps prime the reader for the article, "Prevention in Primary Care." To the left, we see a potentially lethal combination of "vices": sedentary living, smoking, drug abuse, and a diet of fast food. To the right of the organs, we're shown the more healthful alternative: a lifestyle that encompasses exercise, health education, and sensible foods. Marian Berger, editor of *Hospital Medicine*, writes that "this topic required graphic rather than medical art to illustrate the subject."

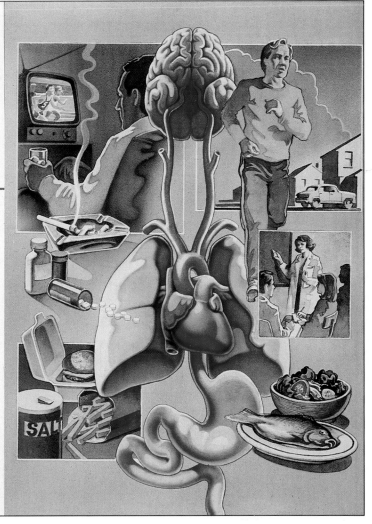

Prevention in Primary Care

Changes in patients' environments and life-styles can enhance their health. Physician-patient communication and dedication to reducing risk can result in healthier, more functional, longer-lived patients.

Clifford J. Hataway, MD
Albert Oberman, MD

For the first time ever in American medicine, the age-adjusted death rate has steadily declined to the lowest levels ever recorded. This decrease, principally in cardiovascular diseases, has led to greater life expectancy for the middle-aged adult population. Current population survival curves (Figure)[1] and information from the United States Surgeon General[2] show a definite increase in survival: the population is living longer and staying healthier than ever before. One explanation is that environmental and behavioral changes have reduced the predisposition to and disability from chronic disease.

Strong evidence exists that intervention to decrease risk factors

Clifford J. Hataway is Assistant Professor and Clinical Director, Division of General and Preventive Medicine, and Albert Oberman is Professor and Director, Division of General and Preventive Medicine, Department of Medicine, The University of Alabama at Birmingham School of Medicine.

yields substantial patient benefits, primarily with regard to cardiovascular disease. Recently, many physicians and lay people have argued that placing more emphasis on preventive measures could reduce the burden of chronic diseases.

The Physician's Role

At least 60% of all health problems may be due to life-style influences.[2] Authorities estimate that cigarette smoking is responsible for 15% of all health costs and contributes to 30% of all myocardial infarctions and 80% of lung carcinomas. Improved hypertension treatment has promoted the 32% decline in cerebrovascular accidents since the 1960s.[2]

Poor dietary patterns play a role in several of the leading causes of death in the United States.[3] These include heart disease, cancer, stroke, diabetes, cirrhosis, and arteriosclerosis. Physical inactivity has been estimated to account for as much as 23% of community cardiovascular risk, and studies show that regular

exercise can reduce coronary heart disease risk significantly, even adjusted for the classic risk factors of elevated cholesterol, smoking, and hypertension.[4] Proper seat belt use can prevent deaths and limit injuries in up to 60% of motor vehicle crashes.[2]

Many people overlook the role of immunizations in preventing serious infectious disease, but their introduction had a major effect on the population survival curve.[2]

Table 1 identifies risk factors associated with health problems commonly encountered in the office. The high prevalence of these factors, the long incubation period of the chronic diseases, and the likelihood that life-style has an impact on them all argue for an active role in prevention for the physician.

The public can practice personal good health habits on its own to reduce the probability of disease. Data from the National Center for Health Statistics, however, indicate that a substantial percentage of adults have poor health habits (Table 2).[5] Clearly, some people *know* about

continued

PROMOTIONS

BOOKLETS, FOLDERS, BROCHURES
VISUAL AIDS
MULTIMEDIA PACKAGES
SALES KITS AND AIDS
ANNUAL REPORTS
CALENDARS
LOGOS

Advertising *sells*; promotion *creates awareness*. In principle, this distinction seems clear enough. But in practice, the boundaries often overlap. Advertising can be used simply to generate product awareness (as in a pre-launch campaign). And a skillfully conceived promotion can measurably increase sales.

So what is it, precisely, that distinguishes the promotions in this chapter from the medical ads in chapters 1 and 2? One difference seems obvious: advertisements use media space; promotions don't. But what about a space ad that announces a sweepstakes?

A perplexing issue, this distinction between ads and promotions. If we can propose one generalization that would apply to *most* of the entries in this chapter, it's simply this: that a promotional piece ostensibly provides something of value to the recipient—information or free samples or art for the office walls. The selling message is relegated to secondary status.

Take the double-duty patient education aids furnished by several companies: the nutrition pamphlets and accompanying stand promoting Lopressor®, or the interactive urinary tract diagram kits (complete with reusable "slate" pad) produced for NOROXIN®, or Merck's handsomely illustrated Patient Education Guides. These promotions were designed to provide a valuable service to physicians and their patients—and at the same time, they put in at least a brief plug for the company or product.

The message may be perfunctory, but these promotions succeed in one area where even the best ads fail: *they stay visible.* An educational booklet—or a 3-D anatomical model, or a wall calendar—will continue to serve as a visible product reminder for as long as the physician chooses to keep it in his or her office. The greater its appeal to physician and patient, the longer it will stay in use—and the longer it will deliver its promotional message to the intended audience.

In the case of over-the-counter preparations, it's more important to get the promotion into the hands of the consumer. The multicomponent Stomach tlc™ kit enlightens ulcer patients with an informative cassette, a booklet, a poster, and a sample of Tagamet®, along with a coupon for their next purchase.

Other educational promotions instruct patients in the use of the product: for example, the large, illustrated flip chart designed to help medical professionals explain the Today™ Contraceptive Sponge to women. Or the ingenious rotating wheel on the Aristocort A® promotion, with its alternating "dry" and "moist" illustrations (used by the physician to explain the healing action of the drug).

Some promotional giveaways are intended specifically for the physician's own use: the makers of ECOTRIN® distributed a series of travel guides imprinted with anatomical art across the spines. (The art would form a complete picture when the physician invited the sales rep back to deliver the subsequent volumes.) And physicians received a portfolio of exuberantly imaginative Folon prints, their subject matter only obliquely related to the benefits of Ativan®.

Product information booklets can resemble scientific monographs or extended advertisements. But even where the selling aspect is more pronounced—as in the handsome showcase for the new antibiotic PRIMAXIN®—the emphasis is on imparting detailed information about the product rather than simply touting the benefits.

Corporate promotional booklets follow the same pattern. While they're obviously developed to strengthen the bottom line by attracting new business, they also furnish prospective customers with the information they need to move toward a decision. Schering-Plough's booklet stresses the company's range of plant facilities; Squibb introduces prospects to its top management team. (For an intriguing corporate visual, see Searle's symbolic spheres.)

Sales aids offer marginally less information and more of a sell. After all, they're developed to help sales reps make an effective multidimensional presentation. These visual tools can take the form of flash cards (like the ones for Femstat®), brochures, or just about anything else (e.g., the NOROXIN® kidney pill dispenser with its selling message on the back).

When it comes to publicizing *events*, the masters of promotion often pull out all the stops. 3M Riker enticed physicians to its booth at a San Francisco convention with free mime entertainment, balloons, T-shirts, and other promotional lures. And an allergists' conference in Boston attracted participants with an elaborate sweepstakes mailing centered on Paul Revere's legendary "midnight ride."

In short, the dimensions of promotion are restricted only by limitations of budget and human imagination. On the pages that follow, you'll be able to examine some of the best current work in this wide and diverse field.

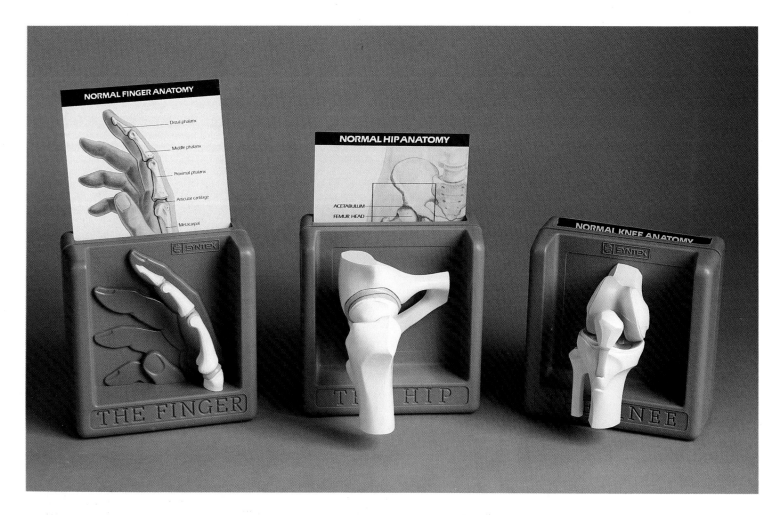

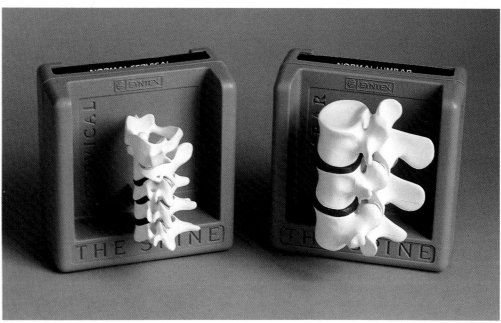

Product: **NAPROSYN®**
Ad Agency: **Vicom/FCB**
Client: **Syntex Laboratories, Inc.**
Art Director: **Lester Barnett**
Illustrator: **Vincent Perez (Insert Cards)**
Model Designer: **Jolly Major**
Copywriter: **Cari Weisberg**

GOLD. Educational and engagingly interactive, these anatomical models help physicians instruct their patients about various spinal and joint conditions. At the same time, they help Syntex Laboratories sell NAPROSYN® to the physicians. Winners of the Rx Club Gold Award, the models feature moving parts as well as illustrated laminated cards that slip into the display for further patient education. Creative Director Lester Barnett writes that a rheumatologist, an anatomist, and an industrial designer collaborated on the project under the supervision of the agency's art director and production manager. Model designer Jolly Major had to recreate the different movements of the joints while adapting each version to fit the same standard platform. The models were produced in the Orient to remain within budget.

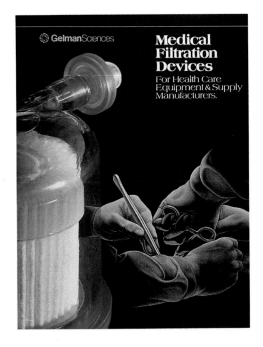

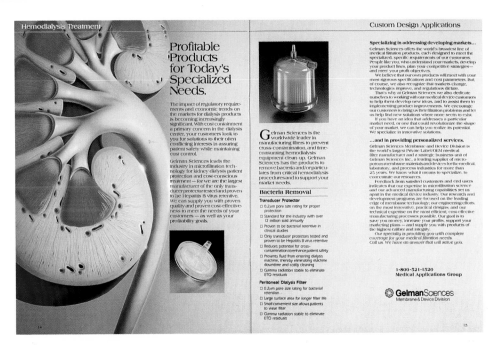

Title: **"Medical Filtration Devices"**
Design Firm: **Robert Drinnon & Associates**
Client: **Gelman Sciences**
Art Director: **Val Hawksley**
Illustrator: **Christopher J. Burke**
Copywriter: **Val Hawksley**

SILVER. One generally wouldn't expect a brochure on medical filtration devices targeted at equipment manufacturers to be graphically exciting. But illustrator Christopher J. Burke has transformed this piece with his spectacular visions of human anatomy. According to Burke and Valerie Hawksley, promotions products manager for Gelman Sciences, the design firm was "directed to create a 'cutting edge' image to emphasize the company's high-technology product line. The illustrator was challenged to go beyond the typical textbook approach...." The resulting unconventional images in this exceptional piece are almost surreal: the eye in profile, its cornea curving like a vast glass dome...the kidney with its seven "lanes" converging into the tunnel of the ureter.

Product: **OMNIPAQUE**®
Ad Agency: **Lavey/Wolff/Swift Inc.**
Client: **Winthrop Pharmaceuticals,**
Diagnostic Imaging Div.
Art Director: **Bob Olson**
Illustrator: **Vladimir Pechanec**
Copywriter: **Linda Culvert**

SILVER. Sleek graphics and a bold red/blue color scheme distinguish this Rx Club Silver Award winner for OMNIPAQUE®, a product used in diagnostic imaging. The centerpiece of the promotion is the "Omni Triad," a gleaming tripartite motif that symbolizes "the three factors demanded by the diagnostician in the conduct of contrast-enhanced imaging." Positioned on the converging lines inside the triad are three angiocardiographic images. The agency used the same basic art in more than one promotional piece for OMNIPAQUE®, each targeted at different specialist audiences; these used the same format, with a different color scheme and images of different organs inside the triad.

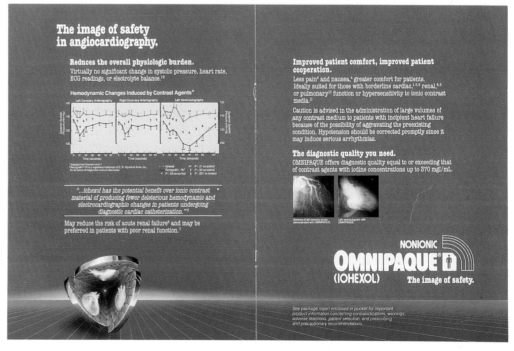

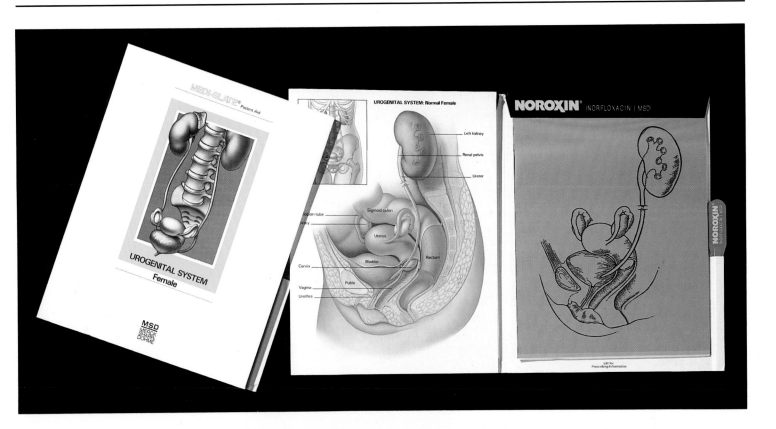

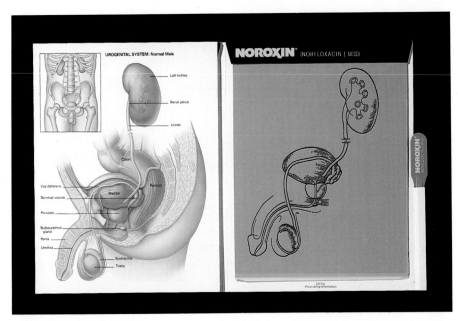

Product: **NOROXIN**®
Design Firm: **Medical Multimedia Corp.**
Client: **Merck Sharp & Dohme**
Art Director: **Gilbert R. Albright**
Illustrator: **Robert Demarest**
Copywriters: **Stanley Waine,**
Jeff Jenkins (Female, Male),
Scott Bolenbaugh (Unisex)

SILVER. Remember those toy "slates" with the plastic film you could lift to make your writing vanish? Medical Multimedia Corporation uses the same concept in these interactive MEDI-SLATE® kits for NOROXIN®. Designed as educational tools for physicians to use with their patients, the illustrated kits focus on the human urinary tract: unisex (with male and female insets) in the first version, followed by separate single-sex spinoffs. (It was the female kit that won the Rx Club Silver Award.) In each package, the "slate" is imprinted with a diagram of the tract, on which the physician can visually pinpoint problems with the accompanying implement. A printed pad enables patients to take home a diagram of their disorder for further study.

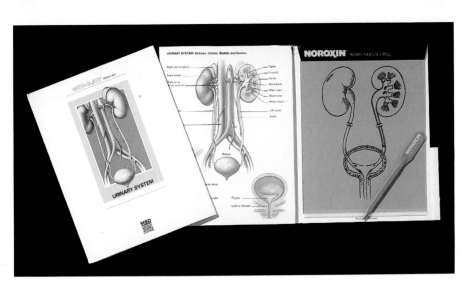

IN MILD-TO-MODERATE HYPERTENSION

Patients prefer the medicine they wear

Product: **Catapres-TTS**®
Ad Agency: **Barnum Communications, Inc.**
Client: **Boehringer Ingelheim**
Art Director: **Monica Garb**
Photographer: **Ken Nahoum**
Copywriter: **James Pelletier**

SILVER. Sixteen engaging photo portraits by Ken Nahoum grace the cover of this Silver Award-winning sales aid for Catapres-TTS®, a skin patch containing antihypertensive medication. The warm, friendly faces, most of them looking directly at the reader, represent a cross section of patients who can benefit from the medication. Inside, general benefits copy and graphs are followed by tabbed spreads on the three targeted patient types: active patients, the elderly, and those with concurrent disorders. Monica Garb, art director of this piece, tells us that it was designed to provide sales reps with clinical support—"an educational and convincing message which would motivate the physician to prescribe Catapres-TTS® for appropriate hypertensive patients."

Product: **DYAZIDE**®
Ad Agency: **Salthouse Torre Norton Inc.**
Client: **Smith Kline & French Co.**
Art Director: **Mike Lazur**
Photographer: **Donato Leo**
Copywriter: **Mike Norton**

SILVER. "Going bananas" is the theme of this wild 14-panel brochure for DYAZIDE®, a blood pressure medication. Featuring a 40-inch banana as its centerpiece, the piece explains how the drug helps reduce blood pressure without depleting the body's supply of potassium. (Hypertensives on diuretics traditionally consume bananas to combat potassium loss.) According to Senior V.P./Account Supervisor Barbara Falco, the banana graphic demonstrates "how much banana is needed to be consumed to replace lost potassium when taking a diuretic." She adds that the piece was designed to "stimulate interest and excitement among the sales force," who had been experiencing "product fatigue" with this long-established drug.

Title: **"Stick this on your phone."**
Ad Agency: **Lally, McFarland & Pantello**
Client: **Lally, McFarland & Pantello**
Art Director: **Jim McFarland**
Photographer: **Dennis Kitchen**
Copywriter: **John Lally**

SILVER. Lally, McFarland & Pantello devised this shrewd promotional piece to lure prospective clients away from rival ad agencies. This is a fairly aggressive tactic by any standard, but LM&P brings it off with a disarming touch of humor. The premise is that prospects should peel off the attached sticker bearing LM&P's phone number, affix it to their phone in a visible place, and watch visiting account execs squirm in their seats. (To rub it in, the prospect is supposed to "wonder aloud why it's so hard to get the kind of advertising you really need these days.") If this ploy improves the quality of their advertising, so much the better. If not—well, they know who to call.

Title: **"The Cholesterol Connection"**
Ad Agency: **Gross Townsend Frank Hoffman, Inc.**
Client: **Merck Sharp & Dohme**
Art Director: **Orin Kimball**

Bright primary colors add pizzazz to the cover of this lead-generating package aimed at decision makers in hospitals. Designed to help hospitals set up community cholesterol screening events, "The Cholesterol Connection" encompasses mail, telemarketing and personal consultation to encourage participation "for the heart of your community." Inside the kit are a video and a sales brochure outlining the program.

When moisture makes the difference...

TURN

Turn to
Aristocort A
Triamcinolone Acetonide
Cream 0.1% with AQUATAIN™ hydrophilic base

For moisture that makes the difference
- Enhances steroid delivery to the inflammation site
- Penetration is enhanced up to 100 times when the skin is hydrated.[1] "Any delivery system that enhances penetration significantly should increase efficacy."[2]

Soothes and moisturizes damaged skin
- Softens damaged skin as it penetrates dry, scaly lesions and thickened crusts

The proven effectiveness of triamcinolone
- Promotes healing of atopic, seborrheic, contact, and other eczematous dermatoses
- Close to 30 years of proven success in the treatment of mild-to-moderate steroid-responsive dermatoses
*Trademark, American Cyanamid Company

Also available in a self-occluding ointment

Gentle and easy to use
- Comfortable—less stinging and burning than fluocinonide[3]
- Contains no parabens, lanolin, or propylene glycol
- Mild enough for pediatric use[1]
- Available in 0.025%, 0.1%, and 0.5% strengths and a variety of sizes

Wetter is better™

Prescribe Aristocort A—effective therapy enhanced with the power of water

[1] Children may absorb proportionally larger amounts of topical corticosteroids and thus be more susceptible to systemic toxicity.

Please see last page for full Prescribing Information.

Product: **Aristocort A®**
Ad Agency: **Dugan Farley Communications Associates, Inc.**
Client: **Lederle Laboratories**
Art Director: **Eric Rathje**
Illustrator: **E.T. Steadman**
Copywriter: **Mike Marino**

The circular panel shows a parched landscape bisected by a bone-dry stream bed. Then you slowly turn the handle of the wheel apparatus 180 degrees, and *voilà*—the same scene reappears, magically transformed, as a lush meadow with a rippling blue stream. The theme of this imaginative sales aid is stated in the headline: "When moisture makes the difference." The product is Aristocort A®, a healing agent with a water-containing base that helps soften skin lesions. According to Michael Marino, copy group supervisor, the long-established product "required a new and innovative sales promotion piece." Utilizing existing art, the wheel device was deliberately designed so that the transition from dry to moist landscape would "take as much time as possible to keep the physician audience involved."

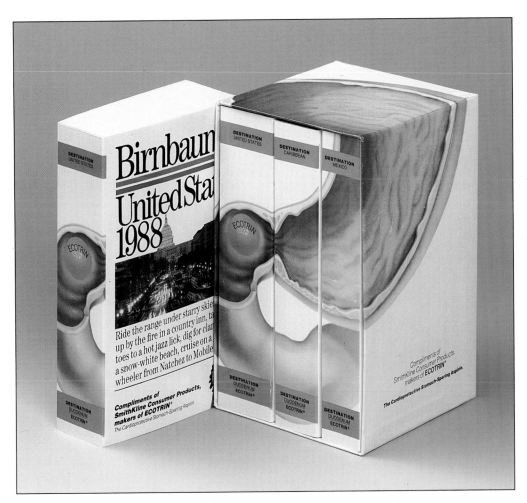

Product: **ECOTRIN**®
Ad Agency: **Lavey/Wolff/Swift Inc.**
Client: **SmithKline Consumer Products**
Art Directors: **Peter Zamiska, Jane Zusi**
Illustrator: **Bonnie Hofkin**
Copywriter: **Al Gerstein**

Here's an ingeniously designed premium aimed at office-based internists and cardiologists. Together, the spines and slipcase of three travel guides form an illustration of the duodenum and vicinity. The "Destination Duodenum" theme promotes one of the major benefits of ECOTRIN®, a safety-coated aspirin that travels past the stomach to prevent gastric upset. Developed to provide sales reps with an entrée into physicians' offices, the set was delivered one volume at a time; the plan was to create initial excitement on the part of physicians so that follow-up appointments would be scheduled. V.P./Account Supervisor Eric S. Malter writes that the premium successfully opened doors for the recently formed sales force.

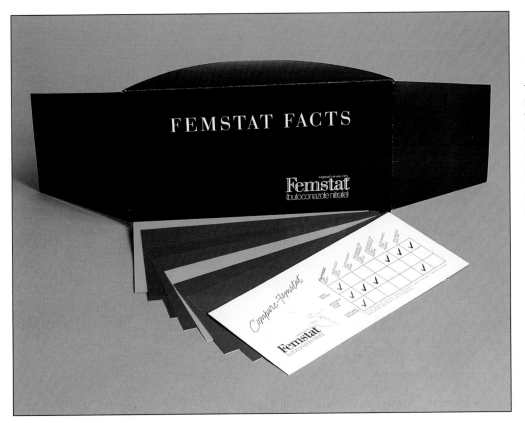

Product: **Femstat**®
Ad Agency: **Vicom/FCB**
Client: **Syntex Laboratories, Inc.**
Art Director: **Penny DeWind**
Copywriter: **Bob Finkel**

These colorful flash cards for Femstat® serve as quick-hitting visual aids for sales presentations to MDs. On the back of each color-coded card is a different benefit, stated succinctly and convincingly, with the key phrase underlined for even greater impact. After the rundown of benefits, a chart compares Femstat® favorably against other treatments for yeast infections in women. The Femstat® logo of a confident woman links all the cards visually. Creative Director Lester Barnett writes that the cards "had to be easy to handle and fun to use."

Product: **Tagamet**®
Ad Agency: **Northstar Productions**
Client: **Smith Kline & French Laboratories**
Art Directors: **Mike Lazur, Neil Paulino**
Illustrators: **John Holmes, Ed Renfro, Chris Butler**
Copywriter: **Joe Harris**

This multi-component stomach care kit from Smith Kline & French Laboratories was designed for physicians to give to their ulcer-prone patients. Part of the firm's integrated promotional/educational Stomach tlc™ program, the kit informs patients about ulcers while treating them to a free sample of Tagamet®, the ulcer-healing preparation from Smith Kline & French. The spunky Claymation stomach character serves as a mascot for the program and has appeared extensively on TV. The kit includes several items—all assembled in a compact package that generates friendly reassurance as well as awareness. Illustration credits go to John Holmes for "Welcome to Stomach tlc®," Chris Butler for the diet poster, and Ed Renfro for "Hi! I'm Your Stomach," the coupon, the magnet, and the cassette and kit covers.

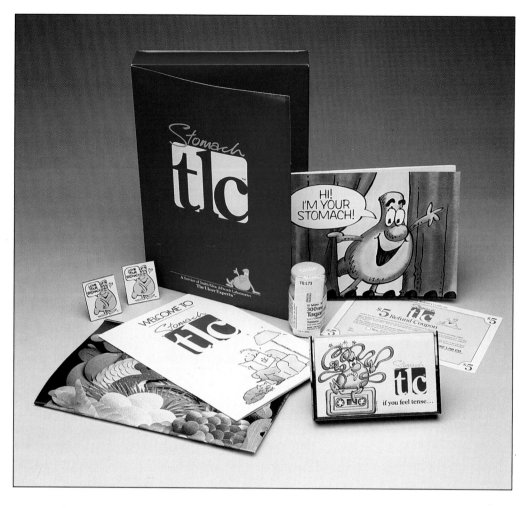

Product: **THEOLAIR**™-**SR**
Design Firm: **Hedstrom/Blessing, Inc.**
Client: **3M Riker**
Art Director: **Heather Olson**
Illustrator: **Robin Moline**
Copywriter: **Sue Gustafson**
Production: **Wendy Danko, Jan Holland, Joe Radick**

The famed "midnight ride" of Paul Revere called America's allergists to the fore in this appealing invitation, which urged them to visit the 3M Riker booth at an annual ACA/AACIA convention in Boston. The promotion included a self-mailer and a poster—both featuring the indefatigable Mr. Revere on horseback. The mailer opens to surprise readers with a "pop-up" of Boston's Old North Church. Depending on whether the steeple has one or two windows punched out ("One if by land, two if by sea"—remember?), the mailer could be a Grand Prize-winning ticket in the sweepstakes held during the show—but you had to bring the piece to the booth to find out.

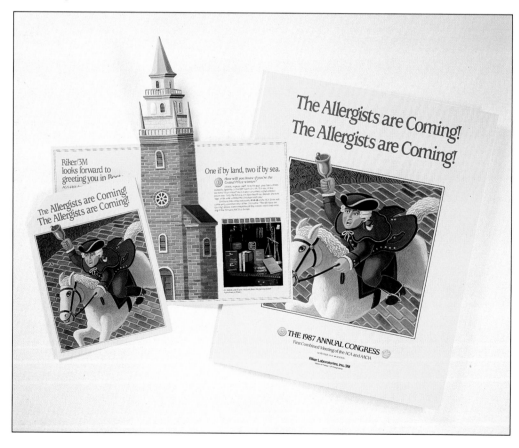

Products: **Riker Product Line**
Design Firm: **Hedstrom/Blessing, Inc.**
Client: **3M Riker**
Art Director: **Dick Pynn**
Illustrator: **Andrea Roads**
Copywriter: **Sue Gustafson**
Production: **Joe Radick**

"Mime's the word" in this multifaceted promotion from 3M Riker. Designed to publicize the firm's booth at the American Association of Family Physicians (AAFP) show in San Francisco, which featured mime entertainment for MDs and their families, the program reaps puns from the word "mime" and cheerfully exploits San Francisco's favorite song to tug at the reader's heartstrings. The promotion encompassed premiums (heart-shaped "Be Mime" helium-filled balloons and four-color silkscreened "I Got Mime in San Francisco" T-shirts), a big self-mailer with magenta hearts and a silvery foil mirror pasted inside, and of course, the mime act, featuring a local professional mime, to draw crowds to the booth. Account Executive Rebecca McManus tells us "there was no question, the show was highly successful for 3M Riker."

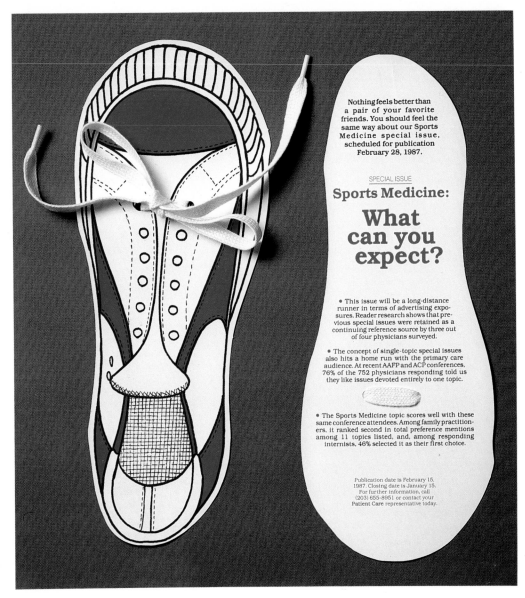

Product: *Patient Care* **Advertising**
Design Firm: **In-house**
Publisher: **Medical Economics Co. Inc.—**
Patient Care
Art Director: **Elizabeth R. Pollack**
Illustrator: **Roy Doty**

Here's a memorable magazine promotion that makes a good run at drumming up advertising dollars. To promote a special issue devoted to sports medicine, *Patient Care* created this engaging sneaker piece complete with an actual, neatly tied shoelace. On the back, the copy persuades potential advertisers that the issue will be a success with the physician audience, characterizing it as a "long-distance runner in terms of advertising exposures." In other words, the magazine would be kept by physicians as "a continuing reference source." The copy also cites physician surveys that demonstrate the popularity of sports medicine as a topic and single-subject magazine issues in general.

Product: **Orimune**®
Ad Agency: **Carrafiello, Diehl & Associates, Inc.**
Client: **Lederle Laboratories/Lederle Biologicals**
Art Directors: **Bill Alderisio, Caron Leeds, Loren Mork**
Photographer: **Allen Vogel**
Copywriters: **Bill Green, Leo Vanderpot**

The image of a discarded leg brace commemorates the 25th anniversary of Orimune®, an oral polio vaccine that has been available longer than any other in its class. Wrapped around a tissue box that serves as a promotional giveaway, the graphic was intended to symbolize polio without showing an actual victim. In addition, writes Senior V.P./Creative Group Supervisor William Green, the empty brace also celebrates "the victory over this virus achieved by this vaccine," which has virtually wiped out polio in the U.S. The confetti streamers pictured around the leg brace add a jubilant note.

Product: **NAPROSYN**® **B.I.D.**
Ad Agency: **Vicom/FCB**
Client: **Syntex Laboratories, Inc.**
Art Director: **Stephen Mullens**
Copywriter: **Bob Finkel**

This big (12½" x 16") flip chart for NAPROSYN® B.I.D., the well-established arthritis medication, provides the sales rep with enough material for a complete presentation to groups of physicians in hospitals and nursing homes. Positioned as the "#1 NSAID worldwide," the drug is portrayed as a versatile, effective, low-risk therapy throughout an extensive series of benefit statements and colorful charts. It's worth noting that, in addition to the many benefits to patients, the piece also conveys the advantages of NAPROSYN® for the physician: "flexible dosage," "physician maintains control of therapy," and more. Also mentioned are the numerous educational and counseling tools supplied to physicians by Syntex Laboratories, Inc., makers of NAPROSYN®.

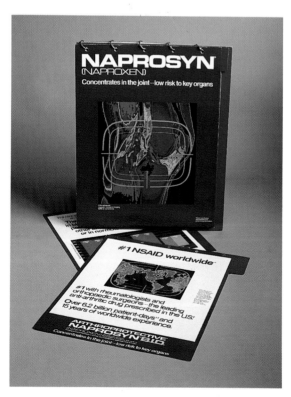

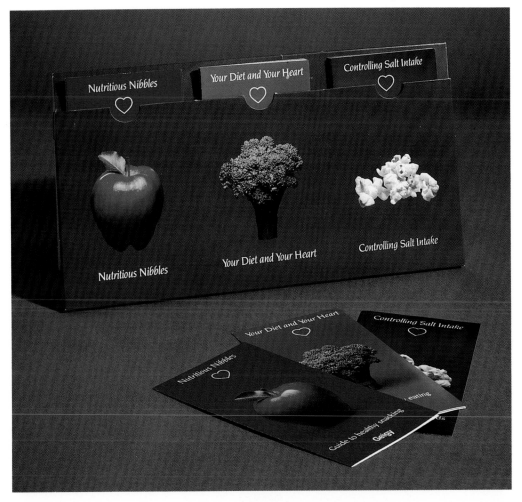

Product: **Lopressor**®
Ad Agency: **C & G Advertising Inc. (In-house)**
Client: **Ciba-Geigy Pharmaceuticals**
Art Director: **Myrtle Johnson**
Photographer: **George Diebold**
Copywriter: **Pat Wisnewski**

This tabletop display unit holds three different pamphlets aimed at patients on restricted diets. A wholesome food item appears on the front beneath each pamphlet; the back of the display states the benefits of Lopressor®, a preferential beta blocker, in concise bulleted form. So, while the front of the display was directed at patients, the back would be used by sales reps during presentations to physicians. The idea for this double-duty sales tool originated with the in-house agency at Ciba-Geigy.

Title: **"Quality of Life Across the Continuum of Cancer Care"**
Ad Agency: **Gross Townsend Frank Hoffman, Inc.**
Client: **Adria Laboratories**
Art Director: **Carveth Kramer**
Illustrator: **Rich Grote**
Copywriter: **Ronnie Hoffman**

Addressed to oncologists, this five-part multi-dimensional mailing eventually assembles inside a slipcase to form an image of two hands stretching across the spines of the packages. Clasped in a gesture of communication and support, the hands represent the relationship between oncologist and cancer patient. The five albums take an in-depth look at the needs of patients on chemotherapy, as well as the doctor's role—both emotional and medical—in conducting their therapy. Each package deals with a single topic. According to Executive V.P./Creative Director David Frank, the albums—which include video and audio cassettes as well as booklets—presented physicians with "tools they could use with their patients to counter negative feelings and false information about chemotherapy."

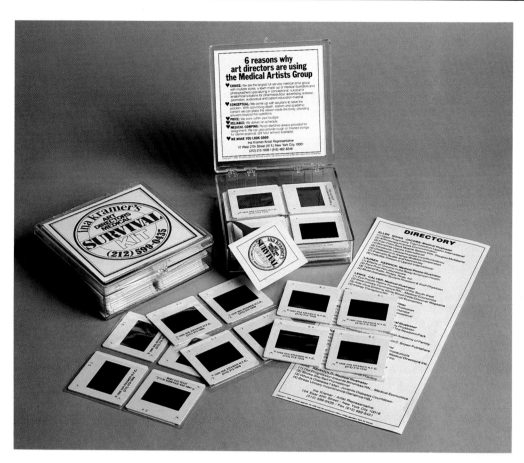

Title: **"Ina Kramer's Art Directors Medical Survival Kit"**
Design Firm: **Lois Muller Studio**
Client: **Ina Kramer**
Art Director: **Ina Kramer**

Here is one of those proverbial "good things" that come in small packages: a unique promotional tool aimed at the people who usually do the promoting. Targeted at art directors, this compact "Survival Kit" helps agent Ina Kramer sell the services of the medical artists and photographers she represents. At the same time, it furnishes the art directors with ready access to top talent. The "kit" is a clear plastic box measuring just 4³/₄" x 4³/₄" x 1¹/₂" high; neatly stacked inside are transparencies of works by several artists and photographers. (These are keyed to an enclosed directory for easy reference.) On the cover, the agent's phone number is prominently displayed in a circular logo that would be readily identifiable throughout a series of mailings. On the underside of the cover—which stays visible as the prospective client examines the slides— the selling copy persuasively communicates six key benefits of the Medical Artists Group.

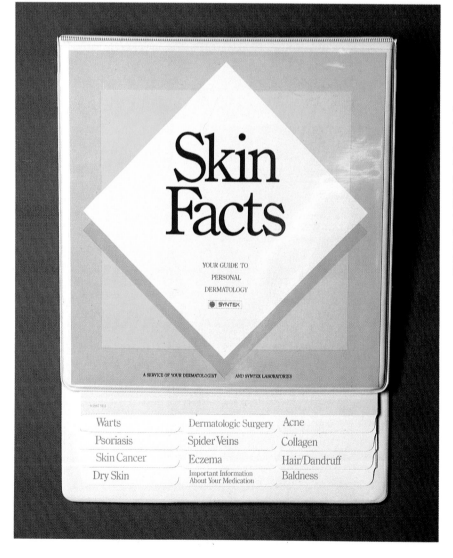

Title: **"Skin Facts"**
Ad Agency: **Vicom/FCB**
Client: **Syntex Laboratories, Inc.**
Art Director: **Vanya Akraboff**
Illustrator: **Luther Knov**
Copywriter: **Caren Spinner**

Educational but accessible, this "Skin Facts" guide from Syntex Laboratories, Inc., informs patients about various dermatological conditions—from warts to baldness. Designed to be read in the dermatologist's waiting room, the 9" x 12" loose-leaf guide is tabbed at the bottom so all topics are readily visible (the cover is shorter than the back panel so that the tabs are clearly displayed). Creative Director Lester Barnett writes that the agency was given instructions to make the piece "look authoritative and thorough," yet keep the "educational style light and inviting." The articles carry this out: they're engagingly written yet full of useful information. Cartoons add a light touch and break up the text.

Title: **"Toxicodendron Recognition Guide"**
Ad Agency: **Vicom/FCB**
Client: **Syntex Laboratories, Inc.**
Art Directors: **Stephen Mullens, Joseph Rozon**
Illustrator: **Will Nelson**
Copywriter: **John Gorham**

Toxicodendron is the generic term for those familiar "poison" plants that lie in wait for careless hikers and picnickers. They're better known by their common names: poison ivy, poison oak, poison sumac. To help dermatologists warn their patients about these outdoor nuisances, Syntex Laboratories furnished these vividly illustrated Toxicodendron Recognition Guides. Developed by Vicom/FCB and illustrated by Will Nelson, the guides unfold to depict each plant as it appears at different times of the year. Range maps are also included. Creative Director Lester Barnett writes that the success of the program prompted the creation of pocket-sized versions as giveaways for patients.

Title: **"MED Start™"**
Ad Agency: **C & G Advertising Inc. (In-house)**
Client: **Ciba-Geigy Pharmaceutical Co.**
Art Director: **Ron Vareltzis**
Designer: **Pat Pickard**
Copywriter: **Kevin Purcell**

One of the tenets of marketing is to establish brand loyalty while the customer is still young. Ciba-Geigy seized a ripe opportunity by developing the MED Start™ kit for a target audience of medical students and interns—all potential customers for life. Not overtly commercial in appearance, the package includes two audiocassettes about the legal and economic considerations of starting up a medical practice. Tucked inside the cover flap are two publications: *MED Start™ Magazine*, subtitled "Winning strategies for starting your medical practice"; and *MEDirectory*, a guide to services offered by Ciba-Geigy. Both publications include advertising and prescribing information for specific Ciba-Geigy products.

Product: **NOROXIN**®
Design Firm: **Hal Lewis Design**
Client: **Merck Sharp & Dohme**
Art Director: **Gilbert R. Albright**
Copywriter: **Scott Bolenbaugh**

This appealing NOROXIN® promotional display dispenses samples of the drug. Developed by Hal Lewis Design, it features a playful visual device that deserves notice. Look closely at the packaging: the two pills take the place of kidneys in the illustration of the urinary tract. The display doubles as an attention-getting sales kit for reps from Merck Sharp & Dohme.

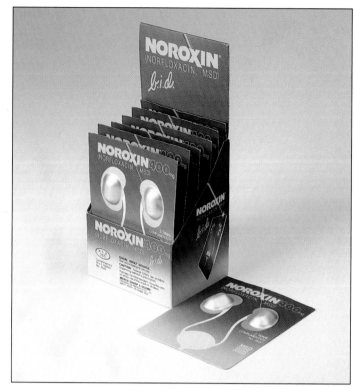

Product: **WyTensin**®
Ad Agency: **Materia Medica/Creative Annex Inc.**
Client: **Wyeth-Ayerst Laboratories**
Art Director: **Don Kahn**
Illustrators: **Lowren West, John Trotta**
Copywriter: **Amy Schachter**

The Salt Watch Program comes with a supply of diet booklets aimed at hypertensive patients and those concerned about their salt intake. The booklets contain not only helpful dietary information, but also *coupons* for low-sodium foods found at most supermarkets. Because the package opens to reveal an advertising spread for WyTensin® aimed at the physician, the Salt Watch Program serves as a sales promotion tool as well as a source of information for the patient.

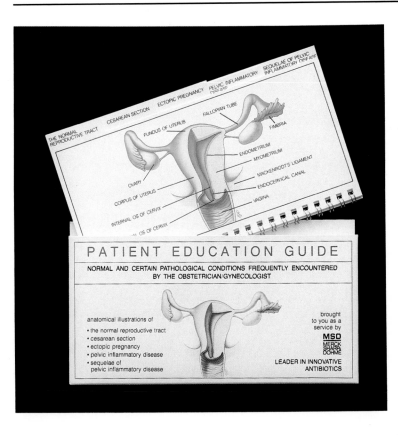

Products: **Mefoxin®, PRIMAXIN®**
Design Firm: **Hal Lewis Design**
Client: **Merck Sharp & Dohme**
Art Director: **Gilbert R. Albright**
Illustrator: **Robert Demarest**
Copywriter: **Howard Pien**

Developed as a teaching aid for OB/GYNs to use with their patients, this *Patient Education Guide* also promotes two antibiotics from Merck Sharp & Dohme: Mefoxin® and PRIMAXIN®. Like the similar general guide produced for Merck (also shown on this page), this booklet is spiral bound and printed on heavy laminated stock, with the five charts step-indexed for easy access. The difference is that this guide focuses exclusively on the female reproductive system. Each chart depicts a variety of related disorders—from ectopic pregnancy to pelvic inflammatory diseases—and is accompanied by a separate chart of the normal anatomy.

Products: **Mefoxin®, PRIMAXIN®**
Design Firm: **Hal Lewis Design**
Client: **Merck Sharp & Dohme**
Art Director: **Gilbert Albright**
Illustrator: **Jane Hurd**
Copywriter: **Bonnie Piestrak**

Illustrator Jane Hurd created the clear, accurate anatomical drawings for this spiral bound *Patient Education Guide*. Supplied to surgeons by Merck Sharp & Dohme, the booklet is step-indexed for quick reference to full-color plates of the respiratory tract, upper GI tract, lower GI tract, urinary tract, and leg/foot. Printed on heavy laminated stock, each chart shows the highlighted area in its normal state, accompanied by details of various pathological conditions to facilitate explanation to patients. The booklet also promotes two of Merck Sharp & Dohme's products—Mefoxin® and PRIMAXIN®. Prescribing information is included.

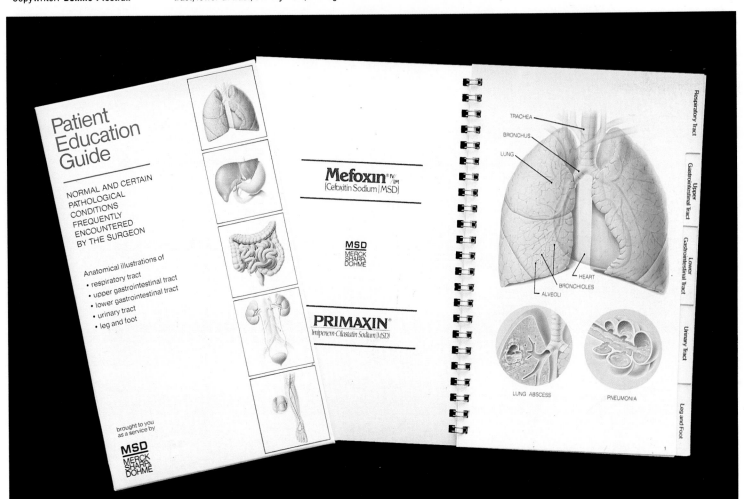

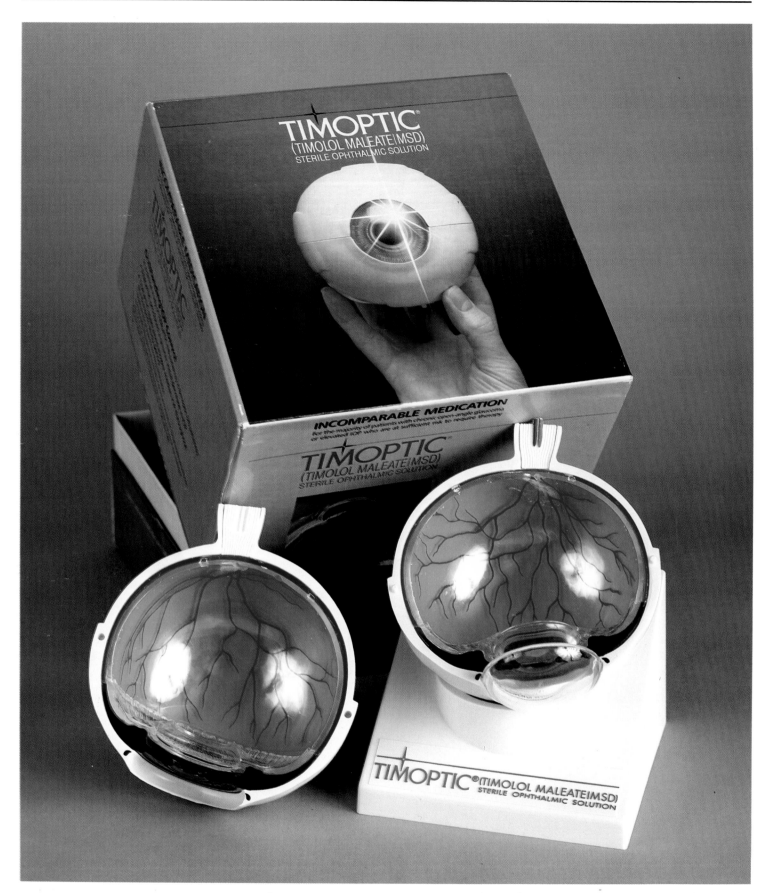

Product: **TIMOPTIC**®
Design Firm: **Hal Lewis Design**
Client: **Merck Sharp & Dohme**
Art Directors: **Don Kruzinski, Matthew Bennett, Pat Sinclair**
Illustrator: **Vicom/FCB**
Photographer: **Hal Lewis Design**

This handsome model of the human eye features a transparent cornea and lens, with a realistic brown iris sandwiched between them. The model opens up to reveal the inner structure of the eye, complete with the intricate network of blood vessels. Developed to promote TIMOPTIC®, an ophthalmic solution, the model serves as a useful educational tool for patients. At the same time, it reminds ophthalmologists about the benefits of TIMOPTIC®. Art Director Don Kruzinski writes that the packaging utilizes artwork designed and used in ads.

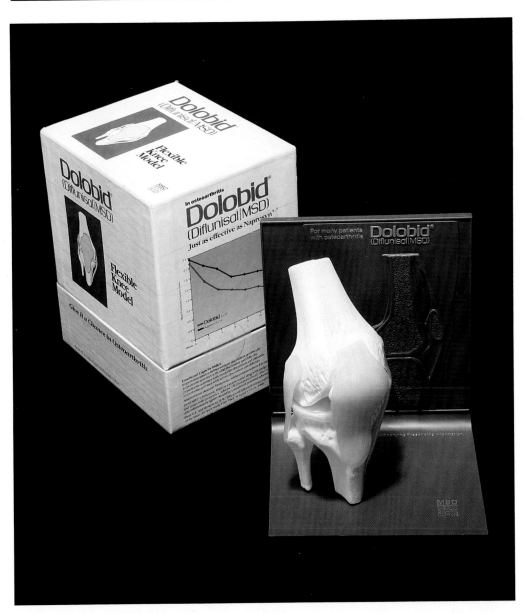

Product: **Dolobid®**
Design Firm: **Sulpizio Associates**
Client: **Merck Sharp & Dohme**
Art Directors: **Matthew Bennett, Don Kruzinski, Fred Sulpizio**
Model Maker: **Kurt Loeb**
Copywriter: **Steve Tom**

This working model of a normal knee serves as a sales tool for Dolobid®. Thoroughly researched and anatomically precise, the knee simulates real-life motion with the aid of flexible rubber ligaments. Model maker Kurt Loeb rendered all the surfaces with painstaking attention to detail. Besides serving as an educational tool for patients, the knee is packaged in a box that promotes the benefits of Dolobid® to physicians. A graph compares the drug with NAPROSYN® while the copy asserts that Dolobid® is just as effective.

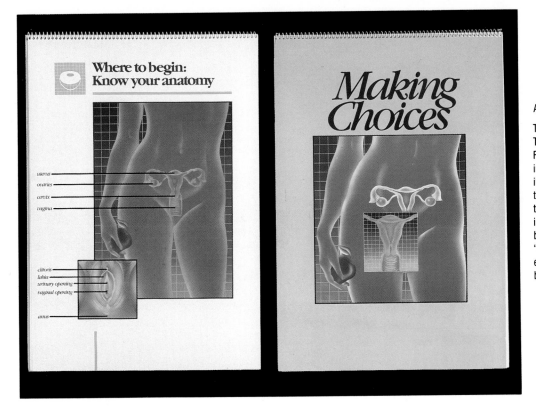

Product: **Today™ Contraceptive Sponge**
Ad Agency: **Gross Townsend Frank Hoffman, Inc.**
Client: **VLI Corp.**
Art Director: **Karen Klein**
Illustrator: **Carol Gillot**
Copywriter: **Marietta Abrams**
Account Person: **Jane Townsend**

To introduce a new concept in birth control—the Today™ Contraceptive Sponge—Gross Townsend Frank Hoffman, Inc., created this 12" x 17" flip chart to instruct women on how to use the product. Tastefully illustrated, with an orchid color scheme that echoes the product packaging, the chart takes women through the insertion procedure one step at a time. Each illustrated page is duplicated in black-and-white on the back of the chart, complete with a running script. This "cue card" approach enables physicians and nurses to explain the procedures shown in the illustrations while behind the chart.

Product: **Bactrim**™
Design Firm: **Medical Art, Inc.**
Client: **Roche Pharmaceutical Co.**
Art Director: **Judith Glick**
Illustrator: **Judith Glick**

This versatile sales aid functions as a patient education device, a memo holder for the physician, and a promotional tool for Bactrim™. Since the drug is used in treating chronic bronchitis, emphysema, and bronchial asthma, the anatomical model focuses on the lungs. All three lung disorders are illustrated on removable slides that can slip into place to depict the patient's condition. According to Judith Glick, president of Medical Art, Inc., the unit was "well received"— possibly because, as she tells us, "Doctors love things like this model."

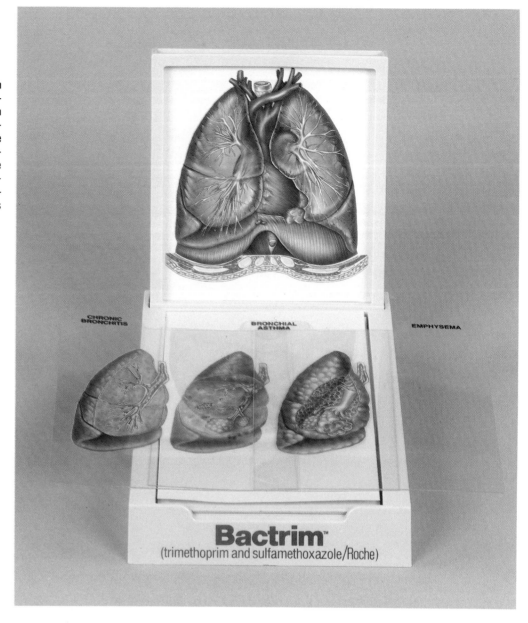

Title: **Milestones (Premiere Issue)**
Publisher: **Thomas L. Maloof**
Sponsor: **Miles, Inc., Pharmaceutical Div.**
Art Director: **Joseph Santoro**
Marketing Firm: **TM Marketing, Inc.**
Photographer: **John Ford**
Managing Editor: **Michael Kaufman**
Production Manager: **Donald J. Stein**
Product Manager: **Michael Wokasch**

The premiere issue of *Milestones*, a publication that bills itself as "The Healthcare Economic Advisory," combines bold graphics with coherent design. The red border and lettering of the cover reappear inside as sharp visual accents, nicely complementing the cool green-gray marble insets.

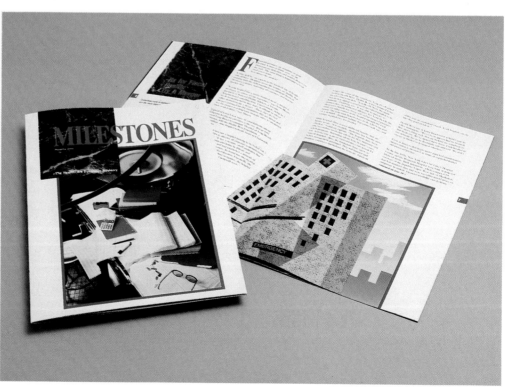

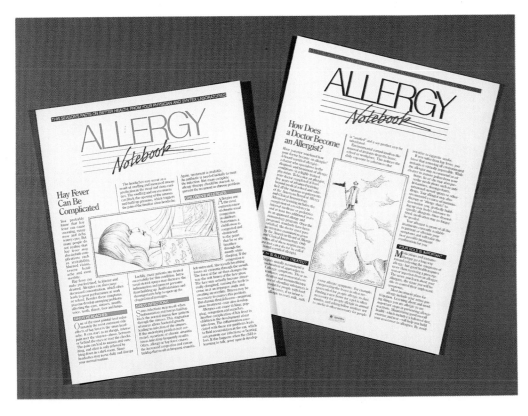

Title: **"Allergy Notebook"**
Ad Agency: **Vicom/FCB**
Client: **Syntex Laboratories, Inc.**
Art Director: **Gail Perry**
Copywriter: **Linda Lipman**

"Allergy Notebook" is a quarterly publication distributed to allergists by Syntex Laboratories, Inc. Intended for the allergy patient, each issue contains articles of interest as well as a question-and-answer column, news about drugs and recent advances, and a quiz (complete with answers printed upside-down). Here's how the program works: the sales rep from Syntex leaves two complimentary copies for the physician; the accompanying letter encourages allergists to make photocopies for distribution to their patients. (Each issue includes a blank space for the physician's imprint.) Copies can also be left in the waiting room. Produced on a tight budget, the publication appeals to the patient while reflecting the professionalism of the practitioner.

Graphic: **Public Health Service Brochures**
Design Firm: **Susan Foster Graphics**
Client: **National Institutes of Health**
Art Director: **Linda Brown**
Illustrator: **Susan Foster**

Four distinctive yet visually related brochures alert the public to the current state of knowledge on four different diseases: Paget's disease, cystic fibrosis, osteoporosis, and epidermolysis bullosa. Designed by Susan Foster (illustrator) and Linda Brown (art director) for the National Institutes of Health, the brochures use single colors and symbolic graphics that visually capture the essence of each disease. According to Foster, the designs had to "work within the format already established by the Institute."

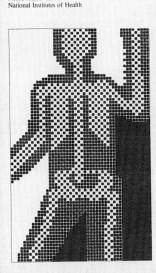

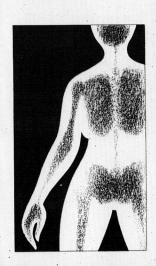

Title: **"Macular Degeneration"**
Design Firm: **Palay/Beaubois**
Client: **The Retina Research Fund,**
St. Mary's Hospital
Art Director: **Betsy A. Palay**
Illustrator: **Betsy A. Palay**
Photographer: **Howard Schatz, MD**
Copywriter: **Howard Schatz, MD**

Created for The Retina Research Fund at St. Mary's Hospital, this handsome booklet treats the subject of macular degeneration, an eye disease that can lead to blindness. Appropriately printed in large type for the sight-impaired, the booklet uses color diagrams and photographs of the eye, as well as numerous "people photographs" to humanize the subject. Written by Howard Schatz, MD, the booklet was designed to assist patients and family members in coping with the disorder and making decisions about treatment. Betsy A. Palay of Palay/Beaubois writes that it was also intended to "allay fears as much as possible within the context of truthfulness."

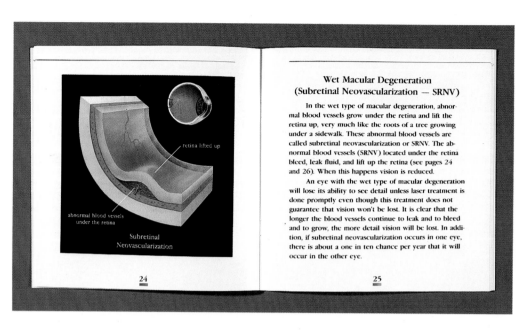

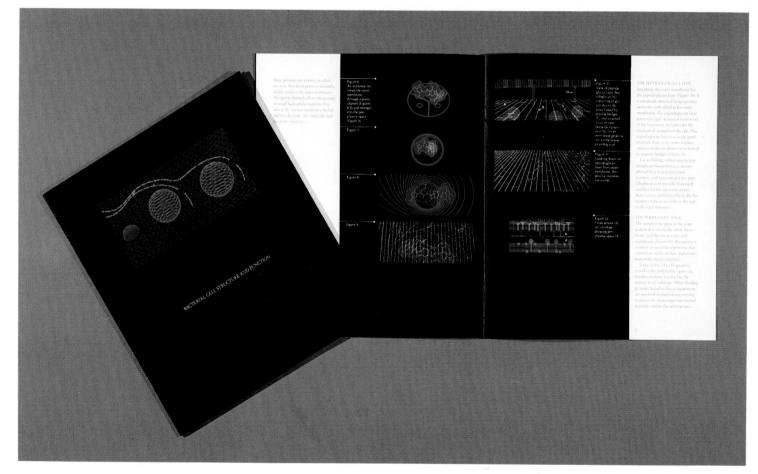

Title: **"CinEcoli™"**
Ad Agency: **IntraMed Communications**
Client: **Roche Laboratories**
Art Director: **Ida Jennings**
Graphic Illustrations: **Robert Abel Associates**

Microbiologists, physicians, designers, printers, and medical writers all collaborated on this strikingly illus-trated monograph from Roche Laboratories. Designed to accompany a stereographic film, the booklet examines the structure and replication of the familiar bacterium E. coli, as well as the means by which antibiotics are known to interfere with its functioning. The spectacular computer graphics are spot-laminated on a matte black background.

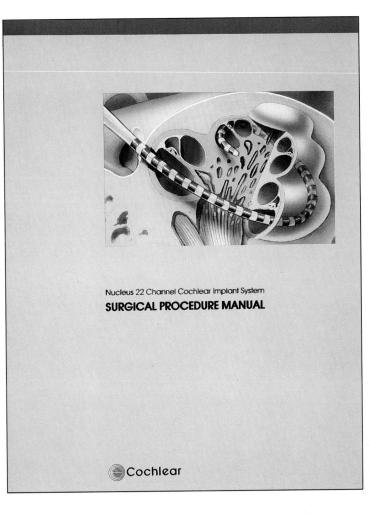

Nucleus 22 Channel Cochlear Implant System

SURGICAL PROCEDURE MANUAL

Cochlear

Product: **Nucleus 22 Channel Cochlear Implant System**
Design Firm: **Zilberts & Associates**
Client: **Cochlear Corp.**
Art Director: **Ed Zilberts**
Illustrator: **Ed Zilberts**
Copywriters: **Graeme M. Clark and others**

Written by a team of medical experts, this richly illustrated *Surgical Procedure Manual* shows otologists how to perform a cochlear implant. This delicate procedure, which involves drilling through the skull to reach the innermost region of the ear, is clearly presented in nine stages, with numerous color illustrations by Ed Zilberts, design firm president. The piece was developed both as an educational tool to be used in conjunction with training courses, and as a marketing tool for Cochlear Corporation. Writes Zilberts, "There is always something exciting about creating communication tools for leading edge medical technologies."

5.0 The Receiver/Stimulator Package Bed The receiver/stimulator package bed should be made so that the package will be stable and not slide forward or rock. The disc-shaped template is sited over the mastoid region (Figure 11). The anterior edge must be at least 1 cm behind the postauricular sulcus, to allow clearance for a patient's eyeglass frame. The center of the package bed should not be too high to encroach on the thin bone over the squamous temporal bone, and not too low to rock on the curved part of the skull behind the mastoid process. Use a 2 mm cutting burr around the inside of the ring to delineate the site of the bony excavation.

Using the cutting burrs, a circular bed is then drilled to fit the receiver/stimulator (Figure 12) and its sides and bottom are smoothed using the special diamond paste

milling burrs (Figure 13). The siting of this bed is made by releasing the retractors and positioning the dummy package so that the anterior edge lies at least 1 cm behind the postaural sulcus. During the drilling dura may be exposed. The mastoid emissary vein can be encountered and bleeding can usually be controlled with bone wax. Pairs of holes may be drilled on either side of the bed and also more posteriorly in the region that will underly the antenna in order to accommodate the receiver/stimulator package stay sutures, which will be used later to secure the receiver/stimulator.

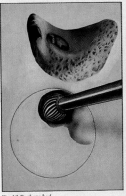

Fig. 13 Milling burr

"The disc shaped template is used to ensure that the bed is just larger than the package, so that a snug fit will be obtained."

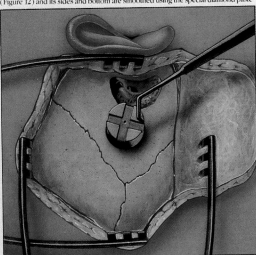

"The anterior edge must be at least 1 cm behind the post-auricular sulcus, to allow clearance for a patient's eyeglass frame."

Fig. 11 Disc template

Fig. 12 Package bed   Fig. 14 Disc template

After removing the bone and completing the package bed, the disc shaped template is used to ensure that the bed is just larger than the package, so that a snug fit will be obtained (Figure 14).

In some cases it may be difficult to drill the bed deep enough to accept the receiver/stimulator without exposing dura. In this case, the bone may be drilled down to dura circumferentially leaving a free island of bone in the center which can be depressed for proper package placements.

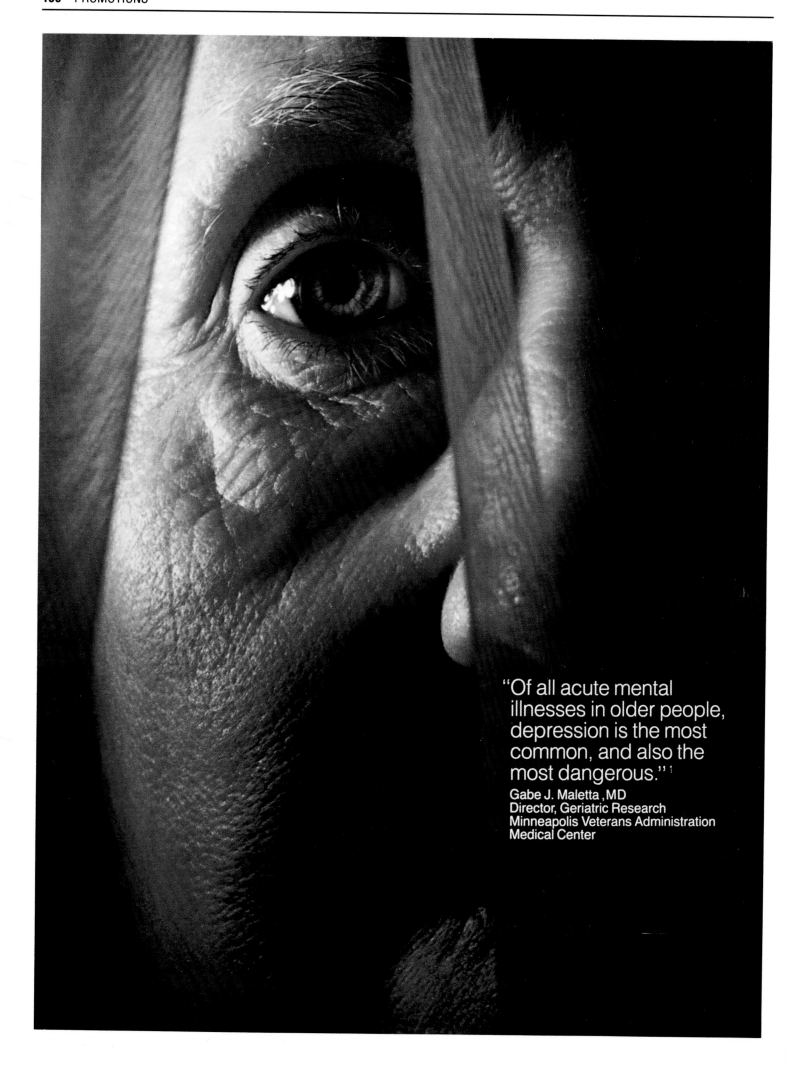

"Of all acute mental illnesses in older people, depression is the most common, and also the most dangerous." [1]

Gabe J. Maletta, MD
Director, Geriatric Research
Minneapolis Veterans Administration
Medical Center

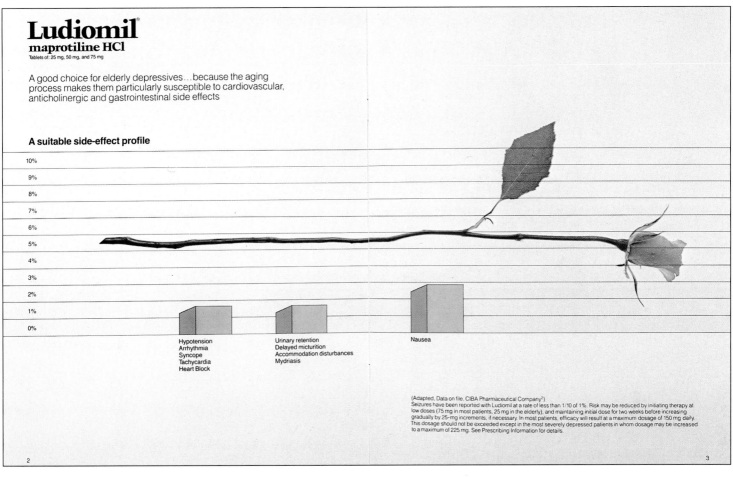

Ludiomil®
maprotiline HCl
Tablets of: 25 mg, 50 mg, and 75 mg

A good choice for elderly depressives…because the aging process makes them particularly susceptible to cardiovascular, anticholinergic and gastrointestinal side effects

A suitable side-effect profile

10%	
9%	
8%	
7%	
6%	
5%	
4%	
3%	
2%	
1%	
0%	

Hypotension
Arrhythmia
Syncope
Tachycardia
Heart Block

Urinary retention
Delayed micturition
Accommodation disturbances
Mydriasis

Nausea

(Adapted, Data on file, CIBA Pharmaceutical Company[2])
Seizures have been reported with Ludiomil at a rate of less than 1/10 of 1%. Risk may be reduced by initiating therapy at low doses (75 mg in most patients, 25 mg in the elderly), and maintaining initial dose for two weeks before increasing gradually by 25-mg increments, if necessary. In most patients, efficacy will result at a maximum dosage of 150 mg daily. This dosage should not be exceeded except in the most severely depressed patients in whom dosage may be increased to a maximum of 225 mg. See Prescribing Information for details.

2

3

Product: **Ludiomil®**
Ad Agency: **C & G Advertising Inc. (In-house)**
Client: **Ciba Pharmaceutical Co.**
Art Director: **Bob Talarczyk**
Photographer: **Michael Furman**
Copywriter: **Pat Blagden**

A haunting image of an elderly face, viewed in startling close-up, reminds psychiatrists and GPs about the seriousness of depression in older patients. The single quotation on the cover affirms this message, while the stunning photograph of the face drives home the emotional side of the message. Inside, the first spread (shown here) documents the favorable side-effect profile of Ludiomil®, an antidepressant. In the second spread, the mysterious rose reappears in a domestic setting—along with a distance shot of the woman whose face gazed out at us from the cover.

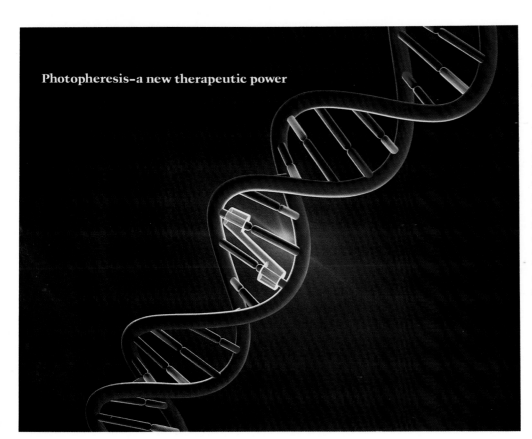

Photopheresis–a new therapeutic power

Title: **"Photophoresis—a new therapeutic power"**
Ad Agency: **Falcone & Associates**
Client: **Therakos—A Johnson & Johnson Co.**
Art Director: **Frank Chesek**
Illustrator: **Earl Quam**
Copywriter: **Alan Blackburn**

The double helix of a DNA molecule graces the cover of this booklet announcing an important new cancer therapy: photophoresis, a technology that blocks replication of abnormal T cells by bombarding the DNA with ultraviolet rays. The handsome cover art clues us in to the procedure: two of the nucleotides in the DNA of a cancerous cell are bonded together, keeping the two halves of the molecule from separating and replicating. The faint gleam of sunlight in the background represents the UV rays that form an integral part of the therapy. William Falcone, agency president, writes that it is "always great to work on a new technology that saves lives."

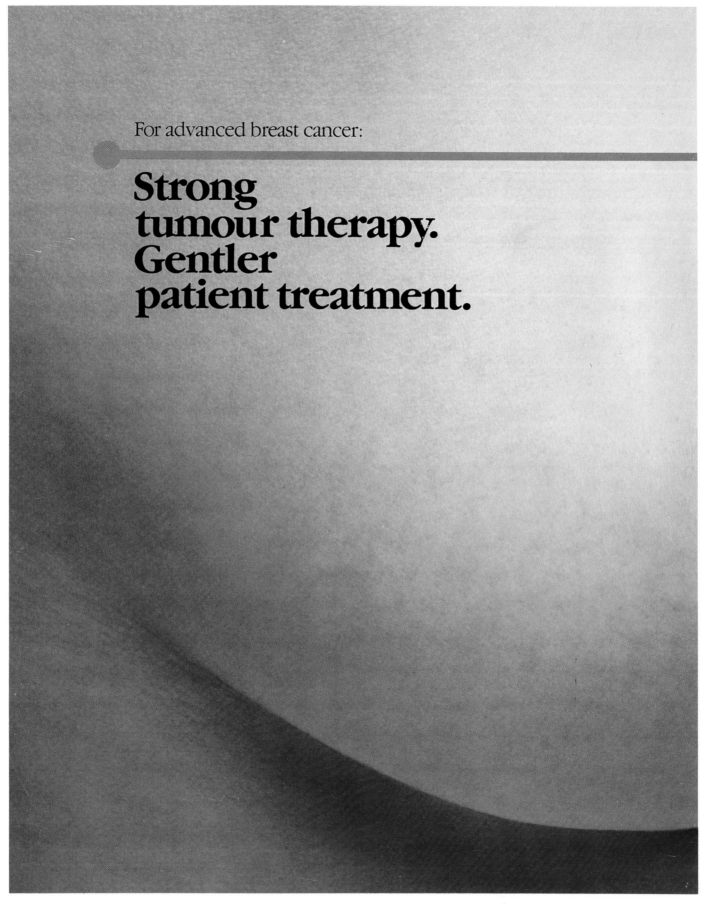

For advanced breast cancer:

Strong tumour therapy. Gentler patient treatment.

Product: **Pharmorubicin**
Ad Agency: **Gross Townsend Frank Hoffman, Inc.**
Client: **Adria Laboratories**
Art Director: **David Frank**
Copywriter: **Jane Harper**

Strong yet gentle—that's the theme of this brochure for Pharmorubicin, a drug used in the treatment of advanced breast cancer. The cover photo discloses the soft, curved lower contour of the breast without revealing all; inside, an X-ray discloses the dreaded tumor. Here, the bulleted copy pinpoints the benefits of the drug; subsequent spreads provide test data to sub-stantiate the claimed benefits. According to Executive V.P./Creative Director David Frank, the agency had to tread cautiously in positioning Pharmorubicin against Adriamycin® (the leading drug for treatment of breast cancer), since both are manufactured by the client. What they did was to position Pharmorubicin as the preferred treatment for three high-risk patient groups.

"**I** DON'T KNOW OF ANY OTHER HUMAN OCCUPATION, EVEN INCLUDING

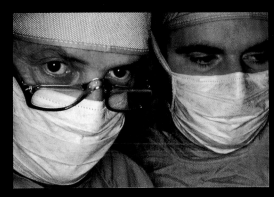

WHAT I HAVE SEEN OF ART, IN WHICH PEOPLE ENGAGED IN IT ARE SO CAUGHT UP, SO TOTALLY PREOCCUPIED, SO DRIVEN BEYOND THEIR STRENGTH AND RESOURCES."

PASSING THE TORCH

THE THIRD CENTURY OF HARVARD MEDICINE

Title: **"Passing the Torch—The Third Century of Harvard Medicine"**
Design Firm: **Barton Gillet**
Client: **Harvard Medical School**
Art Directors: **Claude Skelton, William Shinn**
Photographer: **Ken Haas**
Copywriter: **Kim Carlin**

"Passing the Torch" is the theme of this 24-page fund-raising booklet for Harvard Medical School. Designed to mark the entry of America's premier medical school into its third century, the oversized (9" x 12") and appropriately distinguished-looking publication exhorts potential contributors to join the campaign "for the sake of our children and all future generations in their struggles against disease and toward better health."

On the cover, a prominently displayed quotation refers to medicine as an occupation that drives its practitioners "beyond their strength and resources." The close-up photograph of two suitably intense surgeons helps reinforce the message. Inside, the booklet relates the long, distinguished history of Harvard Medical School and presents profiles of notable alumni and faculty members.

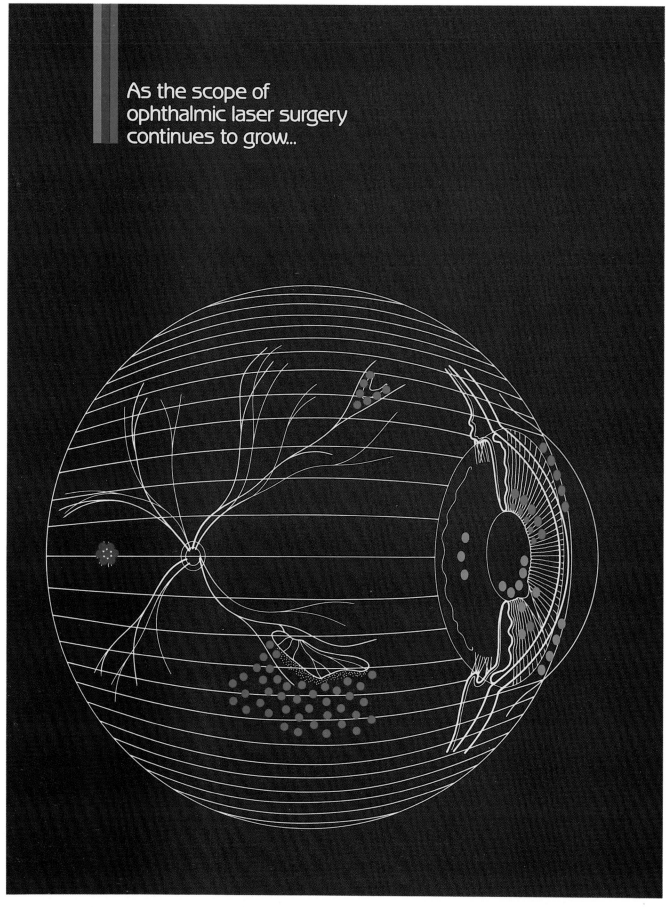

As the scope of
ophthalmic laser surgery
continues to grow...

Product: **9900YAG Ophthalmic Laser**
Ad Agency: **Rainoldi Kerzner & Radcliffe**
Client: **Coherent Medical**
Creative Director: **Charles Schmalz**
Art Director: **Brian Collentine**
Illustrator: **Douglas Wittnebel**
Copywriter: **Barney Currer**

Aimed at ophthalmic surgeons, this high-tech insert for the 9900YAG ophthalmic laser combines sleek architectural graphics with high-impact medical diagrams. Printed on heavy dark-gray stock with brightly colored, sparingly used highlights, the piece attempts to translate laser technology into the physician's frame of reference. Writes V.P./Account Supervisor Susan Hempstead, "Instead of introducing the product in technical terms of watts, nanometers and pulse widths, we focused on the surgeon's need to understand where, when, how and why to use a laser." This was in keeping with the client's desire to position itself as a medical company rather than solely a maker of instruments.

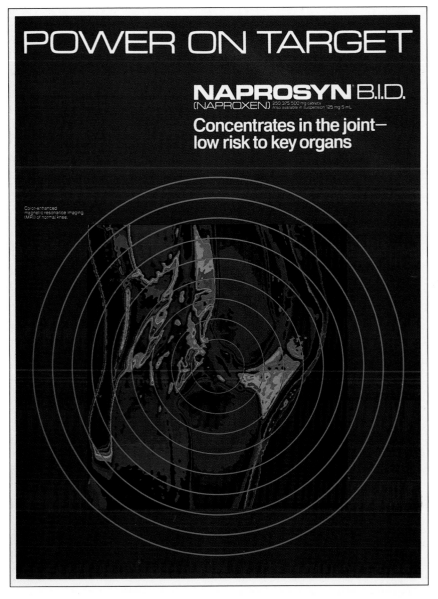

Product: **NAPROSYN**®
Ad Agency: **Vicom/FCB**
Client: **Syntex Laboratories, Inc.**
Art Director: **Stephen Mullens**
Copywriter: **Bob Finkel**

Economical, "on-target" cover copy sets the stage for this effective promotional booklet on NAPROSYN®. The two lines of benefits copy ("Concentrates in the joint—low risk to key organs") position the drug from the outset. Supporting the copy message is a concentric target superimposed over a high-tech image of an arthritic joint. Inside, handsome data presentations and color-enhanced magnetic resonance imaging help drive home the specific benefits of the drug : its efficacy in targeting pain and inflammation, and its low risk of GI and renal side effects. Across the bottom of each spread is a banner that re-emphasizes the targeted nature of the drug.

Title: **"Searle Licensing and Development Brochure"**
Ad Agency: **Hamilton, Carver & Lee**
Client: **G. D. Searle & Co.**
Art Director: **Thom Qualkinbush**
Photographer: **Michel Tcherevkof**
Copywriter: **Jim Lee**

Aimed at CEOs, this appropriately important-looking booklet invites pharmaceutical companies to enter into a special licensing/development agreement with Searle. The cover art symbolically depicts Searle and the target company "coming together" in a mutually favorable relationship. With this vividly hued, futuristic art, the cover effectively conveys a progressive corporate image. At the same time, the tipped-in plate, silver embossed lettering, and sober gray cover stock balance that image with a classic, established look. Inside, the "coming together" visual reappears in different forms, tracing the process by which a company discovers a drug, then turns it over to Searle for development and marketing. The booklet explains the process, outlines the benefits, and supplies biographical profiles of Searle's CEO and V.P. for Licensing and Commercial Development.

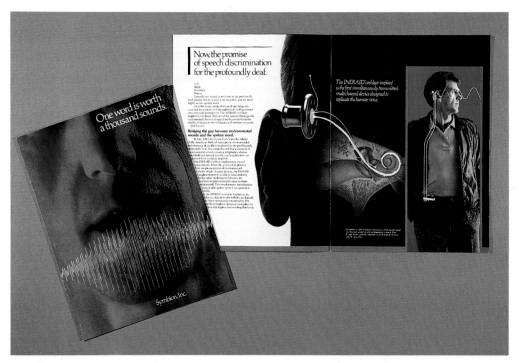

Product: **INERAID™ Cochlear Implant**
Ad Agency: **Forsythe Marcelli Johnson Advertising, Inc.**
Client: **Symbion, Inc.**
Art Director: **Vic Marcelli**
Photographer: **Stan Sholik**
Copywriter: **Jim Forsythe**

Forsythe Marcelli Johnson developed this impressive promotional piece for the INERAID™ cochlear implant, a breakthrough hearing device for the deaf. The cover visual shows a sound wave pattern in front of a speaker's mouth, with the headline message, "One word is worth a thousand sounds"; the reference is to the product's "promise of speech discrimination for the profoundly deaf." Inside, we're shown how the system works, followed by a discussion of the underlying technology and a summary of the client's comprehensive program of testing and education before, during and after the implant. On the back, we read the intriguing case history of a deaf man who can now converse on the telephone, understand foreign accents, and even distinguish between the sounds of a dime and a quarter dropped on a lunch counter.

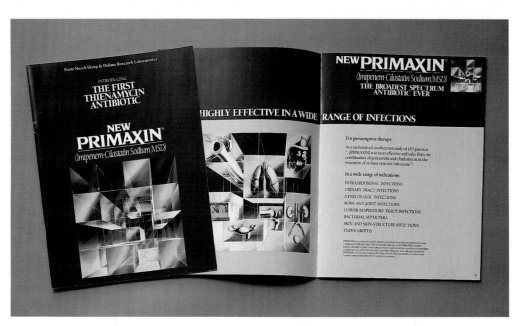

Product: **PRIMAXIN®**
Ad Agency: **Vicom/FCB**
Client: **Merck Sharp & Dohme**
Art Directors: **Gilbert R. Albright, Tom Domanico**
Illustrator: **Gary Meyer**
Copywriter: **Joseph Trudelle**

To introduce Merck Sharp & Dohme's PRIMAXIN®, the first thienamycin antibiotic, Vicom/FCB developed a promotional booklet with a symbolic graphic device: a highly imaginative, optically intricate arrangement of mirror-like planes, glittering with all the colors of the rainbow. Since the drug is positioned in the booklet as "the broadest spectrum antibiotic ever," the visual motif is appropriate as well as dazzling. Inside, illustrations of various organs appear on the same grid, representing the wide range of disorders for which the drug is indicated. Following this grid are single-page breakouts of the individual organs, accompanied by favorable statistics for the treatment of infections in each area. These pages are short-trimmed at the top, leaving the headline message and "spectrum" motif visible throughout.

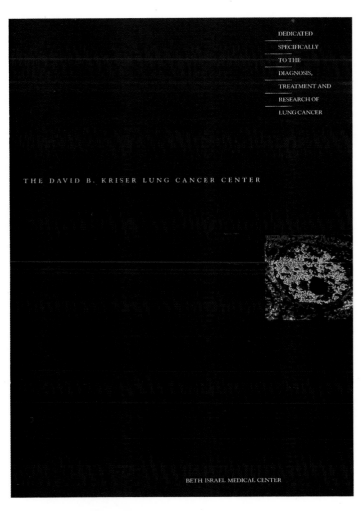

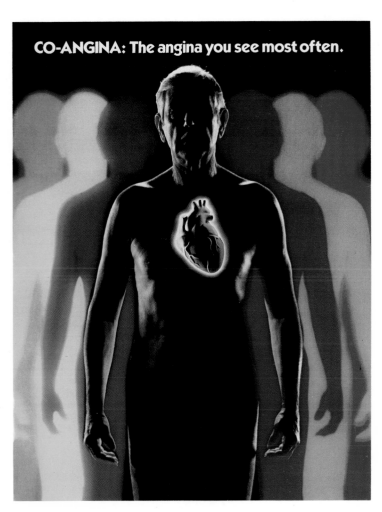

Title: **"The David B. Kriser Lung Cancer
Center"**
Ad Agency: **Friedberg-Feder, Inc.**
Client: **The Kriser Lung Cancer Center**
Art Director: **Steve DeMasi**
Photographer: **Jeffrey Fox**
Copywriters: **John Friedberg, Bonnie Gorsica**

Part of an overall marketing communications program, this brochure for The David B. Kriser Lung
Cancer Center conveys a soothing, upbeat image. Only
the cover is high-tech, with its small thermographic
inset photo on an uncluttered background; inside, the
booklet is filled with human interest photos and warm
colors. Yet there's a nice sense of visual unity about the
piece. According to John Friedberg, president of
Friedberg-Feder, Inc., the purpose of the brochure—
and the overall marketing program—was to create
awareness of the Center's unique, multidisciplinary
approach to treating lung cancer, and to help persuade
physicians to direct their lung cancer patients to this
innovative institution.

Product: **Adalat**®
Ad Agency: **Carrafiello, Diehl &
Associates, Inc.**
Client: **Miles Pharmaceuticals**
Art Director: **Paul Nemesure**
Photographers: **Shig Ikeda, Simpson Kalisher**
Copywriter: **Leo Vanderpot**

The figure of an older man stands out in sharp outline
against a bright background; inside his silhouetted
form, the heart glows as if to convey the pain of angina.
To either side of the central figure, the man's outline is
duplicated in several different colors. This graphic
device suggests the variety of medical problems that
can accompany angina—resulting in the "co-angina"
referred to in the headline. Aimed at a broad spectrum
of physicians, this promotional piece positions Adalat®
as a beneficial therapy for angina in the presence of co-
existing conditions. Copywriter Leo Vanderpot and Art
Director Paul Nemesure tell us that, to their knowledge, this was the first promotion to focus on "angina
with other conditions" and to coin a new word for it—
"co-angina."

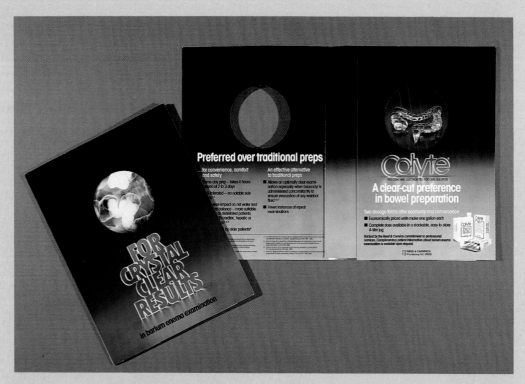

Product: **Colyte**®
Ad Agency: **M.E.D. Communications, Inc.**
Client: **Reed & Carnrick**
Creative Director: **Edward Cohen**
Art Director: **Nancy Martino**
Model Maker: **Ron Terrill**
Photographer: **Neil Molinaro**
Copywriter: **Sally Paull**

In this promotional piece for Colyte®, an oral prep solution used in colon examinations, the headline theme of "crystal clear results" is visually translated into a crystalline sculpture of the large intestine. The fact that this unglamorous organ becomes a thing of beauty is noteworthy in itself, but the paper engineering is even more remarkable. The two covers (the piece can be opened from the front or the back) represent the twin uses of Colyte®: as a prep for colonoscopy and barium enema examinations. Accordingly, die-cut openings reveal a colonoscopic view of the large intestine on one side, an intestinal tract glowing with barium on the other. Then, as the covers are opened, both images disappear from view via retractable slats and leave us with the crystalline colon that stands for "crystal clear results."

Title: **"Partners in Practice"**
Ad Agency: **Thomas G. Ferguson Associates Inc., Pro/Com Div.**
Client: **Squibb & Sons, Inc.**
Art Directors: **Philip Wiener, Donna Modzelewski**
Illustrator: **Elaine Kurie**
Copywriter: **Elaine Heiss**

Targeted at HMOs and chain hospitals, this corporate booklet for Squibb personalizes each of the firm's seven divisions with color photos of the seven division presidents. Adjoining each photo, and serving as a visual link throughout the booklet, is a square inset featuring a portion of the American flag—with a slightly different view of the Stars and Stripes on each page. The purpose of the piece was to sell the audience on "Partners in Practice," a Squibb program designed to help healthcare providers improve the quality of their patient services while keeping costs in line. The booklet manages to touch on the firm's history, philosophy, corporate structure, and current research, as well as the advantages of Partners in Practice.

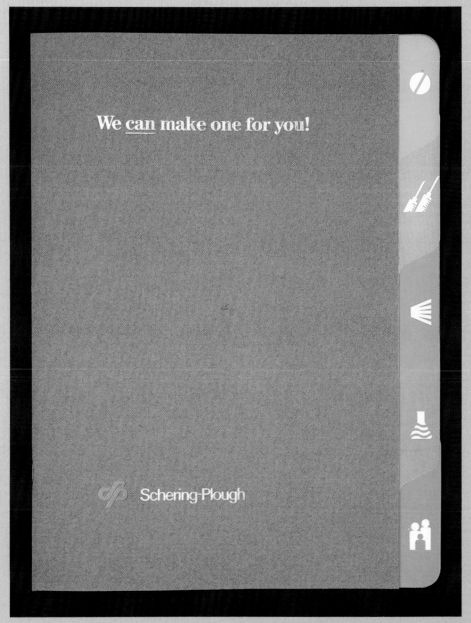

Title: **"We can make one for you!"**
Ad Agency: **Falcone & Associates**
Client: **Schering-Plough**
Art Directors: **Hank Dodd, Bill Falcone**
Photographer: **John Cooper**

Color-coded tabs, each decorated with an appropriate visual symbol, invite the reader to explore the contents of this handsome corporate booklet from Schering-Plough. The tabs each correspond to a different product line, with an added category for "services and support facilities." Designed primarily to promote the firm's manufacturing facilities, the booklet invites other pharmaceutical manufacturers to take advantage of Schering-Plough's "state-of-the-art production capability." Inside, each spread lists the various procedures and services available for each product category. These are accompanied by a series of remarkable close-up photographs that reinforce the "state-of-the-art" corporate image while evoking the tactile beauty of classic still-life paintings.

Product: **LODINE**™
Ad Agency: **F. Scott Kimmich & Co.**
Client: **Wyeth-Ayerst International**
Art Directors: **Richard Malinsky, Barbara Searles, Ralph Schwartz**
Illustrator: **Radu Vero**
Copywriter: **John Schwartz**

Designed for an international product launch, this sales aid series for the new antiarthritis drug LODINE™ emphasizes the medication's power to treat arthritis pain without causing stomach problems. Each cover utilizes symbolic graphics that suggest the action of the drug; inside, colorful three-dimensional graphs relate the benefits in more systematic fashion. Richard Malinsky, senior V.P./creative director for F. Scott Kimmich & Co., writes that, "Since these pieces were to be used throughout the world...the graphics needed to be easily understood." He adds that the copy had to translate easily into other languages, and that each country involved had to approve both the copy and the graphic concept.

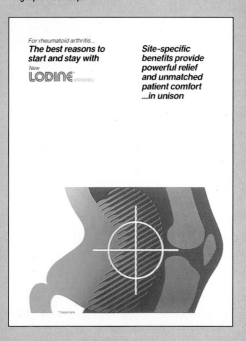

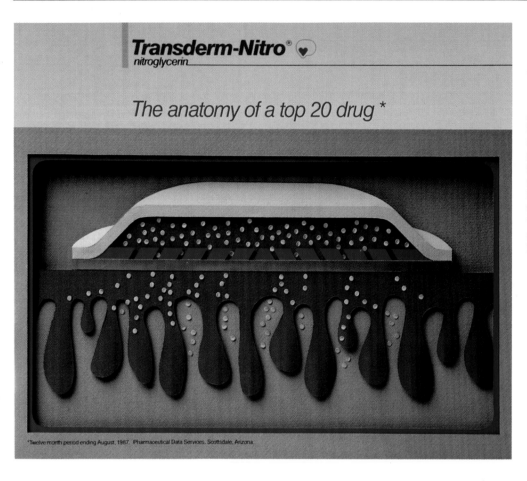

Product: **Transderm-Nitro®**
Ad Agency: **C & G Advertising Inc. (In-house)**
Client: **Ciba Pharmaceuticals**
Art Director: **Ron Vareltzis**
Illustrator: **Don Kahn**
Copywriter: **Kevin Purcell**

A colorful construction-paper diagram by Don Kahn illustrates "the anatomy of a top 20 drug"—specifically, Transderm-Nitro®, the nitroglycerin patch for angina sufferers. The skin surface is depicted in purple, the top of the patch in white. In between, the yellow confetti-like polka dots represent the medication passing through the blue membrane of the patch and through the skin. All of this relates, of course, to the "anatomy" theme in the headline. Used as a selling tool during sales calls, the brochure was designed to stimulate physician involvement and interest.

Title: **"Welcome to the creative world of Dugan/Farley"**
Ad Agency: **Dugan Farley Communications Associates, Inc.**
Client: **Dugan Farley Communications Associates, Inc.**
Art Director: **Eric Rathje**
Illustrator: **Danny Smythe**
Copywriter: **Fran Dyller**

How is a good ad agency like a good restaurant? That's the question tacitly posed by Dugan/Farley in their four-color brochure aimed at prospective clients. The restaurant theme is an outgrowth of the agency's previous slogan, "Advertising in Fine Taste." Appropriately enough, the tools of the advertising trade mingle with those of the medical profession on the handsomely prepared platter. But the agency deliberately ventures beyond the "fine taste" approach in favor of a new emphasis on *creativity*. (In the individual discussions of the agency's services, each headline starts with the word "creative": we read about "Creative Marketing Support," "Creative Production," and so on.) Executive Creative Director (Copy) Marty Ross notes that the piece had to bridge the agency's old and new marketing strategies.

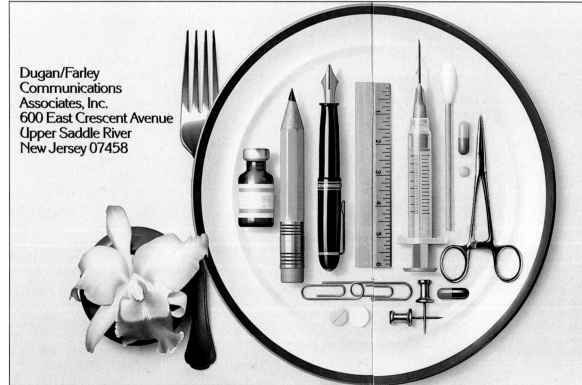

Dugan/Farley
Communications
Associates, Inc.
600 East Crescent Avenue
Upper Saddle River
New Jersey 07458

Here we have only one product to sell. Creativity.

But it comes in many shapes and forms. In many sizes. And with many flavors.

It can be served up piping hot as a small tidbit...

Or we can provide an endlessly replenished groaning board of creative offerings...

A cornucopia of the fruits of our knowledge, skill, and talents.

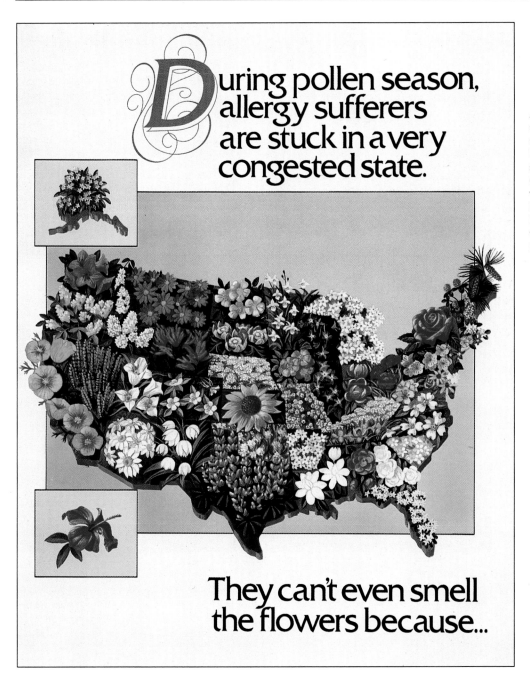

During pollen season, allergy sufferers are stuck in a very congested state.

They can't even smell the flowers because...

Product: **COMHIST® LA**
Ad Agency: **Lally, McFarland & Pantello**
Client: **Norwich Eaton Pharmaceuticals, Inc.**
Art Director: **Nancy Slivka-Bitteker**
Illustrator: **Sean Harrison**
Copywriter: **Susan Greenhut**

A floral map of the U.S. greets the eye in this four-page sales aid for COMHIST® LA, a preparation for allergy sufferers. As students of geography and botany will happily discover, the agency has used all the official state flowers to fill in the state boundaries. Thus, California is composed of poppies, New Jersey of violets—all 50 states literally bloom with their chosen blossom. Of course, the beauty is deceptive: it translates into misery for allergy sufferers—and that's the whole idea of this ingenious piece from Lally, McFarland & Pantello.

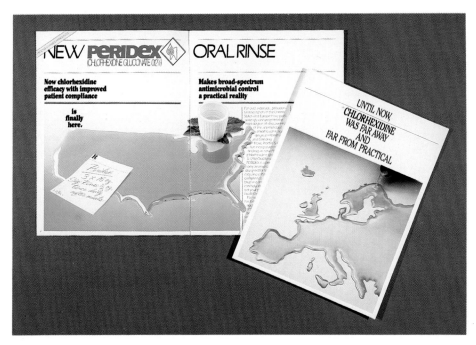

Product: **PERIDEX®**
Ad Agency: **Lally, McFarland & Pantello**
Client: **Procter & Gamble**
Art Director: **Julien Jarreau**
Photographer: **Roger Bester**
Model Maker: **Starbuck Studios**
Copywriters: **John Lally, Susan Greenhut**

As anyone with a smidgen of geographical knowledge can tell you, the pink liquid being poured in the cover photo has taken on the distinctive contours of Europe—complete with Sicily, Sardinia, Corsica, and even the Shetland Islands. With a little help from the headline, this clever visual tells us that chlorhexidine hasn't been available on the American side of the Atlantic—until now. We open the cover, and there it is: a liquid map of the U.S. The message is that, by developing PERIDEX® antimicrobial oral rinse, Procter & Gamble has brought home the benefits of chlorhexidine without its problems. Aimed at periodontists who were awaiting the product in the U.S., the booklet provides ample documentation to show that PERIDEX® was worth waiting for.

Title: **"Critical Care Issues"**
Ad Agency: **Kallir, Philips, Ross, Inc.**
Client: **Glaxo, Inc.**
Art Directors: **Lionel Tepper, Leslie Sisman**
Illustrator: **Gary Carlson**
Photographer: **Clayton J. Price**
Copywriter: **Ron Jastrzemski**
Computer Graphics: **Watson-Manning Blox-Pix**

These visually pleasing brochures promote a series of "Critical Care Issues" multimedia programs aimed at professionals in six different intensive care specialties. V.P./Associate Creative Director Leslie Sisman notes that the client "wanted a high impact graphic, but wanted to keep it clean and clinical." The agency created a distinctive "family look" for the pieces, each of which features a relevant cover shot using diagnostic imaging. An EKG runs across the bottom of each inside spread, and the cover's handsome blue, white, and black color scheme reappears inside as a banner.

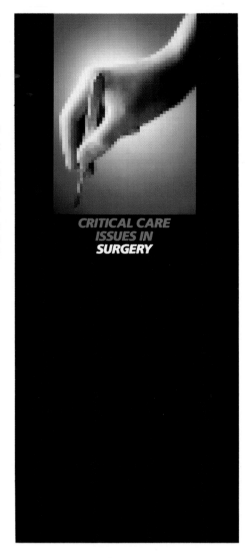

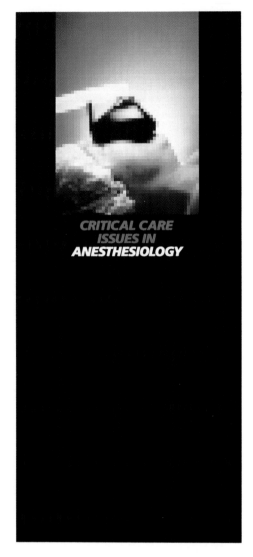

Product: **Norgesic® Forte**
Ad Agency: **Girgenti, Hughes, Butler & McDowell**
Client: **3M Riker**
Art Directors: **Mark McDowell, Ahmed Sadiq**
Photographer: **Bart Gorin**
Copywriter: **Frank Hughes**

Parafon Forte®, an analgesic produced by McNeil Laboratories, was about to bite the dust, so competitor 3M Riker gleefully exploited an opportunity with this lively series of mailings for Norgesic® Forte. In one piece, Parafon Forte® is about to be yanked off the stage by an old-time vaudeville hook—the headline reads, "Going, Going, Gone." (Norgesic® Forte, by contrast, is "Going, Going Strong.") Another brochure shows the McNeil product stamped "DISCONTINUED," while the third one reports the demise of Parafon Forte® in an imaginary front page newspaper story ("Here One Day, Gone the Next"). Turn the page, and the news about Norgesic® Forte bears the headline, "Only the Strong Survive." Each brochure comes with a memo about the discontinuation of Parafon Forte® and the uncertainty of its replacement at McNeil Labs.

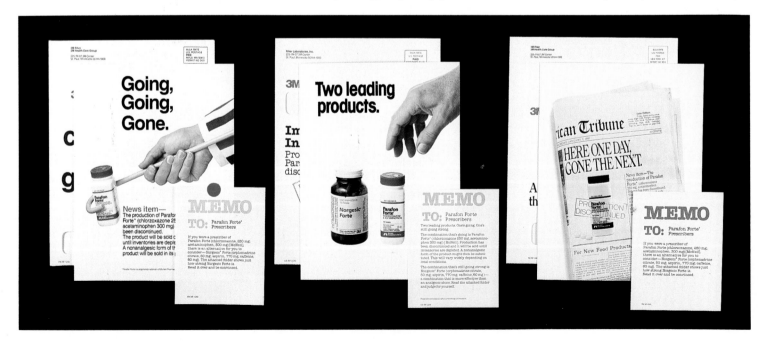

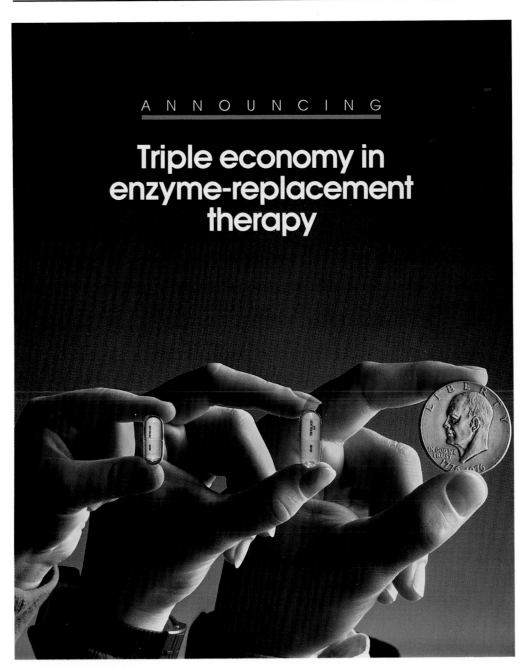

A N N O U N C I N G

Triple economy in enzyme-replacement therapy

Product: **ENTOLASE**®
Ad Agency: **Blunt, Hann, Sersen, Inc.**
Client: **A. H. Robins**
Art Director: **Audrey Artusio**
Photographer: **George Mattei**
Copywriter: **Julia Schroeder**

The theme of "triple economy" works two ways in this promotional brochure for ENTOLASE® and double-strength ENTOLASE®-HP. On the cover, three hands hold up three objects: an ENTOLASE® capsule, an ENTOLASE®-HP capsule, and an Eisenhower "silver" dollar. (The capsules are visible through die-cut openings; they're actually mounted inside the piece.) Is the three-handed cover a visual reference to "triple economy"? Could be, but then we open the brochure and discover what the cover *really* means: that each capsule offers three "economies"—economy of size, of dosage, and of price (remember the dollar on the cover). The brief copy also compares ENTOLASE® favorably with competitor PANCREASE®.

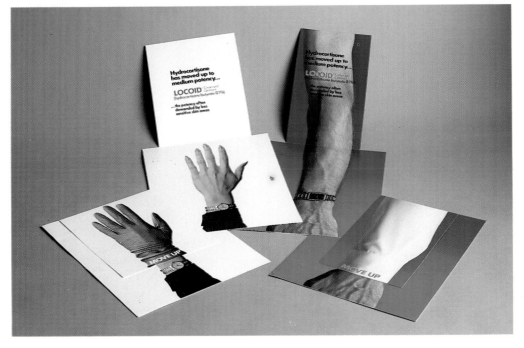

Product: **LOCOID**®
Ad Agency: **Sudler & Hennessey**
Client: **Owen Laboratories**
Art Director: **Margaret Noon**
Photographers: **John Manno, Martin Mistretta,**
Stuart Heir
Copywriter: **Robin Davenport**

"Move Up" is the theme of this interactive folder campaign for LOCOID® hydrocortisone skin treatment. On each cover, we "move up" the covering flap (representing a shirt sleeve, a glove, or a trouser leg) to reveal the perfect skin underneath. The campaign positions LOCOID® as a medium-potency hydrocortisone; the copy invites dermatologists to consider "moving up" from the low-potency alternative. (Just in case they choose not to, the pieces also advertise Owen Laboratories' low-potency product.) Playful and engaging on the outside, these folders follow up with medical inset photos and bulleted benefits copy on the inside.

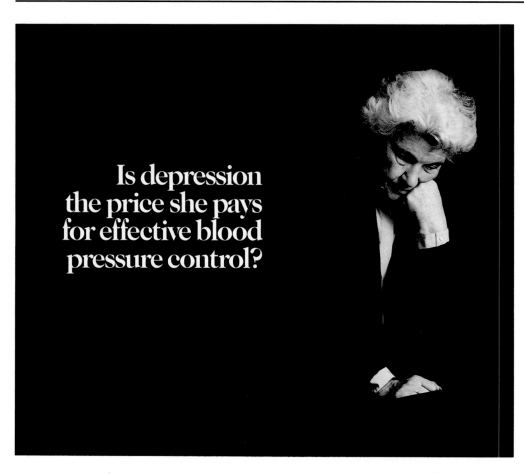

Is depression
the price she pays
for effective blood
pressure control?

Product: **Hylorel**®
Ad Agency: **Sieber & McIntyre**
Client: **Pennwalt Pharmaceutical Division**
Art Directors: **Lin Kossak, Terri DeFino**
Photographer: **Ken Sherman**
Copywriter: **Jon Hughes**

Depression…impotence…fatigue. These three symptoms represent the down side of traditional blood pressure medication. To dramatize the price "one pays," Kossak Design Group created a memorable three-part sales aid for Hylorel®, an antihypertensive drug that had been lagging in sales. According to Lin Kossak, design firm president, the goal was to "establish Hylorel® as highly efficacious with an excellent side effect profile" and to "make noise in a very noisy market." The flash card format was chosen for its "ease of detailing and repetition of message" as well as to create dialogue between sales rep and MD. Each card hits the prospect with a different side effect of traditional therapy (the card shown here deals with depression); on the flip side, convincing statistics demonstrate the effectiveness of Hylorel®.

Product: **Feldene**®
Ad Agency: **Dorritie & Lyons, Inc.**
Client: **Pfizer Laboratories**
Art Directors: **Hector Padron, Mike Lyons**
Photographer: **Leon Kuzmanoff**
Copywriter: **Bill Brown**

Instead of simply describing a multifaceted arthritis management program, this educational folder for physicians goes an important step further. Tucked inside the folder is an in-depth profile booklet on a single patient who has undergone the various evaluation procedures of the program. We see her actual scores on an entire battery of physical and psychological tests. And, in a decidedly understated but persuasive fashion, we're shown how she responded to treatment with Feldene®, the antiarthritic medication from Pfizer. Nowhere does the name of the drug jump out at the reader; it's skillfully woven into the text. (Prescribing information is supplied at the back of the booklet.) Also included for the doctor's use is a guide to evaluation procedures currently used in managing arthritis—complete with sample forms and questionnaires.

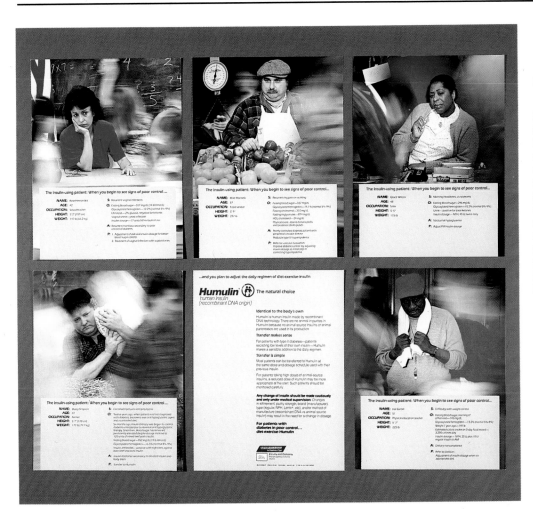

Product: **Humulin**®
Ad Agency: **Deltakos U.S.A.**
Client: **Eli Lilly and Co.**
Art Director: **Dave Seabert**
Photographer: **Rod Cooke**
Copywriter: **Marcia Dunne**

Realistic case studies of diabetics add interest to this series of promotional pieces for Humulin®, a human insulin made by recombinant DNA technology. In each case, the diabetic patient has been experiencing a different set of problems with traditional insulin therapy. The brief medical dossiers supply us with each patient's age, height, weight, and occupation—along with the presenting symptoms, test readings, assessment, and prescribed course of therapy. This involving device commands attention and participation on the part of the physician audience; they're well-primed for the promotional message on the reverse side. (The traditional daily regimen of "diet-exercise-insulin" becomes "diet-exercise-Humulin®.")

Product: **ROXANOL**™
Ad Agency: **Deltakos U.S.A.**
Client: **Roxane Laboratories**
Art Director: **Bill Alderisio**
Photographer: **Nick Samardge**
Copywriter: **Laura Byers**

These life-size "faces of cancer pain" evoke sympathy and involve the reader in a series of case histories designed to promote ROXANOL™, a liquid oral morphine. Each patient is a terminal case; their faces, shot in poignant close-up by Nick Samardge, testify to their pain. On the front, the brief copy lists their name, age, and diagnosis. On the back, we see that each patient has regained "some of the simple pleasures of living." Here, each case study is treated in greater detail: the patient's history, symptoms, and course of therapy are woven into a short profile that culminates with a call for "a convenient pain medication." The accompanying sheet focuses on the benefits of ROXANOL™, with prescribing information on the back.

Superficial bladder tumors are prone to recur...

Artist's conception of the bladder and superficial tumors along the urothelium.

Higher relapse rate without chemoprophylaxis

Although transurethral resection (TUR) is the initial modality in the treatment of superficial bladder carcinoma, the frequency of recurrences after TUR indicates a need for chemoprophylaxis.

Majority of recurrences (50%–70%) occur within 6-12 months.[1]

80%–95% after 8 years[2]

Up to 80% after 5 years[3]

Product: **Adriamycin**®
Ad Agency: **F. Scott Kimmich & Co.**
Client: **Farmatalia Carlo Erba**
Art Directors: **Richard Malinsky, William Vollers**
Sculptor: **W. Parker**
Photographer: **Richard Malinsky**
Copywriters: **John Schwartz, Don Brown**

The image behind the die-cut cover is not an anatomical photograph of a bladder, but rather a photo of a glass sphere in which static electricity has been generated. This intriguing conceptual graphic depicts a new method of treating bladder tumors—by administering the drug Adriamycin® directly into the bladder through a catheter. Senior V.P./Creative Director Richard Malinsky writes that the electrical charge "symbolically represented the drug attacking tumors inside the bladder, therefore showing the administration and action of the drug without using anatomical artwork." The brochure cites evidence that bladder tumors tend to recur sooner and more frequently without the use of Adriamycin®.

Products: **Radiology Catheters and Accessories**
Ad Agency: **Grob & Co., Inc.**
Client: **C.R. Bard, Inc., Bard Europe Div.**
Art Director: **Breda Kenyon**
Illustrator: **Steve Krupsky**
Photographer: **Jim Thomas**
Copywriter: **Larry Grob**

This important-looking promotional folder contains inserts on different products targeted at specialists in an emerging field: interventional radiology. Created by Grob & Co., Inc., the package breaks away from standard sharp-focus "tabletop" photography in favor of richly grainy black-and-white shots, which were deemed more appropriate for radiologists. (Examples of angiography appear throughout.) The copy portrays the company as committed to helping interventional radiologists in their expanding role. According to Lawrence Grob, agency president, the package had "to work by itself, in light of limited sales time available to support this particular product group," and "the various inserts had to tie together yet be quickly distinguishable."

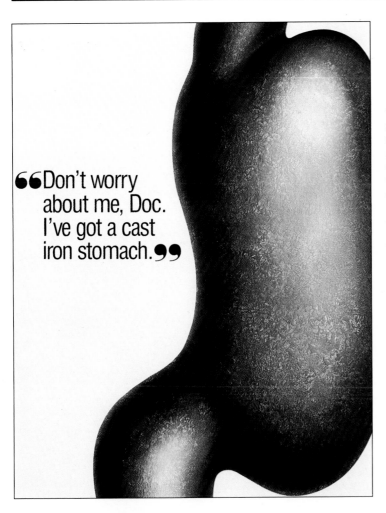

66Don't worry about me, Doc. I've got a cast iron stomach.99

Product: **Disalcid®**
Ad Agency: **Girgenti, Hughes, Butler & McDowell**
Client: **3M Riker**
Art Director: **Mark McDowell**
Illustrator: **Judith Glick**
Copywriter: **Frank Hughes**

"Don't worry about me, Doc. I've got a cast iron stomach." These famous last words appear alongside a *real* cast iron stomach on the cover of this colorful promotional piece for Disalcid® B.I.D. The outer curves of this impressive gastric plumbing fixture coincide with the right edge of the cover. When you flip the cover, the reverse side reveals the stomach lining dotted with small asymptomatic ulcers (shown in actual endoscopic photographs). Colorful charts and concise bulleted copy fill the rest of the piece, effectively selling the reader on the GI safety and other benefits of this aspirin substitute from 3M Riker.

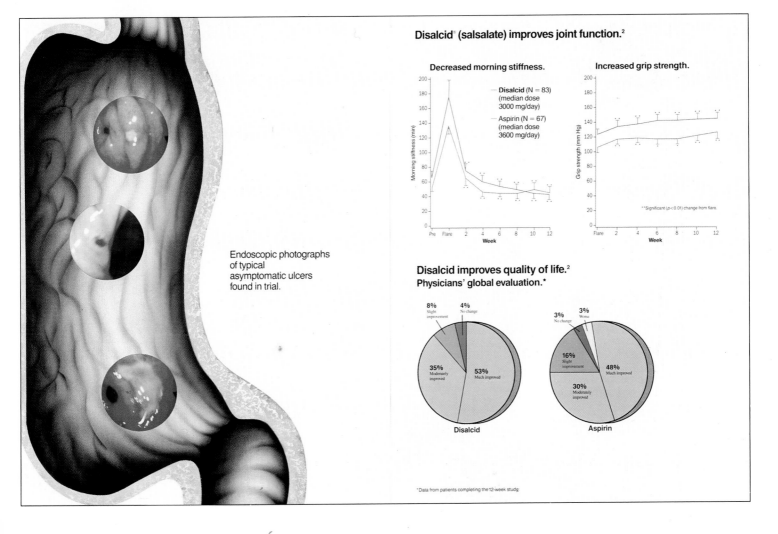

Endoscopic photographs of typical asymptomatic ulcers found in trial.

Disalcid® (salsalate) improves joint function.[2]

Decreased morning stiffness.

— Disalcid (N = 83) (median dose 3000 mg/day)
— Aspirin (N = 67) (median dose 3600 mg/day)

Morning stiffness (min) vs Week (Pre, Flare, 2, 4, 6, 8, 10, 12)

Increased grip strength.

Grip strength (mm Hg) vs Week (Flare, 2, 4, 6, 8, 10, 12)

**Significant ($p<0.01$) change from flare.

Disalcid improves quality of life.[2]
Physicians' global evaluation.*

Disalcid:
- 8% Slight improvement
- 4% No change
- 35% Moderately improved
- 53% Much improved

Aspirin:
- 3% No change
- 3% Worse
- 16% Slight improvement
- 30% Moderately improved
- 48% Much improved

*Data from patients completing the 12-week study.

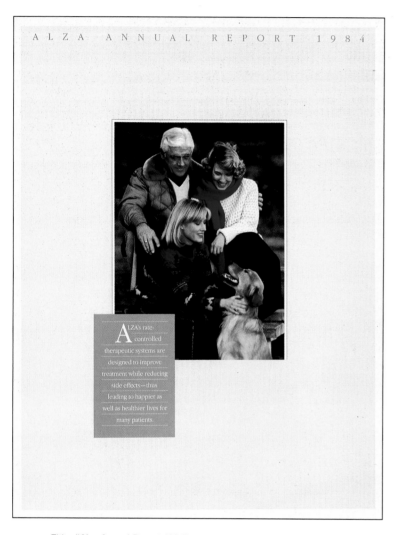

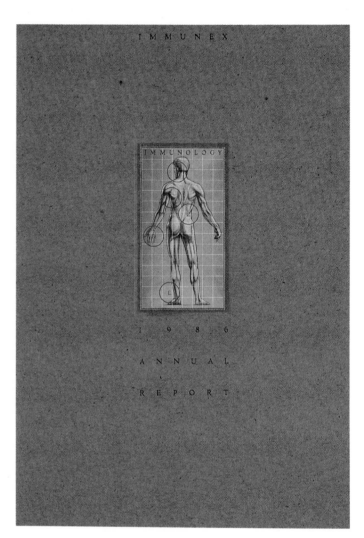

Title: **"Alza Annual Report 1984"**
Design Firm: **Pentagram Design Inc.**
Client: **Alza Corp.**
Art Director: **Neil Shakery**
Photographer: **John Blaustein**
Copywriter: **Bonnie Burdett**

This model American family graced the cover of the Alva annual report for 1984. A visual departure from the company's traditional scientific image, the report is dominated by human interest photographs—with a nod to the company's technological side in the form of small diagrams and product illustrations. Art Director Neil Shakery writes, "Alva's previous annuals had always focused on the research and development aspects of their business. We convinced them that there was a legitimate human interest story to be told by representing the end users of their technology."

Title: **"Immunex 1986 Annual Report"**
Design Firm: **Pentagram Design Inc.**
Client: **Immunex Corp.**
Art Director: **Kit Hinrichs**
Illustrator: **Vincent Perez**
Copywriter: **Delphine Hirasuna**

"Tipped" onto the coarse cover stock of this annual report for Immunex Corporation is a delicately rendered illustration of human musculature in terra-cotta tones. The circled areas of the anatomy, coupled with the heading "Immunology," refer to the corporate goals of Immunex: using hormones to develop products that regulate the body's immune response to specific disorders. The report goes on to discuss some exciting breakthroughs and their applications and positions Immunex as a leader in the biotechnology industry.

ALZA ANNUAL REPORT 1985

ALZA's current products are allowing people to lead more normal daily lives while receiving medication.

ALZA's therapeutic systems can significantly enhance the therapeutic effects and expand the applications for many widely used drugs.

ALZA's future technologies will enable drugs or hormones to be administered in precise, complex patterns synchronized with the body's biorhythms.

Title: **"Alza Annual Report 1985"**
Design Firm: **Pentagram Design Inc.**
Client: **Alza Corp.**
Art Director: **Neil Shakery**
Photographers: **John Blaustein, Rick Wahlstrom**
Copywriters: **Bonnie Burdett, Martin Gerstell**

In its 1985 annual report, Alza Corporation wanted to focus on three aspects of the company's drug delivery technology: products currently available, products under development, and future directions. Art Director Neil Shakery managed to work these three topics into the clean-looking cover design. The photo at left—a human interest shot of a patient enjoying an active life—represents Alza products currently on the market. The center photo, which depicts an Alza employee at work, stands for products under development. And the picture on the right hints at the sophisticated technologies to come. Inside, large photos provide impact while smaller photos, diagrams, and charts amplify the technical details.

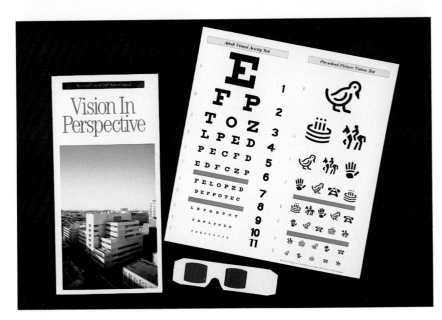

Title: **"Vision in Perspective"**
Design Firm: **Danskane**
Client: **Wills Eye Hospital**
Art Director: **Peg Kane**
Illustrator: **Brent A. Bauer**
Photographers: **Bob Bezushko, George Bezushko**
Copywriter: **Tom Maeder**

Like most annual reports, this booklet for Wills Eye Hospital in Philadelphia provides a yearly update on new programs and facilities, key research studies, and major events of the previous 12 months. But one particular feature made the 1987 report uniquely memorable: it was equipped with 3-D glasses. These red-and-blue shades, familiar to 1950's moviegoers, added an extra dimension to the cover photo and, at the same time, enabled readers to test their binocular vision. Here was a fresh creative departure from typical annual reports—a publication that was not a throwaway, had potential shelf life, and was helpful to the community as a diagnostic tool. The hospital sent out 14,000 copies of the report.

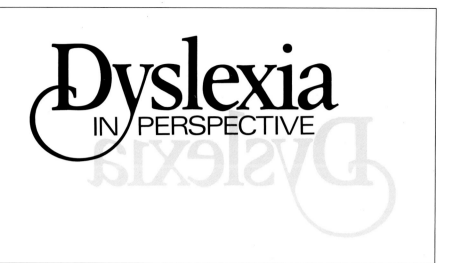

Title: **"Dyslexia in Perspective"**
Design Firm: **Joseph Dieter Visual Communications**
Client: **The Orton Dyslexia Society**
Art Director: **Joseph M. Dieter, Jr.**
Illustrator: **Joseph M. Dieter, Jr.**

Created for the Orton Dyslexia Society's annual meeting, this logotype by Joseph M. Dieter, Jr., speaks volumes simply by reversing the word "dyslexia." It effectively conveys the essence of this widespread reading disability while establishing an attractive and memorable identity for the group. (The logo was used in a variety of printed materials.)

Product: **Children's TYLENOL®**
Ad Agency: **Kallir, Philips, Ross, Inc.**
Client: **McNeil Consumer Products Co.**
Art Director: **Karen Rosen Mauskop**
Photographers: **Tom Arma, Bruce Plotkin, Jade Albert**
Copywriter: **Joyce Hendley**

"Kidspirit" is the name of this lively calendar produced for Children's and Junior Strength TYLENOL® by Kallir, Philips, Ross, Inc. Featuring splashy color photographs of children—and illustrations of TYLENOL® products—on each page, the calendar creates what V.P./Art Group Supervisor Karen Rosen Mauskop calls "a continuous visible presence" for the product line in the offices of pediatricians (as well as primary-care physicians with a large pediatric practice). The moods in the photographs range from serene to exuberant, and most of the children are depicted in a holiday setting appropriate to the particular month. The calendar was designed to appeal directly to mothers and children in waiting rooms, as well as to increase doctors' recommendations for Children's TYLENOL®.

Graphic: **National Arrhythmia Forum Logo**
Design Firm: **Hedstrom/Blessing, Inc.**
Client: **3M Riker**
Art Director: **Tom Roper**
Illustrator: **Tom Roper**

To establish an identity for the National Arrhythmia Forum, Hedstrom/Blessing, Inc., created a distinctive heart logo based on an actual arrhythmic EKG readout. The logo appeared flat-printed in three colors as well as embossed without ink. Account Executive Rebecca McManus writes that the agency positioned the forum, which was sponsored by 3M Riker, as "a serious educational endeavor, as opposed to strictly commercial in content."

A 15-month calendar presented with the compliments of McNeil Consumer Products Company, makers of Children's and Junior Strength TYLENOL® acetaminophen

Product: **Femstat**®
Ad Agency: **Vicom/FCB**
Client: **Syntex Laboratories, Inc.**
Art Director: **John Williams**
Illustrator: **Sandra Bruce**

Sandra Bruce created this graceful, instantly recognizable logo to help establish an identity for Femstat®, a cream prescribed for feminine yeast infections. The figure's body language communicates the new-found joy and freedom of a woman delivered from discomfort. The art seems simple and effortless, although—as Creative Director Lester Barnett points out—it "had to have the precision of figure drawing and the fluidity of calligraphy." Developed to identify Femstat® across all media, the art was designed to reproduce well in color, in black-and-white, and in a wide range of sizes.

Product: **Tokos Perinatal Nursing Services**
Ad Agency: **V. Montegrande & Co., Inc.**
Client: **Tokos Medical Corp.**
Art Director: **Val Montegrande**
Photographer: **Porché West**
Copywriter: **Vicki Grant**

"Proud Parents" is the theme of this compelling wall calendar from Tokos Perinatal Nursing Services. Created on a limited budget and a tight schedule by V. Montegrande & Co., Inc., the calendar utilized existing photographs of patients representing a wide range of backgrounds. According to Val Montegrande, design firm president, the calendar was designed as an aesthetically pleasing "reminder device" for nurses, who it was hoped would refer to it daily and be on the lookout for cases that might be referred to the client. To reinforce the calendar's usefulness to nurses, it included information about preterm labor on each page. The photographs are tri-tones; one of the colors is a special metallic mauve ink.

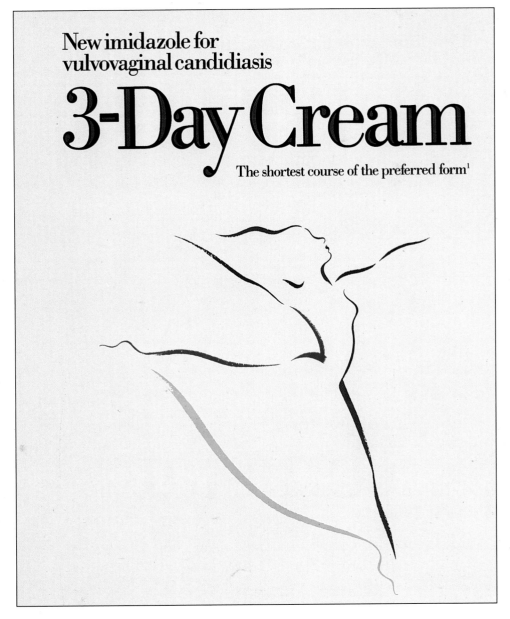

New imidazole for vulvovaginal candidiasis

3-Day Cream

The shortest course of the preferred form[1]

5

DIRECT MAIL

SINGLE PROMOTIONS
CAMPAIGNS

Direct mail used to be the Rodney Dangerfield of advertising: it simply didn't "get no respect." Scorned by the public as junk mail, and typically dismissed by agency creatives as a second-rate outlet for their talents, the medium languished for years as the poor sister of space advertising.

But no longer. Within the past decade or so, marketing-conscious advertisers have discovered the singular advantages of direct mail. For one, the medium can be targeted with greater accuracy than space advertising. You can choose mailing lists that correspond to the precise demographics of your intended audience. And you can reach that audience with a multicomponent package that tells the product story in depth.

There's another advantage, too—one that's especially close to the hearts of all marketing executives. The results of direct mail can be *quantified*. You no longer have to guess at the effectiveness of your advertising; you *know* it from the number of responses. Direct-mail packages can be tested and fine-tuned *ad infinitum* until the response rate is maximized.

As direct mail has gained in popularity, so has its quality. The lively examples in this chapter offer a rousing rebuttal to the notion that direct mail is plodding, unimaginative, and humorless. What you'll be seeing here is creativity at its best.

In fact, these pieces surpass the direct-mail mainstream in terms of creative freedom and flair. One obvious reason is the size of the mailings: when you're targeting a small, highly specialized audience—as is the case in most medical advertising—you can afford to wow your prospects with interactive envelopes, expensive die-cut brochures on heavy stock, substantial giveaways, and other luxuries denied to direct marketers that mail 10 or 20 million pieces at a time.

Another, perhaps less obvious, reason is the peculiar nature of the response sought by the typical medical advertiser. Most direct mail attempts to close a sale…to persuade the prospect to give up a portion of his discretionary income and enclose it in the accompanying envelope. It's a task to be approached with the utmost tact and caution.

Not so in medical direct mail. In the vast majority of cases—especially in pharmaceutical advertising—the physician is not being asked to *purchase* anything. (After all, doctors don't stock their offices with pharmaceuticals; they *prescribe* medication that the patient obtains at a local pharmacy.) This is an important distinction. Instead of making a deadly earnest sales pitch, with the bottom line hanging in the balance, medical direct mail is free to pull out all the stops. After all, the idea is to generate product awareness…to impress physicians so that they'll remember the name of the drug, associate it with some clever advertising, and prescribe it (or recommend it) to their patients.

But it's not *quite* that simple. Direct mail is still supposed to generate a response. And if physicians aren't being asked to purchase anything, how do these pieces deliver quantifiable results?

The answer is *free samples*. The most common response vehicle used in these direct-mail packages is a BRC (business reply card) on which the physician requests samples of the advertised drug at no charge.

To overcome the prospect's apathy barrier, many of these mailing pieces offer an attractive premium that the physician receives along with the samples. (Ciba sent free limited-edition prints to physicians who signed up for samples of Ludiomil®.) Sometimes the enticement is a sweepstakes (see the whimsical "Send Your Nose Seaside" package for Na-Sal™). Or, to generate good will (and a propensity to request free samples), a giveaway of lesser value might be included right in the package. (The makers of Apresazide® provided a uniquely jointed ballpoint pen that neatly tied in with the product's advertised

benefit of "flexibility"—and enabled physicians to sign up for samples at the same time.)

Often, the package provides something of *educational* value. A direct-mail campaign for NAPROSYN® contained a series of "Rheumatological Decisions"—case studies complete with patient background and actual X-ray transparencies. Physicians could formulate their own diagnosis, compare it with the assessment of an "expert," then file away the tabbed folder for future reference. Because such a mailing is "interactive"—that is, it demands some involvement on the part of the reader—the reader is more likely to become involved with the *product* as well.

One popular form of interactive mailing is the pop-up. These structurally complex 3-D pieces have been used as patient education aids (see the detailed shoulder model from Depo-Medrol®), as conveyors of product information (the cross section of the Catapres-TTS® patch is a good example), or simply for dramatic effect (the triumphant man on the mountaintop for PRINIVIL®).

As always in medical advertising, it's important to stand out from the crowd of competitors…to create a package that gets noticed—and *remembered*—for its uniqueness. The brilliantly colored "banana" mailer for DYAZIDE® is like nothing else in medical advertising (or any *other* kind of advertising, for that matter). It's bold, it's memorable, and the banana symbol actually positions the product in terms of its leading benefit.

So, as you can see, medical direct mail is not exactly the province of dullards and hacks. In fact, the packages reviewed on the following pages represent some of the liveliest and most ingenious work to arise from the recent direct-mail renaissance. (They're some of the most *successful*, too—with response rates as high as 42 percent!) A second-rate medium? Hardly.

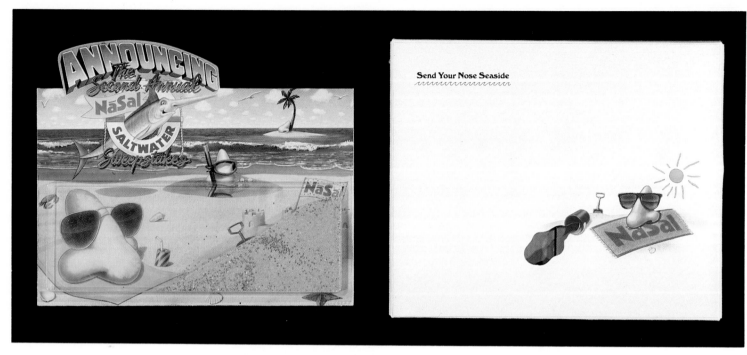

Product: **NaSal**™
Ad Agency: **Sutton Communications**
Client: **Winthrop Pharmaceuticals Division**
Art Director: **Nick Manganiello**
Illustrator: **Tom Gieseke**
Copywriter: **Edie Pargh**

SILVER. Something about the image of a nose (complete with sunglasses) sunning itself at the beach is so absurd that it's irresistible. A window on the mailing envelope for this promotional piece reveals a mound of actual, sparkling sand contained inside a clear plastic compartment on the piece within, and a teaser line— "Send Your Nose Seaside"—provokes even further curiosity. What's it all about? The brochure depicts a balmy beach scene with a group of hedonistic noses at play. Flip the sandy cover, and you read about the Second Annual NaSal™ Saline Saltwater Vacation Sweepstakes. (The grand prize is $2,500 toward any "saltwater vacation" of the winner's choice.) Alongside the sweepstakes offer is concise benefits copy for NaSal™, the saline nasal moisturizing spray. The "saltwater" concept ties in nicely with the product and helps establish top-of-mind memorability.

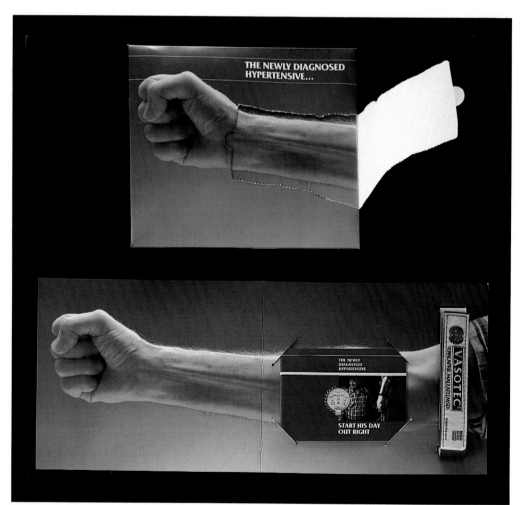

Product: **VASOTEC**®
Ad Agency: **Vicom/FCB**
Client: **Merck Sharp & Dohme**
Art Director: **Patricia A. Senker**
Photographer: **Tripp Von Hoffman**
Copywriter: **Elizabeth Lawson**

SILVER. Even the outer envelope is "interactive" in this ingeniously designed mailer for VASOTEC®, an antihypertensive medication from Merck Sharp & Dohme. To open the envelope, you insert your thumb at the man's shirt cuff and pull away the perforated sleeve. Since the perforated shirtsleeve wraps around to the back of the envelope, you keep pulling until the entire arm—along with the contents of the package—is laid bare. Carefully mounted on the "arm" panel are a 5" x 3½", 28-page booklet promoting the benefits of VASOTEC®, and a rubber tourniquet embellished with a cloth VASOTEC® label (the client hoped that, each time a physician used a tourniquet while taking a blood pressure reading, he or she would be reminded of the effectiveness of VASOTEC® in treating newly diagnosed hypertensives). Patricia A. Senker, senior graphic designer at Merck Sharp & Dohme, writes that "the production nuances of this mailer were incredible!"

Products: **ORNADE®, Albalon-A™**
Ad Agency: **Windermere Communications, Inc.**
Client: **SmithKline Beckman Corp.**
Art Director: **Alison Carson**
Illustrator: **Stanislaw Fernandes**
Copywriter: **Tina L. Bashline**

The two "masks" in this attractive mailer seem identical at first glance. But there's a touch of deep inflammatory pink around the nostrils of the left-hand mask (representing allergic rhinitis), while the same shade of pink appears along the *eye* of the right-hand mask (a clear case of allergic conjunctivitis). Open the gatefold and the remedies for each disorder appear underneath—ORNADE® for the rhinitis, Albalon-A™ for the conjunctivitis—alongside the same two female profiles, now visibly relieved of symptoms. The mailer, which offers physicians free starter samples of both drugs, generated a final BRC response rate of 38%. The project represented a unique use of cooperative advertising funds of two SmithKline Beckman companies: Smith Kline & French Laboratories and Allergan, Inc.

Product: **Allergan Products**
Ad Agency: **Pacificom (In-house)**
Client: **Allergan Pharmaceuticals, Inc.**
Art Director: **Donald R. Meyers**
Illustrator: **Andy Zito**
Copywriter: **Paul Oshinsky**

Shades of Al Capone! The Prohibition Era lives again in this lively party invitation aimed at an audience of ophthalmology residents in Chicago. Created by the in-house agency at Allergan Pharmaceuticals, Inc., the card features authentic period detailing inside and out. (To research his design, artist Andy Zito used an actual double-breasted pin-striped suit from the '30s.) The suit on the cover opens to an impressive 8½" x 13" inside, revealing the gangster's pin-striped shirt, suspenders, and a tie clip inscribed "Big Al." The Chicago speakeasy theme is picked up in the copy, which cheerfully warns invitees: "You'll be dere if you know what's good for you!"

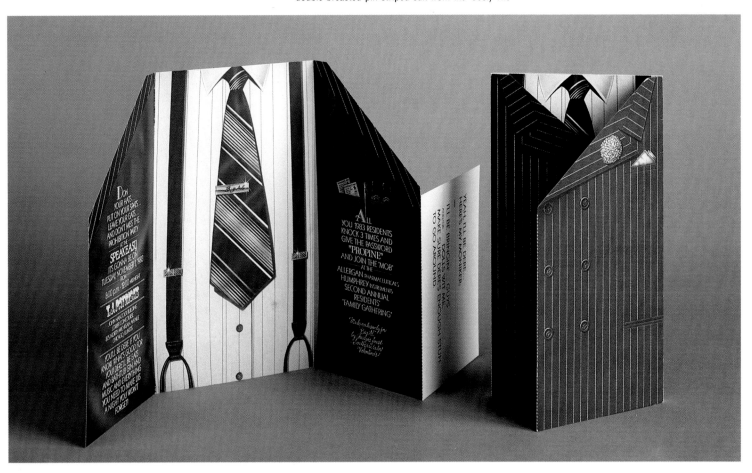

Products: **NASALCROM®, OPTICROM®**
Ad Agency: **Sandler Communications Inc.**
Client: **Fisons Corp.**
Art Director: **Lori Zumatto**
Illustrator: **Marti Shohet**
Copywriter: **Lisa-Stec**

Targeted at physicians who treat allergies, these pop-up mailers for NASALCROM® and OPTICROM® are fun, engaging, and memorable advertising to boot. One piece emphasizes indoor allergy pests—the cozy picket-fenced house shown on the outside pops up to reveal dust mites and other varmints inside. The other mailer gives us a flowery meadow, with the allergy culprits springing into view on the inside. The catchy headlines add to the overall appeal, and the copy is unusual in its parallel treatment of two complementary products—NASALCROM® for nasal allergy symptoms, OPTICROM® for the corresponding eye symptoms.

Product: **NAPROSYN®**
Ad Agency: **Vicom/FCB**
Client: **Syntex Laboratories, Inc.**
Art Directors: **Joseph Rozon, Stephen Mullens**
Illustrator: **Will Nelson**
Copywriter: **Cari Weisberg**

The teaser on the outside reads, "A short message unfolds." Nothing remarkable about that—but the familiar background pattern looks suspiciously like a giraffe. Sure enough, as you "unfold" the message, the 4" x 6" piece grows into a 6" x 22" depiction of a giraffe from the shoulders up. The creative team at Vicom/FCB came up with this memorable visual to gain attention for NAPROSYN®, the antiarthritic medication. At the same time, they've aptly dramatized the dosage "flexibility" of the product for the target audience of primary-care physicians. Creative Director Lester Barnett adds that the agency wanted to develop a piece that "respected the specific abilities of the mail medium."

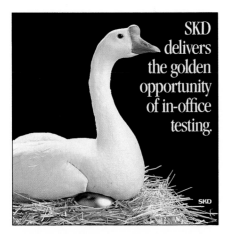

Product: **SKD Products and Services**
Ad Agency: **Rainoldi Kerzner & Radcliffe**
Client: **SmithKline Diagnostics, Inc.**
Art Director: **Paul Harris**
Photographer: **David Tise**
Copywriter: **Daniella Thompson**

The proverbial "goose that laid the golden egg" unifies this handsome campaign for a family of SmithKline Beckman products. Targeted at physicians, the series introduces and positions the products in a "cluttered" market by stressing their profitability. Account Supervisor Eugene Berman writes that the golden goose/nest egg concept was conceived to convey this benefit. He adds that the live goose that modeled for the photography (her name was Harriet) "turned out to be a real prima donna." Staffers feared the photo session would last into the night, but in the end, Harriet "performed like a trooper." Incidentally, the campaign drew approximately 4,300 responses from a 37,000 physician audience.

Product: **DYAZIDE**®
Ad Agency: **Salthouse Torre Norton Inc.**
Client: **Smith Kline & French Co.**
Art Director: **David Recchia**
Illustrator: **Lee Duggan**

Who could resist opening a giant (8⅝" x 16") envelope decorated with ripe bananas in glowing tropical colors? That high-impact image, coupled with the teaser ("Fresh New Data"), compels us to check the contents. Inside, the brochure itself takes the form of an oversized bunch of bananas—skillfully rendered by illustrator Lee Duggan. The brief headline copy talks about the "myth" of hypokalemia (potassium loss) among hypertensive patients on diuretics. To uncover the real facts, we "peel" back the flap and read about the efficacy of DYAZIDE® in preventing hypokalemia. Aimed at physicians who were high prescribers of diuretics and potassium supplements, the mailer commands attention with the irresistible visual, then effectively dispels the "myth" about diuretics by demonstrating that *this* diuretic is different.

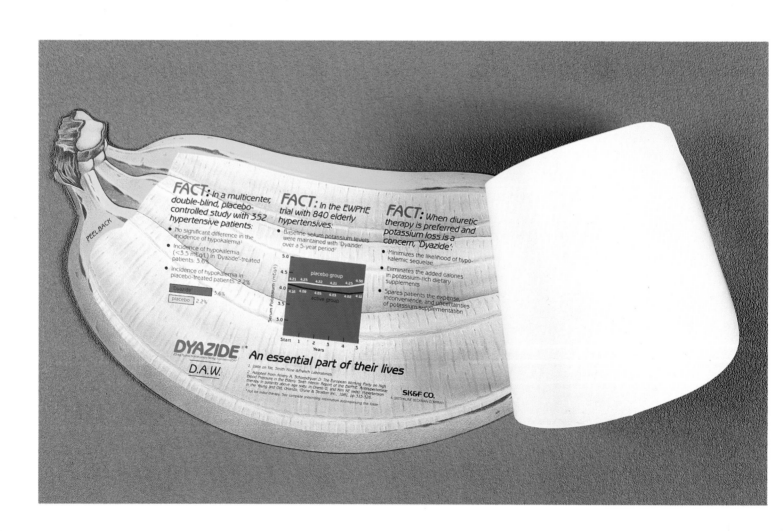

Product: **Norpace® CR**
Ad Agency: **Sutton Communications**
Client: **Searle & Co.**
Art Director: **Nick Manganiello**
Illustrator: **Howard Friedman**
Copywriter: **Norton Bramesco**

Why would a pharmaceutical firm want to convert customers away from one of its own products? When it offers a more convenient variation of the same drug—and that variation enjoys *patent protection* to boot. That's the story behind this eye-catching mailer for Searle & Company's Norpace® CR. A foil package in the form of a big red-and-white pill opens up to reveal a *green*-and-white pill inside (not shown). Both pills are Norpace®—but the green-and-white pill represents Norpace® CR, a controlled-release formula that requires just two doses per day instead of four. Once opened, the green-and-white Norpace® CR brochure reveals a pop-up graph comparing the action of the two versions of the drug over the course of a day. The outer mailing envelope bears a colorful illustration of a prescription pill bottle and the copy "Conversion Kit No. 1."

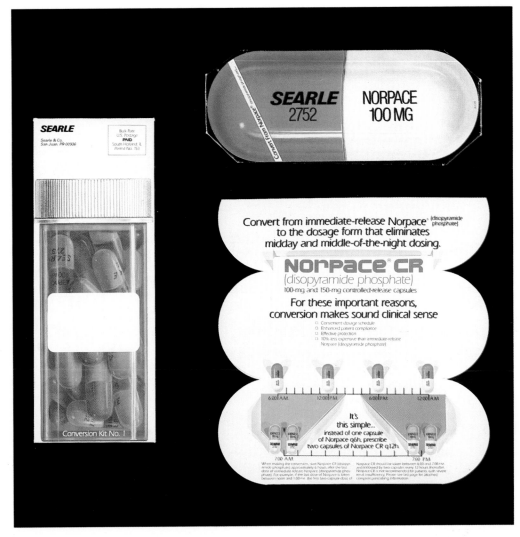

Product: **Tofranil-PM®**
Ad Agency: **C & G Advertising Inc. (In-house)**
Client: **Geigy Pharmaceuticals**
Art Director: **Bob Talarczyk**
Illustrators: **John Hovell, Joe Caggiano**
Copywriters: **Pat Blagden, Ellen Schultz**

Sealed inside an oversized (8" long x 2¼" in diameter) capsule from Geigy Pharmaceuticals is an issue of the

Tofranil-PM® Times. Printed on heavy textured stock, this lively "capsule news" of the '80s devotes just a single brief paragraph to the long-established antidepressant, Tofranil®—but it's enough to get the message across: "Throughout the fifties, sixties, and seventies, Tofranil®…continued as a classic therapy for the treatment of depression. And now, keeping pace with the fast-paced life of the eighties, Tofranil-PM®

remains a classic for today." The rest of the 6" x 16½" newspaper (it opens to 6" x 33") reads like an '80s time capsule, with short features on pop phenomena ranging from yuppies and personal computers to Bruce Springsteen, Rambo, and Princess Diana. A full page of prescribing information and a back-page summary of bulleted selling points round out the promotion of the drug. The package includes a free sample offer.

Product: **Entex® Liquid**
Ad Agency: **Lally, McFarland & Pantello**
Client: **Norwich Eaton Pharmaceuticals**
Art Director: **Jim McFarland**
Illustrator: **Lee Duggan**
Copywriter: **Cynthia Armstrong**

How do you capitalize on the side effects caused by rival medications? These direct-mail promotions cleverly use the term "drybabies" to describe children whose respiratory cold symptoms are treated with antihistamines (and who, as a result, trade their congestion for dried-out sinus and bronchial passages). On the cover of each "Drybabies" brochure is a whimsical cartoon of a truly miserable kid. The intriguing headline—"What turns congested kids into DRYBABIES?"—is common to all the brochures; it prompts us to look inside for the answer. There we learn about the potential problems of antihistamine treatment and the advantages of Entex® Liquid, which combines a decongestant with an expectorant. Each brochure offers physicians a different premium on an attached business reply card.

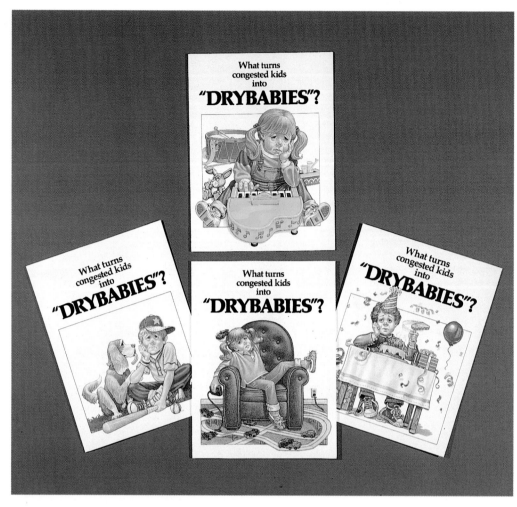

Product: **Entex®**
Ad Agency: **Lally, McFarland & Pantello**
Client: **Norwich Eaton Pharmaceuticals**
Art Director: **Jim McFarland**
Illustrator: **Peter de Seve**
Copywriter: **Cynthia Armstrong**

The bleary-eyed, cold-stricken families who adorn these brochures are obviously suffering. But, in the hands of illustrator Peter de Seve, their misery is so deftly exaggerated, their every movement so suffused with gloom and lethargy, that we can chuckle at their predicament and enjoy the sales pitch for Entex®. The argument is that antihistamines shouldn't be taken to treat advanced cold symptoms; they dry out the respiratory passages and add to the overall discomfort. Entex®, on the other hand, relieves congestion while keeping passages moist. Each piece includes an attached business reply card with a different seasonally related premium offer, from a beach towel to a stadium cushion.

Product: **COMHIST® LA**
Ad Agency: **Lally, McFarland & Pantello**
Client: **Norwich Eaton Pharmaceuticals**
Art Director: **Fred Rescott**
Illustrator: **Shaun Harrison**
Copywriter: **Cynthia Armstrong**

The "State of Allergic Congestion" and the "State of Congestion" are mythical lands of misery—places where pollen hangs oppressively in the air and the wretched citizens sniffle their way through life. The folks at Lally, McFarland & Pantello have spun this concept into an engaging series of brochures for the allergy/cold remedy COMHIST® LA. Each 7½" x 10" piece depicts a different inhabitant of an aforementioned state in an outdoor pursuit, visibly suffering from nasal/allergic symptoms. Inside, Cynthia Armstrong's sprightly copy commiserates with these poor souls, sometimes launching into flights of mock-rhapsodic whimsy. But then the right-hand panel gets down to business by summing up the "extra" benefits of COMHIST® LA. From here it's just a quick step to the "extra" offer presented on an attached business reply card: physicians who send for samples of the drug will also receive a useful premium gift—a different one from each brochure.

Product: **COMHIST® LA**
Ad Agency: **Lally, McFarland & Pantello**
Client: **Norwich Eaton Pharmaceuticals, Inc.**
Art Director: **Nancy Slivka-Bitteker**
Illustrator: **Bob Alcorn**
Copywriter: **Susan Greenhut**

Postcard greetings from the "State of Allergic Congestion" add color and a touch of humor to these mailers for COMHIST® LA. Both "postcards"—a spring scene in a garden and a summer scene by the pool—depict the miseries of seasonal allergies, with a pertinent, legibly scrawled postcard message displayed underneath. Inside, the copy builds the need for "extra help," then reveals how COMHIST® LA meets that need (it combines antihistamine and decongestant action). The business reply card attached inside offers physicians a free leather-covered travel diary (in the "spring" brochure) and a canvas travel kit (in the "summer" brochure).

Product: **QUIBRON®-T/SR**
Design Firm: **Netcor**
Client: **Bristol Laboratories**
Art Director: **William C. Wolff**
Illustrator: **Laura Larson**
Photographer: **Bruno Ratensperger**
Copywriter: **Steven M. Beck**

This brochure doesn't merely *expect* us to look inside; it practically *tells* us to. This disarming directness doesn't hurt, and neither does the intriguing cover art—or, for that matter, the die-cut window. So we open to the inside spread, and out pops a larger-than-life QUIBRON®-T/SR tablet, broken up three different ways. Counting the full pill (shown beneath the pop-up), we have *four* different potential dosages from a single tablet—100 mg, 150 mg, 200 mg, and 300 mg. "Four important reasons to open this brochure," remember? We're not disappointed—in fact, it's a memorable way to create an identity for the product.

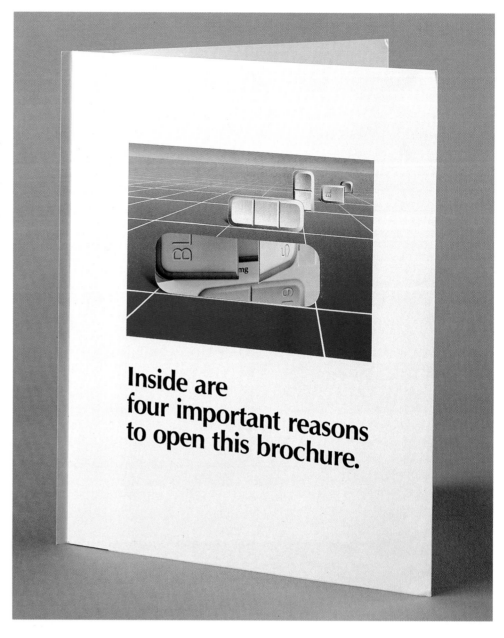

Product: **Catapres-TTS®**
Ad Agency: **Barnum Communications, Inc.**
Client: **Boehringer Ingelheim Pharmaceuticals, Inc.**
Paper Engineering: **Netcor**
Art Director: **Burton Pollack**
Illustrator: **Michel Henricot**
Paper Engineer: **William C. Wolff**
Copywriters: **Burton Pollack, Schuyler Ritter**

The anatomy of Catapres-TTS®, a transdermal patch for the control of hypertension, is brought vividly into three dimensions with this exciting pop-up brochure by Barnum Communications, Inc. Developed in collaboration with William C. Wolff, executive V.P. of Netcor (he served as paper engineer), the cross-sectional model shows the four-layered Catapres-TTS® patch lying atop the skin. The drug molecules are shown passing through the epidermis and into the bloodstream. The model is as intricate as it is colorful and instructive: note the individual hairs popping out of their follicles. Included with the brochure is a sample user guide for patients. To obtain more, the physician must contact a Boehringer Ingelheim representative.

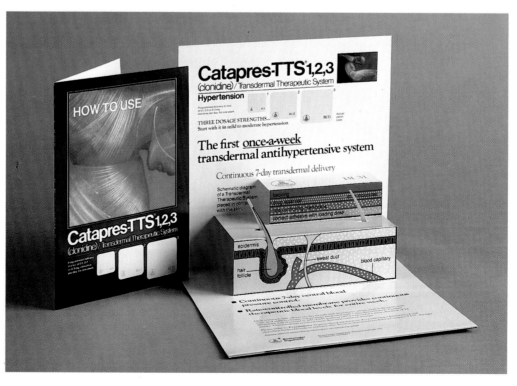

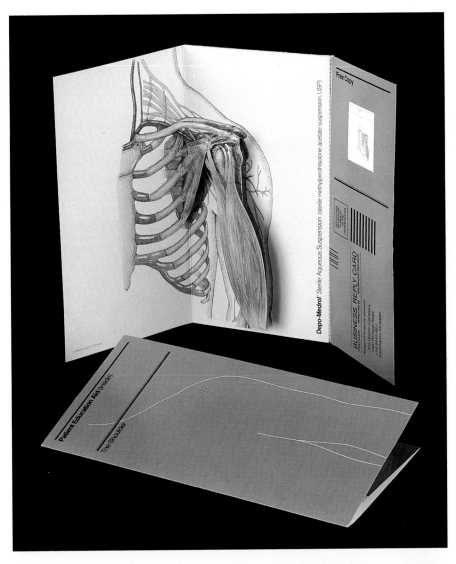

Product: **Depo-Medrol**®
Client: **The Upjohn Co.**
Paper Engineering: **Netcor**
Art Director: **Cliff Keeslar**
Illustrator: **Scott Thorn Barrows**
Paper Engineer: **William C. Wolff**
Copywriter: **Ken Barry**

Here's a 3-D mailer that also serves as a patient education guide. Once inside the envelope, we see a simple outline of a shoulder and arm on the cover of the brochure. Inside, the shoulder has gained an extra dimension: popping up from the brochure is a paper sculpture complete with musculature, bones, and blood vessels. This 3-D model can help physicians acquaint their patients with the anatomy of the shoulder as well as commonly encountered medical problems. The attached business reply card enables the doctor to send for a free copy of *A Reference Guide for Periarticular Injection—the Shoulder.*

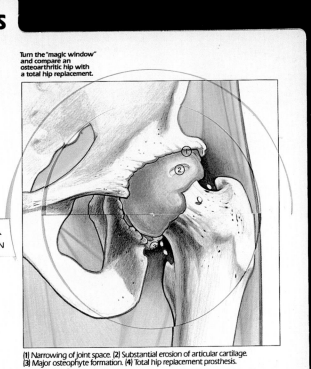

Osteoarthritis of the Hip

Part of a counseling program for your patients with arthritic and musculoskeletal conditions.

Osteoarthritis (OA) is the most common form of arthritis. More than 40 million Americans have this degenerative joint disease.

The cause of the condition is unknown, but it is thought to be associated with the wear and tear of the protective tissue (cartilage) surrounding your joints. As the cartilage changes and its cushioning effect decreases, joints grind together so that even the slightest movement can trigger pain. In addition, small obstructions such as spurs or bone fragments may form in your joints and cause inflammation (swelling and redness). This may add to your discomfort.

Because OA frequently affects weight-bearing joints such as hips and knees, it's often responsible for hampering free movement. The basis for treating a patient with osteoarthritis of the hip is well established: rest, rehabilitation and proper medication. In addition, early detection may enhance therapeutic results.

In more advanced cases, total replacement of the osteoarthritic hip may be justified. For over 20 years, hip prostheses have been used in patients with severe degeneration and intractable pain—often with tremendous success.

Although today there is no cure for osteoarthritis, the disease is not life-threatening. Your physician can develop an individualized treatment program to suit your lifestyle, improve mobility and help alleviate your symptoms.

Turn the "magic window" and compare an osteoarthritic hip with a total hip replacement.

TURN

(1) Narrowing of joint space. (2) Substantial erosion of articular cartilage.
(3) Major osteophyte formation. (4) Total hip replacement prosthesis.

Product: **NAPROSYN**®
Ad Agency: **Vicom/FCB**
Client: **Syntex Laboratories, Inc.**
Art Directors: **Joseph Rozon, Stephen Mullens**
Illustrator: **Vince Perez**
Copywriter: **Bob Finkel**

By using this interactive educational tool from Syntex Laboratories, Inc., patients suffering from osteoarthritis of the hip can learn more about their condition as they contemplate hip replacement surgery. First they see what their osteoarthritic hip looks like anatomically (not a pretty sight)...then they turn the handle 180 degrees and watch a new picture emerge. Now they're looking at a total hip replacement, neatly installed and ready for action. Targeted at orthopedic surgeons, the piece incidentally promotes NAPROSYN®. It was part of a series designed to fit into standard-size file drawers.

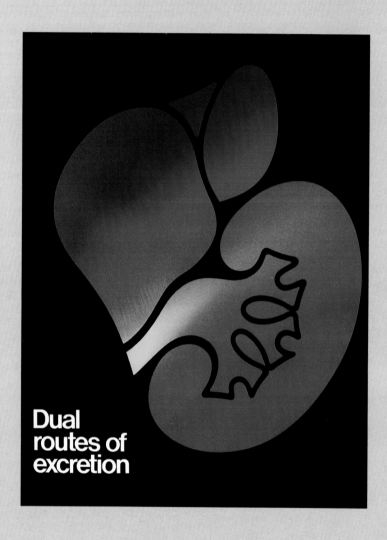

Dual
routes of
excretion

Control
with
once-a-day
dosage...

Product: **Micronase**®
Ad Agency: **Kallir, Philips, Ross, Inc.**
Client: **The Upjohn Co.**
Art Directors: **Gerald Philips, Rose Farber, Al Zalon**
Illustrator: **KPR Studio/Don Martiny**
Copywriter: **Jack Domeshek**

These intensely vivid covers appear to be the work of a single art director, but according to Al Zalon, V.P./ executive art director of Kallir, Philips, Ross, Inc., several were involved. Each mailer focuses on one of the benefits of Micronase® tablets, a treatment for type II diabetes. In each case, the symbolic cover graphic is accompanied by a brief benefit statement that clarifies the visual symbolism and drives its message home. Inside, four major problems of type II diabetes are presented in chart form; on the right side of the chart, the copy describes how Micronase® acts to relieve these problems. In each brochure, black type is used to highlight the "featured" problem (and corresponding benefit of Micronase®); the other three problem/benefit couplings are set in blue type.

1. Endogenous insulin
2. Number of target-cell insulin receptors is increased
3. Insulin receptor binding and sensitivity are augmented
4. Postreceptor-binding events are improved.

Insulin sensitivity restored

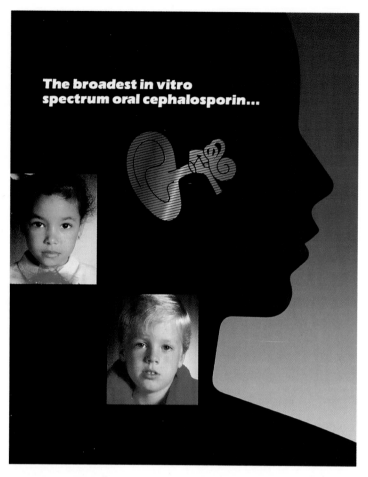

Product: **CEFTIN**®
Ad Agency: **Kallir, Philips, Ross, Inc.**
Client: **Glaxo, Inc.**
Art Director: **Leslie Sisman**
Illustrator: **Walter Thiess**
Photographer: **Paul Chen**
Copywriter: **Ron Jastrzemski**

Developed to introduce CEFTIN®, a broad-spectrum cephalosporin from Glaxo, Inc., these colorful self-mailers take the form of 6" x 7¾" postcards (actually single-folded brochures designed to *look* like post-cards, with prescribing information inside). Each mailer features instantly recognizable graphics that link it to the series: part of the body is depicted in a black profile, set against a violet background, with the targeted area highlighted in a vivid spectrum of color—undoubtedly a visual reference to the drug's "broad-spectrum" action. Color inset photos of patients add a human touch. Aimed at GPs, FPs, and infectious disease specialists, the campaign included over 60 promotional pieces.

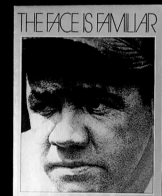

Product: **Diabinese**®
Ad Agency: **William Douglas McAdams Inc.**
Client: **Pfizer Laboratories**
Art Directors: **Patrick Creaven, Diane Lynch**
Photographer: **Time-Life: World Wide Photos/**
Denes Petoe
Copywriters: **Bill Wolf, Noel Holland**

Three great faces of the 20th century, each of them instantly recognizable, lend their presence to this series of mailings for Diabinese®. The headline reads, "The Face Is Familiar"—certainly true for Churchill, Eleanor Roosevelt, and Babe Ruth, but also applicable to the distinctive blue "D" shape of the Diabinese® tablet. Intended to discourage generic substitutions, the campaign won a Gold Medal in the 1985 New York International Advertising Festival. Patrick Creaven, V.P./group head art director for William Douglas McAdams Inc., explains that vintage news photographs were converted to mezzotints and printed with a specially mixed fifth color, a metallic blue ink; this gave the stock photos a contemporary look and visually unified the three mailings. The agency achieved further unity by displaying the distinctive hats worn by each of the three celebrities.

Product: **Ludiomil**®
Ad Agency: **C & G Advertising Inc. (In-house)**
Client: **Ciba Pharmaceutical Co.**
Art Director: **Bob Talarczyk**
Illustrators: **Peter Fiore ("Janet in the Rose Garden"), Dennis Luzak ("Karl in His Workshop")**
Copywriter: **Pat Blagden**

The cylindrical mailing tubes (illustrated with a reproduction of "Whistler's Mother") promise something of value inside. And we're not let down. Ciba has commissioned prominent artists to create a series of "Portraits of Aging." Printed on heavy textured art stock and intended for framing, the prints are part of limited-edition runs exclusively for the targeted physician audience. The handsome "invitation" in each mailing tube entices physicians to sign up for the next free print in the series—along with a sampler set of the antidepressant/antianxiety medication Ludiomil®. The copy makes a smooth segue from discussing the prints to promoting the benefits of Ludiomil® in treating depressed older patients. Three ambitious mailings were carried out through the course of a year, each consisting of a different portrait, a postcard, an invitation, a frame, and a drug sample.

Product: **Ser-Ap-Es**®
Ad Agency: **C & G Advertising Inc. (In-house)**
Client: **Ciba Pharmaceutical Co.**
Art Director: **Bob Talarczyk**
Illustrators: **Janice Townsley, Jeanette Reck**
Copywriter: **Ellen Schultz**

The teaser copy on the cover drops just a subtle hint: "Your chance to unlock the classic combination." But any physician who opens this compact (4" x 6" x 1½") package is bound to be surprised by the contents. Tucked inside is a real combination lock—the kind we all used in gym class. Its three-part combination coincides nicely with the three-part composition (and even the name) of Ser-Ap-Es®, a "combination" of reserpine, hydralazine, and hydrochlorothiazide. Attached to the front cover is an entry form for a random drawing—the winner was to receive 12 classical music cassettes, and *everyone*, six sample mailings of Ser-Ap-Es®. Art Director Bob Talarczyk writes that the piece drew a 42% response (that's right—no decimal point), making it one of the most successful mailings in C & G history.

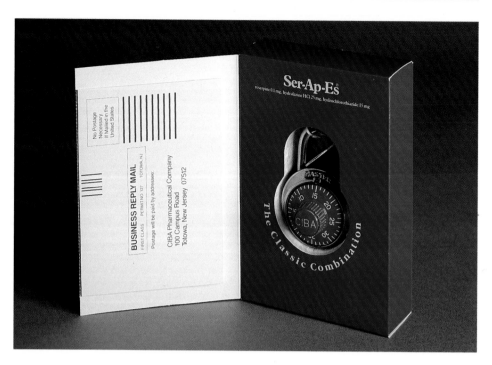

Product: **Today™ Contraceptive Sponge**
Ad Agency: **Gross Townsend Frank Hoffman, Inc.**
Client: **VLI Corp.**
Art Director: **Karen Klein**
Illustrator: **Carol Gillot**
Account Person: **Jane Townsend**

This special demonstration kit for the Today™ Contraceptive Sponge was designed to familiarize patients with this new product and educate them about its use. Aimed at family planning clinics, physicians, and nurses, the kit includes six sample sponges, instruction booklets, and a laminated display card with tastefully illustrated step-by-step directions for inserting and removing the sponge. The kit also provides storage compartments for the product and even includes a Rolodex card with toll-free number for requesting more sponges. According to Executive V.P. Jane Townsend, "It was a totally new concept in contraception and people needed to see it and try it before they could recommend it."

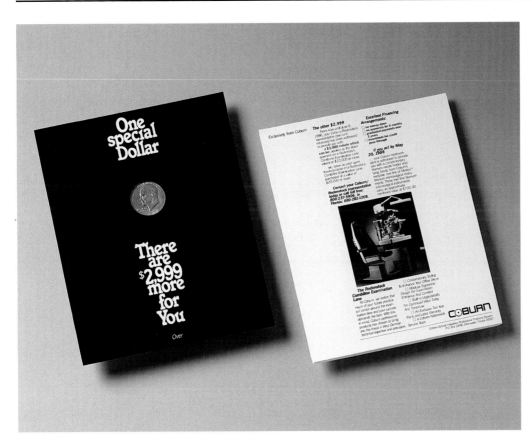

Products: **Coburn Optical Products**
Ad Agency: **Ad-Tech Communications**
Client: **Coburn Optical Industries**
Art Director: **Florian Pfister**
Copywriter: **W. R. Quinlivan**

Targeted at third- and fourth-year ophthalmic residents, this package for Coburn/Rodenstock optical equipment gives away an Eisenhower dollar ("One special Dollar") and promises $2,999 more (the company is offering a $3,000 rebate on the equipment). The idea of establishing an early business relationship with graduating students always makes sound marketing sense, and the generous rebate on highly regarded equipment would certainly make sense to debt-conscious ophthalmology residents. William R. Quinlivan, marketing partner for Ad-Tech Communications, notes that although the Rodenstock equipment is widely recognized for quality, "few residents were aware that it was distributed in the U.S. by Coburn." He adds that "we needed a high opening and read rate"—which the free dollar and offer of "$2,999 more" would certainly accomplish.

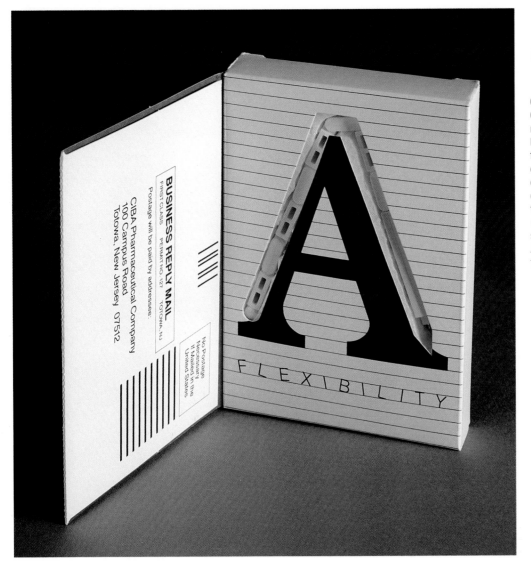

Product: **Apresazide**®
Ad Agency: **C & G Advertising Inc. (In-house)**
Client: **Ciba Pharmaceutical Co.**
Art Director: **Bob Talarczyk**
Illustrator: **Janice Townsley**
Copywriter: **Ellen Schultz**

C & G Advertising Inc., the in-house agency for Ciba-Geigy, developed this petite (3⅝" x 5⅛" x ¾") 3-D mailer to promote Apresazide®. The drug's flexibility becomes the focal point of the piece: a multi-jointed flexible ballpoint pen is tucked inside the package, conforming to the outline of the big letter "A". And the copy on the back reads, "Write for any occasion"—a clever reference to both the free pen and the drug. On the attached business reply card is an entry form for a random drawing; the prize is a genuine leather desk set. All participants receive six sample mailings of Apresazide® throughout the year. C & G reports that this package garnered a whopping 38% response.

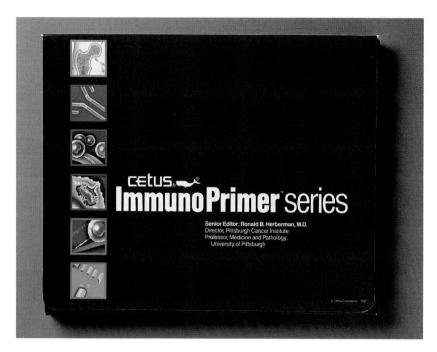

Title: **ImmunoPrimer™ Series**
Ad Agency: **Vicom/FCB**
Client: **Cetus Corp.**
Art Director: **Madeleine Clark**
Illustrator: **Ellen Going Jacobs**
Copywriters: **Caren Spinner, Marjorie Little**

This six-part ImmunoPrimer™ series from Cetus Corporation was designed to educate the entire oncology team—including nurses as well as physicians—about human immunology and new biotech therapeutics. Each unit in the series is a full-color folder packed with concise, well-organized information and educational visual renderings. The copy is sophisticated, yet clear enough to be understood by medical professionals at the sub-MD level. A glossary and reference sources are included on the back; each folder is tabbed and designed to fit into a box that houses the entire series. Lester Barnett, creative director for Vicom/FCB, writes that the agency was "asked to create high awareness and credibility for Cetus with the oncology community."

Product: **NAPROSYN®**
Ad Agency: **Vicom/FCB**
Client: **Syntex Laboratories, Inc.**
Art Director: **Stephen Mullens**
Copywriter: **Bob Finkel**

Aimed at rheumatologists, this exciting series of "Rheumatologic Decisions" presents the physician with challenging case studies for analysis and review. But what lifts these packages above the norm is their *degree* of interactiveness: after reading a hypothetical patient's history and symptoms—and examining the *full-size X-ray transparency* included inside—the physician is invited to formulate a diagnosis and propose a course of treatment. Once this is accomplished, the physician opens the Velcro-sealed panel and reads the actual assessment of Syntex Laboratories' "contributing clinician." Each package is numbered and tabbed for filing purposes, and accompanied by a vibrant promotional panel for NAPROSYN®. Attached to the panel is a questionnaire that continues to involve the physician with NAPROSYN®.

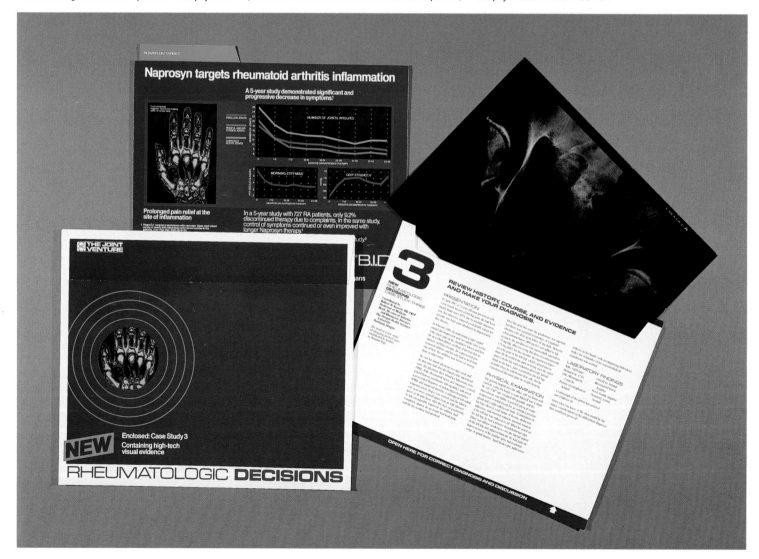

Product: **Tofranil-PM®**
Ad Agency: **C & G Advertising Inc. (In-house)**
Client: **Ciba Pharmaceuticals**
Art Director: **Bob Talarczyk**
Copywriter: **Ellen Schultz**

C & G Advertising devised this ingenious 3-D mailing for the antidepressant Tofranil-PM®. Housed inside the box is a memo pad for the doctor; the image of a faceless man is printed down the side of the pad. This attractive promotional giveaway will sit on the physician's desk, serving as a constant reminder of the drug. But the *box* is even more remarkable. The inside has been designed as a room, with a black "floor" and a featureless human figure in the far corner. The copy on the outside reads, "Breaking Down the Walls of Depression," and sure enough, the "walls" of the box tumble down to reveal the inner room along with promotional copy. Art Director Bob Talarczyk writes that the mailing drew a 37% response rate, and that requests for pads are still coming in.

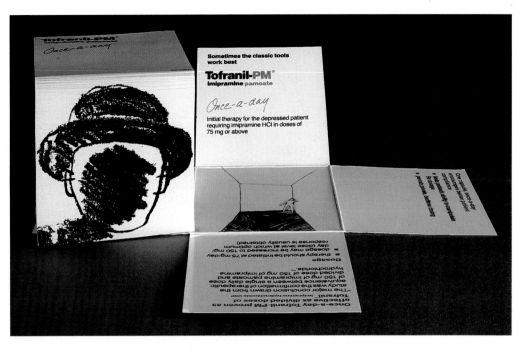

Product: **TONOCARD®**
Ad Agency: **Gross Townsend Frank Hoffman, Inc.**
Client: **Merck Sharp & Dohme**
Art Director: **Jeffrey Pienkos**
Photography: **Jeff Morgan Photography**
Copywriter: **Zoë R. Graves**

TONOCARD® is positioned as the medication of choice for heart patients with "Double Trouble"—that is, a combination of ventricular arrhythmia and underlying coronary artery disease. To promote the drug to cardiologists, Gross Townsend Frank Hoffman, Inc., created this multi-part direct-mail series featuring useful premiums (including calipers and a pointer pen), plus an informative series of "Clinical Applications" in cardiology—as well as booklets combining medical information with promotional messages for the drug. The artwork in the direct-mail campaign was also used in space advertising for TONOCARD®.

Product: **Ativan**®
Ad Agency: **Kallir, Philips, Ross, Inc.**
Client: **Wyeth Laboratories**
Art Director: **John Geryak**
Illustrator: **Jean-Michel Folon**
Copywriter: **Bernie Steinman**

"Is it possible to express concepts of pharmacology and therapeutics in visual terms?" So begins the letter accompanying this portfolio of vibrant prints by graphics wizard Jean-Michel Folon. And, as the letter points out, Folon himself has answered the question. Each of the six images in this portfolio symbolizes a different benefit of Ativan®, a medication prescribed for the treatment of depression-related anxiety. The psychiatrists who received the mailing could learn about the drug while obtaining some colorful contemporary art for their walls.

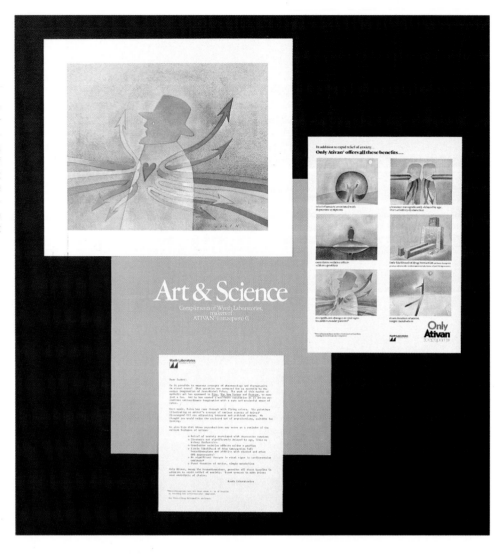

Product: **PRINIVIL**®
Ad Agency: **Vicom/FCB**
Client: **Merck Sharp & Dohme**
Art Directors: **Joe Kamuck, Gilbert Albright**
Photographer: **Marjorie Dressler**
Copywriters: **Joan Marie Washa, Sharon Lantzy**

A golden sunset glows from the envelope of this package for PRINIVIL®, while the teaser copy on the back promises "A New Way of Living with Antihypertensive Therapy." Then we open the brochure and behold an exhilarating mountaintop scene in *three dimensions*. Literally popping out from the background is a jubilant man, arms outstretched in a celebration of life; the two younger mountain climbers look on approvingly. Below the pop-up, the copy puts the emphasis on "LIVING" in a series of four concisely stated benefits. The attached business reply card enables the physician to send for a free starter supply of the drug.

Product: **Tolectin® DS**
Ad Agency: **Thomas G. Ferguson Associates Inc.**
Client: **McNeil Pharmaceutical**
Art Director: **Michael Fiore**
Illustrator: **Bill Haney**
Photography: **F-90 Photography**
Copywriter: **Robert Krell**

A series of three Tolectin® "Living with Arthritis" challenges enables physicians to "experience first-hand the difficulties of arthritis." Each of the "challenges"—the tiny pencil, ballpoint pen, and scissors—appears in the window of the mailing envelope. Art Director Michael Fiore writes that the primary goal of the window envelope was to entice the physician to open the package to discover how the implement "relates to the challenge proposed by the envelope teaser. Once inside," he continues, "the doctor is further challenged to become an active participant by completing the attached BRC using an implement whose 'smallness' simulates the difficulty arthritic patients have in performing even simple tasks." Three separate giveaways—a mechanical pencil, a ballpoint pen, and a sweepstakes drawing for a copy of the *Oxford Textbook of Medicine*—further entice the physician to send for starter samples of the drug.

Product: **VoSol®**
Marketing Firm: **TM Marketing, Inc.**
Client: **Wallace Laboratories**
Art Director: **Donald J. Stein**
Illustrator: **James Whitman**
Production Manager: **Donald J. Stein**
Account Director: **Thomas L. Maloof**
Product Manager: **Eileen Wong-Hart**

It's not all sun and fun for the water sports enthusiasts pictured on these brochures for VoSol®. A fair percentage of them will pay for their pleasure with an acute case of *otitis externa*—better known as "swimmer's ear." Although the action photos vary from one brochure to the next, each piece uses the same headline ("When Fast and Powerful Results Make All the Difference").

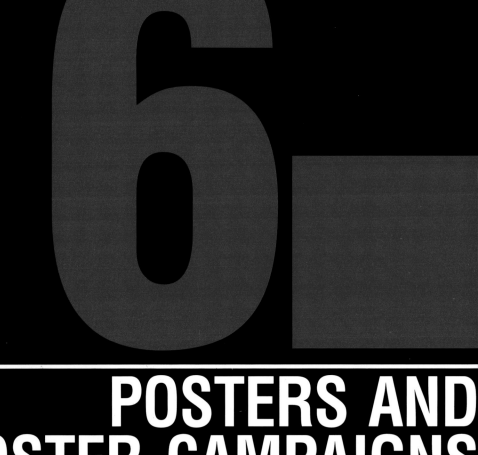

6

POSTERS AND POSTER CAMPAIGNS

PROMOTIONAL
PATIENT EDUCATION
PUBLIC SERVICE

The entries in this chapter are heirs to a grand tradition of popular art dating back over a hundred years. With the development of color lithography, advertisers seized upon the mind-boggling potential of posters for promoting products and events. Nothing could rival the impact of a poster for selling soft drinks or publicizing a show. Yet, over the century that followed, these oversized ads took on an independent life as a uniquely powerful and lively art form.

Through the years, the best posters have ennobled advertising with art, and disseminated that art to a wide public. They also have yielded some of the most memorable images of their times, from the *belle epoque* entertainers immortalized by Toulouse-Lautrec to the psychedelic fantasies of Peter Max in the late '60s.

Posters are mirrors of their age, and the examples on the following pages reflect the suave eclecticism of the 1980s. The styles are diverse—there is certainly no identifiable "sensibility," as with the ornate Art Nouveau style of the 1890s or the exuberantly streamlined Art Deco graphics of the 1920s and '30s. But something about the spirit of these posters is decidedly contemporary.

Like all good posters, they share a few family traits. First of all, they're *big*. Not overwhelmingly so, but they're spacious enough to be glimpsed from a distance. With a couple of exceptions, they're *graphically powerful*—overstated rather than understated. (This is to catch the attention of the viewer.) And they *communicate* clearly and persuasively with their audience.

With their large-as-life dimensions, powerful graphics, and public accessibility, posters have proven to be an effective means of transmitting promotional or public education messages in the medical field. The typical entry in this chapter was designed for display in the doctor's office, where it would serve a dual purpose: to enlighten the patients about health

matters, and remind the physician about the company or product that sponsored it.

Because most of these posters are placed indoors, usually in waiting rooms, they don't have to communicate as rapidly as their brethren on the streets. (There, a passing pedestrian must be able to absorb the message in a couple of seconds.) As a result, medical posters can be designed with interactive features, longer copy, and other devices suited to casual browsing.

One highly attractive example is the allergens poster by artist Heather Cooper. Commissioned by Syntex Laboratories, this elegant garden scene actually harbors about two dozen common allergens—weeds, flowers, pets, and the like. Each item in the illustration is keyed to a list of allergens running down the side of the poster—an effectively involving interactive device for patients in the waiting room.

Another interactive poster—one with moving parts—was illustrated by Radu Vero for Wyeth Laboratories. Developed to warn patients about the dangers of untreated high blood pressure, it includes a number of flaps depicting the vulnerable organ systems in their normal state. When you *lift* the flaps, you see a different picture entirely—each organ is shown as it appears after being ravaged by hypertension.

The cautionary approach shows up in other posters as well. One piece shows us the gradually slumping postures of women as they become afflicted with osteoporosis. Each figure is labeled by age, so patients will know what to expect if their condition goes untreated too long.

Along the same cautionary lines—but more outwardly whimsical in their approach—are the posters warning low-income mothers about feeding "the Sugar Monster"—i.e., letting their kids stuff themselves with overly sweet, highly caloric junk foods and drinks of negligible nutritive value. Each poster in the series depicts a different Sugar Monster—all

of them comically repulsive—representing the various groups of sugary snacks to be banished from the diet.

Yet another "warning" poster—this one promoting auto safety—is more grimly ironic: in cartoon form, people are shown flying from their car upon impact; these human projectiles, hurled like darts toward a dartboard, are accompanied by sobering accident mortality statistics.

More unabashedly humorous is NASAL CROM®'s lively parody of those ubiquitous "Doors of…" posters. In this case, it's "Noses of America." The poster is chockablock with specimens of the native *probosci*—25 of them to be exact—in all their glorious shapes and sizes.

Only a minority of the posters make a direct play for our emotions. One that stands out is the simple message aimed at eye specialists, "To see again what I have seen before," a reference to the restoration of eyesight. Another is Lederle's poster promoting a polio vaccine: it shows a downcast adult polio victim wishing that such a vaccine had been available when she was a child. Still another victim of disease is depicted in a moody poster about herpes; it uses an intriguing photographic technique called "solarization."

Another special technique represented in these posters is paper sculpture ("good" and "bad" food groups depicted in three-dimensional relief). And the poster from Genentech reveals a rainbow-colored Valentine heart etched through a solid black surface.

Lastly, one classic use of posters is to publicize events, and you'll see some noteworthy representatives of that genre: the simple urinary tract symbol for a conference on urology, Ciba-Geigy's expansive "One Heart, One World" poster for the 10th World Conference of Cardiology, and the Rx Club's clever street-sign *caduceus* for the club's first annual medical advertising and art show.

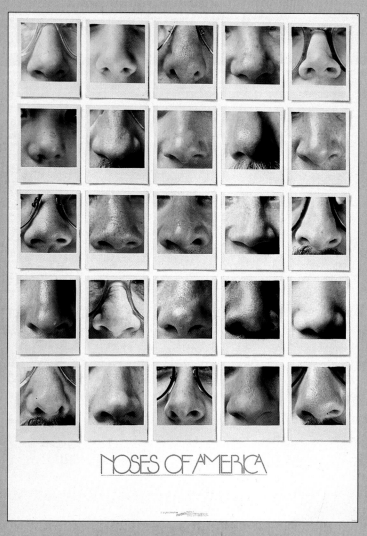

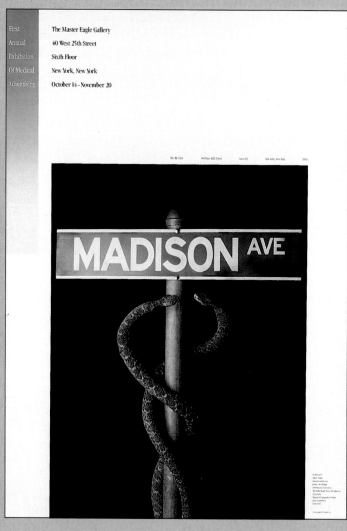

Product: **NASALCROM®**
Title: **"Noses of America"**
Ad Agency: **Sandler Communications Inc.**
Client: **Fisons Corp.**
Art Director: **Jerry Malone**
Photographer: **Tom Holdorf**
Copywriter: **Michael Metelenis**

SILVER. Twenty-five "Noses of America" adorn this tongue-in-cheek adaptation of the familiar "Doors of..." posters. Offered to specialty physicians who treat allergic rhinitis patients, the prize-winning poster was part of a promotion for NASALCROM®, a nasal allergy medication from Fisons Corporation. The participating *probosci* were photographed by Tom Holdorf.

Title: **"Madison Avenue"**
Design Firm: **Jeffrey Pienkos Design**
Client: **The Rx Club**
Art Director: **Jeffrey Pienkos**
Photographer: **John F. Cooper**

SILVER. To promote the First Annual Exhibition of Medical Advertising, the Rx Club used this startling image of snakes wriggling up a Madison Avenue street sign. Their intertwined configuration on the pole suggests the *caduceus*, that time-honored symbol of medicine. The sign for "Madison Ave.," bastion of the American advertising profession, further defines the nature of the exhibition: it can only mean *medical advertising*.

Title: **"Allergens"**
Ad Agency: **Vicom/FCB**
Client: **Syntex Laboratories, Inc.**
Art Director: **Stephen Mullens**
Illustrator: **Heather Cooper**
Copywriter: **Cari Weisberg**

SILVER. A pair of glass doors opens onto an idyllic garden landscape in this elegant poster by Heather Cooper. But anyone who looks closely will notice that the scene is strewn with two dozen common allergens, all of them neatly labeled and keyed to a list that runs semiconspicuously down the side of the door. Created for Syntex Laboratories as a patient education piece, the 18" x 39" poster was offered to physicians in a direct-mail campaign. Lester Barnett, creative director of Vicom/FCB, writes that "physicians are extremely reticent to put pieces up on their wall. This was to break through the barrier." And it succeeded handsomely.

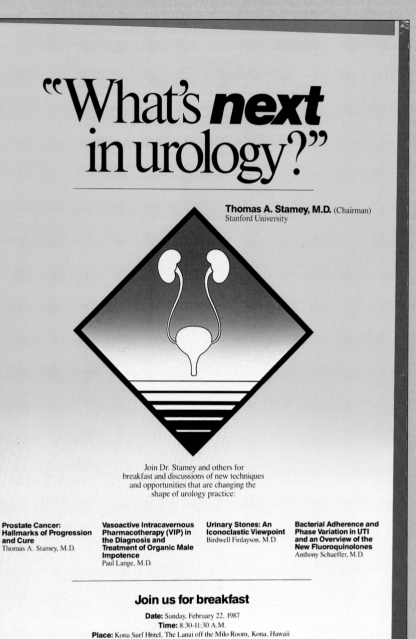

Title: **"to see again what I have seen before"**
Ad Agency: **Gross Townsend Frank Hoffman, Inc.**
Client: **CooperVision IOL**
Art Director: **Debra Prymas**
Illustrator: **Sister Corita**

The inspiring message written across this vivid poster reads, "to see again what I have seen before." By themselves, the words sound lofty but somewhat puzzling; placed in their proper context, they take on a new dimension. What the message actually refers to is the restoration of sight via an intraocular lens from CooperVision IOL. (The dazzling burst of color represents the beauty of restored sight.) According to the agency, the poster was aimed at ophthalmic surgeons and was intended to "press their emotional hot button regarding their pride in restoring eyesight."

Title: **"What's next in urology?"**
Ad Agency: **Gross Townsend Frank Hoffman, Inc.**
Client: **Merck Sharp & Dohme**
Art Director: **Orin Kimball**

SILVER. Designed to promote a conference on future trends in urology, this striking 20" x 30" poster uses two complementary colors—yellow and purple—to draw attention to itself. The diamond-shaped urinary tract motif created an easily recognized graphic symbol for the event, which featured presentations by four prominent urologists.

Title: **"What's your number?"**
Ad Agency: **Gross Townsend Frank Hoffman, Inc.**
Client: **Merck Sharp & Dohme**
Art Director: **Orin Kimball**

Bold, brilliant colors and an instantly recognizable visual of a "broken heart" draw attention to this poster, one of two for a cholesterol screening program. Entitled "What's your number?" this poster shows a multicolored array of cholesterol counts (some good, some not) spilling out of the heart. The other poster (not shown) is entitled "Cholesterol is a heartbreaker" and depicts only the heart itself. Both include a cautionary message about the danger of high cholesterol and the ease of having it checked. Leslie Orfuss, senior project manager, writes that the posters were part of a program called "The Cholesterol Connection"—"a comprehensive package to help hospitals run their own cholesterol screening events."

Title: **"A Work of Heart"**
Ad Agency: **Dorritie & Lyons, Inc.**
Client: **Genentech**
Art Director: **Tom Velardi**
Illustrator: **Tim Girvin**
Copywriter: **Tom Velardi**

A traditional Valentine-shaped heart transforms itself into a sketch of the living human heart in this "Work of Heart" from Genentech. The company is thanking those who helped make its new drug, Activase tPA®, a reality—so in a sense, the "Valentine" concept is entirely appropriate. The graphics for the 24" x 18½" poster appear to be etched through a black surface layer so that the underlying spectrum of color becomes visible.

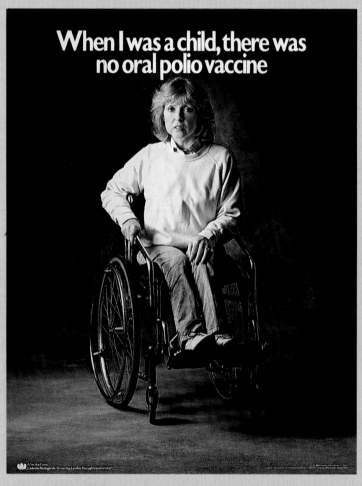

Product: **Orimune**®
Title: **"When I was a child..."**
Ad Agency: **Carrafiello, Diehl & Associates, Inc.**
Client: **Lederle Laboratories/Lederle Biologicals**
Art Directors: **Bill Alderisio, Audrey Artusio**
Photographer: **Nick Samardge**
Copywriter: **Tyler Kaus**

The melancholy face of an adult polio victim adds poignancy to this 18" x 22½" poster from Lederle Biologicals. William Green, senior V.P./creative group supervisor for Carrafiello, Diehl & Associates, Inc., notes that the model actually had polio. The purpose of the piece, he writes, was "to attract interest to a low-interest product that physicians take for granted, and have used routinely for over 25 years." The cautionary tone of the poster reminds pediatricians not to assume that polio has been wiped out, and to protect their patients with the vaccine.

Product: **Lopressor**®
Title: **"One Heart, One World"**
Ad Agency: **C & G Advertising Inc. (In-house)**
Client: **Ciba-Geigy**
Art Director: **Myrtle Johnson**
Illustrator: **Arthur Lidov**

Commissioned by Ciba-Geigy for the tenth World Congress of Cardiology Meeting in Washington, D.C., this vibrant work by Arthur Lidov conveys the theme of "One Heart, One World." The heart is shown in cross section, with deep blue veins and scarlet arteries branching out over the surface of the globe (which itself is depicted in a heart-shaped projection). Below, physicians of all races focus their attention on a human heart; there is a sense of awe as they behold the wondrous pump, which seems to float in midair. An interesting sidelight: the artist put the final brush strokes on the painting at Ciba-Geigy's convention booth; interested attendees could request a copy of the poster from the company's rep.

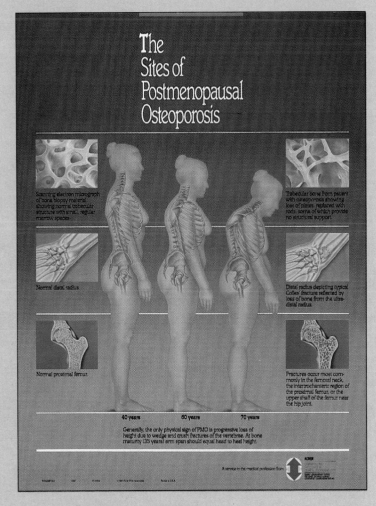

Product: **ZOVIRAX**®
Title: **"Herpes Isn't Hopeless"**
Ad Agency: **Sandler Communications Inc.**
Client: **Burroughs Wellcome, Inc.**
Art Director: **Jerry Malone**
Photographer: **Steve Prezant**
Copywriter: **Dan Sturtevant**

Hope for herpes victims is the theme of this striking 13"
x 17¼" poster prepared by Sandler Communications
for Burroughs Wellcome, Inc. The visual image of the
downcast girl was made through a photographic process called solarization. (Avant-garde photographer
Man Ray used the same technique back in the 1920s.)
Agency President Kenneth B. Sandler notes that "the
poster needed to be large enough to be read across a
waiting room, while not being too large that physicians
wouldn't want to hang it up."

Title: **"The Sites of Postmenopausal
Osteoporosis"**
Ad Agency: **Thomas G. Ferguson Associates Inc.**
Client: **Rorer Pharmaceuticals**
Art Director: **Phil Wiener**
Illustrator: **Judith Glick**

Designed to be displayed in physicians' offices, this
20" x 25¾" poster educates patients about postmenopausal osteoporosis, a serious bone condition that
commonly affects older women. The porous bones are
illustrated in cross section, and the gradually slumping
postures of women shown at 40, 60, and 70 years of
age attest to the ravages of the disease. Aside from its
purpose as a patient aid, the poster quietly reminds
physicians about three medications from Rorer Pharmaceuticals.

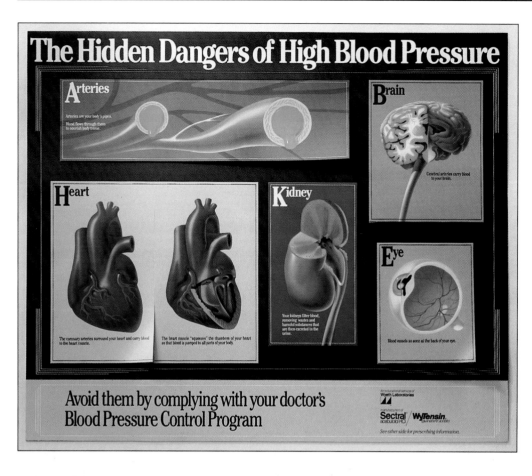

Title: **"The Hidden Dangers of High Blood Pressure"**
Ad Agency: **Materia Medica/Creative Annex Inc.**
Client: **Wyeth Laboratories**
Art Director: **Don Kahn**
Illustrator: **Radu Vero**
Copywriter: **Barbara Slonevsky**

The "Hidden Dangers of High Blood Pressure" are dramatized in this unique interactive poster from Wyeth Laboratories. Designed as a patient education aid for display in physicians' offices, the 25" x 17½" chart features separate illustrations of the key organs that can be affected by hypertension: heart, kidneys, eyes, and brain, along with the arteries themselves. Radu Vero's polished artwork depicts the organs in their normal state, ingeniously positioned on movable flaps. After viewing the normal organs, you then lift the individual flaps and view the same organs ravaged by the "silent killer."

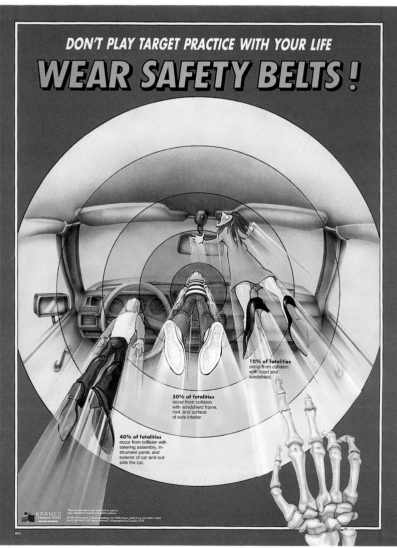

Title: **"Wear Safety Belts!"**
Design Firm: **In-house**
Publisher: **Krames Communications**
Art Director: **Carol Steinberg**
Illustrator: **Fran Milner**

The human projectiles in this safety poster are right on target—quite literally—for sudden death by auto. The grisly statistics beneath each flying body refer to the three categories of impact and their relative incidence in auto fatalities. Note the hand of death in the lower right corner, hurling the victims to their doom. Designed to promote the use of safety belts, the poster sports a cautionary slogan, "Don't Play Target Practice with Your Life."

Product: **Stomach tlc™** ➤
Title: **"Sensible steps toward a healthier diet"**
Ad Agency: **Northstar Productions**
Client: **Smith Kline & French Laboratories**
Art Director: **Mike Lazur**
Illustrator: **Chris Butler**
Copywriter: **Joe Harris**

These ten "sensible steps" toward a healthier diet are not commandments engraved in stone; they're simply helpful eating tips for ulcer-prone patients. Part of the multimedia Stomach tlc™ kit from Smith Kline & French Laboratories, this remarkable poster depicts a wide range of food groups—all in the form of colorful paper sculptures. Healthful foods are presented at the left, the nastier foods to the right.

Tell us where it hurts.

3130 S. McClintock Dr.
4425 W. Glendale Ave.

Tell us where it hurts.

3130 S. McClintock Dr.
4425 W. Glendale Ave.

Tell us where it hurts.

3130 S. McClintock Dr.
4425 W. Glendale Ave.

Tell us where it hurts.

3130 S. McClintock Dr.
4425 W. Glendale Ave.

Product: **The Family Doctor Urgent Care Centers**
Ad Agency: **Frank J. Corbett, Inc.**
Client: **St. Joseph's Hospital**
Art Director: **Chris Heron**
Photographer: **Don Levy**
Copywriter: **Mark Stinson**

The Family Doctor Urgent Care Centers wanted name recognition in the community, so Frank J. Corbett, Inc., developed this series for outdoor display. The simple heading, "Tell us where it hurts," conveys the purpose of the clinics in five words—without a literal description of services. The illustrated scenarios depict common aches and mishaps that mothers (the primary audience) can identify with. Part of a multimedia effort that included ads and direct mail, this series has won numerous creative awards.

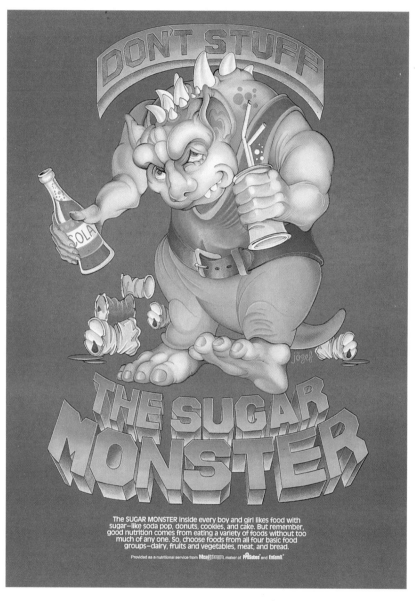

Title: **"Don't Stuff the Sugar Monster"**
Ad Agency: **Frank J. Corbett, Inc.**
Client: **Mead Johnson, Nutritional Div.**
Art Director: **Catherine Pelt**
Illustrator: **Jozef Sumichrast**
Copywriter: **Prill Kozel**

Built like an octopus, the big green sugar monster at right holds a surfeit of sweets in his long tentacles. It's enough to make us turn the same color at the thought of devouring another candy bar. That's the whole idea of this lively poster series from the Nutritional Division of Mead Johnson. Designed to educate low-income mothers about the value of balanced nutrition for their children, the posters balance a whimsical visual concept with a serious message. The other posters in the series depict sugar monsters that thrive on cookies, cakes, and soda pop.

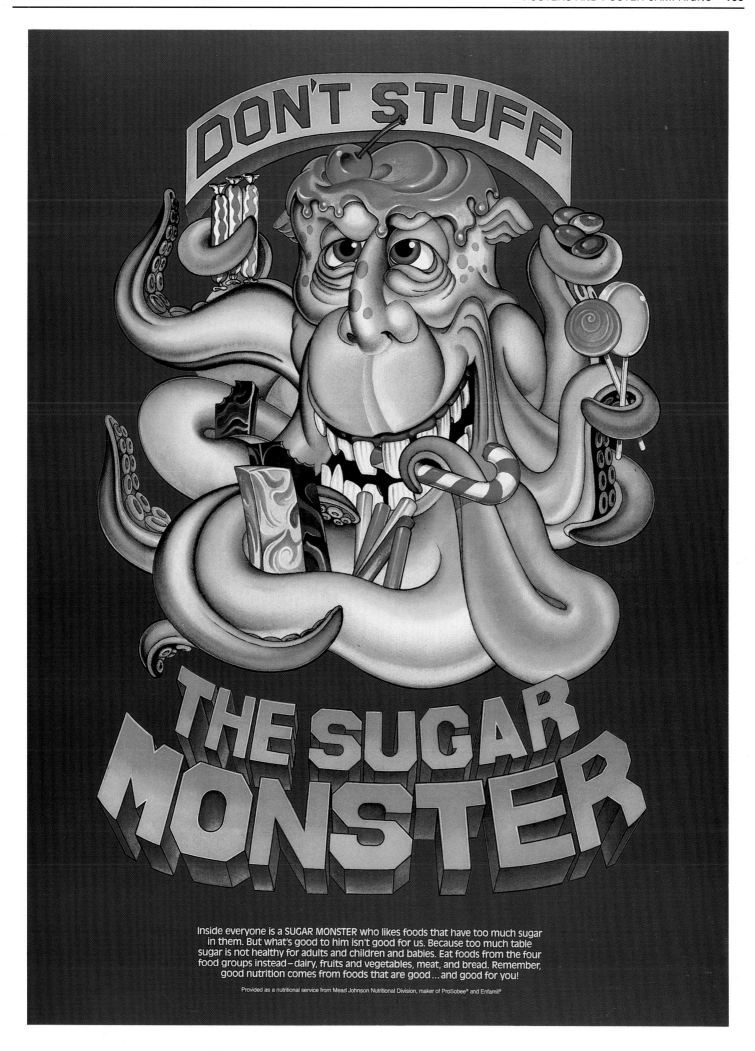

7.

ART AND ILLUSTRATION

ADVERTISING
PROMOTION
EDITORIAL ART

...any in the twentieth century, art that por-
rayed the visible world fell into serious disre-
pute among those who pass judgment on
such matters. Light, shadow, and perspective
were banished into exile; a succession of
styles ranging from Cubism to Abstract Ex-
pressionism trampled the last bonds between
art and nature. A painting was now regarded
as an object in itself, rather than as a *representation* of an object.

During this long period of tumultuous experi-
mentation, it was the *illustrators* who, more
than anyone else, preserved the tradition of
representational art. After all, the primary
purpose of illustration is to represent—and
enhance—the contents of a text. An illustration serves as an accessory to the written
word. It illuminates those abstract black
symbols on the printed page and makes them
more comprehensible, more concrete.

Of course, the best illustrations can stand on
their own as well. They can be savored for
their beauty or inventiveness or depth of
meaning. But unlike a portrait or a still life,
which exists in its own frame of reference, an
illustration explains something outside itself.

All illustrators communicate facts and ideas in
visual terms, but medical illustrators face a
more daunting challenge: their special role is
to explain *difficult* concepts and make them
readily comprehensible—without oversim-
plifying them. The intricacies of anatomy…advances in technology…biology on
the cellular and molecular levels…the action
of pharmaceuticals in the body…even the
complexities of social issues like drug abuse
and institutionalization—all of these topics
must first be understood by the medical illustrator, then be conveyed to the reader, whether
professional or layman, in clear graphic form.

Moreover, the illustrator must be able to
generate enough visual excitement to snare
the reader's attention. (This rule holds true for
editorial as well as advertising illustration.)
Graphics that arouse and intrigue—that give
off *sparks*—stand a better chance of luring

readers into the accompanying copy. And
that, as they say, is the bottom line.

The illustrators represented in this chapter
utilize a broad repertoire of styles, techniques,
and strategies to inform and dazzle the reader.
Let's briefly survey the major categories.

Probably the most prevalent style of medical
illustration today is the slick airbrushed
graphic. Imparting a cool, high-tech glow to
the subject matter, the airbrush technique
creates impeccably rendered surfaces that
seem to bear no visible trace of human handi-
work. Illustrations of anatomical features take
on an almost photographic realism, but are
softer, smoother, more intensely colorful—
and without the distracting surface details that
are prone to crop up in photographs. (For
good examples, see the transplanted heart by
Cynthia Turner, and Ellen Going Jacob's cross-
sectional view of a wound infection.)

Sometimes, for contrast, illustrators will set
off an airbrushed subject with a stippled or
grainy background. This technique, which
focuses attention on the key areas of the
illustration, has been used to advantage by
Jane Hurd in her depiction of alveoli, tiny
structures in the lungs.

Some artists use color rather than background
texture to highlight important features. For the
cover of a textbook, Gustave Falk represented
the entire head and brain in uniform terra cotta
tones—except for the small structures immediately beneath the cerebrum, which appeared
in a variety of hues.

Teri J. McDermott took a slightly different tack
to draw attention to twin fetuses inside a
pregnant mother. While the unborn babies are
depicted in realistic detail inside the womb,
the woman who carries them appears to be
made of stone—merely a decorative, sculp-
turesque framework for the twins.

A few illustrators have capitalized on the potential for visual adventure inside the human
body. William B. Westwood takes us on an

especially exciting subterranean journey
down the esophagus.

Despite the range of styles and approaches, all
of the aforementioned examples depict real
observable subjects—fetuses, internal organs,
cells, and the like. But the next category of
illustration deals with something less tangible, and therefore more difficult to represent
in visual terms: *ideas*. The conceptual illustrator takes the central idea of an article, then
finds a way to turn it into an image. How? By
looking for a symbol, an analogy, an unex-
pected ironic twist. For an inspired example
that utilizes all three, see Gary Viskupic's
powerful metamorphosis of the familiar *caduceus*—that age-old symbol of medicine—
into a straitjacket that ensnares a troubled
teenager in its grip.

One interesting genre that falls somewhere
between the observable and the conceptual is
the depiction of internal processes on the
microscopic or even molecular level. With
their grotesque cellular structures, squadrons
of antibodies, and biochemical bombardments
these exciting visuals conjure up images of
interplanetary warfare. (See Robert Margulies'
depiction of thyroiditis.)

A few illustrators in this chapter deserve special
mention for style. Edward Gazsi's Mad Tea
Party is a treasure trove of sumptuous detail
intelligently conceived and superbly executed.
Enid Hatton has delineated the human back
with classical poise and dignity. Devis Grebu's
patchwork sea of pills is like nothing else in
this book. And Peter de Seve continues to
amuse with his deftly satiric pen-and-wash
sketches.

A final observation: Now that representational
art has regained its stature in the world, today's illustrators seem to be practicing their
craft with renewed zest and unprecedented
sophistication. The field blooms once again
with talent of the first order. And, as you will
shortly discover, the illustrators included in
this chapter represent the cream of a very
impressive crop.

Can you find them?

Lurking in this poster are: Uncle Henry, Aunt Em, the scarecrow's diploma, the tinman's heart and oil can, the lion's medal of courage, an axe, a spear, the witches of the east and west, the witch's broom and hat, an hourglass, three winged monkeys, the wizard, five munchkins, a tornado, a bicycle, a farm wagon, Toto, Dorothy's basket and house, a horse, cow, cat, chicken, goat, sheep, pig, deer, mouse, crow, the magic wand, two slippers, and a hot air balloon.

Compliments of C I B A

Product: **RITALIN**®
Ad Agency: **C & G Advertising Inc. (In-house)**
Client: **Ciba-Geigy Pharmaceuticals**
Art Director: **Myrtle Johnson**
Illustrator: **Edward Gazsi**
Copywriter: **Pat Blagden**

GOLD. They're off to see the Wizard! Designed to hang in the offices of pediatricians and child psychologists, this wonderfully intricate illustration by Edward Gazsi depicts the immortal foursome (the Cowardly Lion, Tin Man, Scarecrow, and Dorothy) in a stylish new interpretation that stays true to the original characters. Woven into the rich tapestry are dozens of "hidden" objects ranging from Munchkins to Auntie Em. (If you look closely, you can probably spot Toto the dog to the lower left of the heart-shaped arch.) Aside from its decorative beauty, this work has another, more practical, side: it should keep the little ones thoroughly engrossed while they wait to see the doctor.

Title: **"Did HMO Cost Controls Kill This Baby?"**
Design Firm: **In-house**
Publisher: **Medical Economics Co. Inc.—**
Medical Economics
Art Director: **Ann Weber**
Illustrator: **Joanie Schwarz**

SILVER. With drama and poignancy, this muted editorial illustration captures the agony of a welfare mother whose baby has just become a statistic. Unfortunately, this is not an artist's hypothetical rendering of a fictitious mother and child. We're looking at a sensitive depiction of an actual case: a five-month-old infant who died in his mother's arms after his HMO pediatrician refused to let him be admitted to a local hospital. (The bereaved mother then sued both the HMO and the "gatekeeper" pediatrician.) The somber color scheme of browns and grays is broken only by the barely perceptible glint of a thin gold chain around the mother's neck.

Product: **HALL® Fixed Mandibular Implant**
Ad Agency: **Maher, Kaump & Clark**
Client: **Hall Reconstructive Systems**
Art Director: **Lori Justice**
Illustrator: **Lauren Keswick**
Copywriter: **K. Angelini**

SILVER. To demonstrate the installation of the HALL® Fixed Mandibular Implant (a device for securing dentures), illustrator Lauren Keswick isolated the jawbone and set it in a beautifully executed see-through face. The implant is rendered in crisp detail; by contrast, the soft, classical features of the face melt into the background so as not to draw attention away from the product. This effect is reinforced by the delicately grainy texture of the face. And note the way the mandible fades into the lavender haze on the far side.

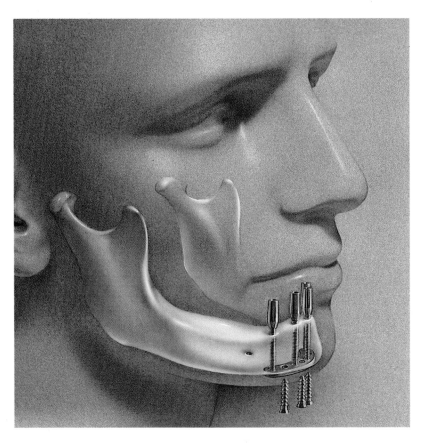

Title: **"Sudden Death"**
Design Firm: **In-house**
Publisher: **McGraw-Hill Publishing Co.**
Art Director: **Tina Adamek**
Illustrator: **Enid V. Hatton**

Cardiac fibrillation is the rapid, random twitching of a heart out of control; death is usually imminent. But an implantable defibrillator can restore rhythm and life, as depicted in this unusual cover illustration by Enid Hatton. The patient is set against the cosmos, his serene face basking in the glow of restored health. The defibrillator mechanism is rendered in light green. Where it joins the heart, beams of white light fan out dramatically in every direction.

Title: *Biological Psychology*
Design Firm: **In-house**
Client: **Holt, Rinehart, Winston**
Art Director: **Louis Scardino**
Illustrator: **Gustave Falk**

For the dust jacket of a textbook entitled *Biological Psychology*, illustrator Gustave Falk produced this softly understated classical profile—complete with brain. Interestingly, he chose to highlight only the intricate structures around the area of the thalamus; these are rendered in bright colors, while the rest of the brain and head are sketched in pale brown.

Title: **"Dizziness, Falling and Fainting in the Elderly"**
Publisher: **Harcourt Brace Jovanovich— *Geriatrics***
Art Director: **Robert J. Demarest**
Illustrator: **Robert J. Demarest**

For a cover article on "Dizziness, Falling and Fainting in the Elderly," illustrator Robert J. Demarest created this clever representation of a brain that pops from the flat cross-section of the head, like a spring from a pocket watch. Unusual in its combination of anatomical and symbolic visual elements, this eye-catching illustration compels the reader to explore further. Demarest notes that, for the conditions described in the article, "there is no visible pathology to illustrate." Hence the use of a symbolic device to suggest dizziness and fainting.

Title: **"Osteoporosis: How to Avoid Its Crippling Effects"**
Design Firm: **In-house**
Publisher: **Medical Economics Co. Inc.—*RN***
Art Director: **Andrea DiBenedetto**
Illustrator: **Sharon Ellis**

What used to be called a "dowager's hump" appears prominently in this striking portrait of an elderly woman for *RN* magazine. In fact, the subject of the illustration is actually suffering from osteoporosis, a disease that weakens the bone structure—most commonly in older women. An interesting design element: the type that originally appeared along with the illustration was set so that its right margin followed the line of the woman's back, emphasizing her stooped posture.

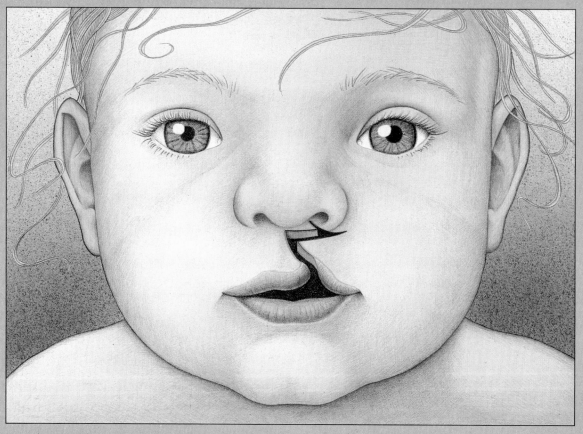

Title: **"Cleft Lip and Palate Surgery"**
Design Firm: **Liska & Associates**
Publisher: **American Society of Plastic and Reconstructive Surgeons**
Art Director: **Steve Liska**
Illustrator: **William Graham**

Most surgical procedure manuals are aimed at surgeons. But the brochure in which this striking illustration appeared was aimed at the *parents* of children with cleft lip/palate. Dramatically close-cropped so the infant's face fills the picture area, the illustration focuses on the cleft that will be surgically corrected. This art was also used in video and slide presentations.

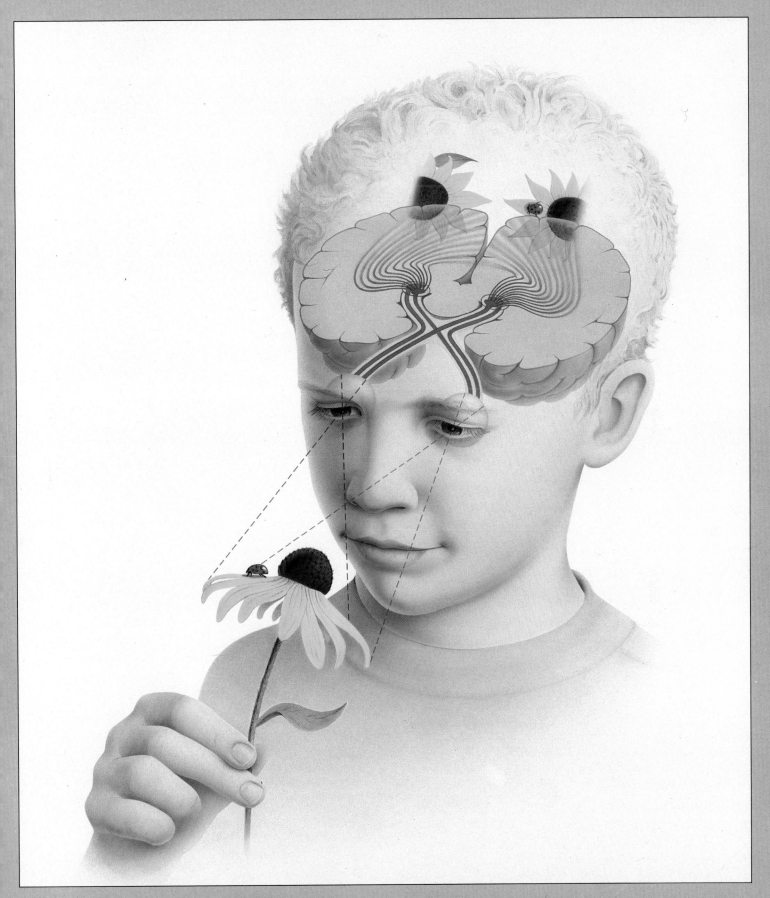

Title: **"The Anatomy of Vision"**
Design Firm: **In-house**
Publisher: **National Geographic Society**
Art Director: **Ursula Vosseler**
Illustrator: **Jane Hurd**

Aimed at young readers, this graphic depiction of "The Anatomy of Vision" appeared in the National Geographic Society's *Books for World Explorers* series.

Illustrator Jane Hurd shows how the image of a ladybug on a flower enters the eyes, becomes inverted, travels along both optic nerves, and reaches the main visual centers in the brain, where messages from both eyes are finally combined and interpreted. By placing the physiological details inside the head of a realistically rendered boy, rather than isolating them as abstract functions, the artist has enhanced the appeal of the illustration for its juvenile audience.

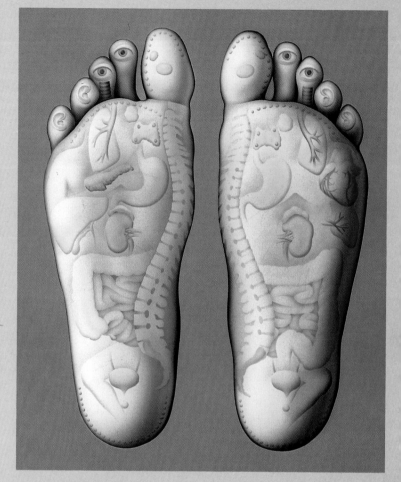

Design Firm: **Kossak Design Group**
Publisher: **Macmillan Healthcare Publications—**
Corium
Art Director: **Lin Kossak**
Illustrator: **Steve Heimann**

This mysteriously symbolic and somewhat metaphysical illustration of hands joined together inside a beaker appeared on the cover of _Corium_ magazine. Illustrator Steve Heimann has placed hands and beaker against a starry night sky. A clue may be obtained by looking at the cufflinks, one of which bears the sign of the _caduceus_, age-old symbol of the medical profession. Aimed at an audience of doctors and nurses, the illustration was created, according to the artist, as "a visual to a narrative."

Title: **"It's Amazing What Some People**
Think Feet Can Do"
Ad Agency: **Frank J. Corbett, Inc.**
Client: **Westwood Pharmaceuticals**
Art Director: **Michael V. Phillips**
Illustrator: **Leonard E. Morgan**
Copywriter: **Rob Kienle**

Imagine depicting the Oriental/New Age pseudo-science of foot reflexology for an audience of skeptical MDs! But this tasteful illustration genuinely stimulates curiosity with a lively rendering of the feet, showing the classic "reflex" points and their corresponding organs in the body. (Massaging those points is said to have a curative effect on the specific organs.) The result is an intriguing, informative, and good-humored look at an offbeat subject—and that's no small feat. The illustration was used in an ad for an antifungal foot cream.

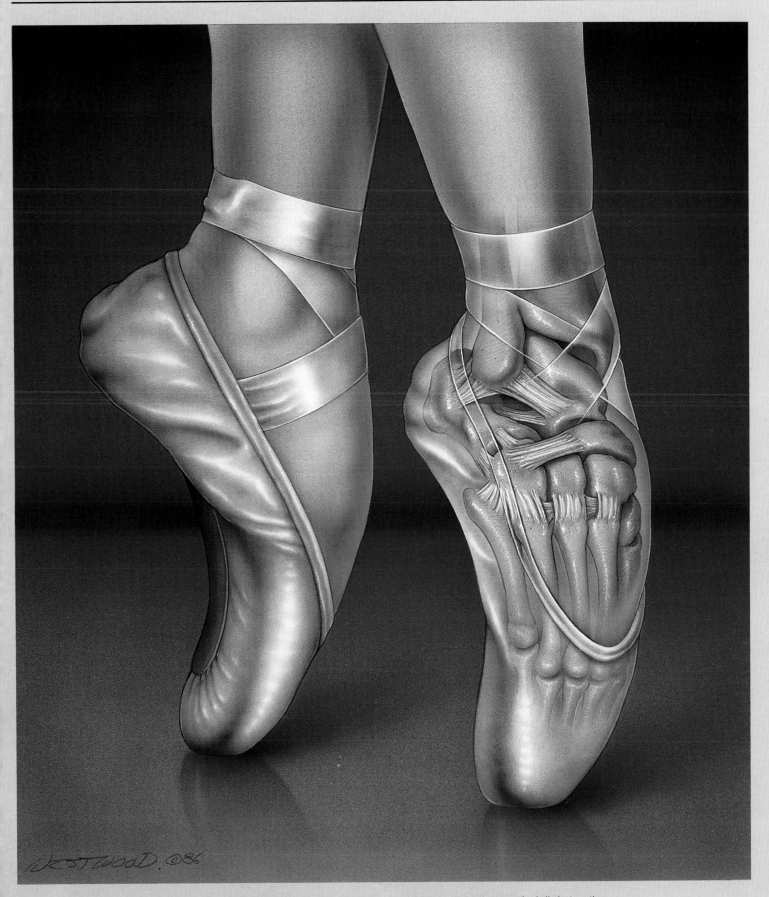

Title: **"Physical Prerequisites for Ballet Dancers"**
Design Firm: **In-house**
Publisher: **Cliggott Publishing—*The Journal of Musculoskeletal Medicine***
Art Director: **Jan Lorrine**
Illustrator: **William B. Westwood**

Beneath the external elegance of a ballerina's satin-clad feet lies a complex structure of bones and ligaments. The illustrator has cast the subject in an ethereal blue-violet light, reflecting the ambience of a lighted stage in mid-ballet. Yet the depiction of frequently injured bones and ligaments had to be clinically acceptable to the audience of physicians. The illustration succeeds beautifully in straddling both worlds—art and anatomy.

Title: **"Anatomy of the Skin"**
Design Firm: **Zilberts & Associates**
Client: **Peter Grotuss, MD**
Art Director: **Ed Zilberts**
Illustrator: **Ed Zilberts**

Beauty may be only skin deep, but skin goes deeper than most of us suspect. In this attractive educational illustration by Ed Zilberts, the largest organ in the human body is viewed in revealing cross section. The amazing intricacy of its underlying structures comes clearly into view: hair follicles, blood vessels, sweat glands, and sebaceous glands—even the muscles (shown as brownish diagonal fibers) that make individual hairs stand erect. For anyone who previously thought of skin as a kind of organic shrink-wrapping, this illustration is a revelation.

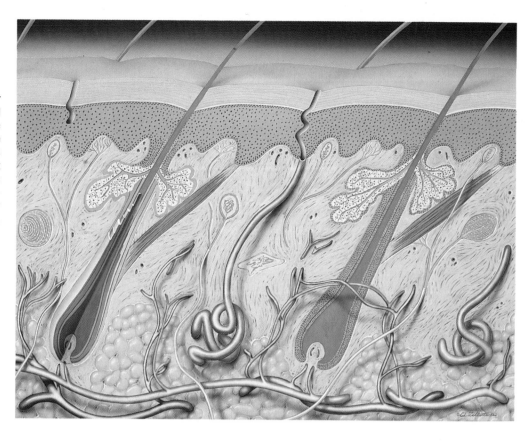

Title: **"Cervical Spondylosis"**
Design Firm: **In-house**
Client: **American Academy of Family Physicians—*American Family Physician***
Art Director: **H. Marshall Wagoner III**
Illustrator: **William B. Westwood**

Winner of the 1987 Silver Medal from the Los Angeles Society of Illustrators, this magazine cover art depicts cervical spondylosis, a neck disorder. Illustrator William B. Westwood shows us the abnormal fusion and growth in the spinal column, resembling, in the artist's own description, "an old gnarled, overgrown tree trunk with the nerves splaying out to the sides like vines in the wind. Even in disease," he writes, "the various elements of our 'fantastic machine' bodies can be wonderfully interesting and beautiful to look at."

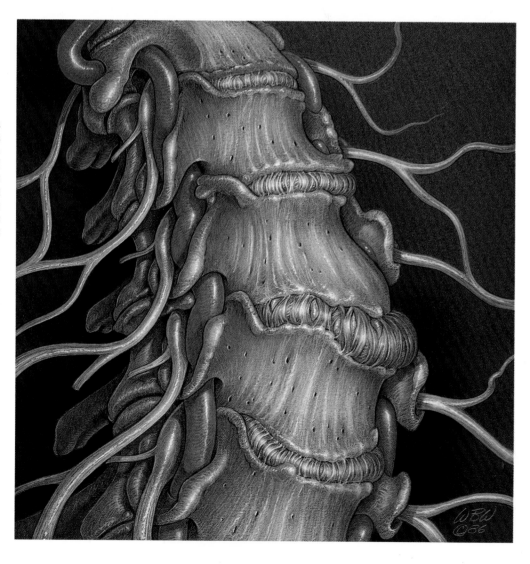

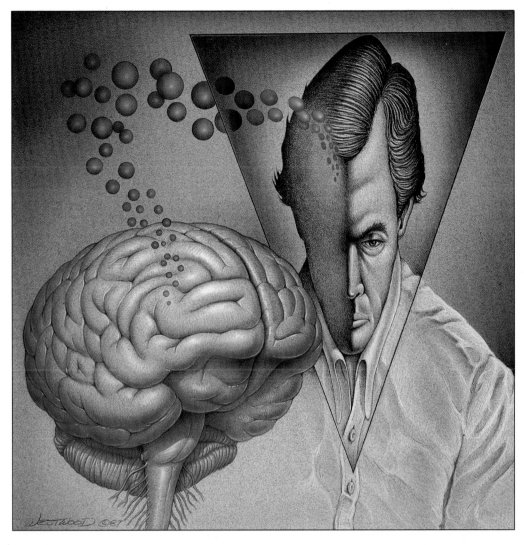

Title: **"AIDS and the Brain"**
Design Firm: **In-house**
Client: **American Academy of Family Physicians—*American Family Physician***
Art Director: **Kathy Gannon**
Illustrator: **William B. Westwood**

Until recently, it was believed that the brain was protected from the AIDS virus by what is known as the "blood-brain barrier." AIDS patients who suffered from mental disturbances were thought to be reacting to the stress of having a fatal disease. But recent research has shown that the AIDS virus does indeed cross the blood-brain barrier and cause mental symptoms. For the cover of *American Family Physician*, illustrator William B. Westwood created this conceptual rendering of the blood-brain barrier as a triangle superimposed over a distorted face. The small spheres represent the AIDS virus penetrating the barrier. The cover article was entitled "AIDS and the Brain."

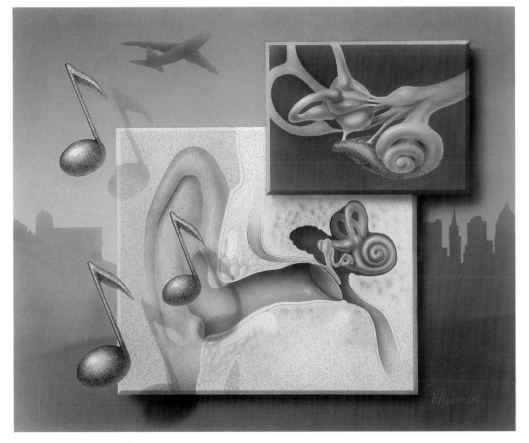

Title: **"Inner Ear"**
Design Firm: **In-house**
Publisher: ***Oregonian***
Art Director: **Rodd Ambroson**
Illustrator: **Rodd Ambroson**
Graphic Coordinator: **Kevin Murphy**

Printed in full color on newsprint stock, this handsome illustration by Rodd Ambroson accompanied an article on hearing loss due to environmental noise. A plane roars overhead in the red sky; a muted cityscape adorns the background. And three heavy notes (they're substantial enough to cast shadows) bounce into the anatomical cross section of the ear. The inset depicts the delicate structures of the inner ear.

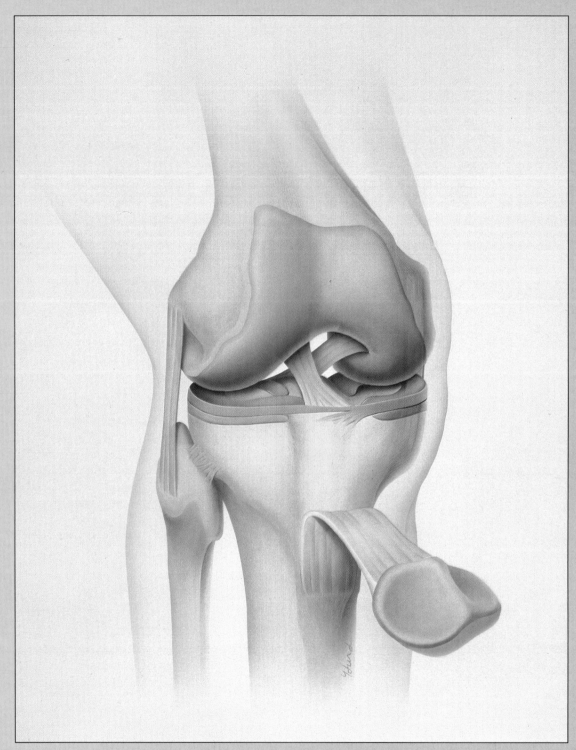

Title: **"Total Knee Replacement"**
Design Firm: **R.A. Design**
Client: **Docere Corp.**
Art Director: **Roger Ashton**
Illustrator: **Jane Hurd**

Conceived as part of a patient education package on knee replacement surgery, these colorful schematic illustrations show the anatomy of a normal knee and the postoperative appearance of a total knee replacement. The component bones, ligaments, and cartilage were numbered and color-coded for easy identification. According to illustrator Jane Hurd, the package, intended to be supplied to patients by doctors, contained a booklet, audio tape, and informed consent forms. Writes Hurd, "These patient education products are intended to help cut down on malpractice suits by thoroughly informing patients and documenting this with many signatures on the enclosed forms."

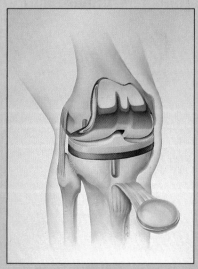

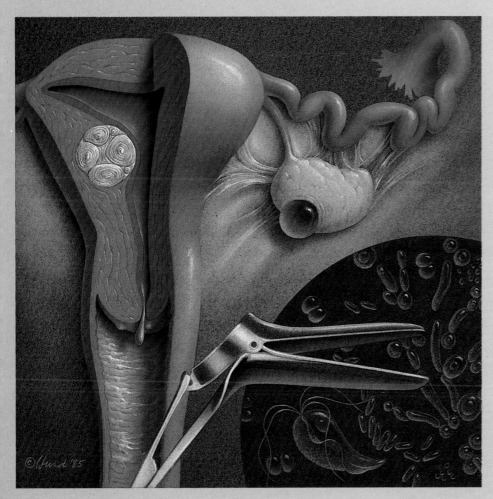

Title: **"Office Gynecology II"**
Design Firm: **In-house**
Publisher: **American Academy of Family Physicians**
Art Director: **H. Marshall Wagoner III**
Illustrator: **Jane Hurd**

For a monograph on office gynecology, artist Jane Hurd designed this cutaway rendering of the female reproductive tract. It doesn't take a trained OB/GYN to note that we're looking at a veritable mine field of gynecological disorders. The diseased parts are smoothly rendered and depicted against a sandy background.

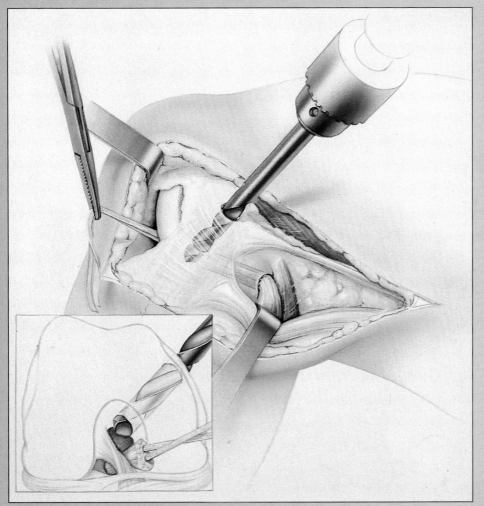

Title: *Manual of Sports Surgery*
Design Firm: **In-house (book interior)**
Client: **Springer-Verlag New York Inc.**
Art Director: **Fredric Harwin**
Illustrator: **Robin Markovits Jensen**

This clearly executed illustration from *Manual of Sports Surgery* depicts the drilling of a tunnel through the femur—part of a procedure to reconstruct a torn posterior cruciate ligament. Such clarity and precision would not have been easily obtained in a photographic treatment of the same subject. This procedure was one of 31 orthopedic surgical procedures illustrated by Robin Markovits Jensen in the manual, which focuses on sports-related injuries.

RN

Acute MI:
the first
crucial hours

Title: **"Acute MI: The First Crucial Hours"**
Design Firm: **In-house**
Publisher: **Medical Economics Co. Inc.—RN**
Art Directors: **Tim McKeen, Andrea DiBenedetto**
Illustrator: **Keith Kasnot**

Acute MI—medical code for myocardial infarction (heart attack)—is grimly depicted as a blackened area around the coronary artery, where tissue has already started to die. This phenomenon is further dramatized by the electrocardiogram that breaks off at the point of infarct. Note how the large blood vessels at the top of the heart nearly fade into the glowing blue background.

Title: **"Sudden Death After MI—
Whose Risk Is Greatest?"**
Design Firm: **In-house**
Publisher: **Medical Economics Co. Inc.—
Diagnosis**
Art Director: **Susan Kuppler Haber**
Illustrator: **William B. Westwood**

An infarcted heart survives its fifth month in this eye-catching cover art for Diagnosis magazine. The heart and calendar tie in with the theme of the article, which examines the critical recovery period for heart attack patients—and their risk of sudden death. The infarcted area (where heart tissue has died as a result of the heart attack) is visible as an ugly scar midway along the coronary artery at right.

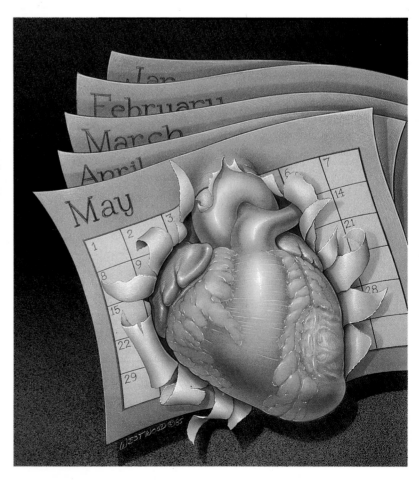

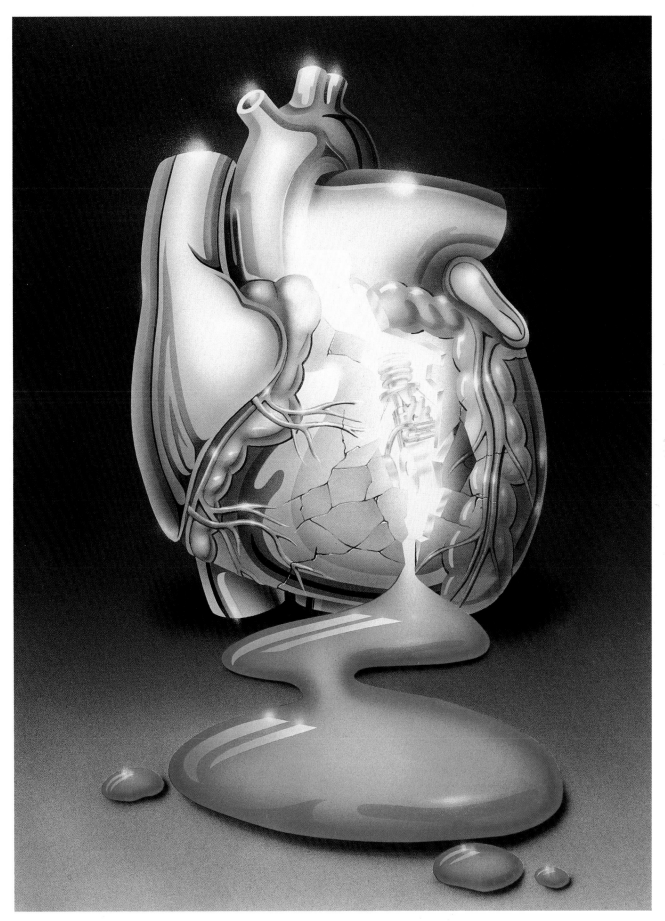

Title: **"Heart Failure"**
Design Firm: **In-house**
Publisher: **Trimel Corp.—*Drug Protocol***
Art Director: **Jean Miller**
Illustrator: **Jean Miller**

For a cover article on heart failure, illustrator Jean Miller came up with this provocative depiction of a broken pump. The gleaming metallic heart displays a wide crack down the front; blood has pooled outside in neatly airbrushed curves. Inside the luminous crack, the emptied pump reveals some of its defective machinery.

Title: **"Placement of Pacemaker Leads"**
Design Firm: **In-house**
Publisher: **Wynwood Publishing, Inc.—**
Illustrated Medicine
Sponsor: **Stuart Pharmaceuticals**
Art Director: **Audra Geras**
Illustrator: **Edmond S. Alexander**

Placement of pacemaker leads is the topic of this instructive illustration for *Illustrated Medicine*. As colorful as it is informative, the art depicts the insertion of the insulated leads through the superior vena cava (the large vein leading to the heart from above) and into the walls of the right atrium and right ventricle. Although the smoothly airbrushed heart is depicted in partial cutaway fashion, illustrator Edmond S. Alexander has used insets to depict the placement of the leads in greater detail.

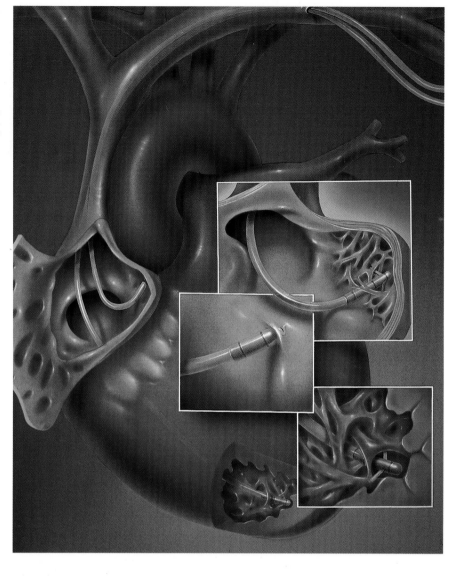

Title: **"Respiratory System…"**
Design Firm: **Watermark Design**
Client: **National Heart, Lung & Blood Institute (NIH)**
Art Director: **Lynne Komai**
Illustrator: **Jane Hurd**

Featured in a public information booklet, this handsome illustration by Jane Hurd depicts a normal alveolus—site of air exchange in the lungs. To establish the scale of the main drawing, the artist has furnished a schematic diagram of the lungs (the area of the drawing is circled). The delicately stippled background offers a nice contrast to the smooth surfaces of the anatomical art.

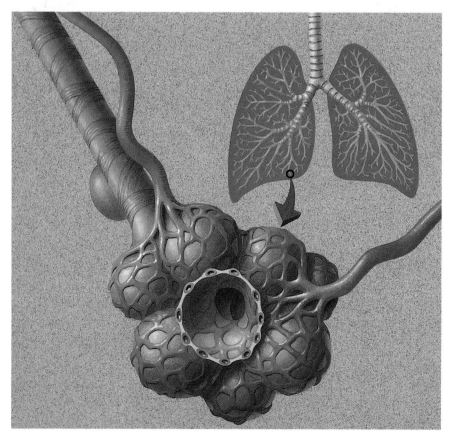

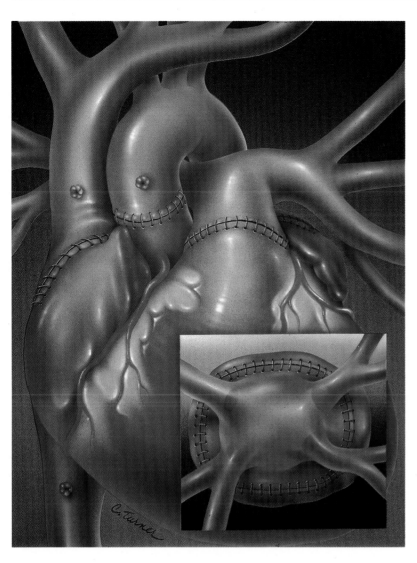

Title: **"The Completed Anastomoses"**
Design Firm: **In-house**
Publisher: **Wynwood Publishing, Inc.—**
Illustrated Medicine
Sponsor: **Stuart Pharmaceuticals**
Art Director: **Audra Geras**
Illustrator: **Cynthia Turner**

This skillful rendering of a freshly transplanted heart (note the sutures across the upper third of the illustration) accompanied an article on "Cardiac Transplantation" for _Illustrated Medicine_. While the quality of the art is exceptional in its realism, illustrator Cynthia Turner has softened some of the details, possibly so the reader's attention will not be distracted from the surgical procedure. The inset shows how the recipient's pulmonary veins are attached to the donor heart.

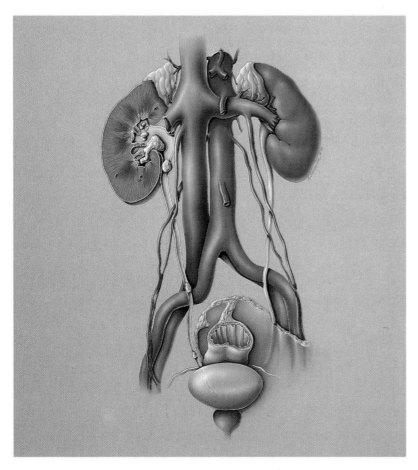

Title: **"Urinary Tract Calculi"**
Design Firm: **In-house**
Publisher: **Cliggott Publishing Co.—_Consultant_**
Art Director: **Tom Jermantowicz**
Illustrator: **Kevin A. Somerville**

This schematic representation of the urinary tract was created to accompany an article on new techniques for managing stones that obstruct the urinary system. Illustrator Kevin A. Somerville has indicated the most common sites for the stones (referred to by doctors as "urinary tract calculi"). Aside from its placement in the text, this clearly rendered illustration was also used as an inset on the cover.

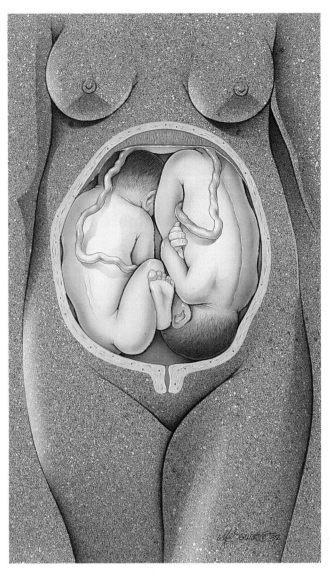

Title: **"Twins: Clinical Management Tips"**
Design Firm: **In-house**
Publisher: **Medical Economics Co. Inc.—**
Contemporary OB/GYN
Art Director: **A. Michael Velthaus**
Illustrator: **Teri J. McDermott**

This see-through view of twins in the womb was designed for the cover of *Contemporary OB/GYN*. Illustrator Teri J. McDermott has rendered the woman's body as a stony, highly stylized form, much like a 1930's bas-relief. The blue tones and stippled surface pattern add to the unreality of the exterior. But the twins are a different matter: the artist has called attention to them by depicting them in realistic detail and natural flesh tones. They're encircled by the pink rim of the uterus for even sharper delineation. The illustrator writes, "I wanted to combine a classical stone-like figure—the mother—with the 3-D look of the twins in order to make the renderings of the babies jump out at the viewer."

Product: **Corometrics Spiral Electrode**
Design Firm: **The Opus Group**
Client: **Corometrics Medical Co.**
Art Director: **Joe Grasso**
Illustrator: **Robert J. Demarest**
Copywriter: **Joe Grasso**

This muted, almost monochromatic rendering of a fetus in the womb demonstrates an obstetrical instrument used in obtaining an FHR signal. Originally part of an ad for the Corometrics Spiral Electrode, the art focuses on the simplicity of the procedure for OB/GYNs. By executing the entire illustration in warm sienna tones, with just a hint of pink in the cross section of the female body, artist Robert J. Demarest has minimized the chance of distraction as we focus on the insertion of the electrode.

Title: **"Male Pregnancy"** ➤
Design Firm: **In-house**
Publisher: **Omni**
Art Director: **Amy Sissler**
Illustrator: **Ellen Going Jacobs**

The title of the article accompanying this visionary illustration says all that needs to be said: *Male Pregnancy*. The article postulates that men may be able to carry implanted embryos, and illustrator Ellen Going Jacobs has given us a startling visual on the concept of man-as-mom. The pregnant male body, viewed from the side, harbors a nearly full-term fetus. A fertilized human ovum and multiplying embryonic cells form a kind of celestial backdrop.

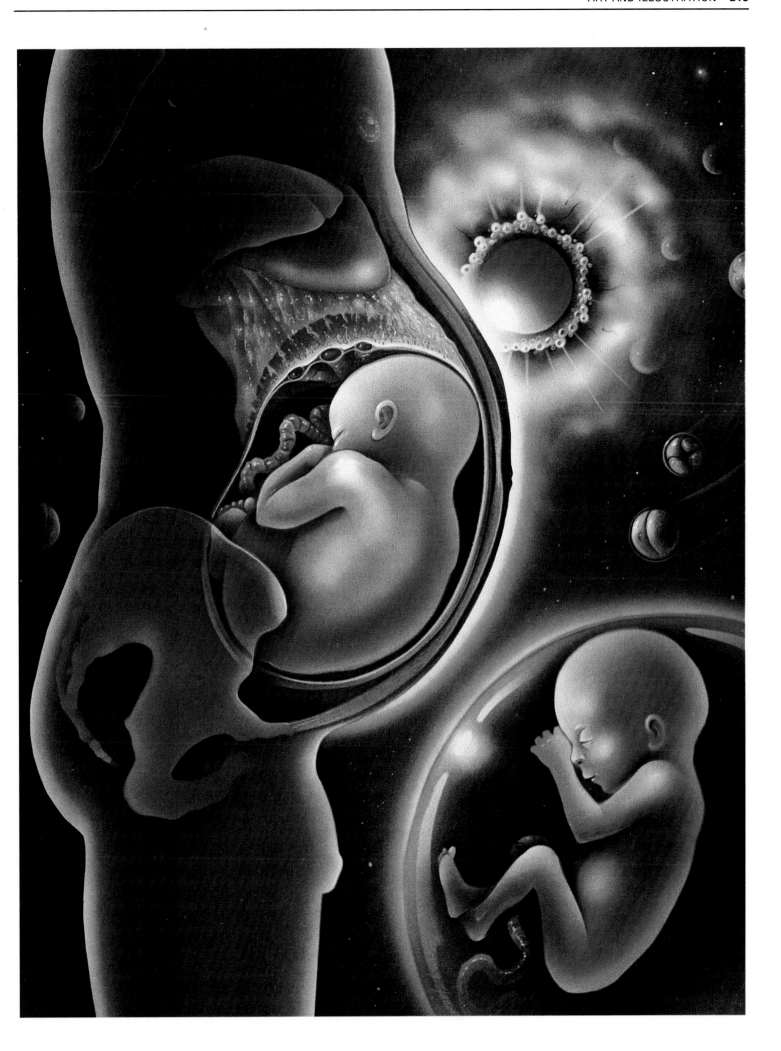

Title: **"Pelvic Inflammatory Disease"**
Design Firm: **In-house**
Publisher: **Medical Economics Co. Inc.—**
Contemporary OB/GYN
Art Director: **A. Michael Velthaus**
Illustrator: **Robin Markovits Jensen**

This surgical view of a swollen fallopian tube illustrates an article on pelvic inflammatory disease (PID) for the cover of *Contemporary OB/GYN*. Artist Robin Markovits Jensen has delineated the anatomical features with a high degree of realism, yet with greater clarity than would have been possible in a photograph. According to Jensen, "It was conceptually very difficult to come up with a view of the anatomy of this area that had not been shown before."

Product: **DALACIN-C®**
Design Firm: **Skidmore Sahratian**
Client: **Upjohn International Inc.**
Art Director: **Jack Roderick**
Illustrator: **Ellen Going Jacobs**
Account Executive: **Richard Hill**

Illustrator Ellen Going Jacobs rendered this deceptively beautiful cross section of a sutured wound to accompany an ad for Dalacin-C®. In the cleft between the finely rendered skin cells, a glowing pocket of pus builds up like molten lava in a volcano. The infection has already inflamed the neighboring cells and reddened the surface of the skin. The gently airbrushed margins of the illustration offer a cool visual counterpoint to the angry-looking infection.

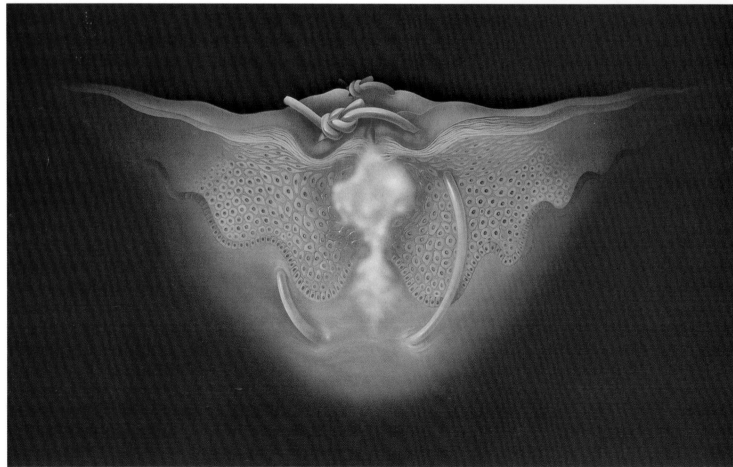

Product: **Karl Storz Hysteroscopic Systems**
Ad Agency: **Forsythe Marcelli Johnson Advertising, Inc.**
Client: **Karl Storz Endoscopy—America, Inc.**
Art Director: **Vic Marcelli**
Illustrator: **Audra Geras**
Copywriter: **Jim Forsythe**

A beam of light penetrates the darkness of what appears to be an underground cavern. But what we're actually looking at is an illuminated Karl Storz scope searching for uterine irregularities. In this imaginatively conceived illustration by Audra Geras, the illuminated hollow of the "cavern" is surrounded by total darkness. With greater distance from the source of light, the colors on the walls fade from brilliant yellow-orange to rose tinged with purple. The rounded nodules, which could pass for cave formations, are intriguingly lit from behind.

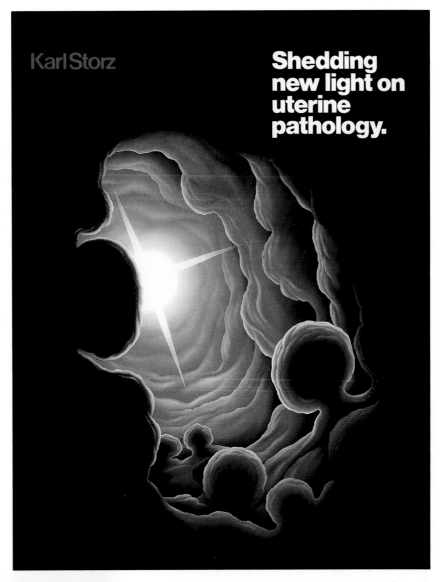

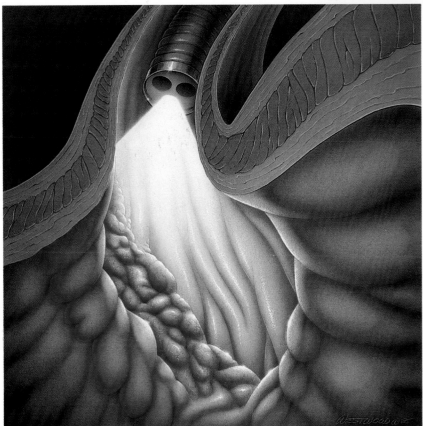

Title: **"Evaluation of Esophageal Diseases"**
Design Firm: **In-house**
Client: **American Academy of Family Physicians—*American Family Physician***
Art Director: **H. Marshall Wagoner III**
Illustrator: **William B. Westwood**

To create visual interest for a cover story on diseases of the esophagus, illustrator William B. Westwood has given us an exciting—even mysterious—depiction of modern technology exploring inner space. The bold perspective and dramatic lighting suggest a subterranean adventure; what the illustration actually shows is a flexible, light-bearing esophagoscope illuminating a cancerous tumor at the junction of the esophagus and the stomach.

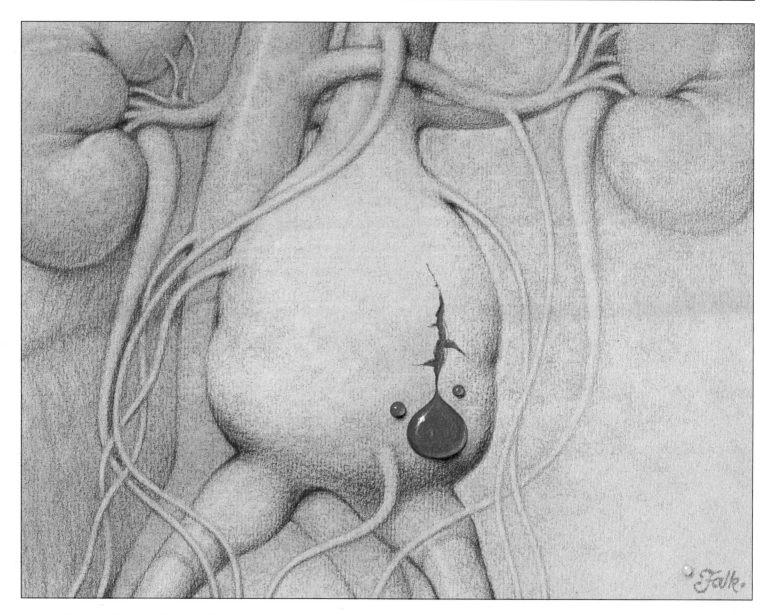

Title: **"Aortic Aneurysms: Causes and Course"**
Design Firm: **In-house**
Publisher: **C.J. Publishing-Bologna Institute—** **CV Review**
Art Director: **Barry Balter**
Illustrator: **Gustave Falk**

The ominous bulge of an aortic aneurysm finally tears open, spewing drops of bright red blood. In this intriguing cover illustration for *CV Review*, Gustave Falk has cast the blood vessels—the entire illustration, in fact—in yellows and golds. Only the blood stands out in its natural scarlet hue to shock the reader and break through the apathy barrier.

Title: **"Thromboembolism: Warning Signs"**
Design Firm: **In-house**
Publisher: **Medical Economics Co. Inc.—** **Diagnosis**
Art Director: **Susan Kuppler Haber**
Illustrator: **William B. Westwood**

On the surface, this cover illustration shows what happens when a blood clot breaks off and starts moving through the circulatory system. But illustrator William Westwood has added a sense of urgency and drama with his unusual perspective—not to mention the jet trails behind each clot. These embolisms are not simply meandering; they're *racing* through the bloodstream to inflict their damage.

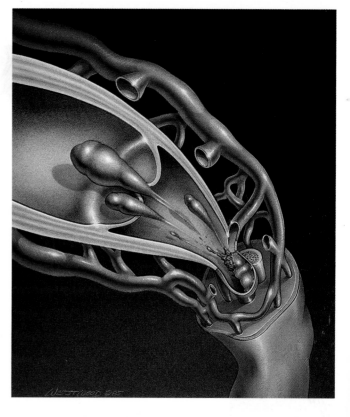

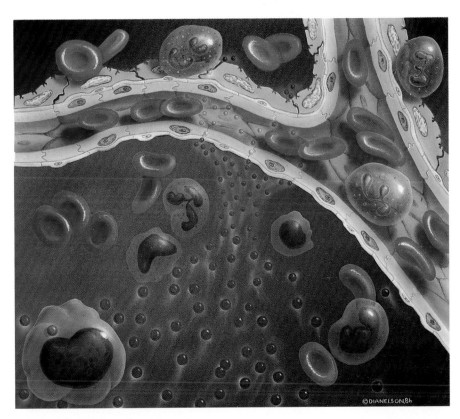

Title: **"Drugs Crossing Placental Barrier"**
Design Firm: **In-house**
Publisher: **Brentwood Publishing—**
Perinatology/Neonatology
Illustrator: **Diane L. Nelson**

For the cover of _Perinatology/Neonatology: The Journal of Maternal-Fetal and Neonatal Healthcare_, Diane L. Nelson has given us a vivid depiction of drugs crossing the placental barrier. The blood vessel is viewed in cross section; its individual cells and even their nuclei are clearly visible, as are the blood cells and the tiny spheres representing the drug. What could have been a dull biological illustration teems instead with life and energy. In developing the image, the illustrator worked mainly from written anatomical descriptions and black-and-white photomicrography.

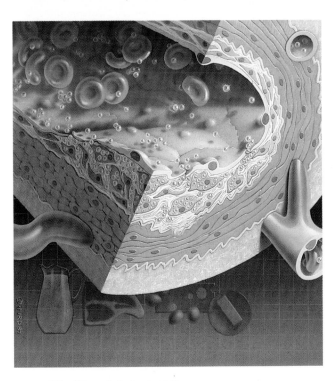

Title: **"Hypercholesterolemia"**
Design Firm: **In-house**
Client: **American Academy of Family**
Physicians
Art Director: **Jane Hurd**
Illustrator: **Jane Hurd**

This striking cover illustration of arterial plaque buildup accompanied an article on hypercholesterolemia in _Family Physician_. Illustrator Jane Hurd has provided both a cross-sectional and longitudinal view of the blood vessel; the tiny yellow spheres are cholesterol molecules being deposited in the artery lining as life-threatening plaque. Below the blood vessel, almost faded into the bluish background, are some of the alleged dietary culprits in hypercholesterolemia: milk, steak, eggs, cheese, and butter.

Title: **"Blood-Brain Barrier"**
Design Firm: **In-house**
Publisher: **Abbott Laboratories**
Art Director: **Coy James**
Illustrator: **Cynthia Turner**

For a monograph on drug abuse, illustrator Cynthia Turner has conjured up a stylized vision of mind-altering drugs permeating the blood-brain barrier. The drug is depicted in the form of yellow balloon-like structures emerging from the blood vessel at lower right and drifting into the cool blue sanctuary of the brain. (The grotesque tentacled objects are nerve cells.)

Title: **"Combination Drug Therapy for Hypertension"**
Design Firm: **In-house**
Client: **Edgell Communications— *Modern Medicine***
Art Director: **Robert J. Demarest**
Illustrator: **Diane L. Nelson**

To illustrate the dynamics of combination antihypertensive therapy (diuretics plus direct vasodilators) for an article in *Modern Medicine*, Diane Nelson took the two interrelated anatomical elements—kidney and artery—and presented them as part of a flow diagram representing the "synergy" of the two complementary drugs. Note the attractive background pattern, which enhances the presentation visually but does not interfere with it.

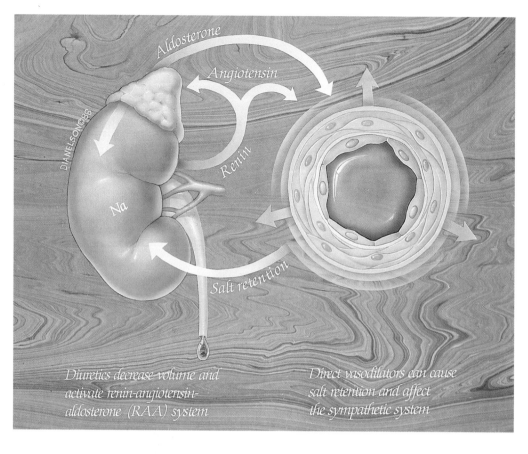

Title: **"The Unique Mitochondrial Gene Complement"**
Design Firm: **In-house**
Publisher: **H.P. Publishing Co.— *Hospital Practice***
Art Director: **Robert Herald**
Illustrator: **Robert Margulies**

A twisted loop of DNA hovers above a richly detailed representation of several mitochondria—the energy-producing structures that play a vital role in cellular metabolism. Designed for the cover of *Hospital Practice*, this attractively stippled illustration ties in with an article on "Mitochondrial Genes and Disease."

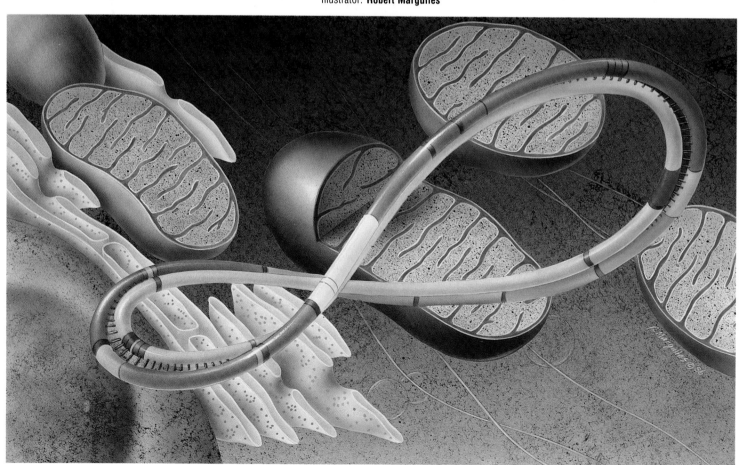

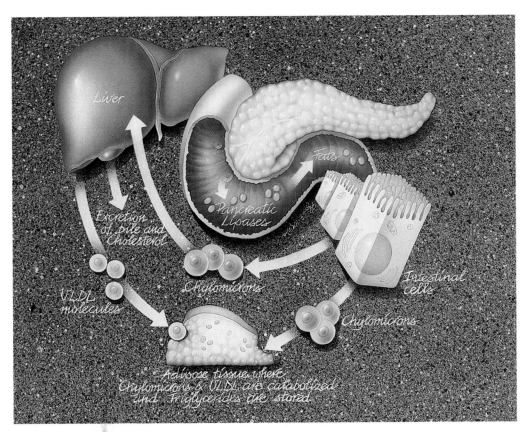

Title: **"Hyperlipidemia—Diagnosis and Management"**
Design Firm: **In-house**
Publisher: **Edgell Communications— *Modern Medicine***
Art Director: **Robert J. Demarest**
Illustrator: **Teri J. McDermott**

In flow-chart fashion, illustrator Teri J. McDermott has visualized the route by which dietary fats become stored in the body as triglycerides. The schematic depictions of the key organs and molecules are set against a stippled background, with each feature labeled in neatly legible calligraphy. This clear treatment of a complex subject was used in an article that appeared in *Modern Medicine*; a cropped portion of the same illustration appeared on the cover.

Title: **"Receptor Stimulation in Autoimmune Pathogenesis of Thyroiditis"**
Design Firm: **In-house**
Publisher: **H.P. Publishing Co.— *Hospital Practice***
Art Director: **Robert Herald**
Illustrator: **Robert Margulies**

Another scene of intergalactic warfare? Not quite. We're looking at "Receptor Stimulation in Autoimmune Pathogenesis of Thyroiditis." With a sense of nightmarish beauty, illustrator Robert Margulies has depicted the bombardment of thyroid cells by a myriad of color-coded biochemical aggressors. This imaginatively conceived and vividly colored illustration graced the cover of *Hospital Practice*.

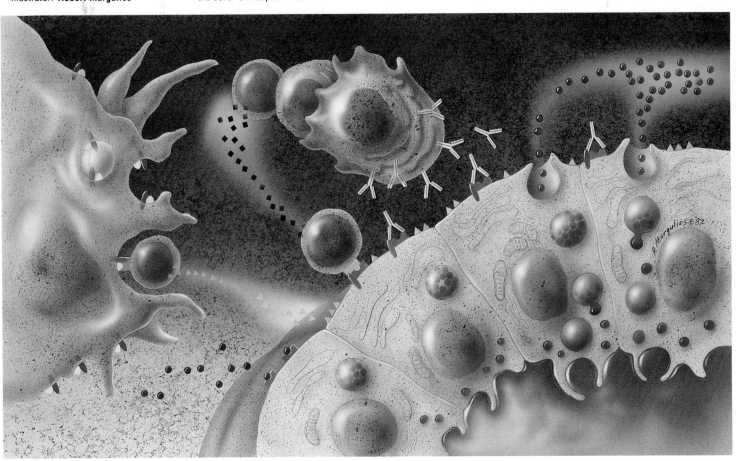

Title: **"Non-Hodgkin's Lymphomas"**
Design Firm: **Graham Studios**
Publisher: **Macmillan Professional Journals— *Current Concepts in Oncology***
Art Director: **Dave Swirz**
Illustrator: **William Graham**

The glowing beauty of this editorial illustration belies the gravity of the subject matter: non-Hodgkin's lymphomas, a family of cancers affecting the lymph nodes and related structures. The lymphatic system is rendered in deep Caribbean turquoise, contrasting handsomely with the mauve of the head. Across the background, set softly in rows of lighter mauve type, is a long roster of known lymphomas. This clever visual device successfully conveys the mind-boggling variety of forms lymphatic cancer can take.

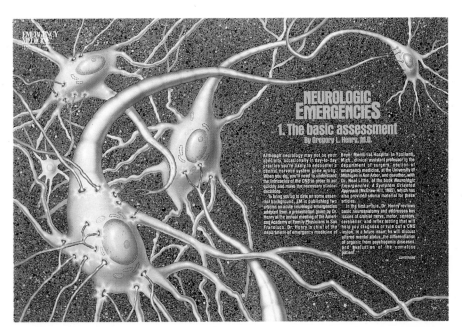

Title: **"Neurologic Emergencies"**
Design Firm: **In-house**
Publisher: **Cahners Publishing Co.—**
Emergency Medicine
Art Director: **Lois Erlacher**
Illustrator: **Teri J. McDermott**

This vibrant rendering of nerve cells accompanied an article on "Neurologic Emergencies" in *Emergency Medicine*. The connections between the cells appear as golden jolts of electricity. The stippled background is lively enough to add visual interest, but does not compete with the subject matter. According to illustrator Teri J. McDermott, the visual had to be "generic" enough for use in two companion articles in separate issues.

Product: **Xanax**®
Design Firm: **Norman Perman, Inc.**
Client: **The Upjohn Co.**
Designer: **Norman Perman**
Illustrator: **Leonard E. Morgan**

The neurochemical action of Xanax®, a widely prescribed tranquilizer, is brought to life by Leonard E. Morgan in this colorful illustration, portions of which are used throughout a booklet aimed at physicians. On the cover, the end of a neuron is rendered in cutaway fashion to reveal the flash of nerve impulses. The tiny red particles at the bottom are neurotransmitters—the chemicals that bridge the gap between nerve cells. Inside, the illustrator shows how Xanax® binds to the receptor sites to relieve anxiety. To depict this process, Morgan used what he describes as "extremely complex and challenging geometric forms."

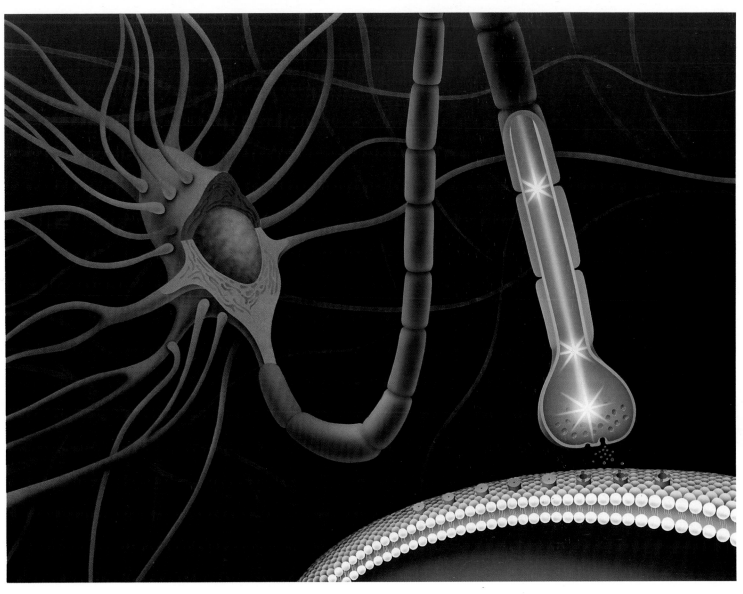

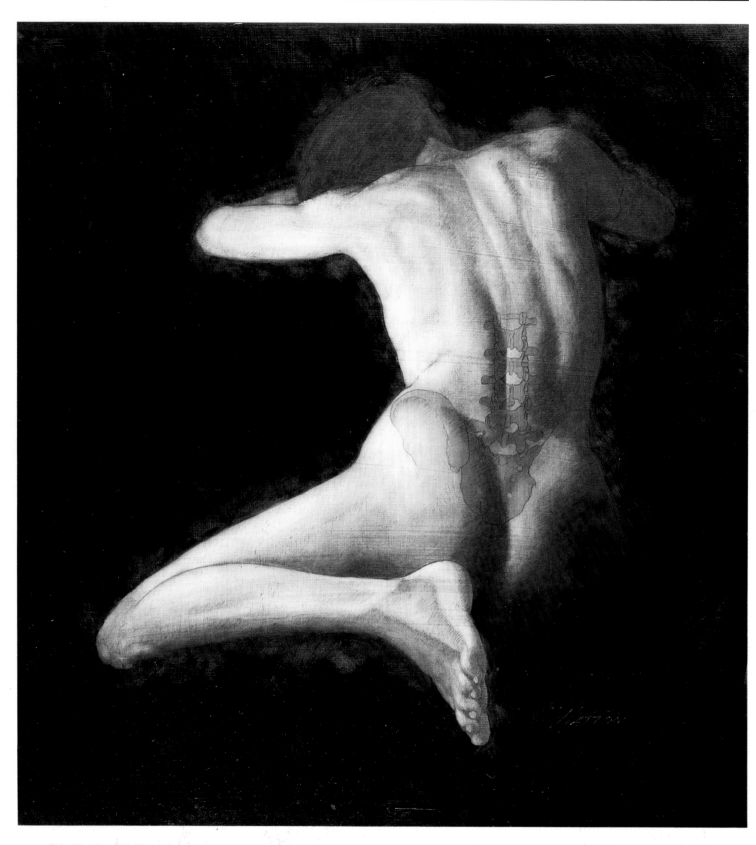

Title: **"Lumbar Disk Disease"**
Design Firm: **In-house**
  Publisher: **McGraw-Hill Publishing Co.**
Art Director: **Tina Adamek**
  Illustrator: **Enid Hatton**

A powerful, almost Michelangelesque nude exposes a sore lower back for a cover article on lumbar disk disease. Illustrator Enid Hatton has lightly delineated the affected portion of the spine and pelvis, but the work as a whole transcends the boundaries of medical art. The dramatic contrast between the flesh tones and the dark background is especially effective.

Title: **"Platelet Inhibitors"**
Design Firm: **In-house**
  Publisher: **McGraw-Hill Publishing Co.**
Art Director: **Tina Adamek**
  Illustrator: **Enid Hatton**

A delicately executed profile of a man, viewed from below in dramatic perspective, serves to depict the subject of platelet inhibitors. Illustrator Enid Hatton has rendered the man's upper body with a glasslike exterior; beneath the surface, we view blood cells traveling to the brain via the aorta and carotid artery. (The narrow platelets are apparently trapped as they exit the heart.)

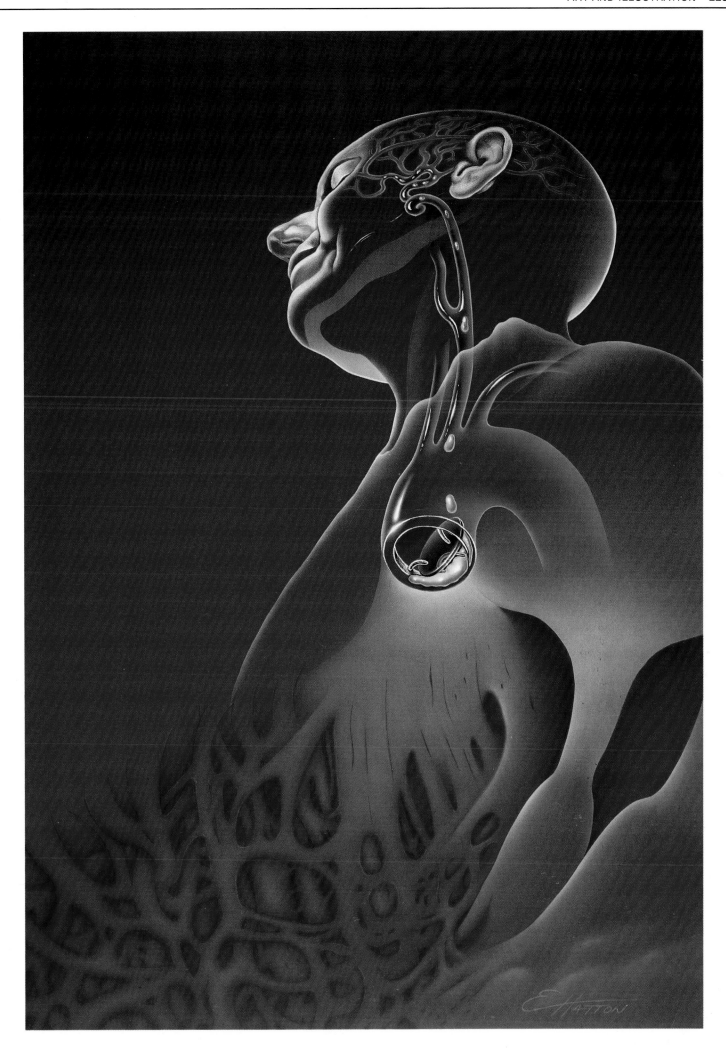

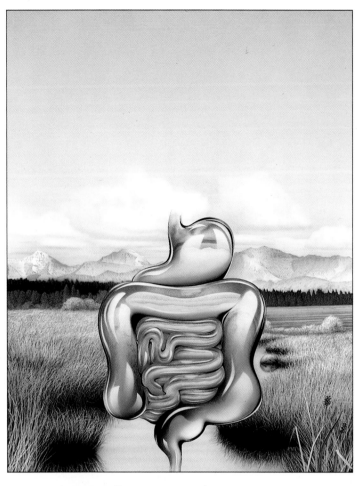

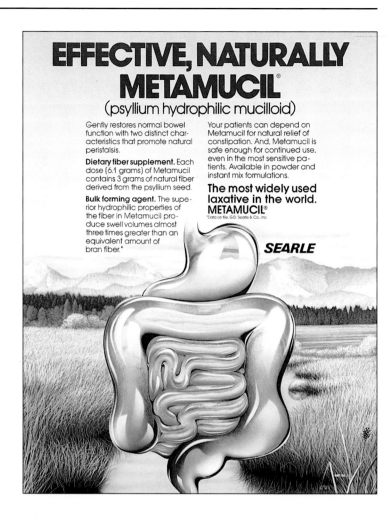

Product: **METAMUCIL**®
Ad Agency: **Medical Directions, Inc.**
Client: **G.D. Searle & Co., Inc.**
Art Director: **Michael V. Phillips**
Illustrator: **Leonard E. Morgan**

A crystal-pure GI tract appears against a similarly pristine backdrop of mountains and meadows in this illustration for a METAMUCIL® ad. On close inspection, one notices that the mountain skyline, the stream, and the tall grass are visible through the anatomy, subtly distorted as they would appear if viewed through curved glass. This meticulously rendered detail helps underscore the natural qualities of the product.

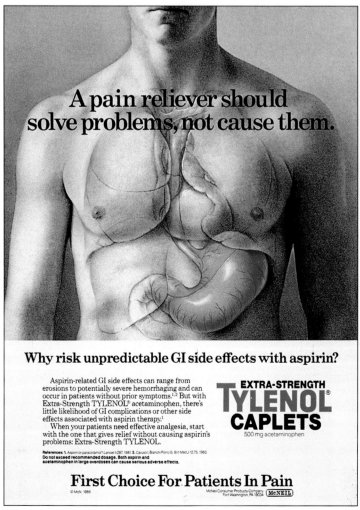

Product: **Extra-Strength TYLENOL**®
Ad Agency: **Kallir, Philips, Ross, Inc.**
Client: **McNeil Consumer Products Co.**
Art Director: **Bruce Tredwell**
Illustrator: **Lauren Keswick**
Photographer: **Raynard Manson**
Copywriter: **Maris Hochman**

Originally appearing in an ad for Extra-Strength TYLE-NOL®, this handsome visual takes us inside the body to view a reddened stomach irritated by aspirin. Intriguingly, the piece combines photography (the torso) with illustration (the internal organs). Artist Lauren Keswick has used color to focus on the stomach; the heart, lungs, and liver are softly delineated in the same monochromatic tones as the rest of the picture.

Product: **TRIAX**™
Ad Agency: **Ad Lab, Inc.**
Client: **Whaledent International**
Art Directors: **Cindy Ho, Jonathan Male**
Illustrator: **Lauren Keswick**
Copywriter: **Dan Zenowich**

For an ad promoting TRIAX™, a prefabricated post and core system for front teeth, Lauren Keswick illustrated the device as it appears implanted in the tooth. The cutaway perspective helps explain the product in visual terms; the lightly stippled background and anatomical features (as contrasted with the sleekly polished surface of the implant) reveal a sophisticated and refreshingly individual technique.

Product: **ALDOMET**®
Ad Agency: **Robert A. Becker Inc.**
Client: **Merck Sharp & Dohme**
Art Director: **Sal Morello**
Illustrator: **Edward Gazsi**
Copywriter: **Norman Franklin**

Illustrator Edward Gazsi created this finely etched portrait for an ad promoting ALDOMET®, an antihypertensive medication said to be gentle on the kidneys. The delicacy of line, color, and shading in the man's face is matched by the artist's equally subtle detailing of the kidney's interior. The gentleness of the melancholy face, coupled with the softly understated quality of the artist's style, helps establish a similar image for the product.

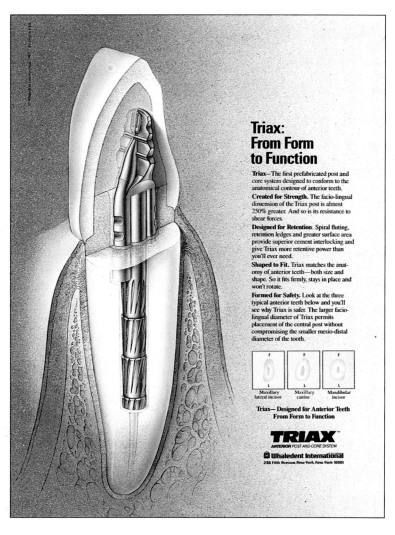

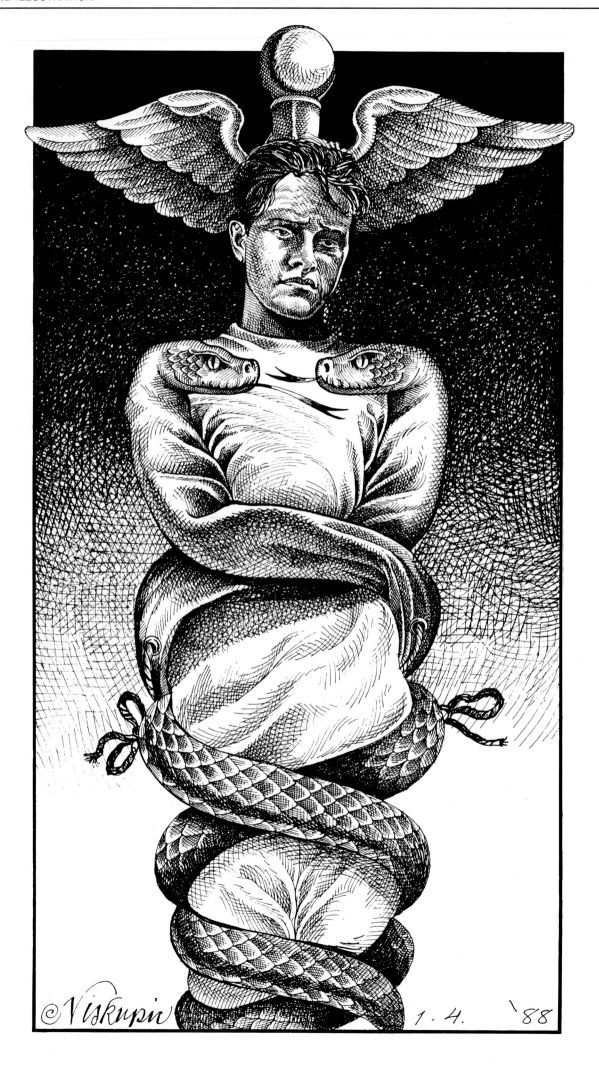

◄ Title: **"The Hospitalization of America's**
Troubled Teenagers"
Design Firm: **In-house**
Publisher: **Times-Mirror/Newsday—***Newsday*
Art Director: **Bob Eisner**
Illustrator: **Gary Viskupic**

The *caduceus*, symbol of the medical profession, presents ripe opportunities for the artist with a satirical bent. The sinister nature of the emblem has been effectively exploited here by illustrator Gary Viskupic, who transforms the serpents and staff into a strait-jacket that ensnares a helpless teenage boy. This dramatic pen-and-ink illustration accompanied an article in *Newsday* about the often unnecessary confinement of troubled teenagers to psychiatric hospitals—a mistake that can stigmatize them for life.

Title: **"Medical Miracles: Who Benefits"**
Design Firm: **In-house**
Publisher: **Times-Mirror/Newsday—***Newsday*
Art Director: **Bob Eisner**
Illustrator: **Gary Viskupic**

For an article on the availability of transplants—and the difficulty of deciding who receives them—*Newsday* illustrator Gary Viskupic produced this darkly ironic view of the human body as a chest of drawers containing spare parts. The uppermost drawer contains the heart (only the crest of the aorta is visible), while the drawer at the lower right represents the bone marrow injections discussed in the article. Viskupic's vigorous ink-and-wash technique adds power and sculptural definition to an ingenious visual concept.

Title: **"The Morally Insane"**
Design Firm: **In-house**
Publisher: **Times-Mirror/Newsday—**
Newsday
Art Director: **Bob Eisner**
Illustrator: **Ned Levine**
Section Designer: **Rita Hall**

For a newspaper feature on the morally insane, which explored the idea that criminal behavior stems from "a lack of infant bonding," illustrator Ned Levine created this troubling portrait of a potentially sociopathic child. The boy's facial expression is vague but unsettling; nestled within the upper reaches of his head is a second, clearly demonic face. Levine writes, "I felt that the eyes of a young child glaring at the reader would be compelling and the eyes of the older face would be disturbing."

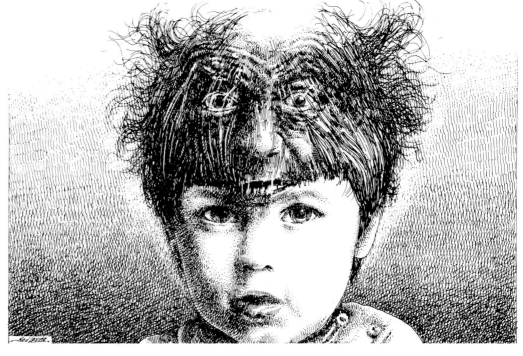

Title: **"Navigating Neuroleptic Malignant Syndrome"**

Design Firm: **B. Martin Pederson Inc.**

Publisher: **American Journal of Nursing Co.— AJN**

Art Director: **Forbes Linkhorn**

Illustrator: **Devis Grebu**

As lightning crackles across the sky, an intrepid nurse guides an unconscious patient through a perilous sea. Devis Grebu concocted this refreshingly different illustration for an article appropriately entitled "Navigating Neuroleptic Malignant Syndrome" in American Journal of Nursing. The "sea" is actually a multicolored patchwork of pills and capsules, complemented by the equally fragmented watercolor sky with its jagged bolts of lightning.

Product: **e.p.t.**®
Ad Agency: **Thomas G. Ferguson Associates Inc.**
Client: **Parke-Davis Consumer Health Products Group**
Art Director: **George Courides**
Illustrator: **Edward Gazsi**
Copywriter: **Robert Krell**

Spectacular is the word for this latter-day re-creation of the tea party from *Alice in Wonderland*. With a passion for detail and an impeccable technique, illustrator Edward Gazsi has rivaled (if not surpassed) Tenniel's famous illustrations for Lewis Carroll's much-beloved classic. The faces, especially, are rendered with superb subtlety and naturalism, while still clearly belonging to the world of imagination; they can stand with the very best work in contemporary children's illustration. The luminous colors are enhanced by deep shading, and the entire surface is composed of tiny flecks of pigment that recall Seurat's pointillism—but even more densely woven. What does this grand tableau have to do with medicine? The March Hare is holding the new e.p.t.® Stick Test, which, as the copy asserts, is "reason to celebrate." Rabbits, of course, have long been associated with pregnancy testing, and e.p.t.® has used them as graphic symbols in previous promotions.

Title: **"Overlooked Anatomy: Examining a Boy's Genitals"**
Design Firm: **In-house**
Publisher: **Cahners Publishing Co.— *Emergency Medicine***
Art Director: **James T. Walsh**
Illustrator: **Peter de Seve**

The article accompanying this whimsical sketch by Peter de Seve is entitled, "Overlooked Anatomy: Examining a Boy's Genitals." And appropriately enough, the army of attending physicians appears to be scouring every inch of the youngster's anatomy except for the part demurely hidden by the fig leaf. De Seve's richly satirical style, with its large areas of watercolor wash and deftly defined details, recalls the work of that preeminent 19th century illustrator Honoré Daumier. But at the same time, he manages to transmit a very contemporary wit and originality.

Product: **WyTensin®**
Ad Agency: **Materia Medica/Creative Annex Inc.**
Client: **Wyeth-Ayerst Laboratories**
Art Director: **Leonard Slonevsky**
Illustrator: **Gerry Gersten**

Why are these organs sitting around in easy chairs when they should be working? Illustrator Gerry Gersten developed this comical visual as part of a promotion for the antihypertensive drug WyTensin®. The four characters in the chairs—the genial, laid-back blood vessel, the morose old brain, the earthy heart with her bandana of blood vessels, and the feisty little kidney—actually appeared in a medical exhibit puppet show created by the agency. Aimed at cardiologists, this "personalized" look at the major organs attacked by hypertension helps drive home a serious message about the disease and the drug.

Product: **PIPRIL®**
Ad Agency: **Warhaftig Associates, Inc.**
Client: **Lederle Div., Cyanamid International**
Art Director: **Matt Warhaftig**
Illustrator: **Joe Ciardiello**
Copywriter: **Jon Hughes**

This visual "cliffhanger" accompanies a case study of a 65-year-old man who died from an infection; it appeared in an ad for PIPRIL®, an antibiotic. Directed at hematologists and internists, the ad was intended to draw attention to European trials supporting the use of piperacillin in combination therapy for treatment of the neutropenic patient. Matt Warhaftig, president of Warhaftig Associates, Inc., writes, "For a graphic this unconventional, we were pleasantly surprised to have the total, unified support among all levels of product management and market research. Although the English found it to be too controversial to run, it has been used extensively elsewhere in Europe."

Title: **"A Few Giants Will Survive"** ➤
Design Firm: **In-house**
Publisher: *American Druggist*
Art Director: **Cheryl Mohrmann**
Illustrator: **John S. Dykes**

To accompany an article on the increasing dominance of large drugstore chains, John S. Dykes concocted this wryly surreal portrait of a pill-headed man (the giant chains) who towers over the childlike figures representing the smaller local chains. The giant appears benign and even paternal, yet he clearly overwhelms the others with his sheer bulk. This subtle ambiguity adds interest to the illustration, as does the artist's deft use of watercolor. He writes that he arrived at this concept "only...after a long time working and playing with many approaches."

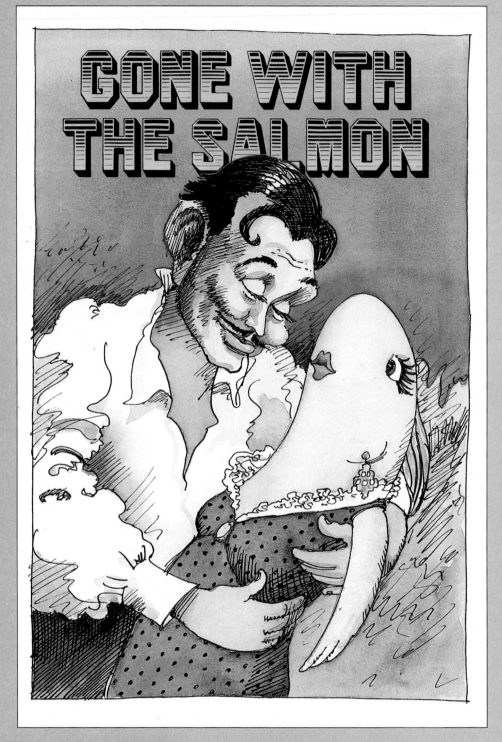

Ad Agency: **Dorritie & Lyons, Inc.**
Client: **Pfizer Laboratories**
Art Director: **Tom Lennon**
Illustrator: **Werner Kappes**
Copywriter: **Irene Biada**

As part of a competition involving its own sales force, Pfizer commissioned these whimsical parodies of Hollywood glamor. The three critters posing arm in arm represent the three prizes to be awarded to top salespeople: a smoked turkey, a smoked salmon, and a smoked ham. In the separate "Gone with the Salmon" enclosure, Clark Gable strikes his best Rhett Butler pose before closing in for the clincher with—well, you get the picture. (She's not exactly Scarlett, but she goes better with bagels.)

Title: **"Protection for Pediatric Patients"**
Design Firm: **In-house**
Publisher: **Cahners Publishing Co.—**
Emergency Medicine
Art Director: **Lois Erlacher**
Illustrator: **Bonnie Hofkin**

For an article entitled, "Protection for Pediatric Patients," illustrator Bonnie Hofkin created this clever visual metaphor. The children, all of them lively and active (check the expression on the Little Leaguer's face), play inside bubbles that shield them from swarms of purple microbes. Two of the kids have just hurt themselves, but presumably the "bubble" of inoculation will keep them out of deeper trouble.

Product: **MEXITIL®**
Ad Agency: **Dugan Farley Communications Associates, Inc.**
Client: **Boehringer Ingelheim Pharmaceuticals, Inc.**
Art Director: **Suzanne Elward**
Illustrator: **David Grove**

Safety is the theme of this evocative depiction of a man and his bicycle. Executed primarily in blue, gold, and brown, with subtle gradations, the illustration highlights the brilliant yellow of the man's reflective safety vest. And with good reason: the art accompanied an actual safety vest used as a direct-mail premium for physicians. The "safety" theme of the illustration and premium tie in with an advertised benefit of MEXITIL®, which, according to Account Supervisor Linda Zani, is positioned as "the safest antiarrhythmic available for the long-term management of ventricular arrhythmias." Illustrator David Grove displays a skillful command of his medium; the figure of the bike rider stays sharply defined against the impressionistic cloud of background color.

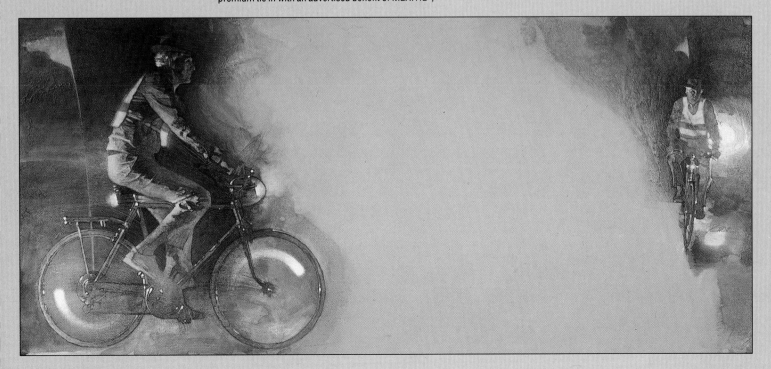

PHOTOGRAPHY AND SPECIAL EFFECTS

ADVERTISING
PROMOTION
EDITORIAL ART

Most of the entries in this chapter are photographs, and at the same time, most of them also involve special effects of one kind or another. In fact, you could say that the typical entry is a photograph *of* a special effect. It seems natural, then, to pair these two categories for the eighth and final chapter of this book.

Special photographic effects can be traced back to the nineteenth century—almost to the beginning of photography itself. Early practitioners of the art delighted in the illusions they could obtain by tampering with photographic images; they must have experienced an exhilarating rush of creative freedom—even a sense of dominion over the natural world. By using double exposures, strobe effects, and other technical tricks of the time, they could transcend the "mere" realism of photography and shape the world according to their vision.

Today, special effects photography still undoubtedly satisfies the creative impulse—the need to control the image and even to outdo nature itself. But one can also point to other, more pragmatic reasons for the prominence of special effects in contemporary medical advertising and editorial work: they catch the reader's eye…they command attention…they arouse curiosity…they encourage involvement…and, just as important, they tend to stay in the reader's mind long after the initial exposure. And, this is what good *advertising* is supposed to accomplish.

Special effects command attention because they introduce an element of unreality into a real-world image. Take the memorable editorial photograph of a young woman "entrapped by her own fat cells." Viewed from above in dramatic perspective, she reaches up to push against the unyielding layer of cells (depicted as a multitude of golden spheres). The same composition *could* have been rendered by an illustrator, but it would not have been as arresting. And an ordinary photograph of a slightly overweight woman would not have captured the drama—or the symbolism—of the individual pitted against recalcitrant fat cells.

By the same token, the cover shot of the man in the square-wheeled wheelchair (a visual analogy for our "crippled" healthcare system) could have been almost as effective in the hands of an illustrator—but not quite. After all, these happen to be *real* square wheels on a *real* wheelchair, occupied by a *real* man. The importance of using photography to capture an implausible image cannot be overstated.

A special effects photograph takes the world as we know it, then gives it a surprising twist that changes our perceptions. The tottering buildings in the ads for Antivert® make us experience the world through the eyes of someone suffering from vertigo. (The effect was accomplished through multiple exposures.) Then, as the scene "stabilizes" before our eyes, we gain first-hand appreciation for the benefits of the drug.

Several of the special effects in this chapter are accomplished with models. Model-making permits the artist to create effects that simply cannot be photographed in the real world. Compared with photographers, model-makers (like illustrators) enjoy a greater degree of control over the final image. They're free to invent, to indulge in abstract symbolism, to build a world to their specifications.

But at the same time, it's important to remember that these models are captured in *photographs*. Unlike illustrations, which exist in their own frame of reference, photographed models *appear* to belong to our world. As a result, any fantastic elements introduced by the model-maker will produce a jolt of surprise and arouse the curiosity of the reader.

Robert J. Demarest's conceptual depiction of dementia uses a model to achieve its impact: an elderly woman's head is composed of building blocks that have begun to tumble down, one layer at a time. For an added touch of surrealism, the blocks blend smoothly into an *illustrated* face. Is the face part of the model, or is it superimposed? That's part of the mystery—and the eye-catching appeal—of this unusual piece.

Just as intriguing is Searle's model of multiple spheres coming together in a central box; the union of a single blue sphere from one side, and a red sphere from the other, produces a brilliant light. So we see that the model itself can be as abstract as the concept it illustrates—in this case, a visually compelling representation of two companies joining in a mutually beneficial relationship.

Models can be symbolic, educational (be sure to see the stunning photographic series on the life cycle of a virus for *Smithsonian* magazine), or more overtly decorative. But whatever their form or purpose, models clearly play an important role in today's medical graphics.

So far, we've been discussing conventional photographs of unconventional things. But holograms are another matter entirely: these remarkable three-dimensional images can make a *paper clip* look breathtaking. The single holographic example in this chapter—among the first of its kind in pharmaceutical advertising—depicts the chemical structure of the key ingredient in Xanax® as part of a ring encircling the human brain.

We've included a few *non*-photographic special effects as well. An ad for OMNIPAQUE® highlights the major blood vessels in brilliant metallic red, set against a subtly shaded metallic *blue* body. Illustrator Mike Dudash produced what looks like a hand-tinted photographic collage (for LEUCOVORIN CALCIUM®)—but, as you'll see, he did more than tint it. Finally, for fans of photorealism, there's the extraordinary image of a bubble being pierced at "high speed" by a tablet of PHAZYME®. And yes, it's an illustration, not a photograph!

Vertigo.*... going... gone

Antivert®/50
(meclizine HCl) 50 mg Tablets

Dosage for vertigo*: The recommended dose is 25 mg to 100 mg daily in divided dosage.

Also available
Antivert® (meclizine HCl) 12.5 mg Tablets • Antivert®/25 (meclizine HCl) 25 mg Tablets

*This drug has been evaluated as possibly effective in the management of vertigo associated with diseases affecting the vestibular system. See Brief Summary.

For Prescribing Information, please see last tab in Compendium.

ROERIG Pfizer

Products: **Antivert®/25, Antivert®/50**
Ad Agency: **Robert A. Becker Inc.**
Client: **Roerig Div., Pfizer Pharmaceuticals**
Art Director: **Frank O'Blak**
Photographer: **Shostal/David Attie**
Copywriter: **Norman Franklin**

SILVER. Two wobbly views of familiar scenes—the lower Manhattan skyline and London's majestic Houses of Parliament—gradually stabilize before our eyes in this striking depiction of vertigo brought under control. Both photographs were used in a series of ads for Antivert®—the London scene for Antivert®/25 and the New York scene for new Antivert®/50. The dramatic two-page format, simple headline copy ("Vertigo…going…gone"), and use of multiple-exposure photography team up to drive home the unmistakable message. Especially noteworthy is the transition from dizzying movement to sharp stability in a still photograph—an effect that simulates motion just as successfully as film could have done.

Vertigo.*... going... gone

Accept no substitutes, specify...

Antivert®/25
(meclizine HCl) 25 mg Tablets

Dosage for vertigo*: The recommended dose is 25 mg to 100 mg daily in divided dosage.

ROERIG Pfizer

Title: **"Are Cost Cuts Crippling Health Care?"**
Design Firm: **In-house**
Publisher: **Time Inc.—*Discover***
Art Director: **Eric Seidman**
Photographer: **Tom Arma**

SILVER. This memorable image of a man immobilized in a *square-wheeled* wheelchair was conjured up to convey the idea of "crippled healthcare" for the cover of *Discover* magazine. Tom Arma stylishly silhouetted the man's face against a smoky backdrop in what is a truly exceptional photographic work.

Title: **"Staging Dementia"**
Publisher: **Harcourt Brace Jovanovich— *Geriatrics***
Art Director: **Robert J. Demarest**
Illustrator/
Model Maker: **Robert J. Demarest**
Photographer: **George Tanis**

A cover article on dementia inspired this fascinating study of a mind tumbling down like a house of blocks. What makes the piece especially poignant is the contrast between the woman's gentle face and the total disarray into which her mind has fallen. Intriguingly, the illustrated face blends almost imperceptibly into the 3-D model of tumbling blocks; Robert J. Demarest, consultant art director, created both the illustration *and* the model. The numbers on the blocks represent the seven levels of dementia: the top level (the sevens) has already collapsed, and the sixes and fives are falling.

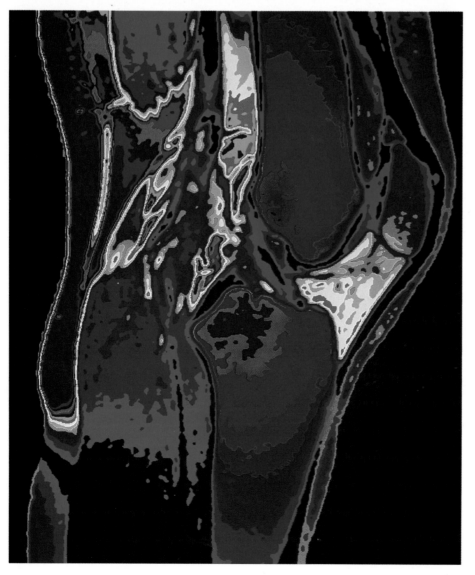

Product: **NAPROSYN® B.I.D.**
Ad Agency: **Vicom/FCB**
Client: **Syntex Laboratories, Inc.**
Art Director: **Stephen Mullens**

These color-enhanced portraits of a human hand (right) and a human knee (left) are stunning examples of magnetic resonance imaging (MRI), an important diagnostic technique of recent vintage. Set against a jet-black background, the hand and knee reveal an array of brilliant colors and intriguing patterns within their familiar outlines. High-tech imaging has transmuted both into abstract and awesome images.

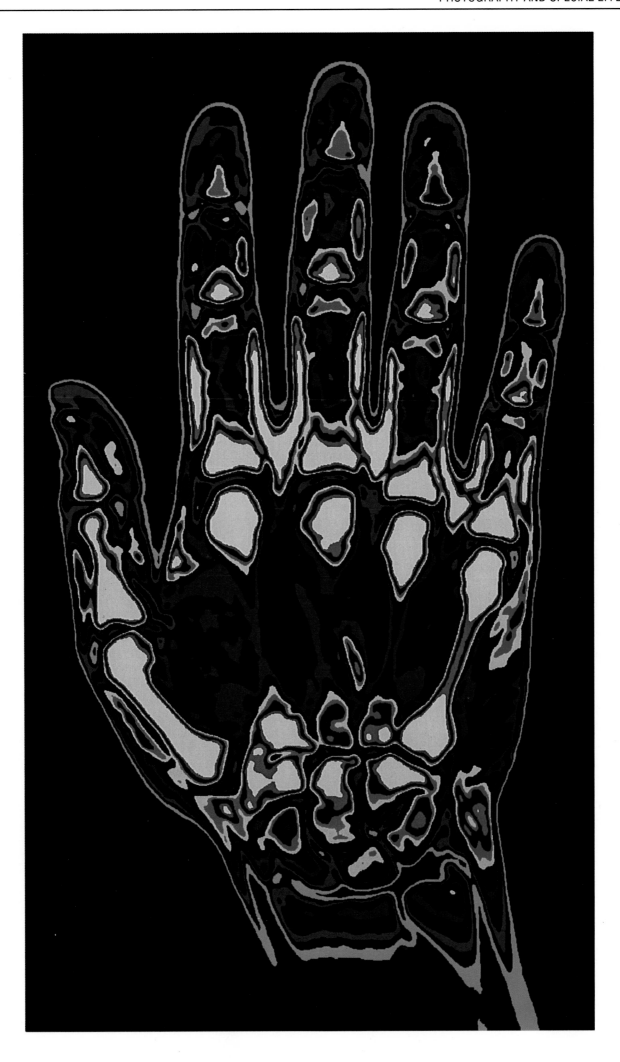

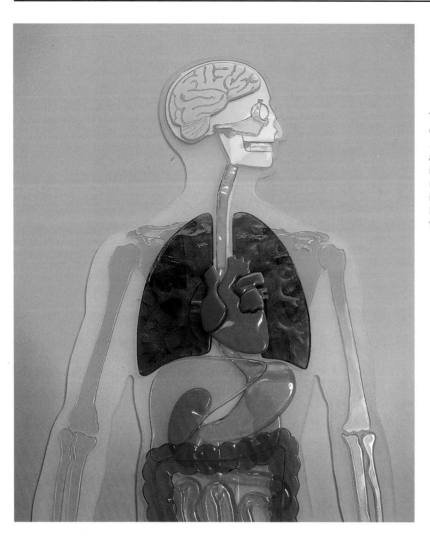

Design Firm: **Dimensional Illustrators Inc.**
Client: **Lippincott Publishing**
Art Director: **Tracy Baldwin**
Dimensional
Illustrator: **Kathleen Ziegler**
Photographer: **Eric Pervukhin**

This translucent Plexiglas model of the human anatomy was created for a book entitled *Structure and Function of the Human Body*. Each piece was hand cut and polished, then assembled in a way that produced interesting juxtapositions of form and color. While undeniably stylized, this rich work also depicts the internal organs and bones with reasonable accuracy. Kathleen Ziegler designed the model; she writes that it took a month to complete.

Product: **OMNIPAQUE**®
Ad Agency: **Lavey/Wolff/Swift Inc.**
Client: **Winthrop Pharmaceuticals**
Art Director: **Dan Smith**
Illustrator: **Natale**
Copywriters: **Al Gerstein, Tony Picard**

Diagnostic imaging has become a highly competitive field in the past few years. As a result, agencies are continually forced to outdo each other in terms of visual innovation. One striking example is this brilliantly executed anatomical art from Lavey/Wolff/Swift Inc. Rendered entirely in *metallic* colors, the human body displays an assemblage of luminous arteries and organs—the precise areas where OMNIPAQUE® is applicable. The rest of the body is rendered in a cool metallic blue that shifts in intensity as you move the page from side to side. Subtle shading brings out the skeletal framework as well as the outlines of the brain, heart, and kidneys.

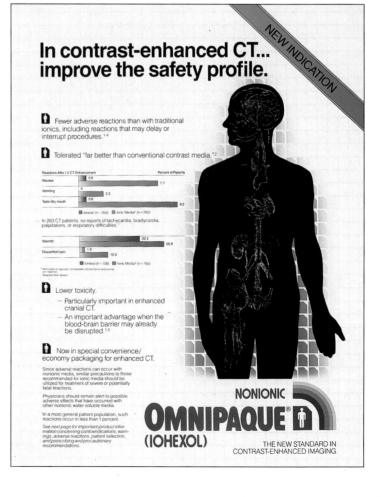

Design Firm: **Dimensional Illustrators Inc.**
Client: **Springhouse Corp.—*Nursing87***
Art Director: **Ed Rosanio**
Dimensional
Illustrator: **Kathleen Ziegler**
Photographer: **Eric Pervukhin**

This dimensional model by Kathleen Ziegler depicts the heart and lungs in polished Plexiglas. It accompanied one installment in a series on major body systems that appeared in *Nursing87* magazine. The other two models represented the endocrine system and the nervous system. Since the three works were part of a series, the style had to remain constant. In fact, the same gracefully contoured body outline was used for all three pieces; only the internal organs changed from month to month.

Title: **"Major Body Systems"**
Design Firm: **Dimensional Illustrators Inc.**
Client: **Springhouse Corp.**
Art Director: **Ed Rosanio**
Dimensional
Illustrator: **Kathleen Ziegler**
Photographer: **Eric Pervukhin**

To call attention to a new series on major body systems, *Nursing87* commissioned this stunning Plexiglas sculpture of the body with its internal organs. The sculpture depicts the major organ systems with accuracy as well as graphic appeal—note the branching bronchial tubes and the transparent bones. The smooth, rounded surfaces and brilliant colors add a toy-like charm that makes this piece a successful audience grabber. Kathleen Ziegler, president of Dimensional Illustrators Inc., notes that the model consisted of 25 separate, carefully hand-carved and polished pieces.

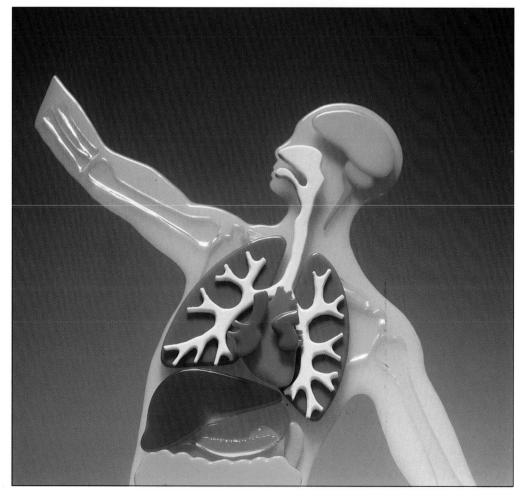

Product: **NASALIDE®**
Ad Agency: **Vicom/FCB**
Client: **Syntex Laboratories, Inc.**
Art Director: **Stephen Mullens**
Photographer: **David Scharf**
Copywriter: **Ann Peterson**

These three superb microphotographs are taken from a poster entitled, "A Closer Look at the Things That Make You Sneeze." Those prickly-looking golden spheres are actually grains of ragweed pollen magnified 2,650 times. The fearsome creature with the segmented legs is, in reality, a common dust mite (magnified 455 times). And that wondrous garden of blue-stalked plants with light purple "flowers" is composed entirely of mold spores (at 255x). Credit goes to photographer David Scharf for this compelling excursion into a microscopic world.

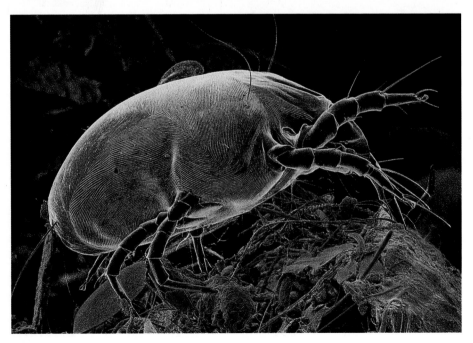

Title: **"How One Virus Tricks a Cell into ➤ Making More Viruses"**
Publisher: *Smithsonian*
Art Director: **Caroline Despard**
Photographers: **Peter Angelo Simon, Yoav Levy/ PHOTOTAKE—NYC**

For an article on viruses in *Smithsonian* magazine, photographers Peter Angelo Simon and Yoav Levy produced these spectacularly colorful—and equally fascinating—images from *models* based on recent research discoveries. The sequence shows how a single virus can "trick" a host cell into making more viruses. In the first photo, the virus makes initial contact with a receptor on the cell. The second image shows the invading virus, now stripped of its shell, heading toward the nucleus of the cell. In the third scene, the virus core splices its DNA onto that of the cell. Finally, new viruses, shimmering like celestial orbs, are released from the cell into the bloodstream. That such a deadly process can be depicted with such unearthly beauty adds even greater impact to the sequence.

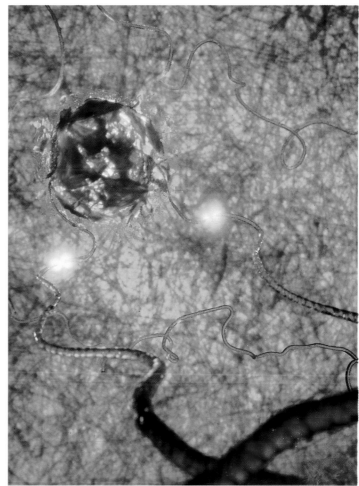

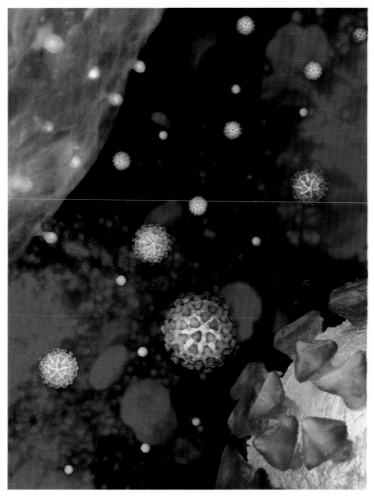

Title: **"Entrapped by Her Own Fat Cells"**
Design Firm: **In-house**
Publisher: *Smithsonian*
Photographer: **Yoav Levy**

"Entrapped by Her Own Fat Cells" is the title of this arresting editorial photograph by Yoav Levy. The underlying concept is that when an overweight person attempts to diet, the fat cells send starvation signals to the brain. As a result, the dieter is compelled to overindulge. Subverted by the body's antistarvation mechanism, the overweight are literally entrapped by their own fat. The photograph of a pleasingly plump young woman uses dramatic perspective—as well as the special effect produced by the golden globular "fat cells"—to sum up the theme of the article in one neat conceptual image.

Ad Agency: **Hamilton, Carver & Lee**
Client: **G. D. Searle & Co.**
Art Director: **Thom Qualkinbush**
Photographer: **Michel Tcherevkof**

Part of a promotional booklet for Searle, this conceptual model illustrates a mutually beneficial licensing agreement between Searle and a potential licensor. As the two companies (represented by the blue and red spheres) meet in the central box, the brilliant glow of a single sphere can be said to represent a perfect union of corporate resources. Graceful, harmonious, and effectively lit, the model conveys a sense of weightlessness. In reality, it was strung together using expertly hidden support wires. Senior Art Director Thom Qualkinbush writes that photographer Michel Tcherevkov made five to six exposures on a single piece of film.

Product: **PHAZYME® 95**
Ad Agency: **M.E.D. Communications, Inc.**
Client: **Reed & Carnrick**
Creative Director: **Edward Cohen**
Art Director: **Warren McLeod**
Illustrator: **Wil Cormier**
Copywriter: **Sally Paull**

This is *not* one of those remarkable photographs taken at a shutter speed of 1/20,000 of a second. Rather, it's an equally remarkable *illustration* patterned after one of those photographs. But instead of a bullet piercing the bubble, illustrator Wil Cormier has substituted a gleaming red tablet of PHAZYME® 95. (The headline of the ad in which it appeared calls it the "Gasbuster.") Note the tiny exploding droplets, the subtle rainbow of color on the bubble, and the visible path of the speeding pill through its midsection. All of this is rendered with amazing technical virtuosity in the best photorealistic manner.

Product: **Lederle LEUCOVORIN CALCIUM**®
Ad Agency: **Dugan Farley Communications Associates, Inc.**
Client: **Lederle Laboratories**
Art Director: **Barbara McCullough**
Illustrator: **Mike Dudash**
Copywriter: **Frank Cordasco**

In this attractive "collage" for Lederle LEUCOVORIN CALCIUM®, the effect of hand-tinted photography is meticulously executed in shades of blue and brown; the brightly colored lines add visual interest. The texture of the canvas, visible in rectangular patches, enhances the collage effect. Although the accompanying ad focuses on a single product, it also promotes the company as a whole—especially its "ongoing commitment to the oncology community." It is this broader theme that Mike Dudash has illustrated in such a remarkable manner.

Product: **Xanax**®
Ad Agency: **Frank J. Corbett, Inc.**
Client: **The Upjohn Co.**
Art Director: **Bill Harrison**
Photographer: **Don Levy**
Hologram Production: **Hologram Design Systems**
Copywriter: **Richard Jacobs**

According to Creative Director Richard Jacobs, this ad for Xanax® marked the first use of a hologram in mass-market pharmaceutical journal advertising. The three-dimensional image shows a brain encircled by a ring, partially broken by a complex molecular structure (the triazolo ring, which differentiates Xanax® from its competitors). The image shifts slightly as the ad is rotated back and forth, and the colors move brilliantly through the entire spectrum as the piece is tilted from top to bottom.

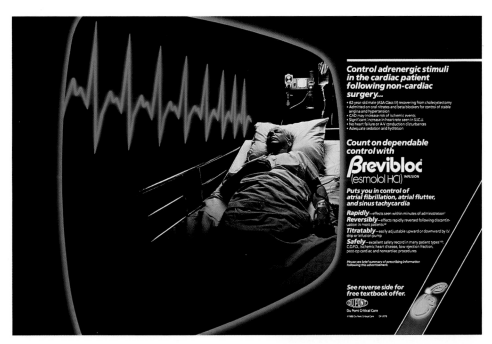

Product: **Brevibloc**®
Ad Agency: **Sutton Communications**
Client: **DuPont Pharmaceuticals**
Art Director: **Stan Dornfest**
Photographer: **Paul Aresu**
Copywriter: **Richard Norman**

Featured in an ad for Brevibloc®, a beta blocker, this recovery room scene appears entirely within the green perimeter of a vital signs monitor. The patient's heart rhythm appears on the screen, just above the patient himself. As Senior V.P. Steve Spittel writes, this visual instantly communicates the indication for the drug *and* depicts the patient in a setting familiar to the audience of anesthesiologists. The electronic green glow of the monitor is picked up in the Brevibloc® symbol at lower right.

Product: **Feldene**®
Ad Agency: **Dorritie & Lyons, Inc.**
Client: **Pfizer Laboratories**
Art Director: **Mike Lyons**
Photographer: **Carl Flatow**
Copywriter: **Bill Brown**

How could a print ad—or any advertising, for that matter—possibly depict the sensations that arthritis sufferers feel in their joints? Dorritie & Lyons, Inc., found the solution. In this innovative ad for Pfizer's Feldene® antiarthritic capsules, the illustrated bones are actually coated with gritty particles. The physicians reading the ad simply had to run their fingers over the rough surface to experience first-hand the "sandpaper joints" so often described by arthritics. This bold example of interactive advertising succeeds in bringing a sense of immediacy to the problem—and in creating name-brand awareness of the remedy.

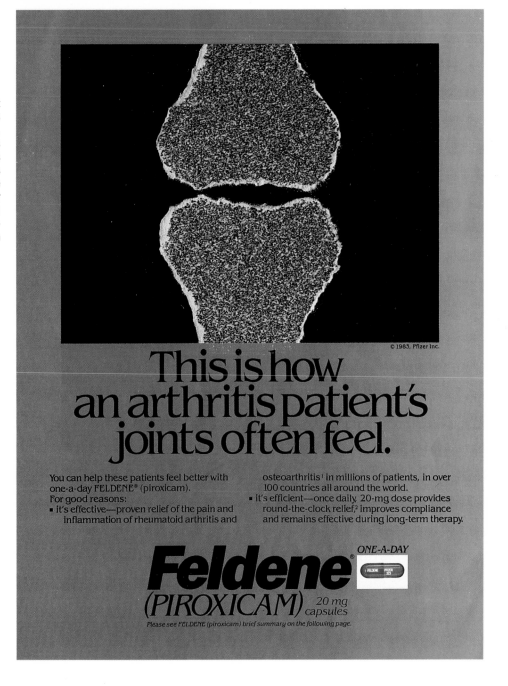

ABOUT THE Rx CLUB

THE PERSON BEHIND THE Rx CLUB SHOW

If you're looking for someone with her finger on the pulse of the medical advertising industry, find Ina Kramer. For the last three years, Ina has been pouring her energy into founding and developing not one, but two, of the most dynamic new organizations in medical advertising and art. Through her efforts, the Medical Survival Group, her agency representing ten of the most exceptional medical illustrators and photographers in the country, has become an industry-wide source of top creative talent. And because of her recognition of the need among industry professionals to view their peers' work and showcase their own, the Rx Club Show—now in its third year—has become a highly regarded and greatly anticipated annual event.

It is perhaps Ina's own training and experience as a designer—she worked in the art field for several years after graduating from the School of Visual Arts—that allows her to serve the needs of medical art directors so knowledgeably. The Medical Survival Group is a highly professional and comprehensive source for a variety of artistic styles—a kind of one-stop shopping for creative professionals in medical advertising agencies, pharmaceutical companies, and both trade and consumer publications. Ina's background also allows her to play an essential hands-on role in the creative process—by effectively relaying art directors' concepts to her illustrators and photographers and helping them transform those ideas into dynamic visual forms.

THE HISTORY OF THE Rx CLUB SHOW

In 1986, Ina Kramer founded the Rx Club Show for art directors and copywriters in medical advertising agencies, client companies, and publications—as well as for independent illustrators, dimensional illustrators, and photographers serving the medical advertising and publishing industries. The first annual Rx Club Show included 102 categories that ranged from medical magazine and newspaper ads and ad campaigns to numerous types of promotional pieces to book jackets, posters, editorial illustration, photography, and special effects.

The response was resounding— the industry entered more than 1500 creative works for

Rx CLUB SHOW CATEGORIES

Medical Newspaper Advertising
1. Less than half page, b/w
2. Half page, b/w
3. More than half, up to full page, b/w
4. Campaign, color
5. Public Service
6. Public Service Campaign
7. Section, Insert, Supplement

Medical Magazine Advertising
8. Consumer, one page, b/w
9. Consumer, spread, b/w
10. Consumer, one page, color
11. Consumer, spread, color
12. Consumer, less than full page, b/w
13. Consumer, less than full page, color
14. Consumer Campaign, b/w
15. Consumer Campaign, color
16. Public Service
17. Public Service Campaign
18. Business or Trade, one page, b/w
19. Business or Trade, more than one page, b/w
20. Business or Trade, one page, color
21. Business or Trade, more than one page, color
22. Business or Trade, less than full page, b/w
23. Business or Trade Campaign, b/w
24. Business or Trade Campaign, color
25. Section, Insert, Supplement

Medical Newspaper Editorial
26. Full page, color
27. Full page, b/w
28. Multi-page Section

Medical Magazine Editorial
29. Sunday Magazine Supplement
30. Consumer, one page, b/w
31. Consumer, spread, b/w
32. Consumer, one page, color
33. Consumer, spread, color
34. Consumer, multi-page, single story, b/w
35. Consumer, multi-page, single story, color
36. Consumer, Section or Insert
37. Consumer Cover
38. Business, Trade or House Organ, spread, b/w
39. Business, Trade or House Organ, spread, color
40. Business, Trade or House Organ, multi-page, single story, b/w
41. Business, Trade or House Organ, multi-page, single story, color
42. Business, Trade or House Organ Cover
43. Consumer or Bus. Mag. Full Issue
44. House Organ Full Issue
45. Single-sponsored Publication
46. Patient Education—4/c
47. Patient Education—2/c

Medical Promotion and Graphic Design
SINGLE ENTRIES
48. Annual Report
49. Booklet, Folder, Brochure
50. Sales Kit—Sales Aid
51. File Card
52. Direct Mail Piece
53. Package, Bottle, Carton, Can
54. Calendar
55. Visual Aid—Special Promotion Piece
56. Letterhead
57. Trademark, Logo
58. P.O.P Design, Display
CAMPAIGN ENTRIES
59. Booklets, Folders, Brochures
60. Sales Kits
61. Direct Mail
62. Packages, Cartons, Bottles, Cans, etc.
63. Trademarks, Logos
64. P.O.P. Designs, Displays
65. Corporate Identity Programs

Medical Books and Jackets
66. General Trade Book (primarily text)
67. Special Trade Book (primarily art/photography)
68. Paperback Book with medical
69. Text or Reference Book
70. Book Jacket: Trade, Text or Reference with medical theme
71. Paperback Book Cover, photo or illustration
72. Annual Report

Medical Posters
SINGLE ENTRIES
73. Outdoor
74. Transit (bus, subway or shelter)
75. Public Service
76. In-store, Promotional, etc.
CAMPAIGN ENTRIES
77. Outdoor Campaign
78. Transit Campaign
79. Public Service Campaign
80. In-store, Promotional Campaign
81. HMO Campaign
82. Hospital Campaign

ART CATEGORIES

Medical Art and Illustration
83. Editorial, b/w
84. Advertising, color
85. Promotion, color
86. Editorial, color
87. Books and Book jackets
88. Section, Insert, Supplement, medical
89. Television News Graphics, medical

Medical Photography or Special Effects
90. Advertising, b/w
91. Advertising, color
92. Promotion, color
93. Editorial, color
94. Books and Book jackets
95. Section, Insert, Supplement

judging. And 18 of the most prominent members of the medical advertising and art fields accepted invitations to act as judges, among them Matthew Bennett, creative director for Merck Sharp & Dohme; Joseph G. Chichelo, director of creative services for Roche Laboratories; Diane Cooney, executive V.P./creative director for Sudler and Hennessey; Robert Demarest, president of the American Medical Illustrators Association; and John Newcomb, design director for Medical Economics Co. Inc.

About 400 works were selected for the first show, which was exhibited at Master Eagle Gallery in New York City, where it attracted a record number of viewers. The second annual Rx Club Show, exhibited at the New York Art Directors Club in October 1988, drew an equally strong response and, again, an impressive roster of judges.

THE JUDGING

The judging for all Rx Club Show competitions is carried out by a panel of experts from the medical advertising and art fields. Each entry is viewed individually by the judges, who look for strong concept, innovative overall treatment, design originality, interaction of graphics and copy, and effective use of illustration, photography, and/or typography. The judges then consider how well all these elements work together to achieve a successful creative solution.

After the judges have carefully assessed all entries and have assigned a rating to each, using a numerical point system, those pieces that score the highest are selected to appear in the Rx Club Show. Those with the very highest scores are gold and silver winners. All those persons responsible for creating each piece in the show—together with the advertising agency and the client company—receive an award commemorating this achievement.

INFORMATION ON ENTERING THE Rx CLUB SHOW COMPETITION

The entry deadline for the Rx Club Show competition varies each year; the show itself is exhibited during the fall. Works created or published within the twelve months preceding the entry deadline are eligible. For further information, contact The Rx Club, 104 East 40th Street, Suite 111, New York, NY 10016; Phone: (212) 599-0435; FAX: (212) 682-5421.

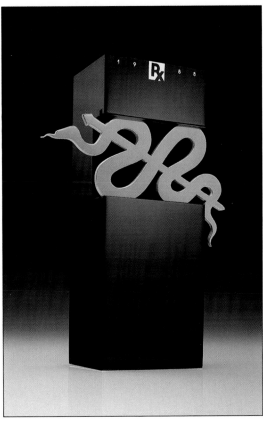

Dimensional award for the 1988 Rx Club Show. Designed by Lester Barnett, executive V.P./creative director, Vicom/FCB, San Francisco and Cliff Wood, Trimensions, New York. Production directed by Judi Craig, V.P., Vicom/FCB, San Francisco.

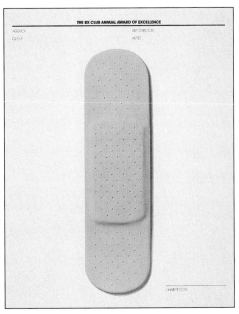

(Left) Award certificate for the 1987 Rx Club Show. Art direction by Carveth Kramer, illustration by Kathleen Ziegler, and photography by Eric Pervukhin. (Right) Award certificate for the 1988 Rx Club Show. Designed by Lester Barnett, executive V.P./creative director, Vicom/FCB, San Francisco. Production directed by Judi Craig, V.P., Vicom/FCB, San Francisco. Typesetting by Petrographics, San Francisco. Lithography by Lasky Company, Millburn, New Jersey.

INDEXES

ADVERTISING AGENCIES AND DESIGN FIRMS

ART DIRECTORS AND CREATIVE DIRECTORS

ILLUSTRATORS, DIMENSIONAL ILLUSTRATORS, AND COMPUTER GRAPHICS

PHOTOGRAPHERS

COPYWRITERS